THE ROAD TO USHUAIA

T0381517

Other books by Patrick Ellam:

Royal Flying Corps Technical Notes

Sam & Me

Some Less Known Words

Sopranino

The Judge

Things I Remember

Wind Song

Yacht Cruising

THE ROAD TO USHUAIA

The World's Southest Town

by

Patrick and June Ellam

www.patrickellam.com

Authors Choice Press
Bloomington

The Road to Ushuaia
The World's Southest Town

Authors Choice Press
an imprint of iUniverse, Inc.

iUniverse books may be ordered through booksellers or by contacting:

iUniverse
1663 Liberty Drive
Bloomington, IN 47403
www.iuniverse.com
1-800-Authors (1-800-288-4677)

ISBN: 978-1-4502-9953-4 (sc)

Printed in the United States of America

iUniverse rev. date: 03/02/2011

CONTENTS

1 - TO THE SEA OF CORTEZ

It was four in the morning when I woke up. The tent was dark but I slid out of our sleeping bag, stepped over June and put on my clothes, without using a light. Outside, the desert sky was bright with countless stars and the branches of a tree were traced in black against them. As I started toward it, I heard a dull, metallic thud - the sound of something heavy being set on the ground - like a machine gun. Quickly and quietly, I went back. Closing the tent (to keep out snakes) I moved the zipper slowly, so that it made a low purring noise, instead of a high screech. And saw the yellow beam of a Chilean Army flashlight, searching beyond the tree. The soldiers had orders to shoot anything that moved, in the hours of curfew. But our tent was in a small hollow, a few yards wide. And lying on the ground, we were below the line of fire of a machine gun, sited over there. So we were safe enough, in bed. After convincing myself that I really did not need to go outside, I closed my eyes and considered how we got to that place.

It had started five years before. June and I had done a lot of voyaging on the sea, in various small boats, and we decided to go travelling over land for a change. But we had seen most of the United States and Mexico, so what next? June wanted to visit Central and South America. And I agreed, because it meant only one language to learn. For Spanish (which is easy to learn) is spoken in all of those countries except Brazil, where they speak Portuguese. And we could get by with Spanish, even here. But neither of us was interested in going by public transportation, because it was too limiting. We wanted the freedom to go as we pleased, when we felt like it, without waiting on lines or worrying about schedules. And we wanted to visit the smaller places, that had no facilities for tourists, where we could meet the ordinary people of other countries.

I must confess I had discovered that sea voyaging was not for me. After going through countless passages shaded as green and blue as the sea herself, I had to admit that voyaging by land sounded good. And South America, a huge piece of the earth so near to the United States and yet unknown to us, sounded interesting. We could have gone by plane. But then you tend to see mostly cities and sky. We would see more of the countryside if we went by bus or train. But more bus stations and train depots than I care to consider. The automobile gives you freedom. Freedom to go when you please, to stop on a whim, to follow a route that looks inviting. Yes, the automobile would be the best way for us.

So we must go in our own vehicle, with our own facilities for sleeping and cooking. But we would have to travel far, often over very bad roads, and sometimes in places where we could not expect to find help. If we skidded into a hole, we must be able to get the vehicle out of it, by ourselves. Yet it would have to carry all our gear for a winter, plus food and water, spare parts and tools. Which meant that we would need a light truck. It would be too small to live in but a tent would do nicely, most of the time. And there should be some sort of bed in the truck, for emergencies. After investigating all the light trucks available, we found that the Scout II, made by International Harvester, came closest to meeting our needs. But their dealers in Vermont could not give us all the details we wanted, so we went to Fort Wayne, Indiana and saw the president of the motor truck division. He was rather surprised to have a customer wander into his office but he soon recovered and sent for the engineer in charge of the Scout II project, who was most helpful. And in a couple of hours, we had the details of our vehicle worked out.

Patrick compiled a list of requirements which he made into a thick file along with all the literature he could find on likely equipment. He sifted through the file, accepting, rejecting, modifying and changing his mind until he had a fairly clear idea of what we could buy to do what we thought we wanted to do. Then the real problem began. Have you ever tried to buy exactly what you want?

Briefly, we wanted it to be as stong and simple as possible. Strong to stand up to long, hard use. And simple, so that we could fix it ourselves, if we had to. Or show a mechanic how to fix it in some remote, foreign village. So the first thing we insisted on was two wheel drive, not four. That surprised the engineer but it eliminated a great deal of machinery, any part of which could go wrong. And it saved us from carrying a lot more spare parts. For in the places where a breakdown was most likely, we should not expect to find spare parts. So we would have to carry every part we might need, with us, all the way.

I wonder if we'll ever use even one of those five inner tubes he bought in case something unrepairable happened to our brand new tubeless tires.

The same reasoning led us to eliminate power steering and brakes, that we did not really need. And a power winch, that could be replaced by a more reliable manual one. For we did not expect to get where we were going quickly or easily. But we wanted to get there alive eventually.

I had only two requirements. Enough water for a good wash, now and then. And a private place for my toilet. Space had duly allotted for not one, but two water jugs. And for my toilet ,a promise of a hardy bush, now and then.

We would sometimes have to go a long way, between places where we could buy gas. So fuel consumption was important and the answer to that was a small engine and a big gearbox. The engine we chose was a six cylinder one that was once used in Rambler cars. It was much easier to get at and fix than a V-8 engine, besides being reliable and economical. And the gearbox was a heavy duty, four speed commercial one, designed to go forever in any gear. So we could climb any mountain in the lower gears and hum along on the level places in the higher ones, much like a heavy truck.

Always a bit embarrassed on these occasions, I found our visit to the factory less painful than several earlier encounters with car dealers. The salesmen never seemed able or willing to answer questions. When Patrick wanted to talk about gear ratios, they wanted to talk about accessories. When he wanted to discuss engine size, the would begin a lengthy monologue which implied that the car which just happened to be standing on their lot was indeed made in Heaven just for us. At the factory, on the other hand, questions got answers and in a short time we had placed our order. Patrick was and still is delighted with his car. The engineers didn't resent his questions and he didn't find it necessary to run red faced and ranting into the distance.

Since we would be going through the tropics, we asked for the best cooling system they could provide, for the engine. And though we knew it would mean a rough ride, we asked them to put on the heaviest springs they could find.

Thus exercising became quite unnecessary. If you are ever feeling flabby, just take our car on a thirty thousand mile spin. What isn't worked off shifting gears, steering and braking, is simply bounced off.

Inside, we asked for two bucket seats, with safety belts, but no back seat. And no radio, since we felt it distracted the driver. But we did order airconditioning, on the grounds that it would be nice while it worked and no serious loss if it failed. And finally, there was the color. They had a light brown, almost gold color that was ideal for our purpose, since it would look nondescript (and therefore attract no attention) in the country-side, when it was slightly dirty. And sort of Upper Middle Class when it was clean, in a city. Which was just the effect we wanted. So we gave them our order and went home while they built the truck.

Since my request for some sort of toilet was ignored, I was a bit miffed by the purchase of airconditioning for the car. An obviously self-indulgent accessory. But our route took us through dust, sand and heat for hours every day. We saw others along the road, lookimg sweaty and dirty, while we managed, with the help of the airconditioner, to stay cool and clean. Once inside the car and moving, we were very comfortable indeed.

It was August when we heard from them and I flew out to Fort Wayne, to drive it back to Vermont, taking care to break-in the engine properly. Then I went to work and built the interior, with the help of a cabinet maker. Just below the windows we put in a deck, from behind the seats, all the way to the back. Under it were lockers for tools, clothes and so on, with lids in the deck to reach them. At the back was the kichen, with an ice box, a gasoline stove and a box for food and utensils. Above those was a place to slide in a folding table. And we covered the tailgate with wood, to use as June's kitchen or my work bench.

The kitchen is much like a boat's galley. Only smaller. And you have to stand out in the open. At least the ground seldom sways under your feet. And we did become adept at rigging elaborate wind or rain shelters. But meals became less elaborate. So many things I thought I couldn't cook without soon were discarded. In the end, we had more space allotted to cooking than we really needed. Two of everything and a frying pan. Quite enough.

When the varnish was dry, I had cushions made of four-inch foam rubber, covered with brown Naugahyde, that went on top of the deck to make a bed in the truck. Or they could be taken into the tent and used on the floor there. The tent we chose was an umbrella type, with the frame on the outside, about ten feet square and eight feet high, made of light-brown canvas. The sides sloped inward toward the top, so that it would not blow over in a strong wind. There was a top fly that went on the outside of the frame, to protect the tent from sun or rain, and a front fly to protect the door, with mosquito netting to go around that. And mosquito netting over the windows. The floor was coated with green plastic and there were zippers on the door which (they said) would keep out snakes. We went to Maine to see it, before buying it. And on the way home, we tried camping for the night.

We arrived in the campground after dark and I set about putting up the tent, while June read the instructions by flashlight. There were a dozen aluminum poles that plugged into each other, to make the frame. And as I tried to spring the last one into place, it flew back and hit me in the face, barely missing my right eye (which is the only one I have, that works). Evidently the ground was uneven and the four corners of the tent were not in the same plane. So we moved it about a foot and the next time we tried, we got it together. But from then on, each time we set up the tent, June would hold onto the last pole while I set it in place. For when you are planning an expedition in which some unusual risks are unavoidable, it is a good idea to eliminate those that are not. But it was nice to wake up in the woods, the next morning and after folding the tent (with the help of the

6

instructions, for it was not simple) we went back to Vermont.

In time, we could erect the tent, single handed or together, in less than five minutes. Even less time than that if rain were beginning to fall. And once inside, with our own bed and table, the round rush mats and perhaps a candle, we were at home. The strangeness of the outside world was held back by that thin shell of canvas. We were safe.

In spite of my inability to cope with the heaving motion of the open sea, I had developed a love for more subdued waters. A river, a saltmarsh. Places where the loudest noise heard is stillness. And we found stillness again on the back roads. Among lakes and ponds, villages and wayside rests. Places where we could now stop because we carried with us what we needed for daily life. There was no longer any reason to rush over superhighways from one mediocre meal to another mediocre motel. With our simple equipment we could live away from the road, seeking out the quiet backwaters, pitching our tent among the trees, with only the sounds of the woods to disturb us. Travelling became a pleasure.

We had some initial problems with the truck, like a throttle cable that let go in the middle of a city, but they were not hard to fix. And otherwise, it was rather grand. It could easily make a U-turn on any normal road. There were four ways of stopping it: Two independent braking systems, an emergency brake and the big gearbox (that we used most). And though it did not have four wheel drive, it had two. In effect, most cars only have one wheel drive. If one of the drive wheels starts spinning, the other gives up. But there is a simple device available to stop that. When one wheel slips, it locks the axle and transmits the power to the other one. So we had one of those. And with deep-treaded tires, the little truck had a good grip on the road. But we needed a place to check it out and the obvious one was Baja California, the thousand-mile-long peninsula that lies parallel with Mexico, between the Pacific Ocean and the Gulf of California. So we read everything we could find on that.

How he became interested in the Baja, I don't really know. He was probably swapping sea stories with someone from the West Coast. We could just as well have driven around in cicles in Death Valley. But at least the Baja run would be a bit more interesting. The more we talked about it, the more logial it seemed.

The northern half was a State of Mexico but the southern part was a Territory and we would need a special permit to go there. But almost the whole peninsula was one vast desert, with hardly any people except in the few, widely scattered towns. And more snakes than anywhere else on earth. After the first two hundred miles, the roads were very bad indeed. In fact, they were just tracks across the desert with no bridges, culverts or signs of any kind. When you came to an arroyo, you found your own way down into it, across the bottom (over the big, smooth stones) and up the far side. Unless there was a flash flood in progress. For when the rains did come, the ground was baked so hard that the water simply ran off it, down into the arroyos. So it was best to travel in the dry season, which was our winter. Even then, there could be sudden storms that would send tons of water rushing down the arroyos. But they were less frequent.

There were two routes down Baja California, which started on the east and west coasts and joined together about four hundred miles down the peninsula. But the winds off the Pacific Ocean were rather strong for tenting, with no trees for shelter. So we chose the other way, beside the Gulf of California, which was known as the Sea of Cortez. By that time, we had made up our minds to go there, of course. It was far too interesting to pass up. And a great place to try out the truck. But we had better be prepared. For weeks we ran around, gathering spare parts, tools and equipment to meet any thinkable emergency: A shovel to dig the truck out. A crowbar to clear a fender, bent against a wheel. A fire extinguisher, first aid kit, snake bite kit and so on.

We drove to Chicago, to meet John Dupre. John was considered somewhat of an expert on desert survival. He had written several articles on the topic. And on the Baja and drivng there. We were full of questions. How rough is it, really? Are snakes a problem? At lunch we swapped sea stories for desert stories. And John always finished his tale (which usually included a snake or two) with a shake of his head and mumble something about not taking women on a trip like that. It was too rough, too dangerous, too .... Too what, John? After the dozenth time, I demanded to know exactly what was too dangerous, too rough? He hesitated and

then said: "Oh, you'll be all right. You're one of the boys."
I decided it best to consider that remark a compliment.

To watch over the engine, I installed a tachometer and a vacuum gauge. For navigation, I calibrated the truck's odometer, installed a marine compass and corrected it for deviation. That was fun. Late one night, I went out to a big parking lot and using the Pole Star, I laid out rocks, maybe ten yards apart, on the cardinal headings. Then in the morning I started driving the truck around, lining it up with each pair of rocks and adjusting the compass, until it was correct. By which time, a great many people must have thought I was mad. Both the gearshift lever and the airconditioner affected the compass, so I made it read correctly in third gear, with the airconditioner on, which seemed to be a likely configuration in the desert, where we would most need it. And to give us further clues as to where we were, I installed an altimeter.

With so much equipment aboard, we had to consider the posibility of theft. The truck came with a self-locking steering wheel and the hood could only be opened from inside but I added a locking gas tank cap and an electric alarm that blows the horn when the truck is moved. Then I cut the fuel line between the gas tank and the engine and installed a shut-off valve under June's seat. That should do it. We would have to carry enough fuel, water, food and ice to go from one town to the next in Baja California. The food was not critical. We could go without eating for a few days, if we had to. And the ice was mainly to preserve the food. But the fuel and the water were important. If we ran out of either of those, we could be in real trouble.

The gas tank held 20 gallons and the truck went more than 18 miles to a gallon, so we put aboard two red plastic cans of 5 gallons each, which gave us a range of 540 miles on good roads and about two thirds of that in the Baja. For though we would be in the lower gears there, most of the time, we would be going much more slowly, which tends to save fuel. The water we carried in 4 white plastic cans of 2.5 gallons each and we knew from our days on the ocean in small boats that we could easily get by on half a gallon a day each. So that was enough for 10 days and we could make it last longer. But we also carried material to make solar stills.

Those work at night. In the evening, you scrape out a depression in the desert, about 3 feet across and a foot deep, and in that you put any vegetation you can find, like old bits of dry cactus. Then you place a cup in the middle of the hole and stretch a piece of clear plastic across it, with stones around the edge to hold the plastic in place. And in the middle, over the cup, you put one small stone. During the night, the air is much colder than the ground and moisture from the vegetation condenses on the under side of the plastic, and runs down into the cup. And in the morning, if you are lucky, you should find half a cup of drinking water. So if you make 3 or 4 of them, you can stay alive. But we did not take any guns, dogs or radio transmitters, since we felt that anyone who could not get by without shooting, biting or shouting for help should not be there. And suddenly we were ready to go. Late in October we left Vermont and drove across America to California, taking the smaller roads and camping each night, mostly in quiet, wooded parks. Each time we set up the tent, we got better at it and we soon found that spending a night in our tent suited us far better than staying in a motel.

Patrick bought a red carpet at a dime store and cut it to fit inside our tent, wall to wall. It was a great improvement. Now we could step out of bed onto the warm carpet. And with our table and stools in place for dining, it was very cozy.

Instead of stopping by a highway after driving all day, we would follow a lane into the country. And instead of being cooped up in a room, we were free to stroll in the woods. We were used to naming our boats, so we called the truck Minim, which is a small thing of no importance (the opposite of a big deal). But in a dictionary it has other meanings: The shortest note in music, the smallest kind of soldier ant, a tiny stroke in caligraphy and an order of mendicant monks who roamed Europe in the nineteenth century. We fell into the habit of calling Minim 'she', as if she were a boat, and we never could decide whether she was a car or a truck. For though she was clearly a truck by birth, she was our only car for many years. But in Latin America, the problem was solved, because they have a word, Camionetta, that means Little Truck, which suited her nicely.

At each border it was required of us to fill in every inch of a long form.

SEA OF CORTEZ

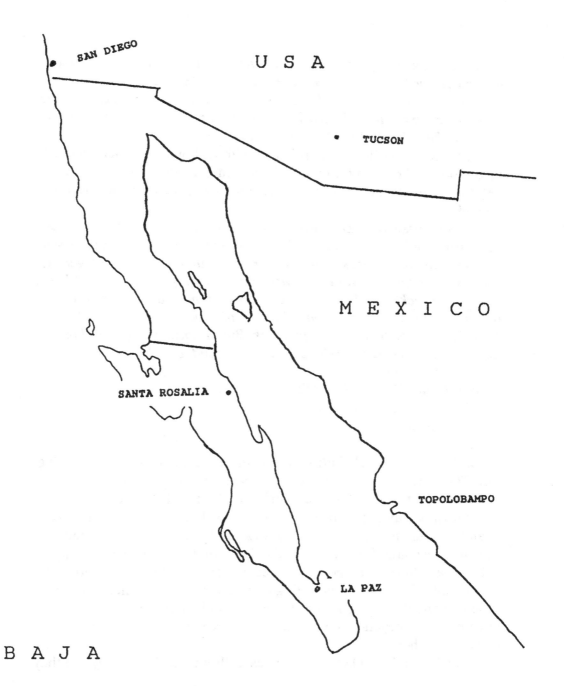

SAN DIEGO

USA

TUCSON

MEXICO

SANTA ROSALIA

TOPOLOBAMPO

LA PAZ

BAJA

CALIFORNIA

They all wanted to know my occupation. Which we dutifully listed as housewife until we learned the Spanish term - 'Ama de casa'

Since we didn't have a house, and were living for months at a time in and around our little truck, I soon became 'Ama de camionetta' Much to the delight of the border officials.

At El Centro, California we filled up with fuel, water and ice, stocked up on food and headed for the Mexican border, ready (if we ever would be) to make the thousand-mile run down the Baja to La Paz, near the far end.

It was thanksgiving Day when we crossed the border and we had been prepared to spend the whole day going through Customs inspection, for Minim was packed to the bursting point with enough gear to last us through the winter. I was wondering how to explain U-bolts, bushings, shock absorbers, oil filters, cans of meat and engine oil, pots of jam, even an anchor and 100 feet of Dacron line, that Patrick thought might be handy if we got stuck. But the customs officer glanced at the car, then asked: "Where do you to intend to go?"

"La Paz", I said.

"Puertecitos?" I nodded, "Yes."

"El Arco?" I noded again, "Yes."

"San Ignacio?"

"Yes."

"La Paz," he stated flatly and shrugged his shoulders. And writing DESTINATION LA PAZ across our papers, he waved us on.

We got lost twice, before we found our way out of Mexicali (you can never trust a navigator in a city) but beyond, the road was paved and straight; with mountains in many shades of gray on the right and low, flat land reaching far away, on the left; all the way to San Felipe.

That was a small village on the Sea of Cortez but it was overrun by Americans. The older ones sitting in chairs by their vehicles along the beach, while the younger ones roared around on motor cycles and dune buggies. And beyond the village, there was a rough gravel road, parallel with the shore.

For a while, a few bikes and buggies followed us but one by one they turned back, while we rattled on down the coast to the tiny fishing village of Puertecitos, its few houses built on the barren hills surrounding a small cove. And there we set up our tent on a rocky ledge, to get a night's sleep before tackling the next section of road, that we had been told was the hardest of any major route in Baja California.

Our tent site was just to the south edge of the cove and a little higher than the village, giving us a lovely view of the sea, soft against the curved sandy beach that led up to the settlement. All of the wooden shacks faced the water, one above the other in rings up the steep slope. And near each one perched an outhouse. Some were elaborately decorated with color and bric-a-brac. Some had windows. Each had a spectacular view.

But the ground beneath the tent sloped down on one side, making it hard to stay on the cushions. And there were stones under the floor. So we did not sleep much. And soon after dawn we had everything back in the truck, ready to go.

We were too excited to sleep. Or apprehensive. We knew we could sail a boat across an ocean, but a people-less land, a desert? It could be very different.

We had read that the next 10 miles would not be too bad, then there would be an abrupt change for the worse, so we were surprised to find how bad the road was, right after Puertecitos. It was scarcely wide enough for one car and the hills were so steep that coming to the top of one, you had to look out of the side windows to find out which way the road went next. The turns were often so sharp that you could not see the road for more than a few yards ahead and the surface was much like the bed of a mountain stream, with large outcroppings of bare rock, between which were loose stones of varying sizes. But that section was not hard to negotiate if you took it very slowly. So we heaved and lumbered along, trying to avoid the worst bumps, until we came to a straight, level stretch of coarse gravel, where we could rattle along at a solid 15 miles an hour. And so it went on for several miles, until we went around a corner, started up a steeper hill than usual and Minim came to a stop.

I braked to hold her where she was but she started going backward down the hill, with all four wheels sliding over the loose stones, so I let her roll to keep her under control and we went smartly back to the bottom. We had come to the hard part. The road ahead wound far up a mountain, so we backed up and took a run at it, going at full speed in first gear, and Minim was fine but it was not exactly a peaceful trip, for it was a goodly clip at which to proceed around blind hairpin corners, over a surface of bare rock and loose stones, in a heavily laden truck. But in all such endeavors there comes a time to stop worrying and get on with it, so June watched the road ahead for signs of other vehicles, while I picked out the best line and Minim leaped merrily from rock to rock, flinging the smaller stones up in her wake, all the way to the top. Then we teetered over the crest, looking for the road down the other side. But once we found it, going down was easier, for we could take it much slower. As long as the brakes held.

In the valleys below were the hulks of cars that never made it. Only a few, but at each dangerous spot along the way we would see rusted steel frames down below. Occasionally there was a pile of stones marked by a cross at the road side, and at the summit of the most incredible climb there would be a modest shrine. You had made it. Now it was time to give thanks.

Finding a wide place in the road near the top of the next mountain, we stopped to let the brakes cool, while we secured everything aboard Minim and tightened our seat belts as hard as we could, to stop our heads from hitting the roof. And so it went on: Up and down a couple of mountains, find a place to stop, check everything and off you go again. Then suddenly the hard part was over. One last, long descent took us down to a flat, level plain where a white gravel road ran straight and far into the distance. And late in the afternoon, we came to the village of Bahia San Luis Gonzaga.

The Skipper has forgotten that, every now and then, the way would suddenly drop out of sight down the side of a small arroyo and directly ahead, before the rear wheels reached the bottom, the front wheels had to start a seemingly vertical climb back to the level road at the top.

Turning off the road, we followed a long, dusty track that widened out as we approached a cluster of small buildings, so that we had the feeling of coming into a harbor in a small boat after a passage from a distant port.

Indeed it was much the same, for there in the wilderness, the few settlements lay like islands in a great sea, the trucks that came and went their only contacts with the world outside. As in a small island, the stranger was always welcome and he was glad of anything he might find, however modest. In which light the village looked pretty good, for there we found gasoline. It was poured from old, rusty drums and was of the lowest grade that Mexico had to offer but that was the only kind we found in all the Baja until we reached La Paz.

We were twice asked for bullets. The government in Mexico had recently put a restriction on the sale of ammunition. We did not carry a gun, so we could not help. But it was quite clear that the bullets were for rabbits, not men. The fishermen lived on fish unless they could find game. If they wanted meat, they had to shoot it. Money was of little value, for there was nowhere to spend it. Only something tha would help get you another meal really meant anything.

Altogether, there were maybe five families in the village but no one spoke English and at that time we knew so little Spanish that we could barely communicate with them. But beyond their houses lived a lone, elderly American who gave us some valuable information about the road ahead. He told us of the time, some years before, when his truck had broken down and he waited for nine days beside the main road for the next one to come by. Then he had survived because there was plenty of food and water in his truck and he did not try to walk across the desert but rigged a shade against the sun and conserved his supplies and stayed where he was. We should not have to wait that long, for there was more traffic on the roads by then. But there were bandits in the area ahead and it would be unwise to camp for the night beside the road, where they might find us. However, there was an onyx mine a day's drive from there, set well back from the road, where he sometimes spent the night. And he told us how to find our way to that.

Our host was a collector. Mostly of empty tin cans. The building with its screened porch, unfinished walls and bare floors, was sparsely furnished. A few benches, a straight-backed chair, wooden tables and crude shelves nailed to the wall studs. All covered with tin cans. A space on the largest table had been cleared enough for a plate and a coffee cup. There must have been a can opener someplace. Perhaps supporting loops of wire and rope that hung on the walls, with his fishing equipment. Poles, lines, tackle. And there must have been a cache of full cans. Perhaps under a cot, barely visible in a corner behind the clutter. Light was fading, the kerosene lamp hanging from a nail in a roof rafter would soon be lighted. Best for us to find a campsite and leave this happy fisherman.

Behind his house was a high, steep hill and driving over it, we came to a lonely beach. Leaving Minim on firmer ground, we carried our gear down to the soft, white sand and there we made our camp, close to the sparkling blue Sea of Cortez. And soon we were celebrating the Crossing of the Mountains. As the sun went down, the moon and all the stars came out, shining bright and clear overhead. The wilderness was silent but for the lapping of wavelets along the shore and we slept soundly through the night, to awaken before dawn and watch the sun rise out of the sea, turning the rugged hills behind us to gold against the pale blue sky. When we had finished the important things, like washing and having breakfast and searching for interesting shells along the beach, we carried our gear back to Minim and set out on the long climb up unto the central highlands. And jogging slowly along, we had time to look around us.

The air was so clear that from the top of a hill we could see far into the distance and begin to understand the vastness of the wilderness. For in hundreds of square miles, the only vegetation to be seen was cactus. Big and small, fat and thin, they clung resolutely to the barren land wherever they could find a crevice to get a root in. And the only living things we saw all day were an occasional bird or desert rat. Late in the afternoon we came to a high, flat plain, almost circular and maybe five miles across, green with cacti, within a ring of brown mountain tops under the blue sky. Down to the left of the road, we saw the white ruins of an old monastery. And soon, on the right, we found the track that led away from the road, over a slight rise, to the onyx mine. It was being worked by two men. One ran a bulldozer that turned up the rocky ground to expose the boulders containing the onyx. Then they both split them by hand until they had a pile of prepared stones, each a foot or so square, that the other man hauled away in a rickety old brown truck. As we approached, he was standing by his truck, quite still, watching us discreetly over the top of the open door. But since it was a high truck, all of him from the waist down was showing beneath the door, which gave an odd effect.

He was a young man and when I asked if we might camp there for the night, he smiled happily and said: "Yes."

"Where?" I asked.

"Anywhere" he replied with a grand, sweeping gesture. So we chose a spot that was less rocky than most and set up our tent, facing across the plain, with Minim close behind to break the wind and ropes from her to steady the tent.

The two men lived in an old bus nearby and as we ate our dinner, we could hear them playing a harmonica and singing, so I walked over to give them some cigarettes. The bus was quite bare inside, a couple of windows were broken and there was no heat. Clearly they had nothing the bandits would want. And our tracks to the mine would be lost among those of their truck. So it was indeed a fine, safe place to spend the night. But going to bed, I was careful to close up the tent, to keep out the snakes. They come out at night to hunt for food and we had no wish to find one in our sleeping bag. On the beach, the night before, there was little risk of that, since a snake will generally avoid crossing an open area, without any cover. But there in the onyx mine, we were surrounded by rocks and boulders, each with a deep shadow beneath it. And the mere thought of a snake gave both of us the willies. But if you choose to sleep on the ground in a wilderness, you just have to be careful. So we made our bed in the middle of the tent, well away from the sides, and went to sleep.

All of John Dupre's snake tales came back to us. We both checked the door closure, zipping it up to the last tooth. Yes, we both remember the manufacturer's claim. But how could that thin bit of canvas possibly keep out a determined rattlesnake? We placed the bed dead in the center of the floor and, packing duffle bags and sweaters around the edge of the tent, we settled in for a bad night's sleep.

Later that night, a cold wind came down from the mountain behind us, tugging and shaking our tent. And in the dawn, we saw clouds overhead.

Clouds that could bring rain and cut off the road ahead. So we ate in haste, packed quickly and left. Beyond the plain, the road wound up through a canyon toward a gap in the mountains, crossing a small river from side to side and sometimes going straight up the middle of it. The surface was of mud and stones and the water was not very deep, so it was not difficult to follow, though one could get stuck and that would be emarrassing in a river, with those clouds around. But after a while, the road moved over to one side and we relaxed a little, bowling along over a smooth, sandy surface. And came to a sudden stop. Trying reverse, I found that Minim's wheels would not turn at all. Her tires bit down into the deep sand and locked solidly. For a moment I wondered what would happen if the clouds above let go and sent a raging torrent of water down the canyon, as they certainly could. Then we went into our underditching routine.

June took the shovel and dug away the sand in front of each wheel, while I attached our hand-operated winch to the front bumper. Next, I set the anchor in the ground ahead of the truck and led the Dacron line back to the winch. Then we took up the strain on the line, that has a certain amount of stretch to it, started Minim's engine and drove her straight out, onto firm ground. And soon we were out of the canyon, bouncing happily along over the bumpy, twisting road through a forest of candlestick cacti, many of them as high as telephone poles, while the clouds dropped away behind us and the warm sun came out overhead.

I wondered, when Minim became embedded in the sand, just where, if necessary, we could camp. The canyon was narrow at that point. And deep. High on each side, jagged rocks climbed steadily up. Every inch of earth supported cacti, more than we had seen before, fresh and deep green. The river must be an awesome sight in the rainy season to support so much growth. There was even an honest-to-goodness, full sized palm tree near the road. The river bed was the only place for a camp. And Minim neatly blocked the road. We had not seen another vehicle that day and I thought of the man who waited nine days beside the road for help to come.

But before long we met a truck coming the other way, old and heavily laden, grinding along at 4 or 5 miles an hour. So we backed up to a place where he could get past us. One problem there was the frequency of Multiple Choice Roads. We would come to a place where the road ahead branched out in 2 or 3 directions, all of which looked the same. Most likely they would rejoin within a mile but one might be an old section, no longer used and now impassable.

There was always one clue available when deciding which route to take: The one with the most litter by the side of the road. Besides the hulks of old cars that didn't make it and had been stripped of anything usable, the way was strewn with bottles, oil cans, mufflers, tires, rims, anything not wanted. Each camp used along the way was clearly evident. The remnains of the camp fire, the litter of the evening meal. There were no labels on the bottles, so some of the sites must have been many years old.

June did the navigation and found it easier than we had expected. Of course, there were no road signs to follow but for anyone experienced in marine navigation, it was not hard. When we came to the top of a hill, we could see far ahead and by comparing what we saw with the map, we could figure the average direction to go in. Then each time there was a choice of roads, she would read the compass and tell me which one to take, to stay in the general direction we wanted. At the same time, she kept a note of our distance run, so that by measuring how far we had gone since our last 'fix', she could always tell approximately where we were, on the map. A 'fix' in navigator's jargon is a point where you think you know exactly where you are. As for example, when we came to the village of Punta Prieta. That was just a dozen houses and nowhere was the name to be seen but it was the only village on the map or many miles, in all directions.

Beyond it, the vegetation was more varied, with boojum and elephant trees among the cacti. And soon we began to see ranches, though mostly they would be little more than a corral and a shack, with a few cows nearby. Then nothing for miles ahead. Perhaps the distances seemed greater because we went very slowly over that rough, rocky ground. Each hour, June would note our distance run and 8.8 miles would be quite normal, while 11.5 would be a good hour's run.

There was no feeling of slowness. I was bouncing in my seat at about 80

18

miles an hour.

But after a while, we left the ranches behind and came out onto a vast, cactus covered plain, green close by and blue in the distance, with sometimes a glimpse of the Pacific Ocean, far off to our right. By then we had joined the road that came down the western side of the Baja from Ensenada but still we did not see any sign of traffic, all afternoon.

A sign appeared in the dust ahead. We stopped briefly to decipher the sun-bleached message: In San Ignacio (several hundred miles ahead) was the New Oasis Motel. With Hot Showers.

Just before dark, we reached the other side and came to a ranch beside the road: Two large corrals, one for horses and one for cattle, a primitive shack that served as a kitchen for the hands and restaurant for passing truck drivers, a small bunk house and a smaller one for the family. Between the bunk house and the corrals were two covered, fenced enclosures, one for gasoline and one for saddles. And each was guarded by a silent, watchful brown dog on a leash just long enough to let him bite anyone who went in. At the suggestion of the older lady, we pitched our tent close under the lee of the bunk house, with the saddle enclosure on one side and Minim on the other to break the wind, and there we were very snug. True there was a strong smell of manure, and our bed was more comfortable after I removed an old gear wheel from under it but the dog in charge of saddles kept an eye on our gear and we had a good night's sleep.

The head rooster strongly objected to our tent. We were much too close to the heap of discarded oil barrels where he preferred to preen himself in the evening. One of the young girls came scolding out of the kitchen, tucked him under her arm and shoved him into the chicken run, He was not at all pleased.

Just before dawn, the cocks started crowing and the whole place came alive. Cattle were loaded into trucks, engines grumbled, coughed and roared, a huge flight of doves soared into the clear morning sky and came fluttering back down. And amid the cheerful confusion we took our leave.

The buildings were framed with the inner core of cactus, walled and roofed with palm leaves. You wondered how they withstood the ever present winter wind. The floors were dirt and yet every piece of simple furniture was scrubbed clean and bright. The women cooked on stoves made of old gasoline barels. The fuel seemed to be dried cactus. Tortillas, gray and pasty, browned unevenly on the barrel top.

After a while, the road dropped down through a canyon onto another broad plain but there the vegetation was not nearly so lush. The few cacti that we saw were brown and scraggly, the land was hard and bare, turning easily to dust in the wind. And alone we jogged and rattled through the wilderness. There you got the curious effect of many mountains but few valleys. Mostly they were great plains, each ringed around by mountains or by the sea and connected by deep, twising canyons, until we came to El Arco, the half way point of the Baja, that lay in the northeast corner of the Vizcayne Desert. It was indeed a desert town, a collection of dusty buildings through which the desert seemed to run with scarcely a break. And out ahead for another 75 miles, clear to San Ignacio.

We had been warned of the dust. Everything we read about the Baja mentioned the dust. And it was dusty - but nothing like we expected. Perhaps because we didn't go in a convoy - following in the wake of another vehicle - we were spared that.

The desert ahead was much like the wilderness before El Arco, perhaps more brown and barren, perhaps more rocky and sandy. And crossing it, the scene changed little for several hours. Then suddenly, trusting the navigator for there were still no signs, we turned off onto a road that wound steeply down into a ravine. And there at the bottom lay San Ignacio, a true oasis. The first things we noticed were the palm trees. Acres of them, tall and strong, with dark green tops and sweeping gray trunks, swaying gently in the breeze and casting deep shadows in the desert sunlight. Then houses, lots of houses. And some substantial buildings. And a lake, shimmering and cool, with black water birds (ducks, I think) swimming like ships in formation. Then we came to the plaza, with the Mission and a large general store and many smaller shops. And people going to and fro, looking busy.

San Ignacio was the first true town we had seen since leaving the border. Small orchards of huge old date palms were scattered through the town. The oasis itself, cool green reeds and grass against the bright blue water, filled us with pleasure. We stopped and stared at the sight. And further on we found the tree-lined square, the beautiful old cathedral, the various general stores, the movie house, the bank and the police station. Ahead were more adobe-walled dusty streets.

After driving around, admiring all that activity, we went back to the edge of town, to the Oasis Motel, which was built of palm leaves. There were ten neat little huts with thatched roofs, dirt floors and open work in between them, so that you could see right through them. And each one was furnished with two cots. But the owner was quite agreeable to our pitching our tent beside his huts, for a small fee. And across the road, he had a shower that we could use, though it would take half an hour for the water to get hot. The building he showed us was maybe ten feet square, made of concrete blocks, with a flat roof. Inside, it was pitch dark but opening a small window brought in a blinding shaft of sunlight and a clear view of the street. And down from the iron roof came one small pipe, with a valve on it.

Opening the valve released a thin, round stream of water and quickly we found that it was boiling hot. Then we found out why: There were relays of small boys, bringing buckets of steaming water from the kitchen across the road, climbing up a ladder behind the building and pouring it into a funnel on the roof, with a thunderous noise on the corrugated iron. But after they had taken so much trouble, we cold hardly spurn their efforts, so we skipped to and fro under the stream of boiling water and managed to get clean without being burned. In fact, it was our first shower since leaving America and by the standards of the desert, it was a rare luxury.

The entire passage from Puertecitos to San Ignacio was made on a road void of a bridge, void of a culvert, lacking even simple grading. Each mile was hacked out of, though or over the land itself. The road simply followed the easiest route between two points. From village to mission to ranch, probably first a foot or burro track - now wide enough for a small truck. Never the most direct route - often the only possible route. We drove on mountain ledges, on river beds, over walls of rough lava. At times the road stretched straight ahead as far as you could see through the desert forest - a dry, sandy track. It was not built up over the desert floor but worn out of the earth. At times the edges of the road were two or three feet high, on each side of you. And the endless cacti towered overhead.

Leaving San Ignacio in the morning, we saw construction work beside the road. Great bulldozers of the largest size thundered and roared. Fussy little yellow trucks buzzed to and fro. Men stood around in twos and threes, working. Soon we came to a wide, smooth gravel highway and went humming along it for mile after mile, until it ran into a mountain and stopped. Then there was the old kind of road, a single lane track over the rocky terrain, that went over a brow and dropped down a fine, exciting series of switchbacks called the Devil's Stairway, toward the valley far below. Minim can turn like a London taxi but I was winding the steering wheel all the way to the end stops as we swept around corner after corner, with a solid wall of rock on one side of us and a sheer, unguarded precepice on the other. June kept watch for other vehicles but the road ahead was not hard to see if you looked straight down and luckily we did not meet any, all the way to the bottom, where the fine new road started again, wide and straight, good for a solid forty miles an hour. Then we came to a brand new, hard surfaced road and swept down it, in a series of gentle curves, to the town of Santa Rosalia on the Sea of Cortez, where we were stopped by a man with a red flag while a construction crew let off some explosives ahead of us.

Waiting there, we commented in our halting Spanish on the fine new road and he agreed that it was indeed so. Then we asked him how the road to La Paz was and he said: "Equal." It took a moment for that to sink in. Then we tried again and he assured us that the new, paved highway indeed ran from where we were, all the way to La Paz. It was so new, there was no line down the middle yet but that did not matter, since there was hardly any traffic on it. And the surface was so smooth that Minim seemed to glide along, with scarcely any effort. It was all very strange. And soon we came to the Bay of Conception, where we camped for the night, alone on a wide beach, close to the water's edge. But somethig was wrong. We were not as pleased with the fine, new road as we should be. We missed the old one.

We shared the feeling of disappointment when we finally realized that a paved highway would carry us to La Paz. At first we had been a little wary of the land - like the sea, it had its own ways - and we wondered just how we would fit in. But with each day, we felt more at ease with the mountains and desert and the enduring life arund us.

Certainly it made the rest of the run down the peninsula very easy. And coming over a hill, we saw the city of La Paz in the distance, across the wide bay that formed its harbor. As we drove around the bay, we could see buildings, white and in pastel colors, along the shore. And houses, rising up the hills behind them, with mountains farther back. And at the edge of the city, we came to El Cardon Trailer Park. That was a surprise: A fine, new park with palm trees and fresh, green grass between the neatly laid out sites. And except for one small trailer, belonging to the Naural Resources Survey people out of Mexico City, they were all empty. The owner, Mr. Hahnel, came to greet us. He was an eldely German who had been in the merchant navy and the trailer park was his retirement project, almost completed. Soon our tent was set up beside a shady ramada, with Minim backed into the little driveway beside it. And a water tap, all to ourselves.

A few weeks later, we were honored with an invitation to the home of Senor Hahnel and La Senora, The blue stucco front wall, facing the malecon (sea wall) and the bay, was broken by a dark wooden door and a shuttered window. The shutters opened into an office where Senor Hahnel conducted his business as a bondsman. The passage from the door led past the office entrance to a secluded patio and the private quarters. There, half indoors and half out, under high ceilings or the sky, the Hahnel family had lived for many years. Senora Hahnel spoke often of her childhood on the mainland in Chihahua. But here, in La Paz, she had come to love the old house. It was just a block from the activity of the center of town and each time she walked from the front door, she saw the harbor, the curving beaches and the sea. Senor Hahnel was building a new house for her at the trailer park. I don't think she was enthusiastic about it. It would mean living along the highway, the noise and fumes of every passing truck invading her life. But El Senor was too excited about his new venture to notice. The activity bound to come with the completion of the new road to

California was luring him to his trailer park. He wanted it to be the best in La Paz.

Patrick, of course, knew exactly what was needed to draw in the traveller. A sign. A huge sign on the highway that would announce to the American camper exactly what was available at El Cardon: Hot showers, a swimming pool, a laundry and full hookups. A term that meant sewer, water and electic connections at every campsite. In due course, Patrick completed a detailed drawing of the proposed sign and delivered it to Senor Hahnel. But we had given up hope of seeing it. Week after week passed and the sign did not appear. Then on our last day in La Paz, as we drove past El Cardon on our way out of town, it was there. A big, beautifully executed sign, just as Patrick had designed it. Except that, besides hot showers, pool and laundry, the tourist was being offered full hangups.

A few yards away, Mr. Hahnel proudly showed us a small, red brick building in which he had installed showers, with hot water and even a laundry machine. Then he introduced us to the guard who would keep an eye on our gear, and left us alone. It was all too much. Reclining in the white painted chairs under the ramada, we felt as though we had suddenly stepped out of the Baja we knew, into something quite different. And in fact we had, for the southern end of the peninsula was connected with the outside world by air and sea, giving it the feeling of an island in the Caribbean, 20 years before. Its warm winter climate and good fishing had been attracting the wealthy for many years and small resorts had been built for them, along the coast south of La Paz. More recently, irrigation had turned the desert lowlands, north of the city, into rich farm land. And La Paz itself had grown quickly but it still looked like the sea port of a small island.

Along the beach there was a sea wall, with a wide sidewalk on it. Then came a road, another sidewalk and the first row of buildings, commercial ones near the center of the town and houses farther out. In the middle, there was a jetty that went straight out into the harbor, with room for several trading vessels along its sides and one small ship across the T-head at the end. And beyond the jetty, lying to their anchors, were usually a couple of ships and a dozen smaller vessels.

Anyone cold walk out along the jetty, if he felt like it, though he took a chance of being hit by something dangling from a crane. And across the road, waiters in white jackets served drinks in the bar of the Hotel La Perla, that was open to the street on two sides and cooled by great fans.

The Hotel La Perla turned out to be the 'in' spot for all sorts of activities. You could sit at one of the tables, sip a coffee and local life would come to you. We were offered pearls, among other things. Since pearling had ceased years ago in La Paz, we guessed these to be Japanese imports. La Paz was a free port, full of transistor radios, TV sets, stereos and hundreds of other consumer goods in great demand on the mainland. One gentleman we met at La Perla, when questioned about his occupation, said quite openly that he was a smuggler. We're not sure just how he operated his business, but it evidently wasn't anything to be hush-hush about.

We both agreed that La Paz would be a fine place to spend the winter and I had a book to write, so we went looking for an apartment. But there were none available, except in one building that was not finished yet. And eventually we persuaded the owner, Raoul Castro, to rent us one just as it was. To be more accurate, his wife did the persuading for us. She was a bright, attractive woman in her late 30's who had been christened Jesus because her father wanted a boy and went under the name of Quichu, as a compromise. Raoul was out all day, minding their fabric store in the center of town, and the new apartments were being built across the street from their house, half a block from the sea wall in the residential section. But the work on the project was behind schedule and Quichu decided to rent one to us, anyway.

There were three floors, each with four apartments and we picked the nicest, on the top floor, with a view of the harbor. But it was a modern building, with floor-to-ceiling windows, the whole width of the living room and the bedroom. And there were no curtains yet. So we set up our tent in the bedroom, to give us some privacy, and furnished the apartment with boxes and such, coveed with cloth or quickly painted. The rooms were starkly white, with tiled floors, and when Quichu saw what we were doing, she brought over some old tables that we could paint, then went off and came back with several big plants in pots, for decoration. There was no kitchen but she had a sink and a water tap put in for us, where it should be, and we used our gasoline stove and things for cooking. There was a shower (cold at fiest but warm, later) and a safe place in the yard for Minim. What more cold one ask for?

Quichu was an angel. When she saw we needed something, she would provide it. So with our collection of odds and ends we were quite comfortable in the empty apartment. Years of living in boats had taught us how little we really needed to survive. But there were problems that even Quichu couldn't solve. One was the noise. Trucks did not have mufflers. Cars did not have mufflers. But they all had horns and screeching brakes. Then came the dogs and after dogs came the roosters. Siesta was the only time of the day everyone got together and shut up. The dogs barked all night long. You would hear the barking start in the distance and one by one each section of the sprawling city would come alive wih howling. They were passing messages, chit-chatting. The dead of night was the only time they could hear each other above the traffic noise. Just before dawn, when all the news had been exchanged and the dogs were barked out, the roosters took a crack at it. They held their gab sessions until the trucks took over around 5 AM. The roosters knew they hadn't a chance against the cocky truck drivers.

The other big problem was having to share the apartment with a growing family of tarantulas. I never got used to having them around. Highly visible against the white walls and white tile floor, the hairy black creatures made my skin crawl. But the woodwork and the doors were all painted black. And the only closets lined one side of a long, dark hall. I carried a pair of twelve inch kitchen tongs whenever I went to a closet. With the tongs, I could take a dress from a hanger, shake it, and with some degree of safety, put it on. One day I stepped out of a hot shower into a tarantula infested bath towel. Now the bath towels were shaken daily too.

Quickly we settled into a routine. For seven hours a day, I worked on the book while June went shopping and learned how to get things like laundry done in the new environment. After lunch, a young typist from a shipping company came to give us an hour's lesson in Spanish. And before long, June was giving English lessons to a doctor's wife on the other side of town.

First Lourdes (short for Maria de Lourdes) would come, after her noon dinner and while others enjoyed the siesta, we would sit around a little card table in front of the huge window overlooking the bay. The hot sun glittering on tin roofs and sand beaches. And until time came to return to her job, young Lourdes would diligently attempt to teach us some simple Spanish. Food, furniture, things, lists of words that some day might be useful. All wasted on me, but Patrick did quite well. Then, when he returned to writing and Lourdes to the job that would keep her at a desk (and out of trouble) into the evening, I would drive to the other side of town, to Graciella's house. While her husband praticed doctoring in the little office at the side of the house, Graciella and I would chatter. She in Spanish and I in Englsh. We had very little difficulty understanding each other. We drew many pictures, used much sign language, laughed a lot and learned little, except that living in the United States isn't really that different from living in Mexico. Even the Avon lady called one day while I was there.

It was a surprise to see the doctor go off to make house calls each day, in his white coat, with his black bag. And there were other things that seemed odd: Sidewalks, for example, that suddenly dropped straight down, as much as five feet on a steep hill, with no railing or anything. If you were stupid enough not to look where you were going, it was too bad.

I remember walking along a street at New Year's time, waiting at a corner to cross an intersection. A policeman stood in the middle of the confusion, directing traffic. One of the cars pulled alongside him and the driver handed the policeman a brightly wrapped package, which he placed at his feet. Moments later, when the cars were stopped and the pedestrians began to cross, a child rushed up to him with another present. The policeman beamed a thank you, placed the gift at his feet and continued his work. Soon the pile of presents stood a foot or more high.

The small shops looked like houses, from the outside. In fact, they were exactly the same, because the older, Spanish-style houses were built to serve any purpose - home, warehouse or shop - that succeeding generations might have for them. But there were also two supermarkets in La Paz, in which it was easier for us to do our shopping, since we did not have to tell anyone what we wanted - we could go and get it. In the evenings, we would stroll along the sea wall, like eveyone else. And beyond the jetty, there was a restaurant called the Yacht Club, which had one dessert: A slice of white cake with pink icing, that was kept under a clear plastic cover. Each time we ate there, we would ask about dessert and each time the waiter would proudly offer it to us. There was no alternative and it was still there, three months later.

On weekends, we would take Minim to secluded beaches like the one at Los Frailes, south of La Paz. There we would set up our tent on the hard, while sand and walk over to the settlement nearby, to order a fish. That was for delivery the next morning but we paid in advance, which made us customers. As such, we had a position in the community and no one ever bothered us. We would spend the night in peace, under the clear, starry sky and just before dawn, there would be a grating noise as the fishermen beached their boat in front of our tent, to deliver a fine, fresh mackerel. The fishing was a cooperative venture. The government supplied the outboard motors (25 HP Johnsons) and the men built the boats, to a standard design, big enough for 3 men and their gear. In the afternoon, the whole village would turn out to drag them up the beach, as they came in. Then the women would do the sorting and the next morning, the catch would leave in an old truck, owned by the community, to be sold in the city.

Later, we drove to the southern end of the Baja, via the west coast, and beyond Todos Santos we spent a night alone on a huge, crescent-shaped beach with mountains around it. There was no sound but the surf, sighing on the pebbles, until just after dawn, when a voice greeted us in English, though the tent. It was Father Theodore Hessburgh of Notre Dame, out hunting birds with three friends, and they stopped briefly to chat about Michigan (where June was born) and the problems of writing (that took much of his time) before continuing on their way. But that was rare, indeed. Usually we met only people who spoke Spanish, fishermen on the coast and farmers inland. Before camping near a farm, we would ask permission, which was always given but usually we would be directed to a spot near the house and as soon as the tent was up, the women would come by, one at a time, ostensibly to hang a few items of laundry on a thorn bush. Of course, what they really wanted was a look inside the tent but they were too polite to ask, so June would invite them in and show them around.

Then the children would come and for those we had balloons, candy and long, yellow pencils. We had assumed that the candy or the balloons would be what they wanted but it was the pencils that fascinated them, for in school they were given only short, well-used ones. And we have seen a boy go off, very happy, saying: "There is much writing in this." Camping in the remoter spots, away from people, we had to be more careful of snakes. In fact, one morning we awoke to find a Gila monster sunning himself on a rock outside the tent. But when I clapped my hands, he left quickly. And some of the lonely places were the most interesting. One was near Cabo San Lucas, at the end of the pennsula, on a small ledge between the old road and a cliff that dropped straight down into the sea. The water must have been deep, near the shore, because in the night, ships came by so close that we could see every detail on their decks.

Back in La Paz, we had a problem transferring money from the United States. In theory, it was easy enough but in real life, there were interminable delays. And one day, when Raoul came by to collect the rent, we did not have enough. The apartment building was his first business venture, other than the shop, and he seemed hesitant about what to do. We explained that we had the money, we just could not get our hands on it. And he went away, quietly. Then, five minutes later, he was back to offer us a loan, until our money came through. We had enough to eat for another week and before then, our money arrived at the bank, so we did not need it, but we were really impressed by his offer.

By then, one other apartment was occupied, by Mr. Jajan, a businessman from Argentina who bought fish in bulk, for shipment to Mexico. He left very early each morning and was back before noon, his day's work done. And he was always very well dressed, courteous and polite. But he smelled so strongly of fish that when he opened his window, on the first floor, we had to close our windows, two floors above.

Senor Jajan would often join us on our evening walk along the malecon.

He was freshly bathed and dressed in the evening, smelling fragrantly of after shave lotion. But he couldn't fool the neighborhood cats. There would always be one or two following us along the quay on those clear, starry night strolls.

Most Americans who visited the Baja came to La Paz on the scheduled flights and went on by chartered airplane to the fishing resorts, south of the city. But a few came by road, after crossing the Sea of Cortez by ferry. There were two ferry services from La Paz, one southeast to Mazatlan and one northeast to Topolobampo, and a third service that went from Santa Rosalia, across to Guaymas. The ones to Mazatlan and to Guaymas were government owned, with modern ships but the one to Topolobampo was an old Chesapeake Bay ferry, run by a private company. And that was much cheaper, so many of the Americans used it. Until the day it sank.

We got the story a bit at a time, from different sources but it seems that the captain sailed from La Paz in the evening, as usual, and stood out beyond the offlying islands. There he ran into seas out of the northwest, that made the old ferry roll heavily, which of itself was not serious. Until a truck broke loose down below and started a severe leak in the hull. He immediately turned back and with great skill he nursed the wallowing old ferry back into the calm water of the harbor, where he put her ashore on the beach. So no lives were lost but many of the vehicles were submerged in oily seawater. And it was several days before they were brought ashore. We saw the ferry on the beach, from the sea wall and heard there were Americans aboard, so we went to the trailer park to find out what happened. And it was a mess. The vehicles were put back in running order, of a kind, but the gear in them was mostly ruined. And since the people who owned the ferry also owned the insurance company, they decreed that it was an Act of God, for which no payments would be made.

We were told by one of the passengers that a certain amount of hostility developed between some of his shipmates and the men who rowed out in small boats to rescue then, the night the ferry sank. The sailors, while helping the passengers into the boats, would unceremoniously toss the passengers' dogs into the sea. The owners were horrified, but as far as I could tell, all the dogs made it to shore.

So when the time came for us to leave, we drove to Santa Rosalia and took the government owned ferry across the Sea of Cortez to Guaymas in Mexico. The ship was built in Finland, quite new and in excellent condition. But all the notices to the passengers, on important matters like lifeboats and fire drills, were written in Finnish. And though the passage itself only took about six hours, the officials made it last for days. First we had to get a permit to go from Baja California to Mexico. Then we had to make reservations and buy our tickets in La Paz. Then we were required to be at the dock in Santa Rosalia by 9:00 AM on the sailing date, so we got there in the previous afternoon and waited. But it was not until 6:00 PM the next day that a peevish official strode down the dock, glanced at our papers and allowed us to board the waiting ship, that sailed after dark and was off Guaymas before dawn. And by the time we were off the dock and on our way, it was mid morning.

Driving north, we came up behind a truck with some men in it who were evidently out to fix the road, for they had a bucket of tar hanging from a hook, from the back. As the truck swayed, the bucket swung to and fro, spilling a few drops of tar but not much, and the men on the truck grinned happily, so we decided to pass them. But just as we did, the truck hit a bump in the road and the bucket went spinning in the air, throwing tar in all directions. Miraculously, hardly any of it hit us and we soon had it cleaned off but the truck did not stop and the men seemed to be quite unconcerned about losing their bucket.

We had truly enjoyed the passage south from the States. So much so that we often talked about returning that way. Just to see it again. To enjoy the quiet of the desert, to explore the tracks and trails and cactus forest once more. With all due respect to the survival experts, our first journey into their area was pure duck soup. The kind of preparation needed for an offshore passage in a small boat was totally unnecessary for land voyaging. One could get by with crude equipment, we were not once harrassed by rattlesnakes, and except for the jogging of the car, the earth didn't shake beneath our feet.

Otherwise, it was an easy day's drive to Arizona and from there, we had a pleasant camping trip across America to Vermont, where we arrived late in May, with the first phase of our plan (the initial research) completed. Minim was fine, though she had far more aboard her than we really needed. And we were beginning to understand the Spanish language and outlook. But we should learn more about how to behave and how to get things done before making a really long journey into Latin America.

CENTRAL AMERICA

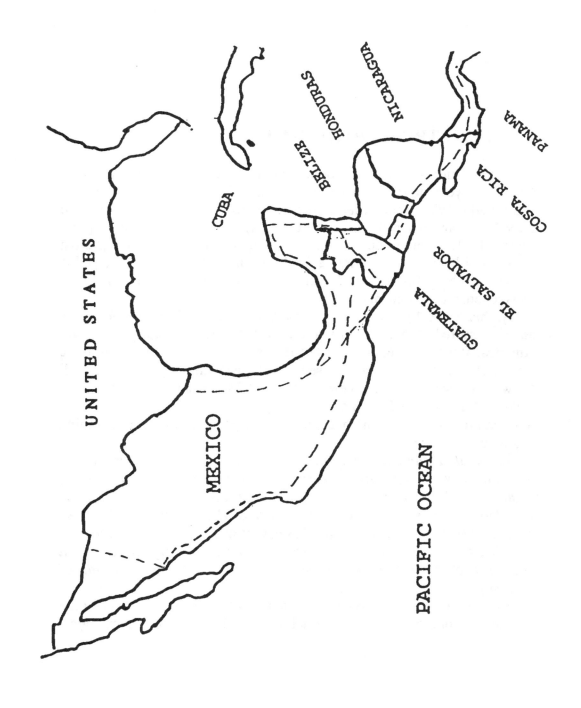

2 - THE STREET WITHOUT LUCK

That summer, I finished the book I had been writing in Baja California (about our years together in small boats) and June added her comments. We called it Wind Song, after a boat we sailed from the Virgin Islands to New York, and when the final draft was typed, we sent it to our agent. Then Julie Hall turned up, with Cynthia Burski. Julie was a young artist who had illustrated a children's book for me and her friend Cynthia worked in the public health department of the Agency for International Developement in Guatemala.

Cynthia was delighted with Guatemala. She had worked there for years and she assured us that it was quite the most interesting country in Central America. It was easy to get to, since it was just beyond Mexicio. And we were welcome to stay at her house in the capital, until we got organized. So we took some of the excess gear out of Minim and left Vermont in October (just ahead of the snow) for Corpus Christi, Texas where we got our visas for Guatemala and made last minute peparations for the camping trip across Mexico.

This would be an easy one. There were no long sections ahead without food stores. We stopped at a supermarket just before the border crossing to stock up for two or three days, just in case. But after our winter in La Paz, I was pretty sure we could get all we needed along the way. What we couldn't get, we didn't need. And besides, it was much more fun to stop and find the butcher and the local market and the bakery. It gave us a chance to chat with the people and see the things that they considered everyday but were novel to us.

One thing we missed in Baja California was classical music, so this time we took my old tape recorder, a small loudspeaker and a dozen cassettes.

But otherwise, we took less of everything and Minim was happier, though still too full. Going across Mexico, we followed a route that we already knew, past Mexico City to Oaxaca and on to Tehuantepec, where we camped under a tall palm tree and I worried all night, in case a coconut should fall on the truck. And in the morning, we set out for Guatemala, via the coastal route that was strongly reccommended by the American Autmobile Asociation. It was only about 250 miles to the border at Tapachula and the road was mostly over low, flat country but the wind was something else. Before we got there, we saw six big trucks lying in ditches, where they had been blown off the road; some on their backs, with all their wheels in the air, like dead beetles. We saw waves breaking, in ditches. And concrete utility poles, snapped off like carrots, half way up. And large, heavy trees torn up. And in one place a big puddle of water, maybe twelve feet in diameter, was picked up by the wind and went sailing across the road ahead of us, retaining its shape for a moment and leaving behind, where it had been, a patch of bare ground.

Luckily, Minim was heavy for her size but going straight down the road was not easy, even at 30 miles an hour, for we had to turn the steering wheel toward each blast of wind, then quickly turn it the other way in the lulls between them. And once we met a big, heavy truck coming toward us with a smaller one hiding from the wind, beside it. On a two lane road. But as we approached Tapachula, the wind eased off and by the time we got there, it was light enough for us to spend the night in our tent, in the shelter of some heavy bushes.

After creeping along all day in airconditioned splendor, the still, muggy hot evening of Tapachula surprised us. As the sun set, the air turned black with insects. We were only too happy to turn-in early. We zipped the fly screens of the tent tightly closed behind us and waited for some cool night breezes from the Pacific shore, a few miles away from our campsite.

Crossing the border at that point was slow and tiresome, for there was a long line of vehicles waiting, trucks laden with goods and cars full of people, their drivers competing for the attention of the harrassed officials in the sticky heat. But eventually we were dealt with and allowed to proceed. The road went through the lowlands of Guatemala and was full of trucks, many of them trying to pass each other in its two narrow lanes, as far as the big agricultural town of Esquintla, where we turned off to start the long climb up into the mountains, toward Guatemala City.

How can countries, right next to each other, be so different? After all, a border is merely a political boundary. Tapachula, as we drove through early that morning, was already crowded with people and traffic. The gutters were littered with trash. Old adobe buildings, covered with garish signs, crumbling with time, lined the narrow streets. New buildings had been started, never finished, half used, and were already falling down. But a few miles into Guatemala and we were speeding along a well-maintained highway with green ribbons of sugar cane planted on either side. Gas stations, instead of being dirty white, oil encrusted concrete, were mostly gleaming glass with pruned hedges and flowers near the pumps. There were signs like 'Shell' and 'Texaco'. All names we knew. And no trash. Only miles and miles of perfectly rowed fields. Then, as we turned inland, we began to see the people. The faces were more Indian than Spanish. High foreheads and bronzed leathery skin. Their clothing, clean and faded, mostly ill fitting. Walking erect or squatting beside rough stands piled high with coconuts, grapefruit and oranges, waiting for a bus to stop and for a few cents to take them up the road.

Our route wandered through towns, Palin, Amatitlan, where bare-footed women walked over the cobblestones with brightly painted water jugs perched on their heads. Through dark openings in the adobe walls, we would glimpse shelves of canned goods, piles of bread, the gleam of glass showcases. A goatherd led a leashed nanny through the crowds, stopping to fill a cup handed to him by one of the residents along the way, with warm milk. Men stood, leaning aginst the walls with their hands in their pockets, watching or chatting with their neighbors. Color, bustle, smiles, sun. And behind them the stately volcanoes gently belching whisps of gray ash. We climbed high into the mountains and there were no longer open fields, just ravines, barrancas. Then over the ridge to a high plateau, to wider streets, to newer. more conjested habitations, to La Capital.

As we went up, the countryside changed from lush, tropcal lowlands to cool, beautiful mountains and in a wide valley, five thousand feet above sea level, we came to the busy, modern city. Luckily we had directions from Cynthia, for it was a big, sprawling city and late in the afternoon we found her house, on a tree-lined road in a quiet residential section. In the high, white wall there was a pair of gates, covered with iron, painted black. And when we rang the bell beside them, a peephole soon opened, through which an Indian girl examined us before letting us in. But we had been warned not to leave our truck on the street, so we drove through the gates and parked it in the front yard, in the care of a large, fierce-looking German shepherd called Lobo (which turned out to mean wolf). The house was modern, with several rooms on two floors and a garden (with a high wall) behind it. And soon, people began to arrive, for Cynthia had many friends who stayed there, when they came to the city. Most of them were Americans who worked for the Peace Corps, out in the country and when the phone rang, any one would answer it in quiet, fluent Spanish.

We had no intention of staying with Cynthia. We're not very good house guests, much preferring to be on our own. But we didn't feel at ease yet in Guatemala. Not quite sure where we might fit in. Perhaps she could steer us in the right directon. So we stopped. Cyn wasn't home from work yet, but when Margarita saw a gringo face at the gate, she unhesitatingly opened the door for us. We were led to an unoccupied room. So-and-so had just left and what's-his-name wasn't due for several days. No problem. So we relaxed and watched the comings and goings. A good deal older than most of the other guests, but years behind them in exposure to the endless variations of Spanish and Indian culture, we watched and listened to these young Amerians with their myriad stories.

Cynthia's office was in the Embassy, across town and when she came home, she filled in the details for us. The house was leased by the American government and was believed to be bugged, so it was all right to shout obscenities at the lamp. Her Indian maid, Margarita, was unmarried and pregnant, which was difficult, since Cynthia's job was to promote birth control. And Lobo was a great, big sissy (but not to tell a soul). At dinner, I asked about flying and Cynthia said she twice bought a share in an airplane. But the fist time, a Guatemalan Air Force plane landed on it, while it was parked. And the second one flew into the side of a mountain, with the other owner in it. So she took up horseback riding, instead. And Bob Braaten of the Peace Corps told us about a road to a remote village, that caved in. Before they could fix it, they had to get rid of a broken culvert, so he went to the Guatemalan Army for some explosives. But they turned him down, saying they would handle it, so he went back to the village. A few days later, a big airplane came droning overhead and a bunch of parachutists jumped out of it, in army uniform, with guns and radios and eveything. Carefully they approached the culvert and while some of them covered the operation with guns, others put charges on it. And as they withdrew, the culvert went up in a series of fine, loud explosions.

Later that evening, we asked Cynthia where would be a good place for us to spend the winter and she suggested Antigua Guatemala, the Old Capital, which was in another valley, about twenty five miles away. Her boss, John Long, lived there so she called him on the phone and the next morning, he came to see us. John was a doctor, born in England, who was on loan from Duke University to serve as head of the medical section of A.I.D. in Guatemala, a job that entitled him to a follow car: A Jeep to follow his, wherever he went, with a driver and a machine gunner in it, to protect him from bandits. But John felt he was really safer without it and he usually travelled alone. He explained that Antigua was a beautiful old city, now a National Monument, where many people lived because it was quiet and peaceful. We might find a house to rent but there were no agents, we would have to ask around. And for a start, he gave us the address of Jim and Alice Bell, who had a shop there.

Driving through Guatemala City at a quiet time of the day was no worse than Mexico City in the rush hour but the road over the mountains to Antigua was exciting, since the drivers of the trucks and busses competed to see who could come closest to disaster as the narrow, two-lane pavement wound and twisted over a 7,000 foot ridge and down the other side.

The way out of town, to Antigua, was much like the way in we had driven, except that the housing looked even newer and more prosperous. There were movie theaters, supermarkets, American and German drug companies, a Swiss watchmaker. Smaller plants making concrete laundry tubs, building blocks. Stores selling hardware, electrical supplies, paint. Anything that might be useful to the new developments along the route. Then as we climbed out of the plateau, the steep hillsides came right to the edge of the pavement. Leaving barely enough room for a single file of countless pedestrians with their carts and cows, packs and sacks either balanced on their heads or held on backs by straps pulled tight over foreheads. Monstrous loads. The road would cross a gully, a barranca, and there would be a narrow footpath leading into the dense, dust-covered vegetation. We would glimpse a corner of a thatched roof or shiny corrugated metal. Home for someone. Sometimes a stucco building would be perched on the downhill side. Nothing but space, dusty space around it. At San Lucas Sacatapequez, the road was lined with stalls. This time cloth was for sale. Loud, bright hanks of cloth. Women washed the materials in the communal fountain, then spread them out on the coarse stubby grass to dry, then hung them on the stalls to sell. We left the main road, this time to head down the mountains into another high plateau and Antigua.

But the old city of Antigua, with its Spanish-style buildings and plaza and many churches, was quiet and charming, so we went to see Jim Bell about renting a house there. For a moment, he could not think of one that was for rent, then he remembered one that might be. It belonged to a young man who was moving to Guatemala City, so Jim took us to see him and the house was indeed available. It was near the edge of the city, on a road called (in Spanish) the Street Without Luck. We mentioned that but the owner said it was an old name, no longer used. The new name was Fifth Avenue. And the house was set back from the road (we went through a gate in a wall) in a coffee plantation, shaded by tall eucalyptus trees. Downstairs, it had two bedrooms and a bathroom. And upstairs, there was a long living room, with windows overlooking the plantation, and a small kitchen. It was all we needed and the rent was reasonable, so we paid for three months, in advance. He would need a few days to move, so before going back to Cynthia' place, we took another look at Antigua. The mountains all around it went up into the clouds but we were told that was unusual. Generally, the sky would be clear. And when we returned, with all our gear for the winter, it was. At the end of the Street Without Luck, starting near our house and rising majestically up, was the biggest volcano I ever saw. Thirteen thousand feet high. And wide. Even handsome, in a macabre sort of way. If that thing ever went off .... But we were assured it would not. At least, it had not for many years. Its name was Agua (Water) and it was believed to be connected, by underground passages, to two others, called Fuego (Fire) and Achetenango (High Place). So long as those passages remained open, the pressure was vented through Fuego. We looked behind our house and there was Fuego, with smoke coming out of the top of it and drifting away on the wind. That was the year when the earthquake flattened Managua, the capital of Nicaragua, about 350 miles away. Nobody expected that, either. But the people in Central America accepted such things, just as Americans accepted traffic accidents, as a part of ordinary life. So we said no more and moved in.

The white front wall on the street was broken only by a small black door. Once through that, there was a tiny patch of grass, a pila (place for washing clothes) concealed in a corner, and the front door of the house itself. There were three levels inside. At the entry was a dining area, the kitchen and a stairway. Up six steps to an open gallery with sofas and tables and a long wall of windows facing the cofee finca (plantation) behind the house. Or down six steps to the bedrooms and bath. A fireplace stood at one end of the gallery and behind the kitchen door stood an honest-to-goodness stove with an oven, and a refrigerator. What more could anyone want?

Most of the people on the street, outside our house, were Mayan Indians, short and dark, the women usually with things balanced on their heads, the men always with large knives (machetes) which they used for every kind of work, from building houses to cutting grass. They were gentle people, who would not rob you, so that it was quite safe to walk across the city, at any time of the day or night. But they were nearly all very poor and if a car was left on the street, they would take anything they could from it, such as mirrors or tools. When that happened, one could go to an automobile parts store across town, that was unofficially known as the Redemption Center. One would describe the part one wanted and the owner would say that he did not stock that item, but he could get it in a few days. And in a week or so, with luck, one would buy one's own part back. So we arranged to keep Minim in the enclosed parking lot of the Antigua Hotel, half a block away. Then I started work on another book, while June went to school.

One of the best places to learn Spanish, outside Spain, was there in Antigua, at a school that catered mostly to people who needed the language to work for the Peace Corps and similar agencies. The teachers were young men and women, educated in the local schools and trained in their field, who spoke no English at all. And there was a teacher for each student. Every week, a list was put up at the shool, saying which teacher would have which student, and it was all in first names, except for June. Ever since our days at sea, she had been called Junie, because it carried better than June when shouted over the noise of a gale. And there in Antigua, she was the oldest of the students, so they gave her the title of La Dona Junie.

There was no laundry in town, since the poor washed their clothes in the public pilas (shallow sinks for scrubbing, with deeper ones from which to dip cold water) and the rich had servants to do it, in the pilas at their houses. Our house had a concrete one, in the garden by the kitchen, but June was not enthusiastic about using it and after a while, all our clothes were dirty, so we decided to hire a maid. June asked one of the teachers at her school if anyone was available and soon Victoria de Estrada, a stocky, bustling woman about 50 years old, came to see us. While June explained what we wanted, Victoria took off her coat and insisted on washing the dishes. And from then on, she came five days a week.

Hand washing our clothes wasn't the problem. I'd rinse out a few things each day in the bathroom bowl and they would be dry in ten minutes on the line, hung out in the sun. But sheets and towels were another matter. There must be a laundry in a town that size. Yet no one I asked knew of one. The stack of sheets supplied with the house was impressive. I watched it dwindle, until there was only one pair left clean. Something had to be done. I'd hire a maid. She would surely know about laundry. When asked about laundry in general and sheets in particular, Victoria led me to the pila in the front garden with its one cold water tap and built-in concrete washboard. Was that really the way people washed sheets, was she willing to do it? Of course, you silly gringa. Every few days I would sheepishly add a soiled sheet to the laundry bag, until Victoria found my cache. Shaking her head and smiling to herself, she washed and ironed them all in one morning.

She arrived at eight in the morning, while we were having breakfast, and washed the previous night's dishes. Then she did the laundry (including sheets) and hung it out to dry while she cleaned the whole house - even the windows. At first, I worried about her standing on a narrow ledge to clean the upstairs ones but when I offered to do it, she told me firmly that it was not my place. Then she took her basket and went off to the market to do our shopping before she cooked lunch. June came back from school at noon each day and insisted that Victoria have lunch with us. That took some persuasion, in the beginning, since it was unheard of for a servant to sit down and eat with her employers. But she soon got used to it and because she did not speak any English, we all spoke Spanish. Our conversation would include a wide variety of subjects, since Victoria was highly intelligent. And when June or I made a mistake, she would interrupt and correct us. After lunch, Victoria would clean the kitchen and by two o'clock, she was on her way home, since we preferred to be alone in the evenings. And we paid her a dollar a day, though we were told by several people that it was too much.

Too much? She left us after lunch to go to her next job as a laundress for a large family. She was paid two dollars a week for that. So for five mornings with us and six afternoons with the other people, she amassed seven dollars a week. Of course, things were very cheap there. Her room was only ten dollars a month. Food was dirt cheap to us. As long as you don't go to a doctor when you are sick, or wash your hair with shampoo or a million other things, you too can live on seven dollars a week. But Victoria had other responsibilities. One daughter, 20 years old and unable or unwilling to hold a job, lived with her. Her other daughter was married but her husband had difficulty feeding his pregnant wife and small son on his six dollar a week carpenter's pay. We knew the food we gave her for her evening meal went to her children and grandchild, so we insisted that the noonday meal with us be a feast. After a fierce bout of shyness, Victoria relaxed and began to eat. It was a pleasure to watch her. We all enjoyed those meals.

In fact, her finances were hard to believe. One day, she had a headache, so I gave her a couple of aspirins and suggested that she keep a bottle of them handy. But she explained that she could not afford to tie up the money. Instead, she bought two at a time (at a higher price) from a local store. She was completely honest. When we gave her money to buy things for us, she would account for it, without being asked. If she had too much, she would come back with flowers or maybe a newspaper. But there would always be a few pennies change. So we put a bowl on the refrigerator, with some money in it for her to take as she needed it. And on Fridays, we would leave her pay there, so that she would not have to ask for it.

Soon Victoria made the daily market visits. They were important excursions to her. She had money for a few purchases and time to dally a bit and chat with friends. She would pass through the crowded, dark alleys lined with produce, smiling and nodding and haggling with the Indian women, the basket on her arm full of good things to eat and always a bunch of flowers.

We did some of the shopping ourselves and gradually found the best places to go. One shop, that was full of old fashioned electrical equipment, also sold rum and vermouth. Another shop, that looked like a private house, sold home-made candles in all shapes, colors and sizes. And so it went on. For fruit and vegetables, we went to the market, which was in the ruins of a large church that had fallen down in an earthquake. Most of the roof was gone but pieces of cloth and matting had been rigged to keep the sun out, leaving a huge labyrinth of dimly lit areas, each packed tight with individual stalls, among which the throng of people pushed and squeezed their way. At first we were uneasy in there and of course it would be stupid to carry anything of great value, such as a gold watch or a large sum of money, but the avacados and melons, tomatoes and beans were fresh and good. Things that you cold hold in your hand were usually sold by the mano, or handful, which might be three oranges or five small tomatoes. Other items were weighed by the woman who sold them, in a pair of scales that she held out for her customer to see. And we were charged a little extra, as rich foreigners but the prices were low and we felt that they needed the money more than we did, so we only pretended to bargain. Near the market was the Plaza, a well kept park with paved walks and shade trees and a fine, large fountain. Facing it were a cathedral, two banks, some government offices, a movie house and several shops. And in one corner was the bus stop.

In the corner of the fountain stood four nymphs, painted stucco faces faded from the sun and water. Streams of water flowed from their nipples. There was a touch of amusement in their smiles that seemed to reflect the expressions of the people lounging on the benches around them.

The drivers and their helpers must have been paid for each passenger they carried, becuse there was always a great deal of shouting around the brightly painted busses, as each crew filled its old vehicle, far beyond its obvious capacity, before rushing off in a desperate race to their destination, often passing each other on blind corners in the mountain roads, so as to be first to pick up extra passengers along the way. But only the very rich could afford cars and for most of the people a bus ride was an adventure, comparable in our terms to a mid-winter flight on a secondary airline. In fact, the bus drivers were treated much like airline pilots, admired by girls and cheered by their passengers when they arrived safely.

Twice a month, we drove Minim to Guatemala City (which was known as The Capital) to visit a supermarket and buy fresh meat at a shop called the Three Little Pigs. And sometimes we found a copy of Newsweek. But the book store we went to only received ten copies each week, so we were lucky to get one.

We could have bought meat in the Antigua market. There were butchers, but no sign of refrigeration. Anyway, I had no idea of what was being sold. The meat was cut into thin strips and piled high on tables covered with blood and flies. A red flag hanging at the stall signalled that the animal had been slaughtered that day. I just wasn't up to that. There were several smaller shops where milk and cheese were sold from refrigerated cases. And my favorite, Tienda Santa Fe, also had a freezer full of plastic-covered steaks and chops! Patrick refused to let me buy bread at a tienda near us. The little girl who waited on us always had a cold and would carefully wipe her running nose with her hand before she picked the bread out of the huge baskets behind the counter. He is so fussy.

On weekends, we went to places like Chichicastenango, high in the mountains northwest of Antigua, where the Mayans brought their textiles and pottery for sale in the market. Driving there, we passed men walking up the steep road with huge loads on their backs, literally dozens of heavy earthenware pots. But the market was bright with displays of hand woven cloth, in vivid colors and bold designs, under thin white awnings against the hot sun. And it was crowded with cheerful people, coming and going, eating and drinking, comparing goods and arguing about prices. Between there and Antigua, a side road wound steeply down to beautiful Lake Atitlan, the largest in Guatemala, deep and mysterious in the high mountains, And at the bottom of the road, beside the lake, the American hippies hung out. When the wind was right, you could smell the 'pot' a mile away. White children, naked and filthy, roamed the village while their parents sat around all day, talking. And the Mayan people, so clean and hard working, pretended not to notice. But the Government was concerned about the problem and once in a while, the police were told to straighten things out.

I stopped the truck to give a couple of young Americans a lift. They had quit college and were wandering around Central America. Why didn't they take a bus up the mountain road to the main highway? It was so very cheap. Oh no, it was much more fun their way. They had the money, that wasn't the point, but they wanted to rub shoulders with The People. In places like Guatemala, where about ninety percent of the wealth is in the hands of about three percent of the people, it was hard for me to understand just who they thought they would meet by hitch hiking. Next time, walk or take a bus, I advised as they pulled their aluminum-framed back packs from the car and I opened all the windows to get rid of the odor of unwashed bodies.

We pick up Indians in those areas. It is often hard to get them in, with their parcels and machetes. We sit tightly packed, with me on a pillow over the drive shaft. Sometimes there is the smell of sweat but more often a

clean leathery odor prevails. And I marvel at these people who must carry
water from a public fountain or bathe only in a cold stream.

Down on the Pacific coast, the beaches were of black sand, ground fine
from volcanic lava. And in the tropical lowlands, between the beaches and
the mountains, were fields of sugar cane and lush pastures for cattle. But
except for the one paved highway, from the Capital down to Esquintla, the
roads from the montains down to the lowlands were primitive. And one
Sunday, when we went for a drive, we had to ford five rivers. The first
ones were narrow, with stony bottoms, and were easy to cross but lower
down they became wider, with bottoms of sand and mud, until we wondered about turning back. But since we were only out for a day's drive, we
had not bothered too much about navigation and we were not at all sure
where we were. Or how to get back. So we went on down, to the next
river, which was even wider than the last one. The only way to the other
side was down a steep bank, then diagonally across the river in a foot or
so of water for maybe a hundred yards and up a steep bank to the level
ground beyond. But over the far bank, we could see the top of a truck. So
there must be a road from there to civilization.

Minim rushed down the bank and went churning up the river, with a
wake like a motor boat, her back wheels sometimes losing their grip on the
slippery bottom, then catching again, her tail swinging from side to side
as I corrected a series of skids. But she hit the far side with enough speed
to carry her up the bank and over the top. And there was the truck we
were aiming for: A stripped, rusting wreck at the end of a muddy track.
Keeping up our speed, we followed the track and gradually it became
firmer, until we came over a rise and found it blocked by a cart full of
sugar cane, drawn by a bullock. But the driver signalled us to go around
him, so we bumped across a field, past a whole line of carts, and came to
a refinery, from which it was easy to find the paved road back to Antigua,
via Esquintla and the Capital, having gained a little more experience of
driving in out-of-the-way places.

But most of the time, Minim stayed in the enclosed parking lot of the
Antigua Hotel. Every morning, I would walk over there to see that she
was okay and on my way, I would have a word with the beggar who stood

outside the hotel. He was partly paralyzed, needing crutches to walk, and his hands would not open far, so that he could not get a job. And in that society, begging was the only way he could make a living. But he had a good pitch, outside the hotel, and on weekends he did quite well. So I gave hime something every Tuesday and Thursday and when I greeted him on the other days, he would respond with a shy smile and a polite remark. There were other beggars, both men and women, in Antigua but we did not feel that we could give to all of them, so we settled for helping the one we knew and occasionally giving to others who were crippled. We would have liked to have done more but the problem was too large for us to tackle. But the children who hung around the tourists' places were often professional beggars, operating under the instructions of their parents, who stayed out of sight around a corner.

We had watched well dressed Guatemalans step into the street from a day of sunning and dining around the pool at the hotel. They would dutifully pass out a few pennies to the beggars at the door. It was the custom. So we learned to keep a pocketful of change when we went out. It needn't be much, but a dime would make a difference. There were those, as Patrick mentioned, who would send their children to beg from you while they hid around the corner. We both would react badly to that. It is hard to think of a parent teaching his child to beg. But when you consider the unemployment that you see at every turn, perhaps the parent is teaching a valuable lesson. It may be the child's only way to survive in the years to come.

There was an official Tourist Office on the Plaza, staffed by a big, bossy woman and a meek little man, both of whom spoke English. And they had very definite ideas as to how the tourists should behave: They should arrive in airplanes, go straight to the tourists' hotels, take tours in proper tourists' busses, buy things, get back in their airplanes and go away. They were polite enough to people like us, who came in our own cars, but did not really approve of us. For it was obvious to them that a safe and secure life depended on firm control by the Proper Authorities. And how could you control people who went where they pleased, whenever they felt like it? In fact, the man told us that he would not dare to go from Antigua to the Capital - about 25 miles - without his papers.

Most of the tourists came on package tours, herded aound like sheep by English speaking guides, but there were some foreigners living in Antigua, like Jim and Alice Bell. They had come down from California and bought a small shop which they stocked with textiles and other things that were made by the Mayans in different parts of Guatemala. Jim would go all over the country, buying some items but more often arranging to have things made, that he would pick up a few weeks later. And back at the shop, Alice would make up men's ties and women's dresses, out of the brightly colored materials. Altogether, it was the best place in town to find such things and they made a living at it, though it had its frustrations. For the Mayans had little sense of time and often when Jim went to a remote village to pick up some things, they would not be ready. Or the maker had got bored with doing several things of one kind and switched to something else. And communication could be a problem, even within the country.

Not many people had private telephones and there were few lines from Antigua to the Capital, so to call someone as little as 25 miles away, you generally had to go to the Telegraph Office and wait an hour or so to get through. The banks overcame the problem by having their own radios, in gray metal boxes, that squawked and muttered in corners. But otherwise, there was nothing unusual about them, except for the young soldier with a machine gun in the lobby and another one covering him from across the street. One day we were waiting at a traffic light in the Capital and a white Mercedes drew up beside us. Alone in the back was a well-dressed man with a gray mustache. And in the front were his driver and his bodyguard, holding a machine gun. Whether they were really necessary, we could not be sure. Perhaps they were more symbols of power and status. In any case, we never saw John Long with one, though he was entitled to it. But then he was tall and distinguished and had a superb command of Spanish, including seventeen different words for 'buttocks'. Bob Braaten, who worked for the Peace Corps in some remote areas, always went unarmed. And one day when he was alone in his house, he saw some soldiers approaching, their guns at the ready. He looked out of a window and there were more of them, coming the other way. So he did nothing and soon there was a knock on the door. It was the Captain, formally asking for a drink of water. And when Bob gave it to him, they went away.

It was generally believed that most of the Peace Corps people were really working for the C.I.A. and when you were talking to one, it was considered wise not to stand too close to him, in case someone took a shot at him. But the winter climate in the mountains of Guatemala was superb, with warm days and cool nights and scarcely any rain. There were beautiful woods of tall pine trees. And farms on land so steep that a man could fall off it. And high valleys where flowers were grown in the rich volcanic soil, watered each night by the mountain mists and brought on each day by the strong, clear sunlight. And lower down, serious Germans growing coffee. And in Antigua itself, marimbas like huge xylophones run by nine men, all looking straight ahead and banging out cheerful music. And the inconveniences seemed petty, indeed.

We learned to avoid sickness by soaking our vegetables in a pan of water with a couple of teaspoons of Clorox in it, and discovered bundles of small sticks called Alote, that were great for lighting fires. And found a drink called Jocote, made from the fruit of the cashew, that was cheap and quite good, though we laid off it one day a week to avoid going blind. But once a month, we had to go to the Customs headquarters in the Capital and apply for a permit to keep Minim in Guatemala. Each time, I would spend the best part of two days, standing in lines at different offices in the huge, gray building, while June sat outside in the hot sun, guarding the truck.

Only once, when we both had to appear before an official, did I go with Patrick and leave the car locked but uguarded. We returned in time to see a group of young men running a wire coat hanger between the window and the door frame.

One day, there was a young American just ahead of me, who had come down from Washington, D.C. on a 10 speed bicycle and he really had problems, for the bike was not registered (his State did not require it) and he had no Operator's License to ride it. But on the second day, he told me he had made the necessary contacts to have the whole matter straightened out. So I went to a Customs Agent, whose office was just across the street, and asked him to get the next month's permit for us. Which was a great success, for he knew just what to do. First, he typed up some impressive looking documents, then he asked me for ten dollars, which he put in a plain white envelope and gave, with the documents, to a young man who disappeared for half an hour. And came back with an official permit to keep Minim in Guatemala for as long as we liked that winter. That showed the value of learning how to get things done, in Latin America. For it was not enough to behave normally, by our standards. We had to do things their way, if we were to go from country to country without making waves. For the same reason, we were careful to confirm to their standards of dress and behaviour. We were always neat and clean, my hair was kept short and Mnim was washed frequently. And when we approached a stranger, no matter who it was, we did so with the elaborate courtesy that they considered normal.

In Antigua, we sometimes had guests for dinner and one evening a school master told me that his class could not have their annual outing, because they lacked a female chaperone. So I told him that June would be happy to do it and we agreed to meet at the Esso station on the mountain road, two weeks later. When the bus arrived from the Capital, it contained about 40 boys and girls, from 15 to 17 years old, with two masters in charge of them. And as we followed them over the mountain road in Minim, we wondered what chaperones do. Late in the afternoon, we arrived at the camp site, in a high meadow of long grass with a narrow brook winding through it and beyond, a steep hill covered with pine trees. Quickly the boys and girls set up their tents, along the edge of the trees. And by the time we got ours up, they had vanished.

I thought of striding up the hill, shouting "Don't do it" but it hardly seemed likely to do any good. So I went back to our tent, beside the brook, where June was cooking dinner. Soon the two school masters joined us, with the news that the trees were the edge of a forest. And as June poured the wine, she said: "Don't worry. We won't be here in nine months." It was cold there at 8,500 feet when the sun went down and after putting up a light to guide any strays home, we went to bed. All through the night we shivered in our tent, wondering how the kids were doing but when the sun came up, they were all there. So we took them to a church, with the thought that it might do them some good, before sending them back home.

Another time, we found a Volkswagen camper parked outside our house, with a young couple from Germany in it. So we invited them in for a shower and after chatting for a while, we decided to climb the volcano called Agua together. That was the big one, at the end of our street, and it was not active but it was 13,000 feet high and we were at 5,000 feet in Antigua. So before dawn they took everything out of their car and drove us up to the village of Santa Maria de Jesus, at 7,000 feet on the shoulder of the volcano, where they parked it in the middle of the plaza. And as the sun came up, we set out on foot toward the crater 6,000 feet above us. Already the village was bustling with activity. Everywhere people were going briskly about their day's work. The little engine that powered the corn mill chugged away, one bang at a time. And there was a feeling of cheerful cooperation, all around us, as we left the small Mayan community.

There were no cobblestoned streets in Santa Maria de Jesus, just dry, rutted, dusty alleys leading from the barren town square over the sides of the mountain. The town had been built long before anyone thought of traffic. Even today, the possibility of more than half a dozen people living in the town being able to afford or even want a car seemed unlikely. Around the square were a few adobe buildings but for the most part, the population lived in thatched huts that spilled down the mountain. A sita, a plot of arid volcanic ash, was fenced off by thatch walls. Inside, there would be a shack or two: Shelters for the family and their livestock, if they had any. A section of the sita was planted. Mostly corn and tomatoes, squash or melons, foods that were staples in their diets and that could be sold in the market. The area also served as the family toilet. But you didn't see the dust or the mud when it had rained or the calloused gray feet of the children. You saw the warm red shawls, intricately woven with yellows and blues and greens. You saw the washed and faded blue wrap skirts bunched around the waists of the women and tied with loops of heavily embroidered belts. The geometric flowers and birds of the designs. You saw the beauty these people had brought to their lives with their artistry.

The trail was not steep, most of the way, but the volcano was made of fine ash and climbing it was like walking up a huge pile of sand. Each time you stepped forward a foot, you would slide back six inches. So it was slow going. For a long way above the village, the land was cleared and people were farming it. Then we came into pine trees, higher up, where we met men coming down the mountain with bundles of wood on their backs. But as we went farther, the trees became smaller and there were no more people around. We walked up into the clouds and through them - gray and foggy and damp - and out into the sunshine above them, to look far out over their billowing white tops. And between the clouds, way down below, we could see Antigua, red and white in its valley. And at noon, the sound of a factory whistle came up to us, clearly, as though it were close by. Just below the top, the trail became steep and exercising my privilege as the oldest of the party, I sat down in the shade of a bush - for the sunlight was harsh in the clear, thin air - to admire the view, while the others went on.

We hadn't worn the right shoes. We had to borrow hats. We didn't have proper sweaters and had entirely failed to bring sufficient water. Our young friends had brought exactly what they needed. They kindly shared what they could with us. But they had climbed the Alps. They knew what it was all about. I was horrified when Patrick dropped out. How could he possibly let our side down like that? He's the athlete of the family. But he had simply stopped. We were perhaps a hundred yards from the rim - straight up. I would put a hand around a clump of grass, pull myself up, find a footing, and look for the next hand hold. I dare not look down. Dripping with cold, clammy sweat, the grass slipped from my wet hands and I tugged at clumps of earth just inches from my face. The roots of a few skinny pines formed a narrow ledge. We stopped and my young friend called to her husband that she could not possibly go on. We should go, she would stay there. "No, let him go if he wants, but we are getting too split up. It is best that I stay here with you. He'll be all right." I wrapped myself around a thin trunk and thankfully slept.

When we took off our shoes to rest our feet, we discovered that the fine volcanic ash - which is widely used as an abrasive - had found its way inside our socks, even between our toes. And walking down the mountain in our bare feet was more comfortable. But soon we dipped down into the clouds and through them and out beneath them. And the trees became taller, as we went on, until we reached the land cleared for farming. By then it was late in the afternoon and we were thirsty, so we were thankful when a farmer allowed us to cut bamboos to drink. The rings on the bamboos were about 15 inches apart and in each section, between two rings, there were a couple of ounces of liquid which tasted like carrot juice. And by cutting a hole near one end of a section, you could drink it out of the bamboo. So we had several of them, between us and paid him for them and continued down the mountain, feeling much better.

It was getting dark when we reached the village and after driving back to Antigua, we all took hot showers and slept for ten hours. But in the morning, we were very stiff and it was two weeks before June and I felt normal again.

Patrick handed me a bottle of cold beer as I stood in the shower. Nothing before or since has tasted so good. Afterwards, we made a pact that AGUA would be our LAST volcano. We solemnly shook hands.

Meanwhile, the young couple left in their camper, to drive through Central America to Panama and back to America by way of the Yucatan Peninsula. We thought them brave to try it, since we knew so little about those countries, and they told us that they had no insurance on their car, because the AAA in California wanted $400 for the trip. But they were both in the business of growing flowers, in Germany and they had people to visit in each country, who might be able to help them. So we wished them good luck and they promised to let us know how it went.

Every few days, that winter, there was a small earthquake. They came in various kinds. One made a creaking sound in the roof, moving rapidly along it. Another made all the doors in the house shimmy. And a stronger kind set the chandeliers in the living room swinging from side to side. When we saw that, we stepped into the street, in case the heavy tiles should start falling from the roof. But the strongest earthquake occurred while we were asleep in bed. It was after midnight when we suddenly awoke, to find our bed hopping up and down, first on one leg, then on another, on the tiled floor. So we turned on the light and both peered under the bed. But there was no one there, so we ran around the house, turning on all the lights. By which time, it was over. And shortly after that, one of the volcanoes behind our house - Fuego, I think - erupted, sending a column of black ash about ten miles straight up into the sky.

Everything about it was on a grand scale. For more than a week, noises like thunder rolled down from the mountain, rattling the windows of our house. By day, we could see a black cloud of ash, drifting far across the country - in fact, it threw so much material up into the atmosphere that it changed the weather all over the world. And at night, it was truly spectacular. A wide column of red flames roared out of the mouth of the volcano, high into the air. And huge rocks were flung out, one after another, curving white hot across the sky and back down to join the stream of molten lava rolling down its side, turning pale red and dark red and vanishing in the night. There was a fine view of it from the corner of our street and in the evenings we would stand there, chatting with a group of our neighbors as we watched the show. For though it was only a few miles away, there was a valley between the volcano and us that would stop the lava from reaching Antigua. And the general reaction of the people was "How pretty""

Old houses in the city often have a narrow stone stairway leading to a roof garden where you can sit and enjoy a clear view of the natural wonders around you. Our house was new and rather modern for Antigua. Highly functional but lacking in old Spanish charm. So we went out into the street with everyone else who hadn't a better view at home.

But one day the whole volcano, more than twelve thousand feet high, split down one side with a great roar. And that night we decided to sleep a little farther away from it. So we drove up to the Esso station on the mountain road, where the side road from Antigua joined it, and spent the night in Minim, parked in a corner. We could still hear the volcano and see the red flames shooting up into the sky but nothing new happened and in the morning we went to Antigua feeling that we had been unnecessarily cautious. That night we slept soundly in our house, for we were very tired, and completely missed a major earthquake alarm. It came from the Capital and everyone in Antigua, except us, spent the night in the parks and open spaces, away from the walls and roofs that would come crashing down when the earthquake started. But it never came, that year.

By then it was nearly time for us to go back to Vermont and one day, when we went to start Minim's engine, we found the battery was flat. So we took it across town, to a shop that specialized in batteries. And after examinimg it, the man said "Sir, this is a fine battery. One cell is dead but that can be fixed. And the acid is weak. Perhaps you would like it replaced?" So we left it with him and the next day we picked it up, repaired and recharged. All for three dollars, with the acid. But since we were thinking about leaving, we checked our passports. And in each one there was a red stamp, saying 'Report to Department of Immigration within 30 days'. They must have been put there when we came into the country, months before, but they were in Spanish and we had not noticed them. Which left us with a problem, for if we went to the Immigration people in the Capital, there would surely be all kinds of proceedures to go through and forms to fill out and penalties to pay before the whole thing was straightened out. But we planned to leave Guatemala by the border crossing into British Honduras, at a remote village, far from the Capital. So we decided to take the chance that they would assume we had complied with the regulations, at the border, and let us through.

As Holy Week approached, there was great activity in Antigua. Floats were prepared for processions. The people who were to carry them got out their purple robes. And all over the town, brightly colored carpets were being made in the streets. A wooden frame was laid in the road, outlining the area to be covered, and that was filled with sawdust, a couple of inches deep. Then more sawdust, dyed in bright colors, was used to make a design, in a thin layer on top. A carpet might be as small as twelve feet square or more than fifty feet long and almost as wide as the street. Each one was different, being made by the people in the houses nearby. And when it was finished, the wooden frame was taken away. After which, it was sprinkled with water every day, until the procession came.

Neighbors would get together and make a carpet in the street in front of their houses. Sometimes fresh flowers were used. And green pine needles and white lilies were strewn over the cobblestones too. But many of the carpets, made by using the wooden frames and sawdust and stencils, looked as if they had been flown in from the Orient.

The procession on Good Friday lasted all day. Huge, heavy floats carried by as many as eighty men came slowly down the street, followed by bands playing mournful music that was even more effective because it was often off key. And when they came to each carpet, the shuffling feet went through it, stirring up the sawdust and destroying it completely.

On evening walks through the streets we would hear bands practicing somewhere out of sight. We marvelled that anyone who practiced as much as they did could be so bad. But on Good Friday, the tedious, sour dirges couldn't have been more perfect for the scene before us.

Thousands of Mayans from the mountains jammed the streets and as the procession went by, the incense was so strong that it was hard to breathe, or even see far. But there were two men in purple robes, ahead of each float, with tridents on long poles to lift up the overhead wires. And when the procession came back in the dark, the floats were lit by fluorescent lights, powered by a gasoline engine on a small cart behind each one.

The last float was the most impressive of all. In its center, a figure of Christ bent beneath the weight of a massive, gilt encrusted cross. At each corner stood an ornately robed apostle, his painted eyes staring out over the now black robed entourage. Everything swayed to the rythm of the mournful music; the censers of burning incense, the men bearing the float, the musicians, the onlookers. As the float passed, the spectators fell into a swarming mass behind it and followed the procession to the other side of town. There, in a centuries old church, another statue of Christ was raised to a cross.

But as soon as the Crucifixion was over, the Mayans went home, and by Saturday morning, the town was empty. The Church went bravely on with its program but no one was watching, any more. A tiny procession went quickly through the streets, almost at a trot. And soon there were piles of smouldering sawdust where the brightly colored carpets had been.

We were told that the Mayan ruins at Tikal, in the jungle of northeastern

Guatemala, were especially fine. So we planned to drive out that way and continue through British Honduras and the Yucatan Peninsula to Mexico and the United States. The young German couple wrote to tell us that the roads in British Honduras were very bad. But otherwise they got through without any problems. And Cynthia told us that all the snakes in the jungle, including Feu de Lance and 25-foot boa constrictors, had been migrating to the areas designated as public parks, so that it was unwise to camp there. She also mentioned that there were places where the road to Tikal was made of red clay, which was extreemly slippery after a rain. And she advised us to spend the first night by the Rio Dulce (the Sweet River). So we packed our gear into Minim, said goodbye to all our friends and drove up the winding road, out of Antigua.

We told Victoria not to come that day. We would be leaving much before her regular time. And I wanted her to do a thorough cleaning before returning the key to the landlord. The tourist season was nearing an and, and with it her chance of finding another job. So we gave her some money to get her through the next few hard months. But bright and early, she was at the door. She had a shawl for me and a shirt with a quetzal bird on it (Guatemala's national symbol) for Patrick. We hadn't given her the money for that, she needed so much herself. But we hadn't the heart to scold her for bringing gifts.

In the Capital we stopped to buy food, at the shops that we knew, for the first few days. And beyond the city, there was a paved road across Guatemala, toward the Caribbean Sea. A car full of people had been killed with machine guns on a side road, the week before, in broad daylight. But the main road was secure, they said. And leaving the high mountains, it followed a lovely valley across the country, to the place where the gravel road branched off toward the Rio Dulce. It was late in the afternoon when we came to the river and found a fine camp site, next to a swimming pool and a bar. But it was still hot, near sea level in the tropics, and going into the bar, I said (in my best Spanish) "My God, it's hot. May we have two rum punches, please?" The barman went away and rattled in a back room and came out with a small sauce pan (which should have aroused our suspicions), went away again for quite a while and finally brought us, with great pride, two hot rum punches. They were made with milk and scalding hot, with nutmeg on top of them. And we were so hot that we were pouring with sweat. But after he had taken so much trouble, we could only drink them, a sip at a time, and say how much we liked them.

The next morning, we crossed the river on the ferry and headed north up the road, into a range of steep hills where it narrowed to one lane and the surface changed to red clay. But since it was dry, we were able to keep going and after a while, we were on a two-lane gravel road, through rolling hills covered with dense jungle, sometimes passing a plot cleared for farming and more rarely, a small village. About noon we came to a large, open truck broken down in the road, with a dozen men standing mournfully around it. They had been there since eight in the morning and the temperature was well over a hundred degrees. And they thought they knew what was wrong with the engine but they could not fix it. They said there was a mechanic in a village 20 miles down the road but my Spanish was not good enough to explain the problem to him, so I offered to take one of the men to see him. And since Minim only had two seats, June stayed behind.

I watched Minim disappear in a cloud of dust. This couldn't be happening. He would never calmly drive off and leave me. The men stood around, smiling and showing open patches of gums where teeth had once hung. They fidgeted with their machetes and quikly exchanged some information. Then one gently touched my arm, stepped back and pointed to a hut across the road. In the heat and confusion I hadn't noticed it. They all escorted me to the door. There, a young woman welcomed me, offered me a hammock or a stool, I accepted the stool and they all left.

The dirt floored interior was divided into two tiny rooms with a partition of old cloth and cardboard. The cardboard was from a UNICEF box and I wondered if they had gotten the contents too. A baby was crying behind the wall. A table in one corner held several pieces of cutlery, stuck handles down in a chipped glass. More hammocks were hanging from nails against the poles that supported the roof, waiting for night. There was nothing else in the room, except of course the chickens who wandered in and out though a side door. I got up to take a look.

Under a thatched shade a leathery old woman was frying tortillas, her griddle on a stove made from an oil drum. The girl I had met before was making tortillas, kneading the ball of yellow corn dough, shaping in into a perfect circle with the palms of her hands. Then tossing it into the air a hundred times and catching it just where it was a bit too thick, until it was delicate and paper thin and fit to be cooked. On the ground near an open can of water was their metate - the large flat stone on which they ground their home-grown corn into a flour with another rolling-pin-shaped stone. They seemed to be feeding my fellow travellers but offered me nothing and I didn't ask. There were enough unexpected mouths to feed. So I wandered back into the shade of the house to wait.

When we reached the village, we were directed to the river where a man lying in the cool water told us how to find the mechanic, in a walled enclosure behind a house. He was working on a truck and had another one to fix after that but when we told him about the men waiting beside the road, he gathered up some tools and came with us in Minim - sitting on the floor between the two seats - to get their truck going. As soon as we arrived, he climbed up on the big truck and his head disappeared in the engine compartment - just his legs and his rear end remained visible - but I gathered he could fix it. June came out of a hut across the road and as we drove off, the men thanked us politely for our assistance.

Later that day, we came upon a farmer and his young son, walking along the road, so we picked them up. The man had a big machete, of course, but those were gentle people and we had no hesitation about giving them a lift. June sat on the floor, between the two seats, and the boy sat in his father's lap, in the passengers' seat. Though they were Mayans, the father also spoke Spanish and he told us that they walked about 6 miles each way, between their plot of land and their house, every day, unless they were lucky enough to get a ride. But evidently he had never seen an airconditioner, because he said "That's a pretty good idea, reversing your heater."

The last part of the road to Tikal was very bad, with pot holes that you could put a cow in. And in one place, we dropped a front wheel into a good one, bending the shock absorber and breaking its heavy steel bracket in two. But we did not notice it until we arrived at the ruined city, where the soldier who checked our papers pointed it out to us. And by then it was getting dark, so we went to the camp ground. It was a clearing in the jungle, maybe 50 yards across, a round patch of grass with a few trees left for shade. In it were five vehicles, with tents beside them. And all around it were high trees, with dense undergrowth between them. As we set up our tent, we saw toucans (the most ridiculous of birds) in the trees. And spider monkeys. And from the jungle came noises we did not care to consider.

A few yards away, there were two large tents belonging to a group of eight New Zealanders who were going round the world. And after dinner, we sat around their fire (for it was cool when the sun went down) exchanging information. They were travelling in an English van with a small diesel engine, that had given them a lot of trouble, though their trip had barely started. They had shipped the van from New Zealand to Chile and driven it across the Andes into Argentina. But coming back, where the road across the Andes was steeper, seven of them had to get out and push, while the owner drove. That caused some comment, since he had charged each of the others a fee for the trip, that was to continue via Mexico and the United States to New York, where the van would be shipped to Europe and driven through the middle east to India.

Sitting around the fire, a nurse next to me said that she planned to leave the van in London and continue alone. So I told her that I had heard of a bus, driven by an Australian with a Persian as co-driver, that went now and then from London to Bombay. And she said "Yes, I took that last year." Each trip was advertized in the London Times and also in the nursing magazines in England. The bus went across Europe to Italy and was shipped to Greece and on to Turkey. Then they went across the desert, camping every night and taking turns to sit up with rifles and guard the others. And when they came to a big city like Karachi, the driver said "All right, I'll see you in two days" and left them to fend for themselves.

The van that she was travelling in, at Tikal, must have been overloaded, with eight people in it and their luggage piled on the roof. And later, I noticed that there was no tachometer. So the driver had no way of knowing if the engine speed, which is critical with small diesel, was within allowable limits. And it was not surprising that it kept breaking down. But the owner told us that the roads in South America were no worse than those in Guatemala, though the police and military checks were more frequent. And there was a place near the border of Panama and Colombia, called the Darien Gap, where there was no road, so they had shipped the van past it.

In the morning, we rose early and walking along the narrow foot path from the camp ground, we soon came to the ruins of the city of Tikal, splendid in their setting of grass and palm trees, cleared from the jungle that had overgrown them. The ancient city covered nine square miles, with many fine buildings - temples, a ball court and so on - that had been meticulously uncovered and restored by teams of archaeoligists from the University of Pennsylvania, over a period of 20 years. The buildings, with their beautiful stone carvings, were for the church and the government. And between them, there had been the smaller dwellings of the people. So in its day, Tikal must have looked like a modern city, with tall buildings rising out of a sea of houses. But the houses had not survived and now the buildings, one of them 120 feet high, stood alone in their clearings, with small items, such as stelae (stones carved with the stories of important people or events) around them. Among the small items were many of the round stones on which people were sacrificed to the gods, early in the morning, as the sun came up. But now the ancient city was silent, except for a few birds, as the sun's rays slanted down through the trees, casting long shadows in the cool dawn. That was a superb time to be there, alone with a few other travellers, all so impressed by what we saw - and what we could easily imagine - that we spoke in whispers. But by ten o'clock it was hot and sticky and the tourists came in airplanes from the Capital to the gravel strip at Tikal, breaking the spell. So we drove off - slowly, because of the bent shock absorber - to the town of Flores (Flowers) beside a large lake, about 30 miles away. There we asked a soldier if there was a welder in town and he directed us to a house with a lean-to beside it, where a polite, serious man had both gas and electric welders. In less than half an hour, while while we ate our lunch on Minim's tailgate, he took off the shock absorber, bent it straight and got it working, welded the bracket and put everything back. And his charge, as I remember it, was two dollars for the job.

By then it was very hot indeed, so we drove a few miles out of town and found a secluded place in the shade of some trees, where we parked the truck and sat in the Lake of Flowers, up to our necks in the warm, muddy water - wondering if it had snakes in it but really to hot to care - all afternoon. When we got back to the camp ground at Tikal, the water had been turned off - the one tap was only open from 4 until 5 PM each day - so we went to the tourist hotel near the airstrip for a beer. But it was old and run down and the only person staying there for the night was an airline pilot who wished he had a tent. And the next day, after spending the early morning hours in the ruins, we set out for British Honduras.

Since that time, all ruins are compared with Tikal. We don't know exactly what it was that impressed us both so deeply. Certainly there are other Mayan sites that are every bit as interesting. More detailed carvings, more variation in architecture. But Tikal seemed to breathe. It might have been the jungle, full of sounds. Or the immense size of the site, one structure after another, temples to the heavens. Or because we had come early. We were alone much of the time. Too early to be persued by guides. But there was a magic - no question about that. And it's nice to think that Tikal has always been alive.

The official maps of Guatemala showed British Honduras as Territory of Guatemala Held Illegaly by the British, and about ten miles from the border, we came to an ambush. There was a heavy machine gun, hidden in the bushes at a corner, aimed down a straight section of road. And at the sides of the road, there were men with small arms, waiting to move out when the machine gun stopped firing. But they were in Army uniform and they were easy to spot from the west, so we assumed that they were there to stop vehicles coming the other way. And maintaining a steady speed, we waved cheerfully at them as we drove past them.

At the Guatemalan border, we were afraid that we might be told to go back to the Capital, to have our passports checked. So I kept up a stream of chatter, in my best Spanish, about how fine the ruins of Tikal were and what a splendid place Guatemala was, and before I ran out of things to say, the man gave me back our papers with a tired smile and we were free to go. Across the border, in British Honduras, the officials were black and spoke English but they seemed to take a dim view of us and eventually the man in charge said "I'll give you three days" which was more than we needed, so I thanked him politely and we continued on our way.

We had been told that the roads ahead were very bad and we were surprised to find that they were paved. But they were very old and they had not been kept up, so that the pavement was full of cracks, running in various directions. And at each crack, the level went up or down an inch or two, so that driving over them, even at 30 miles an hour, was rough going. The country looked very poor, with its low hills stripped of their mahogany trees, as though the British had taken everything of value and left the inhabitants to eke a living out of what remained. No wonder the officials at the border took a dim view of me, with my English accent. And we had been told that it would be better to avoid Belice, so we took a side road down to the ferry that went across a small river.

That was a flat barge, guided by a wire cable from bank to bank, and it was operated by a man who turned a big brass wheel - working hard at first but more easily, later on - which pulled the barge across the river to the other side. Then there was low, flat country - still poor but perhaps less so - across which the narrow road wound and twisted, until we came to the town of Corozal on the Caribbean Sea. That was near the border of Quintana Roo (a territory of Mexico in the Yucatan Peninsula) and there were two places which offered camp sites but neither of them looked very nice, so we had dinner in the restaurant of a motel by the sea and afterward we asked where we might camp for the night. The owner was most obliging and for a small fee he gave us a beautiful site at the water's edge, on green grass with a small ramada and two chairs and a tall overhead light that he assured us would keep away thieves. And after setting up our tent, we sat watching the lights of small boats, far across the water, before going to bed.

But in the night a storm came up, with thunder and lightning and heavy, driving rain. And a wind from the sea pushed the shallow water of the bay toward us, until it came over the grass and we awoke to find the shadows of large crabs - cast by the light overhead - running up the outside of our tent. Still, the tent was snake proof and therefore presumably crab proof. And I saw no reason to get up and run around in all that wet, so I turned over and went back to sleep. But the storm must have coincided with high water and the Spring tides, because when I woke up again, I could feel waves going under the tent, forcing up the floor. And June thought it was time for us to leave that place. The rain was drumming on our tent and gusts of wind shook it angrily as we pulled on our wet clothes. Outside, each time the lightning struck, we could see low clouds over the breaking seas. And standing beside the tent, we were knee deep in water. So we took a corner each and guided it - propelled by the wind - toward the shore and beached it in the parking lot.

By the time his lordship decided to wake up and do something, everything we owned was floating. We had to get out while there was still time. Grabbing what we could, we dashed for high ground. Then we went back for the tent, pulling the stakes out and lifting the whole wet mess by its aluminum frame. Leeches and crabs covered our bare legs but I couldn't hear myself scream above the noise of the gale.

About then, the owner of the motel came and apologized for the inconvenience - it had never happened before - and gave us a room, into which we carried exveything from the tent. I had left Minim on higher ground, where she was quite safe, and after staking the tent down in her lee, we retired to the room.

We had seen the motel in daylight and rejected it. But now, our foam mattresses full of sea water, we had no place else to go. I opened the door, turned on the light and watched several hundred black things scurry into corners. The bed had been slept it. The towels had been used. We dried ourselves as best we could, shook out the bed clothes and Patrick went back to sleep.

By dawn, the storm had vanished, the sky had cleared and the sea had returned to its proper level. Our things dried fast in the hot sun and by mid-morning we were on our way, across the border into Quintata Roo and northeast up the Yucatan Peninsula to the ruined city of Tulum. That was the only Mayan site by the sea - a small, walled city with few large buildings - but there were enough remains to leave a clear impression of how its people had lived. And half a mile south of it, we found a gap in the sand dunes where we set up our tent, sheltered from the wind by dense bushes but with a fine view, far out across the sea below us.

We had not seen the Yucatan before, so we drove north to the Isle of Women and west across the low, flat land - the road straight and lined with palm trees, mile after mile - to Chichen Itza. But the ruins there were disappointing, after Tikal- just a pyramid and a ball court in a wide, open field beside the highway, with a hot dog stand and a gift shop - so we continued on, by way of Merida and Campeche, to Villa Hermosa. There the only place to camp was in the paved parking lot of the airport, beside the busy highway and across from the fair grounds, that were active until long after midnight. But otherwise, we had a pleasant journey across Mexico and the United States to Vermont and arrived home in the spring time with the second phase of our plan completed. We now knew enough Spanish for ordinary purposes, we could get things done and we knew how to behave. In fact, we were ready for a longer journey, into the other countries of Central America.

INTERMISSION

We could not afford to go south, the following winter, so we drove across the United States to California - sleeping in the tent, as usual - and stayed in a friend's house near Sonoma while he and his wife went to Europe. June worked at the hospital, while I worked on a book and each evening, after dinner, we both studied Spanish for half an hour, in preparation for our next trip southward. In the spring, we heard from friends in Vermont that their son was at a Coast Guard cooking school near Petaluma, so we invited him to the house for a weekend. But how does one entertain an 18-year-old boy on a Saturday morning?

Clearly one goes hang gliding, so we went to Cotati Beach and found an instructor with a glider for rent, which we carried to the top of a large sand hill. And being the host, I felt that I should make the first jump. The proceedure is that you attach yourself to the glider - really, a large kite - and run down the hill. And soon your feet are no longer touching the ground. But before I had decided what to do next, I landed on my head.

There are two other ways to land a hang glider, that I can vouch for. The most comfortable is when it stalls and spins into the ground and you land on your rear end. And the least comfortable is when you go into a dive and push hard on the control bar and start flaring-out into level flight and almost make it and grind into the ground on your stomach at high speed.

But our frind's son had no trouble at all, right from the start - perhaps because he was 35 years younger than I, perhaps because he was 60 pounds lighter - while June had the good sense to stay firmly in charge of the picnic basket, at the top of the hill. And three weeks later, I could turn my head all the way, so we decided to call the whole thing a success. When the owners of the house returned, we went back across America to Vermont, And by the end of the summer, we could once again afford to visit Central America.

3 - SINGING RIVER

This time we decided to go to Costa Rica, where the winter climate - in the mountains - was said to be like Guatemala's but the government did not find it necessary to have an army. Again we tried to reduce the weight in Minim by leaving behind anything that we did not really need - including nearly all gadgets like spotlights and map boards - and we found that having fewer items in the truck made camping for the night much easier. And on or way south, across the United States, we got visas for all the countries of Central America.

In Mexico we found that the premium gasoline which we were used to was no longer available. Instead there was an unleaded kind that we could not use in Minim and a low grade leaded kind on which she made loud, protesting noises if we put the accelerator down too far. But by using the vacuum gauge and keeping the reading above 8 inches, we avoided that and at higher altiudes, where the air was thinner, the problem disappeared. So we took the old highway, over the mountains - avoiding Mexico City - and dropped down to sea level at Tehuantepec.

From there, we followed the mountain road - via the modern city of Tuxtla Gutierrez and the fine, old town of San Cristobal de las Casas - to the border of Guatemala, where there was very little traffic and we were quickly passed through. Then we drove up a beautiful gorge, into the high mountains beyond past the turnoff to Lake Atitlan - and down into Antigua, rumbling over the cobble stones of the ancient city, to a guest house called Casa El Patio, across the road from June's old school. It was owned by Tom and Erika Patterson, an American engineer and his Guatemalan wife, who had met in South America and retired to Antigua. It was an old house in the Spanish style, with all its rooms facing a covered walkway around a central garden of green grass and red, flowering trees. It had been meticulously restored by Tom and it was run by Erika and her staff with a quiet, relaxed efficiency that made it, in our opinion, the nicest place to stay in Antigua. But in a couple of days we had done our shopping and seen our friends and it was time to leave for El Salvador.

There were two roads through that country but according to the AAA, there were a number of dangerous tunnels on the coastal route, so we headed for the inland one, which they recommended. And soon we came to the border, where a woman Customs Inspector took her time examinimg each of our posessions, while a swarm of small children crowded round the truck. Then it was a long, tiresome day's drive over a series of steep hills on a narrow, winding two-lane highway crowded with slow-moving trucks, though the city of San Salvador and on to San Miguel, near the other end of the country, where we arrived after dark and camped in the grounds of a motel. We had been told before we left Guatemala that El Salvador was at war with Honduras and we might not be able to coss the border between them. But when we got there, everything seemed to be quite normal and while the various officials were checking our papers, we asked a few discreet questions. They were indeed at war over a football match five years earlier, which the wrong team had won. But they saw no reason to shoot at each other (though there were soldiers with machine guns on both sides) and settled for charging travellers a little extra to cross the border, in view of the situation.

The highway went across a corner of Honduras, which seemed to be poorer than the other countries of Central America - there were ox carts with big, wooden wheels carrying water to the villages - but near Cholteca we found a Texaco station, run by an American who called himself Gringo Jim, with a trailer park beside it. And soon after that, there was a new road that branched off to the right, toward the border of Nicaragua. The offices of the Customs, Immigration, Health and Police officials were in long wooden huts beside the dusty highway and outside each door there was a line of people waiting in the hot sun - truck drivers, mostly and a few families in overladen cars, piled high with baggage - but inside each office, it was surprising to see how quickly the officials were working.

They had a great deal to do, copying in big books the deails of each vehicle, its cargo, its driver and every one of its passengers, then typing permits, in many copies - typing much faster than I can, on ancient machines - for all of them to proceed. And in spite of the heat and the press of people in the tiny offices, the officials were remarkably polite.

The countryside of Nicaragua was low and flat - lush farm land, with prosperous-looking towns - but sticking up, here and there, were smoking volcanoes. The capital city of Managua had been destroyed by an earthquake two years before, so we avoided it and on the road past it, we came to Nick's camp ground. Nick had spent some time in the United States but he found that, speaking Spanish, he was not treated like a man. So he came back to Nicaragua, where he was glad to accept a lower standard of living, in return for his dignity. And though he had little to offer, he was slowly building up his facilities.

In the morning, we drove past the Lake of Nicaragua, with two volcanoes in it and a range of mountains beyond its distant shore. White-capped waves broke along the beach, near green fields where cows grazed. But beneath the surface of the water, which was quite fresh, there were sharks. Probably they were descendants of ordinary sharks that had lived in the lake many years ago, when it was connected to the sea. And after it was cut off, as the water slowly became fresh, the sharks had adapted themselves to it.

Just beyond the lake was Costa Rica, where the officials at the border had a fine, modern building and little paper work to do and we were soon on our way again. When you enter a country at a border like that, which is far from any major town, you first see a remote, undeveloped part of it and then you come to the normal areas, as though you had entered a large building by a back door. The road, though paved, was full of steep-sided pot holes and the rolling countryside seemed little used for nearly fifty miles, until we came to the town of Liberia, with modern houses and a motel with a coffee shop and tables in the garden beside it, where we stopped for lunch and our troubles began. For I rather liked the modernity and convenience of Costa Rica but June thought it was a bore.

Of course, I was bored. We hadn't stopped since leavng Antigua, unless you want to count gas stations. Our route conveniently by-passed every town of any size or interest. When I had suggested a quick buzz aound San Salvador, I was given about three dozen reasons why that was a terrible idea. Certainly the inevitable road-side craft stands hadn't looked promising. The painted ox carts hauling barrels of water up steep hills seethed with sweat and poverty more than color. Touring Managua after a major earthquake was low on my list, too. And the people along the way had been more hostile than usual. Not really unfriendly, just not very open or relaxed. But I was still willing to take a little time to wander off the main roads. Things might be more interesting away from the highways. No time for that. We must push on. And there was Patrick. Happy as a clam. Ordering a hamburger from a menu printed half in Spanish and half in English. He even ordered a salad. I hoped he got sick.

The road continued - with few pot holes now - over gentle hills for a while, then steeply down to the turnoff to the old sea port of Puntarenas, hot in the tropical afternoon, the road to it lined with shacks and (we thought) not very nice. So back to the main road and up into the mountains, away from the sea - climbing and dipping and climbing again - to the high, green valley where the capital cities of four provinces are clustered together, all within 15 miles of each other. The largest, San Jose, is also the Capital of Costa Rica - a busy, modern city - and beyond it, half way to Cartago in the village of Tres Rios, we found the Singing River Trailer Park, a dozen sites on a narrow ledge beside a rushing river, put there by an American major and run by his Costa Rican Wife. Four of the sites were occupied, one by an American couple who were planning to live down on the coast, the rest by Spanish speaking people in transit. And in a small brick building, below the owners' quarters, were toilets and showers. So we set up our tent, between flowering bushes at the foot of a steep bank, and left it there while we explored the valley, looking for a place to spend the winter.

The countryside was beautiful in a soft, peaceful way but it rained hard each afternoon and there was a strong wind all the time, which we found tiresome after a while. Everywhere we looked, there were American-style houses and in the shops we saw American people, mostly retired on fixed incomes, who spoke little or no Spanish. In fact, one woman came in and said in a loud voice "Who here speaks English?" And when we talked with her, she told us she had lived there for four years and ran a shop in San Jose. But we had not come so far to live in Small Town, USA and I grew less enchanted with the place every day, while June - who had been in a snit since we came to Costa Rica - was itching to get back to Guatemala as soon as possible.

Still we gave it the old college try, searching for some quiet corner where we could avoid the pervading influence of the United States and doing so, we almost got into trouble. We were slightly lost, somewhere to the west of San Jose, so we stopped to ask a farmer (in Spanish) for directions. And he must have thought Minim was an official vehicle, for he told us how to get to La Luz (The Light). That seemed to be a reasonable name or a village in a Catholic country, though we could not find it on our map, so we followed his directions, figuring that we could at least start again from there.

He has it all wrong. The town was on the map. And so was a fine road leading to it and an intersection shown on the other side of the river where, if the map had been correct, we could have joined the highway back to San Jose. But the map wasn't correct. Evidently the road had never been built, just proposed. When I asked the man if we were on the road to La Luz, he said "Yes." So on we went.

But the road got steadily narrower and rougher, until it was just a one-lane track over big, loose stones that suddenly went down a short, very steep hill and came to a dead end at a small electric light plant. Across a deep gorge ahead of us was a foot bridge, barely wide enough for a man to cross. And on the other side, there was a fine, paved road, beside the main building. But there was no possible way for Minim to reach it. So we had to go back. But it is one thing to slither down a steep hill over big, loose stones and it is quite another thing to climb up it, with enough speed to carry you to the top and no room at the sides to dodge the worst of the bumps. And for a moment, we bouth doubted that Minim would be able to make it. We could not blame the farmer who had given us the directions, for he was on foot and no doubt he thought it a perfectly reasonable way for a couple of people to get there. But now we were at the bottom and the World Outside was at the top and the time had come to face that fact.

We both got out of the car and stood looking up the sides of the gorge. It was hard to believe that we had actually driven down the rocky cliff behind us. There was no way out except the way we had come. In fact there was some discussion about the cost of helicopter time and whether or not one could lift Minim. After deciding we really couldn't afford it, Patrick managed to turn the truck around in an area the size of a city street parking space and we were on our way.

I lined her up with the narrow trail, then we cinched our seat belts in, as tightly as we could. And putting her in first gear, I accelerated as quickly as possible, to get the engine's revolutions up to the point where it developed maximum power. After which, the whole thing was a piece of cake, for she just went up that hill as if it wasn't there. Of course it was a bit bumpy, but we were expecting that. And before we fully realized what was happening, we were safely at the top. But Costa Rica was not for us. It was far too civilized. We might as well spend the winter in Fort Lauderdale. So we took our wet tent and headed back toward Guatemala.

This time we went past Nick's place in Nicaragua and spent the night at Gringo Jim's in Honduras, which was nicer. Then we took the coast road across El Salvador, that was faster and more pleasant than the other way, going through flat farm land with little traffic, then close along the shore past well-kept houses - the tunnels were harmless and rather fun - to a quiet border control point where we were quickly processed. On the Guatemalan side, the Immigration Officer was young, efficient and polite but evidently he thought there was something odd about our coming back so soon, for he only gave us three days in which to report to the Immigration Service in the Capital. At moments like that, it is possible to feel apprehensive, for we had been told that the Guatemalan authorities could be quite rough on people who stepped out of line - on one occasion, they were said to have scooped up a bunch of hippies, put them in an airplane and pushed them out over the Pacific Ocean - and he might have noticed the endorsements in our passports, made two years before, which we had failed to obey.

But the three days he had given us were more than enough to cross the country and escape into Mexico, so we decided to take the chance that they would accept or explanation that we simply had not noticed the endorsements. And after following the coast road to Esquintla, we headed up into the mountains, to a camp ground called La Red, on the way to the Capital. There we set up our tent near an old Scout that had once belonged to the US Postal Service, in which a thin, elderly man from Texas was living alone. It only had one seat and where the other one should be, he had installed a Porta Potty. Then he had glued odd bits of carpet of various colors all over the inside - floor, sides and roof - and built a crude kitchen in the back, where he was about to heat up a can of stew. So we invited him to share our dinner and as we ate, he told us his story. He had been in the recreational vehicle business but he got out of it when the price of oil went up, since he felt that people would stop buying them. And he owned a share of an oil well, which used to bring him additional income. But at the new price, he was getting $7,000 a month from it, so he fixed up the old Scout and went travelling.

In the morning, we went into the Capital and found the Immigration Office, in the basement of a large building. So June stayed with Minim while I took our passports and went down to join a line of people, shuffling slowly toward a small window. When I got there, a busy official in civilian clothes asked how long we wanted to stay and I said "Three months, please." He glanced at our passports, which had several entries in them since the trip to Costa Rica, and said "Sixty days. If you want more, you must come back." Then he banged a rubber stamp on a pad of ink, hit each passport with it and said "Next." And I found myself standing on the busy street outside the building in the strong sunlight, holding the passports in my hand.

We had found a parking spot near the Immigration building. The area wasn't very savory. Street traffic was one way, always jammed. Sidewalks were even worse; men leaning against the walls while people tried to push past. After about an hour I noticed one man, in a suit and tie, standing near the front of the car. Others had come and gone but he was always there. He seemed to be known. Men would stop and chat with him. But he would arrange things so that he was always facing me. Street vendors paraded by with lottery tickets, straw hats, three piece suits, tacos, plastic watch bands; the selection was endless. I had locked the car doors but the windows were open. It was like an oven inside. I must have been hotter out on the pavement. Yet the man still stood watching me. I was geting a bit nervous. When Patrick finally arrived, the stranger spoke to him. He scolded Patrick for leaving me alone. It was not a safe place. And then he disappeared into the crowd.

Then we drove over the mountains to El Patio in Antigua, and after telling Tom and Erika about our adventures - it was so good to be back - we went looking for a house to rent. That took several days this time, but eventually we made contact with a tall, imposing White Russian called Musa who was going away for a few months. Her house was on the north side of the city, not far from El Patio, on a street of modest houses and small shops - all in the Spanish style and one story high - but the varnished grillwork over the windows and the new door in the white, freshly painted wall proclaimed that it had been renovated for the use of a wealthy foreigner. For the Guatemalans seldom allowed their wealth to be seen from the street. On the outside, a house might look run down and dingy but suddenly a door would open and a big, white Mercedes would come out and drive off as the door closed again.

And indeed Musa's house was nicely done, with a crucifix and candles on a stone shelf to your right, as you came in, and a big living room to your left, with a high ceiling and wrought iron chandeliers and at the far end, a brick fireplace. The two windows on the street side were of frosted glass, with wooden shutters to close at night, and in the opposite wall were two big, arched doorways that opened onto a patio, shaded by the roof and looking out onto a paved courtyard with flowers on all sides and a fountain in the middle. Along its right side was a high, white wall with flowers in baskets hanging from it and on the left side, behind the beds of flowers, was a narrow pathway beneath the overhanging roof of a low building, with doors leading to a modern kitchen, then a bathroom, then a small study, then a store room. And at the end was a large bedroom, with a double bed and its own bathroom.

I thought it odd that there was only one bedroom but when I raised the matter, Musa gave me her imperious look and said "My dear boy, if anyone sleeps here, he sleeps with me." So we agreed on a rental of $330 a month, to include the services of her Mayan butler Tomas and his wife Hermania. And a few days later, when Musa left, June and I moved in.

That isn't at all the way we found the house. We had met Musa briefly at El Patio on our way south the month before. In fact, we had both gone to the house for a brief look. Musa was out, but Tomas showed us around. And all the way to Costa Rica, I thought of that fountain and the garden and the red tiled roof.

We could not really afford such a grand life style but it was fun, while it lasted. Each morning, we strolled across the courtyard, past the fountain, to the shade of the patio, where Tomas in his white coat took our order for breakfast. And while Hermania prepared it, we admired the view, beyond the far wall, of the pine trees on the distant mountains. Then I went to work, in the study, on a series of articles for Yachting Magazine, while June drove Minim over the mountains - past a place called Swan Lake - to Chimaltenango, where she did odd jobs for Dr. Berhorst at his Mayan hospital.

Most of my visits to Chimaltenango were futile attempts to offer my services. Poor Spanish kept me from trying to volunteer in the Antigua hospital, but certainly in an American administered clinic there might be something I could do. I did not want to bother Dr. Berhorst. He was, when I did meet him weeks later, very charming and very busy. Those around him weren't. After several broken appointments and standard brush-offs (which only made me more interested) I happened upon an American woman who came to work once or twice a week in the office. Since the hospital was supported by donations, mostly from the States, there were indeed some things I could do. But by that time, we had only a few weeks left in Guatemala. The doctor is the center of much needed health care in that old mountain town. It is a privilege to watch him work. From tuberculosis to malnutrition to a broken arm or a tooth extraction. Of course it is an impossible task. What can he do with not enough money, with generations of ignorance and neglect in an uncaring society, with not even a tap of running water in his surgery and knowing that whatever he does today will be there again tomorow? He does what he can. He does a lot.

Chimaltenengo is on the old Pan American highway running along the ridge of the high mountains into the Capital. It is far enough from the city to be unfashionable, yet close enough to provide some escape, so besides the Indian population there is a substantial Spanish group living there, and a few Americans. I drove into a parking space one day near the hospital and watched a taxi unload. It was a small, dust covered car packed with people. The driver, two adults and two children climbed out of the front seat before those in back could exit. From the back came four more adults and five childen. On top were tied the usual array of parcels and crates. Some with chickens. The driver opened the trunk and extracted a couple of suitcases, several more baskets and a very angry pig. I was market day in Chimaltenango.

But we preferred not to have Tomas and Hermania around in the evenings, so they went home - walking across town - after lunch and June cooked dinner, often for a few friends. John Long, the doctor, was training paramedics, recruited from the villages. That was greatly helped by the fact that the Mayans had a tradition by which a man owed two years of service to his community. So they would come to John's organization for training and then go back to put in the remainder of their time, each in his own village, teaching the people there. Jim and Alice Bell were still running their shop - Tienda la Flor (the Flower Shop) - Alice staying in Antigua most of the time, while Jim went around the country, placing orders for the various items and later picking them up. Cynthia Burski and Bob Braaton were engaged to be married and were negotiating to buy land in the lowland jungle, between the Rio Dulce and Tikal, to clear and make into a ranch.

Cynthia had just finished her tour of duty with AID and after driving alone, all over Guatemala, for four years without any trouble, she went back to the head office in Washington and was mugged in the parking lot. But she put up such a fight that her attacker ran off without getting anything. She and Bob were quiet people, soft spoken and easy going, and it was strange to see them sitting on our patio, both doing fancy needle-work while they explained the problems of developing a ranch out of the jungle in Guatemala. One man they knew had bought such a piece of land but when he got there, he found squatters on it. So he told them to leave and they shot him dead, without hesitation.

The land was not cheap. Bob and Cyn were paying $80,000 for their place, that was six miles from the end of the nearest gravel road, through dense jungle, full of snakes. They planned to build their house out of the mahogany on the property but taking in other materials would be slow, since anything they left in their truck at the end of the road would be stolen, so they could only take at one time what the mules they led through the jungle could carry. But Bob had worked on cattle ranches in Montana and knew the business. And he had finished his job with the Peace Corps. And neither of them wanted to go back to the dull, safe life in the United States after living in Guatemala.

For those who were born there it was different. Marta Julia, a young girl who was one of June's Spanish teachers, was anxious to see the United States but for her to get together the necessary money - not to mention the Immigration problem - was nearly impossible, within a thinkable period of time. We tracked down Victoria, who had been our maid two years before, and found that she was having problems. She had been out of a job for a while and was very thin, so we lent her some money - she was too proud to accept it as a gift - and after a while, we found a job for her with an American family. Our friend the beggar had lost his pitch near the Antigua Hotel and someone had set him up with a tray of cigarettes and candy, under an arch beside the plaza. But he was unshaven and looked awful, so we gave him a little and persuaded him to get spruced up, so that the tourists would not avoid him. We were aware, of course, that we were interfering with other people's lives but we could see no reasonable alternative, when we could so easily help them. It was a problem.

Julie Hall, the young artist who introduced us to Cynthia, had given up her job in Vermont and moved to Guatemala. She had a house on a quiet street (near the cemetary) in Chimaltenango, with all its rooms in a row, going away from the street. And the last one (which was kept for visitors) was haunted. Two people slept there at different times, and they both had the same experience. There was no electricity in the house, so a candle was kept by the bed and in the middle of the night, the person woke up to find it alight. So he reached to put it out and a hand out of the darkness grasped his wrist. It was the ghost of a man who once owned the house and he held firmly onto the wrist while he told the person how to find the gold he should dig up and take to the priest to have a Mass said for his soul. But since he said it in Queechee, the person failed to understand it.

Our house in Antigua had no room for Minim but we found a fine parking space nearby. You went though a gate on a busy street and down an alley, past a watchman, to an open lot behind the buildings, with covered spaces all around it, each containing a truck or an expensive car. And there we had our own space, with 24 hour service, for $3.50 a week. We were learning how to do things as the local people did them. We still studied Spanish every day but we were more concerned with how to behave so as not to appear rude or stupid, and to be accepted at least as half-way-civilized foreigners. The music we brought with us was classical and acceptable anywhere but the local newspaper did not have much international news, so we used our short wave radio to get it from Canada in the evenings, for the awareness of world problems was far greater among the people we met in Guatemala than among our friends back in the United States.

One young man had just arrived in Guatemala to join the Peace Corps when he was sent off, alone in a light truck, to a remote village in the mountains. About 15 miles from a main road, he was on a track barely wide enough for one vehicle, with a steep bank on one side and a sheer drop on the other, when he met a truck full of people coming the other way. With much laughter they piled out of the trck, cut down some small trees and built a platform beside the road, over a precepice. And waving cheerfully, they signalled him to drive onto it, so that their truck could get past him. For a moment, he hesitated but the only alternative was to reverse for several miles, with a good chance of going over the edge at one of the tight corners, so he eased his truck onto the platform, as he was directed. And thankfully, it took the weight. But a week or so later, when we met him, he had not fully recovered from the experience.

When Erika knew us better, she told us that her father had come from Germany, many years ago. And as was the custom in those days, he had taken two wives, one Spanish and one Mayan. When he died, he left his money to the Spanish family and his land to the Mayan one. But the money was spent, over the years, while the land became worth a fortune. And she had some Mayan sisters, living in the mountains as they always had - graceful, black skinned women who carried pots on their heads - who were the wealthy members of the family.

But Erika was well connected and through her we met Don Carlos Dorian, a distinguished gentleman who spoke of Guatemala as though it were a family business. His house near Antigua had so many rooms that his wife had numbers put on the doors. It was an old house, built on three sides of a large garden, and its furnishings were unpretentious. But some of the antiques were very fine and wherever you looked, as far as the distant mountains, he owned the land. His wife Chita had been a swimming champion and still pacticed every day in a long, narrow pool beside the house, while Don Carlos had a glass-fronted cabinet full of cups that he had won for automobile racing when he was younger. They both spoke flawless English and he was quite familiar with places like the New York Yacht Club in America.

The house had been built in the sixteen hundreds. Or at least started then. Certainly over the past three hundred years there had been some additions and alterations. There were halls and verandas, stairs and narrow passages, hidden gardens and vistas. Just inside the main entry, the first little room on the left was a chapel. It was a narrow room and in front of the worn wooden pews stood a lovely altar. Don Carlos picked up some hand written pages lying there, near the bible. They had been written at the time of the first Spanish settlement in Guatemala, about the rules that were to govern the community. Nice old things to have around the house.

From a balcony by the dining room, we could see the white church - a replica in miniature of a famous cathedral - that Don Carlos had built for his workers. And below the balcony, there was a big, paved yard where coffee was drying in the sun. He owned several coffee fincas and went to them, from his place in Guatemala City, by airplane. But there was nowhere to land at the one near Antigua, so I asked him what he did. And he said "Usually we drive - it's not far - but when we're in a hurry, we borrow a helicopter from the Air Force and it lands over there, in the yard. It's quite convenient." As a young man, he had put the electric system in Antigua, supervising the installation of the poles and wires, and he told us - with quiet delight, because Erika was across the table - that in those days El Patio was a whore house. Each girl had her own room and asking us which one we had stayed in, he said "That's Rosie's room, I remember it well."

Now he was past seventy but a few years ago he had been driving over the montains from the Capital to Antigua a two o'clock in the morning when he ran into an ambush. He came around a corner at his usual high speed and found two cars blocking the road, so he headed for the narow strip of grass between the road and the dropoff. And before the bandits had time to do anything, he was past them, But someone had left a pile of sand, a little farther on, that stopped him. He was alone in the car, so he grabbed his machine gun, opened the door on the passenger's side and rolled out onto the ground, just as the shooting started. The noise of their guns was very loud, in the still of the night, but he opened fire and put 26 holes (by later count) in their two cars, before they ran away. Then he inspected all the cars and found that none of them was driveable, so he set off down the road toward Antigua on foot.

When he got there, the streets were empty. All the doors and windows were shut and the people were asleep. So he went to a friend's house and banged on the door. After a while, there was a stirring inside. Then a widow opened and a face appeared for an instant and the window slammed shut. And though Don Carlos called out his name and said what had happened, he got no reply. So he walked to another friend's house and the same thing happened there. No one would listen to him. It was frustrating. He was very tired. And dirty. And the machine gun he was carrying was heavy ...... Of course.. They didn't believe it was him. He went to another friend's house and this time, he knew what to do. He kept the gun out of sight and as soon as the window opened, he tossed his American Express credit card through it. And a minute later, his friend let him in.

After telling us that story, Don Carlos excused himself and went off with the foreman of the finca, speaking quietly in Spanish, and we suddenly remembered that he had been speaking English, all though lunch, out of politeness to us. We tried to do the same at our house but our friends came from various countries and sometimes there would be conversations going on around our dining table in English, French, German and Spanish at the same time, which was confusing. And one evening we went to see The Great Gatsby at a movie house in Antigua but the sound track, in English, was so worn that we found it easier to follow the story by reading the sub titles, in Spanish.

As we learned to speak Spanish better, we found it easier to understand how Spanish speaking people think, for the way a thing is put makes quite a difference in how you see it. Where we would say "I just broke a glass" they would say "A glass just broke itself" which is hardly the same thing, at all. And the way government departments operate in Central Amarican countries makes sense if you remember that they were ruled by Spain for hundreds of years, before the days of rapid communication. When a problem arose, the local commander would send a message down to the coast, to be carried by sailing ship across the Atlantic Ocean. Then he could safely file the whole thing for several months until a reply came back.

The system by which local officials get a small salary and make up for it by accepting bribes is really no different from that by which waiters are paid. It simply transfers the cost of their work to the people they serve. And the bribes required for most transactions are quite small. So the person using their services has merely to learn the proper amounts to offer and the proper proceedures for giving them, in each case.

But some of the arrangements that have come down from the days of Spanish rule and been modified to meet today's needs are curious and interesting. Like the water bills in Antigua. Each house there has one or more pajas (straws) of water. That is the amount of water that will flow through a straw in a certain length of time and if you use that amount or less in a month, there is no charge for the water. But if you use more, you have to pay for that. Or you could buy another straw, from someone else, and use more water, without paying for it. And if there is a street light outside your house, the cost of that is added to your water bill. Unless you buy another straw, or maybe half a straw, to offset the overage.

The taxes on a small business in Antigua are decided by a visit to the tax man, once a year. The shopkeeper will admit that he did make a few sales, though business was slow and expenses were very high. And the tax man will look up what that shop paid last year and maybe add a little. And a reasonable sum will be agreed upon. In theory, such a system is open to abuse. But in a place where only a few people pay taxes and they all know each other, it probably results in as fair a distribution of the tax load as we achieve in America with all our complex laws.

Between Antigua and Chimaltenango there is a turnoff to the village of San Andres Itzapa, where a shrine to a new saint called San Simon was quickly becoming famous. Driving there, we picked up a man on crutches, who grinned happily out of the window at his friends walking up the straight, dusty road. And in the village of adobe houses and narrow streets, we left Minim outside a shop, under the eye of a large woman in a black dress, while we visited the shrine. From a small coutyard, two doorways led into a room lit by many candles and at one end, in a glass case, there was a department store dummy, seated in a chair, dressed in a tuxedo and white tennis shoes. In front of the case was a shelf, on which there were offerings of cigars and whisky (that he liked) among the candles and pinned below the shelf was a notice asking you not to put the whisky too close to the candles.

An old photo was propped against a bottle inside the glass case. We couldn't discover if it were a photo of San Simon in the flesh, or of someone who reminded the villagers of their saint. The man in the photo stood in the middle of a dusty street. He wore a dark suit, a bowler hat and a bow tie. He smiled slightly through a bushy, short cropped mustache. Very neat, very dapper - just like the manikin inside the glass case.

The long wall, opposite the doorways, was almost covered with small, framed notes of thanks - each saying that a person had been cured of some ailment - all of them signed and some with passport-sized pictures attached to them. And on the floor, half a dozen people knelt, silently praying. Outside. acros the courtyard, a new shrine was being made for San Simon. And walking back through the village, we noticed - as we had in other villages - that some of the Mayans were very slightly built indeed. Perhaps because of their diet.

Many of the Indians seemed to be around four or five feet tall. Their diet was usually slim. Corn tortillas wrapped around a few scraps of meat or tomato or bean paste. Few suffered from obesity.

You hardly ever saw a woman with gray hair in Guatemala, because the rich women dyed their hair and the poor ones seldom lived long enough to go gray. It was sad to see so many people's lives cut short like that, by sheer poverty. But even the smallest things we could do to help were appreciated. One day we were driving in the high country near Antigua when a farmer ran across the road ahead of us, carrying a piece of burning wood. And as we watched, he ran to and fro in a field, setting fire to small piles of trash. So June insisted that I stop the car and went chasing after him, with a box of kitchen matches. But he was going away from her, down into a dip, and I had to stand on a rock beside the road to see the two figures come together, far across the yellow stubble. For a moment they stood facing each other - she speaking, evidently, and he listening - then she gave him the matches. And sweeping off his hat, he bowed from the waist.

Running through the sandy volcanic soil at seven thousand feet was not easy for me. At least the farmer seemed pleased. His smile was real as he opened the box. He said something about not taking them all, but I explained that we had another box in the car. "Then many thanks" he said, and doffed his hat.

In Antigua, it was surprising how neat and clean the parks were, considering that many of the people were so poor. And the shoe shine boys in the central plaza, who would run after a tourist, shouting "Give me one money" in English, were easy to get along with in Spanish. Usually there was not work for them all, so I would pick an older one, who - I thought - needed the money more. And while he worked, a few of the younger boys would sit around us, chatting and joking among themselves. I was seldom included in their conversation but evidently they liked to be close to a foreigner, who was a symbol to them of wealth and freedom. In the same way, you would often see a boy standing beside an expensive car - his hand resting lightly on it - just to be near so fine a thing. For such boys were young enough, still to have dreams. But their chances of ever possessing the slightest wealth were very slim indeed. And while it was not in their nature to rob anyone, they would steal anything they could.

One day, we went up to the Hill of the Cross - overlooking the city of Antigua - with an American surgeon and his wife. As there were four of us, we used their car and when we got there, June and I rolled up the windows and locked the doors on our side. But the surgeon and his wife left their windows wide open, for it was a hot day. And noticing it, I decided not to say anything, since the car was empty - I thought - and we were only going a few yards away, to see the view. As we stood on the hill, looking down at the city, five small boys came up a path on our left, went past the car and down into the woods on our right. And when we got back to the car, the surgeon's wife said her handbag had gone. She had left it on the seat beside an open window, with their two passports and about $ 2,500.00 in it.

Her two pairs of prescription glasses in their cases had been left neatly on the seat. Very considerate of the thieves.

We searched the car - inside and underneath and around it, for you don't want to believe a thing like that - then we remembered the boys. And while I searched the trails down the sides of the hill, June and the others went off to get help.

The first thing we did was to get Erika from El Patio. We needed a good translator. She called the police and then came to the scene to help.

As I worked my way down the hill, it kept getting steeper and finally dropped down to a road along the bottom, at the edge of the city. There I met Erika and while she made enquiries at the houses along the road, I went back up the hill. Two young men came up one of the trails, which were used as short cuts over the hill, and when I asked if they had seen a bag - a plain, white one with a shoulder strap - they offered to help me find it. So we split up - each taking a trail - and I was peering through the undergrowth, looking almost straight own at the road below, when the police came. They arrived in a Jeep and looking up the hill, they saw me. So they waved their guns and shouted at me, to come down at once. Which would have been easy, if I had just let go of the tree that I was holding onto. But otherwise, I would have to go back up a bit, to get down. And if I did that, they would probably shoot me. So I shouted down the hill, that I was looking for the thieves. And my two friends joined in, from other trails. And there was much shouting, up and down the hill, until Erika came along the road and calmed them down.

We covered that hill for the next few days, in case we might find a trace of the purse or its contents. And I went into every little shop in the area, offering a reward for the return of some of the papers, at least. In one shop, a small dog growled and barked all the time I was trying to speak to the owner. Finally, he apologized. He said he couldn't stop the dog. You see, it didn't like gringos. Later that day we stopped at a friend's house. His dog was snarling and barking as he tried to speak to a Mayan who had arrived just before me. Our friend apologized. He said he couldn't stop it. The dog, you see, didn't like Indians.

By then it was getting dark and the boys were long gone, so we all went to the police station, where the proper reports were filed. And later, Erika told us that she was almost sure she knew who had stolen the bag, from her talks with the people along the road below the hill. But she did not tell the police, because they would be so hard on the boys, if she accused them, whether they had done it or not. And the surgeon, who was staying at the Patio, said it was no loss to him. Most of the money was in traveller's checks, which would be replaced automatically and the rest, that was in cash, was covered by insurance. So there would just be the inconvenience of going to Guatemala City to report the loss of the passports and get temporary papers for the trip home. But to the boys' families, it must have been the windfall of a lifetime, for the passports alone were worth more than a thousand dollars each - we were told - in the black market. And even if they only got ten cents on the dollar for the lot, that would be more money at one time than a working family could ever hope to get by any other means.

Just before Easter, June's parents came from Michigan to stay with us in Antigua. Her father was in his eighties - though her mother was younger - and neither of them spoke any Spanish but they wandered all over the city, having a fine time. Her father was a quiet person, content to stroll in the sunshine and observe the world around him. But her mother was an outgoing type and whenever she saw a baby - which was often - she would go up and say "Isn't he cute?" and "My, what a big boy" and the Mayan women understood perfectly.

She was disappointed that their plane was not hijacked, for she had hoped to see Cuba but we took them down to the Pacific coast to see the black sand beaches, and up into the mountains to Lake Atitlan and the market at Chimaltenango. And one evening when we were at Julie's house there was an earthquake. Dr. Berhorst was there and several Peace Corps people and everyone was talking, when the floor shook - just a little, but enough to be quite unmistakable - and I looked across the room at June's mother and she was so pleased. It was one more thing to remember when she got back to Michigan.

We often took drives into the countryside and I would take scraps of food to give to dogs along the way. Most of the people shared what they could with their dogs, but there was so little to go around. Once we took a plastic bag of bones left from a roast and stopped to give them to a particularly sad crerature. I gave him one bone and then noticed a tiny girl standing in the trees a few feet away, staring at me. She said nothing. Her eyes were black and listless. I handed the bag to her. She thanked me and turned to go. With one hand she steadied an infant strapped to her back and bare footed, dog following, slipped into the underbrush at the side of the road.

Our house in Antigua was on the route of the processions during Holy Week, so they had a fine view of those - Tomas, our butler, went proudly by in his purple robe - and when they were over, the folks flew back to America. All through that winter, we had been enquiring about the road beyond Costa Rica, to South America and we were told that there was a secion called the Darien Gap, between Panama and Colombia, that was impassable. There were rumors that a road might one day be built, but for the time being you had to ship your vehicle from Panama and that was expensive. So we were quite envious when we met a young French Canadian couple who were going all the way to South America. Their truck - an old red pickup with a simple top on it - was parked across the street from our house and since they were obviously travellers, we stopped to speak to them. They had just come from the United States, so we invited them in for a shower and over dinner, they told us their plans.

They were going to drive to Panama and put the truck on a ship - past the Darien Gap - to Colombia, where there was a road that went south, throgh Ecuador, to Peru. And they hoped to see all of South America before flying back to Canada. He had built a wooden platform in the back of the truck, with a mattress on top of it and space below for their gear. And he had welded the tailgate shut, so that you had to lift the mattress and open various hatches to get things out. There were padlocks on the doors and the hood, and inside was a large dog, trained to attack anyone who broke in. The truck, though old, was in good shape and looked as if it would last the trip. And when they drove off in the morning we wished that we could go with them. But the time had come for us to head north once more.

At times I doubted that we would ever travel much farther than Central America. And I wondered if I really wanted to. It's all very well to look down yor nose at tourist facilities but would you really rather travel in a dirty, rusty old truck for thousands of miles, eating God only knows what - - sleeping and washing God only knows where or when? A few years ago I might have thought it a great adventure. But at forty five, I began to doubt. Our sailing days had left us fairly unspoiled. We had learned to survive without the small luxuries of routine life. Well, if those kids could do it in that old heap, I could live through it with our truck and tent. Besides, the best time to fret is if and when the journey is about to happen.

We planned to leave on a Monday, but we heard that there was going to be an anti-American demonstration in Antigua on the Sunday, so we left early on Saturday morning - taking the route over the mountains - and were in Mexico that evening. Arriving in Mexico from Guatemala was like coming to the United States from Mexico. Everything seemed to be so well kept and all the people looked so prosperous. But the whole scene was a trifle dull, until we passed Durango. I had to go to San Diego, to judge some yacht races, so we stayed in the high country as far as Durango, then took the road down to Mazatlan, which was quite exciting.

For the best part of 100 miles it winds through impressive mountains, so steep that the engineers built it along the ridges, near the tops of them. Often there is a sheer drop, of several thousand feet, on both sides of the road and between the ridges, it clings to the walls of rock in a highly unlikely manner. In those circumstances, my hands get clammy and the steering wheel feels slippery, so I hold a spoke of the wheel in my left hand and shift gears with the right one - saving the brakes as much as possible - and concentrate on watching the road close ahead and try not to notice the clouds far below.

But eventually the road dropped down to the Pacific Ocean near Mazatlan and from there it was easy going, all the way to California. And when the yacht races were over, we drove across the United States, back to Vermont, with the third phase of our plan completed. We had reached the point where we could think in Spanish and we were ready for a journey through South America, as soon as we could find a way to afford it.

4 - ONE WAY TICKET

That summer, Tom Follett - who used to work in our yacht delivery business - said that he might be able to take Minim to South America for us, very cheaply. He was now sailing as master of the Sol Reefer, a small refrigerated cargo ship, in the dynamite trade. Every two months or so, he took on a full cargo of the stuff at the Atlas Powder Company's dock in Georgia and went off to deliver it - a little here and a little there throughout the Caribbean and sometimes down the west coast of South America, as far as Peru.

The owner of the ship was David Humphreys, who also used to work for us, and he had no objection to Tom loading Minim on deck and putting her ashore at a suitable port in South America. But the ship was not licensed to carry passengers, so June and I would have to sign on as members of the crew. June would be the cook, while I would be the second mate, and we would be paid one dollar each, for the passage. We would be expected to pay for our food, in the circumstances, plus the cost of the paper work involved. But the whole thing would only amount to a couple of hundred dollars, each way. That was wonderful news and we immediately set about making preparations for a trip through South Amarica - overhauling the truck, that already had 100,000 miles on it, and gathering all the details we could on what lay ahead.

It was wonderful news - all except the bit about cooking. Patrick is always so generous with my time. But Tom quietly assured me that there would be no need for a woman in the galley of a merchant ship. His full time crew had ways of their own. Tom himself travelled with his own bread, wine and cheese. A precaution that saved him from innumerable indigestible meals. So I started the calculations on life expectancy of a thirty pound Vermont cheddar in the tropics.

But information on driving through South America was very hard to find. The American Automobile Association claimed, in their literature, to know it all but when we drove to Washington and visited their World Wide Travel Service there, we found that they had nothing to offer, of any practical value.

The AAA could arrange flights and hotel bookings, just as any travel agency could. We needed driving information: maps, suggested routes, availability of gasoline, months when passes over the Andes might be closed. Surely there must have been some correspondence in their files from the Automobile Clubs of Argentina or Chile or Brazil. But they had nothing, and they didn't want any information either. A pity we wasted their time. Evidently the AAA has more important things to do in Washington D.C. than talk to some nuts who want to drive through South America.

In New York we tracked down a couple of books on the subject but they only gave a few of the details that we wanted, so we decided to keep asking - hoping to find someone who had actually been there - along the way. Most of the countries of South America required a Carnet de Passage en Douane (a customs document, allowing the car to enter a country for a short time, without duty being paid on it) and to get that, you had to put up a bond of a thousand dollars, that we cold barely afford. Then one day we were told that it had gone up to three thousand dollars, which threatened to make the whole thing impossible for us. So I went to see our bank manager in Hyde Park, Vermont and suggested that we take out a personal loan for the $3,000 and give it to him, for the bond. But he said "There's no need for that. Just sign an application for the loan and I'll keep it in my file. Then if something goes wrong and they want the money, I'll activate it. Otherwise, I'll tear it up when you get back." And so we got our bond, for no cost at all.

When we applied for the Carnet, we had to say which countries we would be visiting and that meant deciding on our route. June wanted to see all of South America, which was fine with me, but my own ambition was to get to Cape Horn - to drive Minim the whole length of the continent and put my tent up on the end. After studying the weather patterns of South America, we found that it would be best to go south on the west side of the Andes, as far as the end of Chile, then cross over the mountains into Argentina and head for Cape Horn, so as to arrive there in the middle of their summer - about the 20th of January. Then we could go northeast, through Argentina into Uruguay and Brazil, and northwest, via Paraguay and Bolivia, back to Peru. That made a triangle which took in most of the countries, including all the ones farthest away, that we might never get a chance to see again. For the northern ones, like Venezuela, are just across the Caribbean from the United States and we could hope to see those later. And the total distance, from Vermont to Cape Horn and back, was around 30,000 miles - much of it on very bad roads - that should be enough for one winter.

Meanwhile, Tom Follett firmed up his schedule and we were all set to load Minim aboard the Sol Reefer in the fall, when David Humphreys called up to say that the US Coast Guard would not allow us to load the truck on top of the dynamite. We thought that was picky of them and offered to empty the gas tank but they still said "No" and finally David told us that there was nothing more he could do, as far as the passage south was concerned. But if we could find our own way to South America, he could probably arrange for us to come back on the Sol Reefer, out of Peru, when she would be full of fish. Of course she might not go to Peru in the spring - it all depended on who wanted to buy dynamite then - and in that case, we would have to find our own way back. But we had saved $ 1,000 by not having to put up the money for the bond, which would pay for our passage to South America and by that time, we were in no mood to give up the trip. So we called the Italian Line - which was the cheapest - in New York and booked passage for Minim and ourselves aboard the Rossini, sailing out of Panama on December 13th for Callao (the port for Lima) in Peru. The Rossini would be stopping in Colombia and Ecuador on her way south but the fare was not much more to Callao and Tom Follett advised us to ship Minim there, because the thieves were especially bad in the other ports, along the way.

Years ago we had been caught in a storm off the coast of Maine. The two of us were in a tiny, totally unseaworthy sailboat. We'd misjudged the force of the storm and found ourselves having to turn out to sea to avoid being hurled onto the rocks. Patrick, after tying me to a couple of cleats, went below deck for a rest. I struggled with the tiller, trying to steer the compass course he'd given me. As we neared the offshore shipping lanes, a passenger ship bound for Europe came into view. She was ablaze with lights. A huge floating city sailing past us and then dipping out of sight over my horizon. Later, when it was my turn to rest, I went below (to die, I thought) and fell asleep thinking of the lovely bright ship and all those happy, warm, safe and dry people. Having never sailed on anything but small boats, the thought of even a few days on the Rossini was marvellous. At last it would be my turn to be safe, warm and dry.

We paid in advance, to save carrying the money with us, and a few days later, we found a One Way Ticket in our mail box. So we took everything that we did not need out of Minim, to save weight and space, and on the 20th of October we left our home in Vermont, bound away for Cape Horn.

Cold feet? Too late for that. Our little restaurant in Vermont had been quite busy and as I rushed around with trays of sandwiches, Patrick would rush past me saying something like "Tom will take us on his dynamite ship." And I'd say something like "That's nice, dear." Then, "He can't take us, so do you want to go by passenger ship?" "That's nice, dear." Etcetera.

June's parents lived in Benton Harbor on Lake Michigan about 100 miles east of Chicago, so we went there to say goodbye and left more of our gear with them, for the truck was still too full for such a journey. The problem was to decide what else we could do without and for two whole days we tried diferent ways of stowing Minim - leaving more things out, each time - until we were satisfied that we had done the best we could. There were sacrifices, of course. Like our folding seats that we used in the tent, which had to stay behind. But we found two metal-framed nylon ones, much smaller (and less comfortable) in a local shop and took those, instead.

Patrick complained rudely about our new seats. In fact, he suggested that perhaps they were suposed to be worn internally. I didn't care if or how he used his. Those little seats did the job and saved us many cubic inches of space.

The International Harvester place in Benton Harbor had a good supply of parts for Scouts, so I spent a day there, having Minim prepared for the trip. When they changed the oils, they found filings in the gearbox and differential, which indicated a certain amount of wear but not enough to worry about. Then they tuned up the engine, relined the brakes (for the first time in 107,000 miles) and replaced the two rear brake cylinders. I wanted a clutch plate to take with us but they did not have one, or any spark plugs. Still, they were nice people and they gave us a Fleet Discount for so much work. The next day, we fitted entry-resistant door knobs, on the locks, and bought a 12 volt extension light for camping (so that we could leave our Coleman lamp behind). Then we changed most of our money into traveller's checks and went off to have lunch at the Country Club with June's sister and her husband.

It was odd to sit there, at a table overlooking the river, in an atmosphere of soft music and waiters, and compare our life styles. They were going to spend the next six months doing what all sane, middle class Americans do, while we went off to live in a tent, trying to reach Cape Horn. Why did we do it? There is no quick, simple answer, for it is a question of values and freedom and luck. Most people, it seems to me, have little real choice in how they live, because of the forces that act upon them, from the outside. Typically, a man will get his first job and soon find that he can afford a car and a wife and a house and so on, until the payments, plus his everyday expenses, equal his income. And at that point, he is committed to a life of earning the money to pay for them.

In effect, he has become a slave to his posessions. And many people are quite happy in that role. But there are some who prefer more freedom and see that they can get it by having less things to pay for. And there are fewer still who, mostly by luck, find they can have great freedom and choose to take it, knowing that they must accept a lower standard of living, in most people's terms, than their abilities would otherwise allow. To them - to us - the chance to wander among the lakes of southern Chile, to chat with an Argentine policeman at a lonely outpost in Patagonia, to spend an evening with a Bolivian farmer and to keep forever the memory of those things was simply worth more than anything else that we could hope to get with the same expenditure of time and money.

That evening, we changed into our travelling clothes and put our city ones in a suitcase, in Minim. As with all expeitions, there was a certain apprehension at that moment, when the preparations were finished and we suddenly realized that the time had come to leave. But it would not last - it never did. And in the morning we drove off, heading west and south. Twenty minutes later, the front wheels of the truck began to wobble wildly, with a loud rattling noise, so we stopped and took off the hubcaps. The mechanic who had worked on the brakes had not tightened the wheel nuts. They were all loose but the front ones were worse and the left front wheel was about ready to fall off. So I tightened them all and we went on our way. But from then on, I checked every mechanic's work myself.

Driving across the United States, we fell into our usual routine, stopping at a supermarket to buy food - impressed, as always, by the display of opulence on the shelves - then at a wayside park for lunch. And a State park - the best kind - for the night, among tall trees, out of the wind, with electric heat and light. And drinks and supper - chicken and rice - and wine and laughter in our tent and the stillness outside. When daylight came, we found hot showers nearby and after breakfast we drove south on country lanes, through small towns, to a State park in Tennessee. We were the only campers there and a quiet spoken ranger, who came by to collect the modest fee, told us that we were in a forest of Loblolly pines.

The next day - much relaxed after two nights in our tent - we passed through a town which claimed to be the Home of the Largest Peanut in the World. All through the streets, there were signs - white on blue - with arrows to BIG NUT. That was a last look at the United States, before leaving for a long journey into a different kind of world, and we saw it in a new light. Though the people in each place were provincial in outlook - as they were in Vermont - most of the goods in the stores came from a few giant companies. All the cheese in one shop, for example, was Kraft. And we wondered what would happen when the little firms were driven out of business.

Birds were singing that day - we had come far south - and at lunch time, June had trouble with a wasp. He came to see what was to eat and she took a swipe at him but missed and he was not scared - he hovered, quite still, in front of her face - and she backed away and tripped and lay in the dirt, swiping and missing, until the wasp got bored with the game and wandered off.

I'm not unduly sissy about wasps. But Patrick had been talking of little but South American killer bees for several hundred miles. Visions of swarming insects hovered in my memory as I tried to back away, tried to focus on that thing buzzing three inches from my nose. Until I tripped and he buzzed off. Much to Patrick's delight.

As a spectator, I thought it was rather fun but if ever we should meet up with the killer bees in South America, that would be quite another story and very serious. They had been bred, we were told, by someone in Brazil who was trying to improve their output of honey. But they had strong agressve instincts and would attack people. If you took a swipe at one and missed, he would go and get the rest of the swarm and they would sting you until you were dead. But we could not think about the problems we would have to face in South America, yet. They were too many and varied. So we concentrateed on getting as far as Panama, for the time being. We would worry about the rest, later. Camped beside Lake Texoma, we listened to CBS News on our radio. It sounded more interesting than usual, because we knew that we would not be able to get it, much longer. That night it rained, so in the morning we took the tent, still wet, and went to see friends in Fort Worth. And the next day, when it was bright and sunny, we dried it out in their garden. Then we called the various consulates, about getting visas, but found that we would have to go to Houston for those.

In the evening, over drinks, an 'expert' who had once been half way down Mexico told me that the Most Important Thing was to put a well-known additive in our oil. And he was most upset when I did not agree to do so. But in my opinion, it would have been most unwise to put that stuff in our engine. For there seems to be an American dream that when anything is difficult, you pay money and get a magic potion that makes it easy. But life is not that simple. The stuff he recommended was suitable for cars with new engines, but to put it in a truck with 100,000 miles on it would have been disastrous. And he really resented my trying to explain to him why. Near Houston, we camped in a State park and for three days we went into the city, visiting consulates. The Central American countries gave us visas (mostly large ones, that took up a whole page in our passports) but none of the South American ones did, except Ecuador, where they wanted to know exactly when we would be arriving in the country and where. Going south, we did not plan to visit Ecuador and if Tom Follett picked us up in Peru with the Sol Reefer, we would go past it on the way back, too. But if not, we might have to drive north to get home, so we picked a likely date and said we would be arriving at the frontier of Peru then.

The people in the consulates of Argentina, Peru and Chile all said that there were no political problems and we could camp anywhere in South America. They told us that the Germans and the Scots had settled in southern Argentina, while the English had settled in Chile. Camping in the National Parks was popular and people like us were becoming quite common on the roads in Chile. Also the ferry to Tierra del Fuego was okay and so were the roads there, in January time, which was mid summer there.

Then we visited the AAA office, in case they might know anything - being so close to South America - but they did not. They gave us a road map of the continent - as did all the AAA offices we visited - but said that nobody actually drove around it (or should) which seemed to be the official line. But the people in the consulates were from South America and they saw no reason why we should not do it, if we wished. In fact, they were most helpful and gave us suggestions on places to visit and things to see, in their countries.

Most seaports are infested with thieves, so we decided to screw down the lids of the lockers in Minim at Panama, before putting her on the ship for Peru. And to change the lock on the tailgate, so that the ignition key (which we would have to give to the stevedores) would not open it. When we went to the International Harvester place, to get one, we also found the spare clutch plate that we wanted. And a switch for the backup lights (ours had just failed and they are useful for setting up the tent at night). And driving through a well-kept section of the city, we passed a bar that advertized nude girls, on and off the stage.

We wondered about snakes and found that antivenin was available through doctors for all South American ones but we did not get any, because it can also make you vey sick.

Patrick wondered about snakes. He seemed to worry about them a lot. When in fact, we hadn't seen a dozen in all our years of camping. I remember seeing one frightened snake after three months in Baja California. When I thought of what their snake population is supposed to amount to, I was shy about returning to the States and admitting I'd seen only one.

From Houston we went to San Antonio, where we pitched our tent in a commercial park, right in the city. And across a small river was a chain link fence with a sign on it that said Guard Dog On Duty. Survivors Will Be Prosecuted. But we found shock cord there, after discovering that it was called bungee cord, and replaced all the pieces by which our tent was suspended from its frame - sitting for hours in the shade of the trees, with city noises around us - using a size heavier than the original, to stand up to the winds that we expected to encounter, down toward Cape Horn. Then we had the International Harvester people change the lock on Minim's tailgate and adjust her brakes, and the time had come to move on to the Mexican border.

Headed south, we stopped for lunch at Poteet Canyon Park, where vandals had sprayed paint (Class of 75) on the doors and stonework of the nice new building. Then it was a long, dull drive down a straight road that would be a fine highway in Mexico, to the State park at Falcon Lake, a wide part of the Rio Grande. There were a few campers in the park (all boats and motorcycles and gadgets) but we went past them and set up our tent under a lone tree, by the water, with a view of Mexico. And met a rabbit and a turtle. And the bright moon was half full. But it was windy in the morning - waves were breaking on the grass, along the shore - so we moved to Benson State Park, near McAllan, which was more sheltered.

Going through her notes, June discovered that we would not have to do an inventory until Panama, which was a relief. For we had been told that in some countries we would be required to present a complete list of every item in the truck, in Spanish, and we were not looking forward to making that. But we might be gone for six months or so, depending on how things worked out with the Sol Reefer, and we figured that we should allow ourselves a budget of $ 25 a day, for food and gasoline and everything, to be on the safe side.

That afternoon, we washed Minim and stocked her with food. And the next morning - Friday the 14th of November - we were up before dawn. There was farm news on the radio - Vote Yes for drainage tomorrow - then it said that the State of Texas had a budget surplus of over a million dollars. After folding our tent, we checked the ground where it had been - from now on, if we left anything behind, we might not be able to replace it - then filled up with gas and bought Mexican insurance and went down to the border.

The officials saw the visas on our passports and decided that we were 'transmigrants' just passing through Mexico - not tourists - so we had to pay extra for our clearances. But soon we were driving through Reynosa, reading the signs in Spanish, and out onto the highway, heading south. That is a good way into Mexico. It avoids the busy border towns of Brownsville and Matamoros and takes you down a straight, paved two-lane road over rolling hills to Ciudad Victoria. And on the bypass road, around the city, is a trailer park, owned by an American and his Mexican wife. There we set up our tent, between two rows of banana trees. Then we went into the city - to the tourist office - to make our last telephone call to Vermont. The office was large and bare, with three people in it but little furniture, and the senior man placed our call for us, with a certain amount of ceremony. But the line was good and all was well at home, so we thanked everyone in the office and walked across the plaza to buy fresh, warm bread, before going back to our tent, that was 'home' now.

A bakery in the States displays its wares in glass cases. But once over the border, it is customary to walk into a room full of counters piled high with pastries, breads and cookies. There you take a tray and a pair of tongs and help yourself. I always buy much more than we need. It is all too tempting and so easy to grab.

The owner of the trailer park had spent years teaching school in Wisconsin and he was very happy not to be regimented any more, while his wife was glad to be back in Mexico, where you could buy food that tasted like food - not processed - and real bread. And when we said we were going to South America, he lent us some notes by a man who had been there. It was just two pages, hand written, and mostly they were about places where he had stopped for a night, in Central and South America. But we copied them carefully, since first-hand information like that was rare, indeed.

Were they happy in Mexico after living several years in the States? Well, the plumbing wasn't quite as good, and the houses weren't so fancy and they did have less money to spend but, on the whole, living was much better. There is more to life than plumbing. There was no pressure on them from the community to conform to others' standards. They had bought a piece of land and were building their trailer park as they had time and money and interest to do it. There were no forces from outside telling them how they should dress and how their breath should smell or their teeth should sparkle. And the long days were broken up by siestas and lemonade or cool beer and times of work in the house and chats with their customers. The washing machine was broken but it didn't matter. They would wash things by hand, or perhaps a neighbor would call by and do it for them, for a few cents. The wet clothes would dry quickly in the sun, and if it were raining, all could wait until later, or tomorrow.

Though we were just north of the Tropic of Cancer, it was cool that night and we had our electric heater going in the tent until our long wire melted, where it went into the outlet. But a lovely dawn brought a clear, calm sunny day - the banana palms were quite still - and soon there were trucks and people passing on the road and the dew was drying on our tent. Two cats and six ducks came by to share our breakfast until a donkey showed up, trailing his tether, and chased them all away, flipping the ducks up into the air with his nose as he ran. And soon we were on our way, taking the old Inter American Highway south. At Ciudad Valles, we bought milk and cider and a new plug for our electric wire - people were friendly and shopping was easy, as our Spanish came back - then went on, to Tamazunchale (which sounds like Thomas and Charlie). That was a picturesque village when first we saw it, twenty years before. And now it was a sprawling town, like a big truck stop. But the road beyond it was as beautiful as ever, winding up into the mountains, with spectacular views of green valleys.

The hills are steep sided and every inch has been cultivated. There are patches of banana trees and orange groves. Soft green banana fronds that flutter in the light breeze next to patches of waxy green leaves of citrus trees. Then rows of corn stalks, brownish and dry in the fall. The squares of color and texture forming a patchwork on the mountain sides. Small patches, for all the work is done without aid of horses or machines. The land is much too steep to be worked by anything but man.

As the sun set - its rays slanting through the pine trees - the valleys filled with darkness and at last light, we set up our tent beside the Posada del Rey in Zimapan. The old hotel was a fine building, now empty and sad, for that highway is little used by tourists, any more. And the camp-ground was just a patch of grass - once a tennis court - with no facilities. But it was the best available, there. While June cooked our dinner, a white pony made a pest of himself - poking his nose into everything - and ate a box of crackers, box and all. But he finally left when we locked the truck and zipped up the tent and went to bed.

The pony left only after every bit of food was locked away. As we ate dinner at the table in the tent, he glared through the window, trying to bite the cloth screen. We zipped the canvas covers over all the openings and sat in the dimness, chewing quietly, knowing that those giant yellow teeth were right there, a fraction of an inch away. When we tried to wash the dishes on the tailgate, he put his nose in the soapy water. Finally, we took the debris of dinner, rammed it into the truck, locked the doors and gave up.

It was cold at dawn, at 6,500 feet, without any heat. And the pony was back, so we gave up the idea of cooking and left. But later we found a level place, above the road in a mountain pass, and stopped for breakfast. The sun was hot, by then, but the air was still cool. And trucks full of brown dirt went by, below us, their drivers waving to us in greeting. To avoid Mexico City, we left the highway at Pachuca and took secondary roads across the high, brown, open country - with the snow covered peaks of Popocatepetl and Ixtaccihuatl in the distance - to Cholula, west of Puebla, where there was a trailer park behind a long white wall. We were both suffering from flea bites - probably from the ducks at Ciudad Victoria - so we took showers, washed all our clothes and fumigated the tent. Then I fixed our electric wire and we were in good shape again. There were very few vehicles in the park that night, all of them small and old - no big, new American ones because of higher gasoline prices - and the next day, there was remarkably little traffic on the roads. But the countryside was beautiful. at that time of the year, with many flowers and flowering trees, all the way to the fine old city of Oaxaca (the 'x' is like an 'h' in Spanish, so it sounds like 'Wa-HA-ca').

The highway there snakes along the side of a mountain, above the city, then drops down into the northeastern suburbs. And on the left, about two blocks over, is a trailer park with tall trees that whisper in the breze - like the casuarinas of Barbados - under which we pitched our tent. It was warm in the sun as we did our shopping nearby. And there were good fruits and vegetables but no milk, because it came from Puebla and the truck had not arrived.

Probably, if we had wanted to drive to another part of town, we would have found a shop that sold only fresh milk and perhaps some butter and the beautiful white country cheese. But I would have been expected to provide a bottle or a covered bucket to carrry the milk.

Back in our tent, there were noises of the city and music around us but they were not loud. And there were trees with red and orange flowers on them. And the moon was almost full.

At night most of the activity was centered around the Plaza, a mile or more from our campground. We had spent many evenings there, strolling along the crowded sidewalks, listening to the band playing on the octagonal stand at the park's center. Watching children running happily over lounging parents, young couples giggling and kissing, and watching other tourists watching us watch them. We had stopped to drink beer at a table under the hotel veranda, or eat an ice cream that was served by a boy no more than ten years old. The Plaza would have been fun on a balmy evening like that, but we were much too tired from our long drive to enjoy it.

There was a small van - a motorhome - in the park, which belonged to two elderly Americans who had bought it in England and cruised all over Europe in it, then shipped it from Holland to Mexico. They were concerned that things might be stolen from it, on the docks, so thay packed all their valuables in a metal trunk and sent that separately, with their rubber boat. But the van arrived safely, with nothing taken from it, while the boat and the trunk were stolen from the warehouse in Holland.

Early next morning, we went down to Tehuantepec - past the lonely prison, sweltering in the tropical heat - and on to the junction at Ventosa (Windy) where the highway goes north, back to Veracruz or east toward Guatemala. And since we were going east, we had to show our papers to the man at the check point. He was sad, because we had no American cigarettes for him - I had given them up and never thought to bring him a pack - but he had a fine, new hut beside the road. And the old one was still standing, a few yards away. Why tear it down?

The wind was not strong, that day and we left it behind as we climbed up into the green mountains, toward Tuxtla Gutierrez, modern and prosperous from the oil found in the State of Chiapas. But the tourist office, so neat and new the year before, was run down, its garden overgrown with weeds. And the only place to camp was behind the San Francisco Motel, on the far side of town. We had been there before and knew better than to look in the toilets, which were unspeakable. But we were off the streets of the city and there were some bushes nearby. After eating our dinner in the dark, so as not to attract attention, we slept in the truck and soon after dawn, we were under way again.

The motel has two or three spaces for trailers. They aren't really set up for tenters who need a bit of privacy or a bit of a privy. But being more relaxed about such things than their northern counterparts, they were happy to allot us a section of the drying yard for our night's stop.

An hour or so later, beyond San Cristobal de las Casas, we saw a new trailer park, set back from the road in the pine trees, and we made a note to stay there, coming back. When we got to the border, there was one car ahead of us, belonging to UNICEF. But as we waited for our papers to be dealt with, about forty Germans arrived in a blue Mercedes bus, towing a huge trailer marked 'Rolling Hotel' in many languages. On its left side were rows of tiny windows and on the right were three platforms that could be let down to make more space. It was a National Holiday in Mexico, so the children of the village put on a parade, dancing and skipping down the road. And after consulting with the authorities, the tour leader told his charges that they could get their cameras and take pictures. Then the bus sounded its horn, like a ship about to sail, and we rushed up the hill, to get to Guatemala ahead of them.

Lunch was by a waterfall, in the lovely gorge beyond the border, with white clouds and blue sky and green trees. Then on up into the mountains, where men farm land so steep that they sometimes fall off it, into the valleys below. And past brooding volcanoes, to Julie Hall's house in Chimaltenango. She was out, so we left a message with her tiny Mayan maid and dropped down into Antigua, to Casa El Patio. The new Canadian Ambassador to Central America was staying there, learning Spanish at June's old school, before taking up his post in Costa Rica. And Tom and Erika set up a big table for dinner. Later, Julie arrived, with Bob and Cynthia, who were now married. Julie was doing fine but Cyn's horse was bald and there were two cats and three ducks missing from their finca (probably eaten by boa constrictors). And the anti-American demonstration in the spring had fizzled out, as they expected.

It was good to be back in Guatemala. We stayed four days there, as we had planned, relaxing and getting ready for the trip to South America, for it was the last place where we had friends. Erika went to the bank with us, to change some of our traveller's checks into dollars, and she tried to place a telephone call to the Italian Line in Cristobal. But it was impossible to reach them, due to 'passive resistance' by the Panamanian operators, in protest against the United States for not giving up the canal. So we sent them a telegram with a prepaid reply and hoped that it would get through.

In Guatemala City, we had lunch at our favorite sidewalk cafe - it was much nicer, all fresh and green after the rainy season, than we remembered it - then went to Granai y Towson, in the business district, and bought 30 days' car insurance, valid in all the countries of Central America, or $ 58.22. They have their own bank in the same building and after paying your bill, you go back upstairs, where a serious young man explains all the details of your policy and gives you his card, with his business and home telephone numbers in case you need him.

Back in Antigua, there were parties with John Long and our other friends and we met Ed Shook, the driving spirit behind the restoration of the Mayan ruins at Tikal. Julie had driven an old van from Vermont but someone there put an additive in the oil (the same one that the man in Texas tried to make us use) and it had ruined the engine, so she was trying to get rid of it. But it was not easy, because it had not been imported into Guatemala and the only people she could sell it to were missionaries, who were exempt from paying import duty on it.

Marta Julia, the young girl who had been June's Spanish teacher, was still hoping to go to the United States one day. And Victoria, who had been our maid, was still working for the American family. But they were away most of the time, so she lived alone in the house, with her daughter and grandson. Proudly she showed us through the house, closing the door of each room behind us, and told us what a terrible time she had, getting workmen to fix things properly. But she was rather plump and very happy to be given the responsibility.

What a relief to find Victoria so happy. No thin, wringing hands, no stream of tears or pleas for help. Not that we wouldn't help. It's just that when she was upset, she would carry on so and sob and tell us all her troubles - most of which we couldn't understand anyway, through all the tears. Our Spanish wasn't that good! Her only complaint was that her new employers didn't come often enough. There wasn't enough for her to do.

Our friend the beggar had his tray of cigarettes and candy under the same arch, beside the plaza - in that society, it was not just a 'front', for people would buy one cigarette or a small piece of candy at a time - and he was clean shaven, so that the tourists would not avoid him. We gave him something, and stopped to ask how he was doing, and he seemed as pleased to have someone take an interest in him as to get the money.

On Sunday, the 23rd of November, a telegram came from the Italian Line - in good and exact English - confirming our reservations in the Rossini, sailing from Cristobal on December 13th. And we were preparing to leave Guatemala the next morning, when Erika asked us if we would stay and look after the Patio, while she and Tom went to Miami for a week. That would not leave us much time to get to Panama but the only country that we wanted to see, on the way, was Honduras. So we agreed to put off our departure until December 3rd and sent a letter to the Italian Line, giving them our new schedule. Then we spent the afternoon studying the operation of the Patio. There were no fire extinguishers and no insurance of any kind but Tom told us not to worry about that. In fact, the whole thing was quite simple and each member of the staff - a butler, a cook and two maids - knew what to do, every day. But none of them spoke any English, so we would have to deal with any tourists who showed up. And of course, June would have to plan the meals, buy the food, pay the bills and so on.

El Patio can run itself, Erika has it so well organized. I should have just relaxed, enjoyed the garden and scratched the parrot's chin. But of course I had to try a couple of things in the cooking department. In the end, I couldn't touch her cook's performance because everything I tried required a myriad of unavailable ingredients. Substitutions got me nowhere. My tries were costly and complicated and didn't taste any better than hers. But the cook showed infinite patience and in the end no great harm was done.

While June was shopping with Erika, I fixed a shower head in one of the rooms   there were no spare parts for such things - then rotated Minim's tires and adjusted the tailgate. That evening, Erika told us what to do about the beggars who came to the door all the time. You give them 3 to 5 cents if they may come back but 2 cents is an insult, meaning "Do not come back". It took us three years to find that out. The Pattersons had hardly left for Miami when Lorito the parrot got loose in the back yard. He was a fine bird who would shout "Gringa" - correctly, in the feminine - at foreign women, so there was a great flap until we got him back. And that night, we accidentally locked Lupe the dog (who was American but looked Guatemalan) out of his sleeping place in the workshop. But the only people staying at the Patio just then were the Canadian Ambassador and his wife (Ralph and Louise Reynolds) and a young American Catholic priest called Geoff, on his way to Solola, near Lake Atitlan, to train Indians to be priests. So we put some baroque music on the record player, lit the candles on the dining tables and played host to them.

When June went to the market, a small girl called Carmen insisted on carrying the big basket on her head - following us from stall to stall - and shopping for the Patio, it would soon have been too heavy for her. But luckily we had a string bag with us, so I put the heavy things in that and slung it over my shoulder, and Carmen earned her fee without getting hurt. We were quite relaxed in the market. We could slip though the crowd of Mayan people and make our purchases, without any fuss. But it had taken us years to reach that point.

What a joy to be back shopping in that market. Mounds of tiny potatoes the size of marbles, ripe plum tomatoes, perfectly shaped, small deep-purple eggplants. And cantelope - the flavor of the Michigan melons I remember getting as a child. Perhaps we North Americans eat so much today because what we do eat doesn't taste like food. We keep filling our mouths and salting our cardboard and plastic, ever hopeful.

Geoff went off to Solola and after dinner, sitting by the fire, Ralph Reynolds told us he felt strongly that the United States should get out of Panama without further delay. He was a quiet, reasonable man, whose job it was to evaluate such things and it seemed to me that he was probably right. Then he and Louise left for Costa Rica - after inviting us to dinner at the Embassy, the next Sunday - and we had a trickle of one-night guests staying at the Patio. Two groungy Australian girls, on their way to tour South America by bus, told us that it was important to look neat, to get by - God, what they must have looked like, when they were being themselves - and said that blondes sell for many wives in the Amazon.

And there was a German doctor from the United Nations in Geneva, with a French assistant, who were pushing water systems and paramedics. But they were only in the country for a few days and had never heard of

John Long, who had been training paramedics in Guatemala for years. John explained that malnutrition was the cause of most of the medical problems in Guatemala but helping the people was not easy, since they had a tradition of slash and burn agriculture, which denuded the land, and the population explosion was creating a demand for more food, faster than it could be met.

A young couple we knew in Vermont came from Quetzaltenengo to see us. He was an agronomist with CARE and was doing his best to improve the food situation (though he was required to spend more time on reports than he thought proper) but the erosion in that area was so bad that some houses and even small fields were standing up, as though on islands. And they were using bulldozers to terrace the land, so as to catch the rain water, before it ran off and took more soil with it. By then, we had been given two acounts of Lima. One said it was a nice place with a good climate and the other said it was a miserable, dirty city with a lousy climate. Jose, the Mayan butler at the Patio, was tall and thin and quiet - out of politeness - almost to the point of being solemn. But on his night off, he left in a sport shirt and gray slacks, with bicycle clips on them, looking quite rakish.

Built against the white garden wall at the back of the house were several small cubicles where the staff slept. Each room was barely big enough for a narrow cot and a crude bedstand and chair. Jose's room was a bit larger, but then he was the butler. I think the cook's room had a window. The other two maids didn't fare quite as well. But the rooms were dry, the beds had linen and blankets and the garden was filled with flowers and vines and hanging baskets of orchids. Add a couple of cars and Jose's bicycle. Still, not an unpleasant place, even when the washing machine was noisily jogging in one corner.

And some of the supplies for the guest house came from shops that we never knew existed, after two winters in Antigua, mainly because they did not look like shops at all. Jose took us to the beer place, which was a house on a quiet street, where you put your head in a door and asked if there might be some beer. A man would come out and walk a few paces to a big wooden gate that he would unlock and lead you around, behind the house, to a shed full of beer. And the cook took us to another house, where you rang a bell and a maid let you into a room, bare except for a couple of tables, in which there were small piles of vegetables - on the tables and on the floor - that were fresh every day.

Erika bought some of the vegetables for the Patio from this particular gardener, because no human fertilizers were used. One could safely serve raw vegetables and lettuce. But unless you cooked it, peeled it or soaked it in Clorox, food from the Antigua market could be risky.

Julie Hall was doing well. She was a really good artist and wealthy people were coming from the Capital to her house in Chimalenango, to buy her pictures. In fact, one day, just as we were leaving, a limousine drew up and three well-dressed women went in, whle the chauffeur - who was also, quite obviously, a bodyyguard - waited outside. Driving back to Antigua that day, we stopped to help a young man who had just fallen off a large, powerful motorcycle. But he declined our assistance with polite thanks. It was new and he was just getting the hang of it. And a few minutes later, he passed us on a blind corner, going very fast. Bob and Cynthia went back to the jungle lowlands to finish clearing their land and expected to be in the ranching business soon. With one loan for cattle and another for feed, which made me nervous. But Bob worked on a ranch in Montana, before he joined the Peace Corps, and it did not bother him.

On Tuesday, December 2nd, we went into the Capital to buy food for the trip south. It had rained in the night, which was most unusual, and we wondered if the roads that we wanted to take through Honduras would be passable. But it was clear and windy in the morning and the sun was drying everything fast. So we said goodbye to our frends and packed Minim, ready to go. Tom and Erika arrived back on time and at dinner, we asked two people from Bogota in Colombia about South America. They had a double burglar alarm and two armed guards at their house. And they said that Buenaventura was unsafe at night, though the Army guarded it, so that the advice which Tom Follett gave us, to go by ship as far as Callao, was sound. They had shipped their own household goods from the United States to Colombia by air, to avoid the sea ports, but they had still lost $ 2,500 worth. And they said that the Pan American Highway might never be completed because of Hoof and Mouth Disease, that was nonexistent in Central America, where there was a flourishing cattle business, and prevalent in Colombia. Then we went to bed early, for in the morning we were to leave for Panama and new lands, beyond the seas.

5 - BEYOND THE DARIEN GAP

On the way to Panama, we wanted to see more of Honduras and especially the Mayan ruins at Copan, just across the border from Guatemala. That meant going northeast, toward the Rio Dulce and then taking a back road, which might or might not be passable, through the mountains. So we were both too tense to sleep much and at 5:30 in the morning we gave up trying. As we stowed the last of our things in Minim, the dark of night gave way to a bleak, gray dawn. Shy and polite as ever, Jose came out to shake hands. Then Tom and Erika, full of good spirits, came to see us off. And soon we were rumbling over the cobble stones, through the quiet steets of Antigua, and heading up the winding road toward Guatemala City.

Antigua was quiet, early in the morning. We dutifully followed the one-way street signs, so unnecessary now but essential as the day emerged and the many doors set into the labyrinth of adobe walls opened, spilling the populace into the streets. Barefoot Indians, Latino Donas, dogs, goats and children would press against the walls to let innumerable busses and trucks, cars and bicycles pass. It would be impossible to walk two abreast for more than a few feet at a time.

There was little traffic in the Capital, so early in the day, and beyond it the road dropped down into the lovely valley that runs toward the northeast. Near Zacapa we turned off, onto a secondary road and about 5 miles beyond Chiquimula we spotted the lane, down to the left, which goes to Copan. But it was not as bad as we expected. There were many fords to cross but the water was not high, at that time. And the road, though narrow, was mostly of firm gravel. At lunch time, we stopped beside a wide river. Nearby, three boys were swimming and not far away, groups of women were doing their laundry in the flowing water. A large truck came past us and went down, across the river at a shallow place and out onto a dry bank in the middle, to load soil. But none of the people there paid any attention to us.

For some reason we always expect to be a minor event when we stop in a populated area. Usually small boys crowd around the truck to watch us or to beg. At last we were off the tourist route. Hardly a head turned our way. Half a dozen boys of various sizes passed us, towing a man - perhaps their teacher - behind them. They scurried down the river bank near us, washed quickly in the stream and climbed, dripping and grinning, back up the path. The teacher nodded our way and said "Buenos" as he called instructions to his disorderly flock. Everyone had something to do and we had a peaceful lunch.

Near the border of Honduras, there were several check points, for Customs and Immigration and so on. And though there was no traffic on the road, the work of inspecting us and writing down all the details was lengthy and slow. But early in the afternoon, we cleared the last one and a few miles farther on, we came to the town of Copan.

Wednesday must not be market day in Copan. There was not a soul in sight as we drove into the little town. Around the rustic plaza we saw a few modest buildings, a church and a nearby school, an attractive little building housing the museum, a bank and a couple of shops - closed. Of course, we were early. Perhaps it was still siesta. We drove on through town to the ruins.

The ruins of the Mayan city, just beyond the town, are not nearly as extensive as those at Tikal but they contain many fine carvings in stone. And a steep, high stairway, covered with heiroglyphs, which has one step near the top that tilts when a person steps on it and sends him hurtling down to certain death on the large, flat stone at the bottom. Obviously you have to be careful, exploring such places on your own, but I do not like following a guide around, so we refused a young man's offer to show us the ruins. But soon one of the guardians of the site came by and insisted on telling us about them, so we listened politely. The city had been occupied from 700 BC to 400 AD and the carvings included many parrot-like figures, which we had seen at other Mayan sites. But he showed us a large, clear Star of David, cut in a stone wall, that would be hard to explain. And he told us about the games, played in the ball court.

The court is paved with stone and divided lengthwise into three parts, each about the same width. The two side parts slope down, toward the middle one and where they meet, there is a drop of about a foot, down to its level. The games were played by two teams, each confined to the sloping part on its own side of the court, who threw a large, heavy ball from side to side. And when it fell in the middle, someone was taken away to be sacrificed to the gods. Only the upper classes were allowed to watch the games, from a raised area at one end of the court, and there were elaborate dressing rooms for the players, on each side. And high on a nearby temple are places where the losers were chained to the wall and left to meditate on their fate.

It was dusk when we hurried through the gardens around the site to the gate where we had left Minim. A young boy stood against a tree, watching us unlock the car and whittling on an object with a small pocket knife. He had wanted to guide us earlier in the day but we had refused his assistance. Now he came forward, shyly askng for a lift back to town. We put him on the cushions between our seats. His name was Guillermo. He went to school in the mornings and in the afternoons he would hike out to the ruins in hopes of earning a little money. Evidently a customer had been found, for he offered to pay us for his ride. We declined but he insisted on giving us the piece of greyish-pink sandstone he had been carving. It was a miniature of an ancient Mayan head, the size of a walnut, looking every bit like something he had found at the site.

In the town of Copan, in a small museum, there are stone collars that were put around the necks of the losers, while they meditated. And knives which the priests used, to cut out their hearts. But the upper classes had fine jewelry and their front teeth were often inlaid with jade. There was no convenient place to camp near Copan but the Hotel Marina was rated First Class and had a yard behind it that was locked at night, so we left Minim there and took a room.

It should be clear by now that Patrick valued the car more than me.

Perhaps when marriage licenses cost as much as automobiles, a wife will receive more respect. But he very logically insisted that he could always drive on without me, if he had to, but without his truck the overland journey would be quite another thing.

The bathroom was a toilet and a wash basin, in the room, beside the bed. And the water was cold. But there was a bar, a room where Drinks of Moderation (weak beer) were sold by a small boy. We were his only customers and after placing the bottles on our table, he went to play with his friends, on the steps out to the street. And the whole place was scrupulously clean.

We walked into the high ceilinged dining room. Simple, straight backed chairs and crude tables covered with sheets of patterened plastic. The patterns scrubbed bare in great patches. There were pottery bowls of salt and pepper in the center of each table, with a stack of paper napkins, torn into quarters, a glass of extra spoons, and a small well worn dinner plate at each place. A dark haired girl in a cotton house dress brought dish after dish to our table. We would serve ourselves and then she would carry the dish to another table. There was soup and then a meat stew. There were potatoes and onions and watery pale green squash. Then canned fruit, instant coffee and powdered cream. Very good fare for such an out of the way place.

The other people at dinner were a man from Switzerland and a student of archaeology from Honduras (who had offered to show us the ruins). And at breakfast, there were two elderly American ladies. One was a retired school teacher, now working for the Peac Corps, and the other was a friend of hers, down from the United States on a visit. They had come from Tegucigalpa by bus, which must have been quite an experience, for the road out of Copan was not easy, even for Minim, and we passed several trucks, stuck deep in the mud, before the surface improved to rough gravel. But at Nueva Arcadia we came to a fine, new paved road, running north and south, that we had not expected. And since we had been told that the southern route, through the mountains, was impassable beyond Santa Rosa, we headed north and east, down a long valley toward San Pedro Sula. That route also allowed us to see more of Honduras, which was very lush and seemed to be underpopulated, compared with the other countries of Central America. But near the city, there was a great deal of commercial development and we were glad to avoid it by heading south, toward Lake Yojoa. We had intended to spend the night beside the lake, which was quite beautiful and hardly seemed to be used. But we were far ahead of our schedule, due to the fine roads, so we continued south over the mountains to Tegucigalpa. The big, sprawling city seemed poorer than most, though we did not go into the center of it. And the country to the south of it was more populated than before. Also there was more traffic on the road and there were pot holes in it that were steep-sided and dangerous, especially where they had been squared off to be filled. But it was not far to Choluteca, on the coastal road and before dark we set up our tent in Gringo Jim's Trailer Park.

It is a small place, set back from the road beside his gas station and shaded by high trees, with water and electricity at each grassy site and gravel driveways between them. And that night, there were two American families in it, with their music blaring and their children shouting. But when they went to bed, it was quiet, with just the sound of tree frogs and bright stars overhead and the sweaty, tropical heat. In the morning, Gringo Jim came by. He said he had been an instructor at Annapolis, before retiring from the American Navy. And his business was down, due to problems in Mexico. Tourists were being shaken down at the borders and were no longer allowed permits to keep their vehicles in the country for 6 months but had to renew them every 30 days, for five dollars each time. When we told him we were going to South America, he said the Colombian borders were closed, Chile had economic problems, Argentina was in turmoil and Peru was unstable. And he described the technique that was used for mugging people, in the small towns of Argentina. Four men box you in and take your wallet, right on the sidewalk. But that sounded rather civilized, compared with beating people up, as they do in New York. And in any case, it seemed unwise to take much notice of anything said by an 'expert' who had not actually been to the place he was describing.

Minim was dirty, after the trip to Copan, so I washed her before we went to the border of Nicaragua. And as we closed her up, the 12-volt light on the long wire that we used for cooking got caught in the tailgate and was crushed. But going through the border was fun, because there was a tall Canadian ahead of us, with a short blonde girl in a low cut dress. And she almost came out of it, most of the time. Perhaps the girls who model such dresses are small but when ordinary ones buy them, the effect is dramatic. And she was obviously enjoying it, as were the officials.

Small pleasures. And why not? Anything to break the endless monotony of those border crossings. Always huge ledgers to be filled in by the sweating, grimy officials. Always long lines of travellers, sweating and dirty, swatting flies, trying to keep their passports and travel documents half way tidy. Always the vendors of oranges and Chiclets, of cold Cokes and warm tacos, hovering nearby, trying to keep the dust off their wares. And always the money changers, standing in a bit of shade, nervously counting the limp, soiled bills in sweating hands while children ran from group to group begging, oblivious of the heat and dirt. It was nice to have something to grin about.

Then it was a fast run across Nicaragua - some of it in heavy rain - past the two volcanoes in the lake, to the border of Costa Rica. And changing currency was no problem. In its literature on Central America, the AAA stressed the importance of taking the currency of each country with you. But now that we knew the score, we simply took American dollars in small denominations and changed a few at a time. Then at each border, we changed what we had left over for the currency of the next country. And though the money changers charged a commission, it never amounted to anything significant. There is a trailer park in Liberia, about 50 miles from the border, with a bar and a swimming pool (because it also has hotel rooms) where we met a Mexican couple in a Volkswagen bus, who warned us to beware of thieves in Costa Rica. They told us about two people who had spent a night in a bus like theirs, outside an hotel in San Jose, and had woken up five times, to find people trying to break into it. And they also told us that many Americans were trying to sell their fincas in that 'paradise' because of bugs that raise hard welts, three days after they bite you.

It rained that night but stopped in the morning and I had a cold shower in a neat white building with 3 hornets' nests, 2 large cockroaches and a praying mantis. Then we followed the main road, down past the turnoff to Puntarenas and up into the mountains, where we nearly ran over a large snake. He was right across our path, as we came around a corner, and there was little I could do, to avoid him. But evidently he put on a burst of speed and when we looked back, he was gone. I never knew that they could go so fast. Near San Jose, the traffic was heavy and the macho complex led to a dangerous style of driving. But beyond the city, in Tres Rios, we found a new socket or our light and bought some food, on our way to Singing River.

We shopped in an American style supermarket called Mas X Menos. It was not at all bright and shiny but there were rows of fresh fruits, refrigerated cases of butter and cheese, a meat counter and a separate counter for eggs and chicken. Eggs could be purchased by the dozen only, as oposed to many small shops where you could buy just one if that was all you wanted. And the chickens were dressed, stripped of their feathers, but with their heads still on. Different countries, different customs.

The woman who owned the trailer park greeted us with the news that thieving was rife in Costa Rica that year. We should never leave our car unattended for a moment. Her son's trailer, that was parked underneath her house, was robbed two nights ago. And her guard dog had been killed, so that now the thieves could come into the park whenever they wanted to. She had replaced the guard dog with a new puppy, who was very friendly but farted in our tent. And there were three other vehicles in the park but we heard no American voices. The people next to us were Hungarian and spoke little Spanish or English but we chatted with them in a mixture of the two languages, plus French and German when we ran out of nouns. They had been there for three months and had only lost two broken umbrellas but they never left their trailer at night. And they said that it rained from 2 until 5 each afternoon, at that time of the year.

As the clouds gathered overhead, I adjusted the electric alarm on Minim and put the new socket on our long wire, so that we had a 12-volt light to cook by again. And soon the rain was teeming down but we were snug and dry, in the tent. Checking it, we found the initials 'M.E.'high up in a corner, most likely put there by the person who made it, and promised ourselves that we would send her a message, when we got home.

On rainy days we could open a can of cold fish or, after a bit of elaborate preparation, have a proper dinner. Patrick would reverse the truck to line up with the tent opening. Then lowering the tailgate, he would attach the canvas front awning to the top of the car, rig various side curtains with bits of plastic and clothes pegs and I would have a relatively dry place to cook a meal. It was a bit of a fidget but in the end hot food on a cold wet night in the tent seemed to be worth a little trouble.

On Sunday morning, we telephoned Louise Reynolds, who had invited a few friends to meet us at dinner that night. And she told us how to get to the Canadian Ambassador's Residence. It was a private party but we were not used to dining in such grand circumstances and June, especially, was looking forward to it very much. But at lunch time, I began having stomach pains and by five o'clock, my temperature was 102 degrees. I had caught the 'bug' and could not go. June insisted on staying with me, rather than go on her own, so we made our apologies and called it off. And while I lay in bed, in the tent, June banged and clattered around.

I was annoyed with Patrick. He is never sick. Why, of all times, did it have to be that night? The Reynolds' had invited us while we were all in Guatemala. I knew they had taken trouble to arrange the dinner. It was very bad to cancel so late in the day. Then, on top of that, Patrick was fit as ever the next morning. I would never have sat with him through the night if I'd thought it would be such a short lived illness. The way he was groaning, I expected to have to send for an ambulance any minute.

I was up every hour, through the night but kept taking an amoebicide (Entero-Sediv, put out by Gruenthal) as directed and by morning, my temperature was close to normal. Later in the day, we went to see Louise, with some mail that we had brought from Antigua, and she showed us around the Residence. It is a fine, large house with a sweeping stairway that goes up to four double bedrooms and four bathrooms but they are not divided equally. The master bedroom has two bathrooms leading off it, for the Ambassador and his wife. Then there is a bedroom for Important Guests, with its own bathroom. And the people in the other two bedrooms share the last one. It is not hard to figre how you rate, in a house like that.

Back at the trailer park, we met the owner and when we said we were going to South America, she told us that she had been robbed three times by taxi drivers in Buenos Aires. She paid the first one in American dollars but he gave her the wrong rate of exchange for them. So she changed some at a bank and while she was figuring what to give the next one, he took a 1,000 peso note out of her wallet and left. Then, at the airport, she watched her money carefully but the third one drove off with her suitcases. And she was Costa Rican.

But I was feeling better all the time, and the next day we set out for Panama, to meet the Rossini. The tent was still wet but we did not wait to dry it, for the road ahead was new to us and went over the highest pass in Central America, eleven thousand feet above sea level. And though we saw no gas stations as we passed Cartago, we kept on going, because we knew there was one at the second junction ahead. But when we got to it, both the pumps were dry. And by then, we only had 2 or 3 gallons left. For a while, we hung around the lonely station, trying to cajole a few gallons out of the man who ran it. But he had none at all. And he might not get any, for days. Then he asked exactly how much we had left and when I told him, he said we had no problem. It would be quite enough to get us up to the summit, which was not far. And from there, we could coast down the mountain, all the way to San Isidro del General, where we would find plenty, of all kinds.

There wasn't enough fuel left to get back to Cartago anyway. So we might as well go forward as far as we could. But each time the road went up in front of us, we would feel a little queasy. We saw few cars and few people along the way. The road was narrow, no places to pull over and steep, rocky dropoffs on both sides. The thick tropical vegetation dripped with intermittent rain. What a lovely day to run out of gas.

So we followed the winding road up into the clouds, nursing our small supply of gas by coasting down into each dip, then starting the engine before we lost our speed for the next climb. And when we reached the summit, the gauge said 'Empty' But the road dropped down, on the other side, though the clouds and out beneath them into steady rain. And we coasted for about 13 miles, using the brakes as little as possible - just enough to slow down before each tight corner and letting them cool whenever we could, until they began to fade. That was the first time we had experienced brake fade and even though we were expecting it, there was a tense moment when it happened. For although Minim has three braking systems, they all depend on the same four brakes. And when those stop working, half way down a mountain, it is time to take action.

As we came into a corner, I braked as usual but she did not slow down enough to make it. So I bore down hard on the brake and started the engine and revved it up and slipped it into third gear and we made it around the corner. Then I gave the brakes a rest while I changed into second gear and let her slow down a little before hitting them hard and making a noisy change (with no synchro-mesh) into first. In that gear we were safe, for its drag was enormous, so I gave the brakes a longer rest. And when we came to a suitable place, I brought her to a stop, beside the road. When we got out, all four brakes were hot and the front ones were smoking, with a sharp, acrid smell. But they would cool better and more evenly if we were moving, so we continued down the mountain, keeping Minim under control with the engine and the gears. And hoping we would not run out of gas. But an engine does not use much, with the throttle closed, and it lasted all the way to San Isidro, where there was a fine, large station with plenty.

And we swore that we would never do anything so stupid again.

The brakes were cool, by then. And when we tested them on the level road, beyond the town, they worked as well as ever. But I wondered if they could have suffered any lasting harm, which might show up later, in South America. And I worried about that, all the way to the border of Panama. At first, the officials there seemed rather brusque but they made a competent search of our gear (for drugs, presumably, or arms) and only charged us 50 cents altogether. And a young man from the Canal Zone said that the stories of anti-American feeling, which we had heard, were 'a load of crap' Also, he had seen a trailer park, somewhere near the town of David. Waiting for our papers, I noticed that we were back in the same time zone as Vermont, for we had been going southeast, most of the time, all through Central America. The road ahead of us went east, then northeast to Panama City. And the canal goes northwest from the city, so that the Atlantic end of it is west of the Pacific end. But the Atlantic is north of Panama and the Pacific is south of it, which is why the Pacific Ocean was known to sailors as the Great South Sea and the islands far out in it are still called the South Sea Islands.

Beyond the river, the country was sparsely populated and we did not see any trailer park near David, so we kept on going. Soon it was pitch dark and the thought of setting up our tent in that soggy, tropical place - surely full of snakes - was hardly attractive. But at Santiago there is a Texaco station and behind it is a curious structure called the Motel Manson. The station is very large, with a high, overhanging roof of corrugated iron that shelters a wide sidewalk, off which are various glass doors. One leads into a restaurant, another to a gift shop and another to a small room where the men of the local Rotary Club were earnestly holding a meeting. And the motel looks like a mobile home park, with an elaborate system of covered walkways between the units, which led us to believe that it often rains there. Each unit has a bedroom at either end, with a bathroom, kitchen and living room in the middle. But most of them were empty and when we enquired about them, we were offered a whole one to ourselves. Inside, most of the light fittings were missing or broken and the water heater did not work. Outside the back door, there were steps leading down into the jungle. And back inside, a huge cockroach scurried into a closet. But we did not expect to find anything better in that town and there was an armed guard on the parking lot, so we took it.

The armed guard was wearing a military uniform. Evidently the local powers felt it necessary to patrol the area. Perhaps trouble was expected. Where were the other guards? One man, even with a machine gun, could hardly be expected to protect all the cars in the lot from a determined group of trouble makers. We decided not to ask questions. If we were too inquisitive, someone might think we were up to something. The soldier politely ignored us as we gathered our things together to carry into our room.

We brought our supper into our unit but we had to eat it cold, because the kitchen stove did not work. And we had missed lunch, that day, so we ate it next. While June was tidying up, I thought about the brakes but decided that they were probably all right. Then we turned in, with a window open toward the parking lot, so that we could hear Minim's alarm. It rained hard in the night but by dawn it had stopped and the young soldier guarding the parking lot he was helping the police had cornflakes and coffee with us, standing beside Minim. And he said it was the end of the rainy season.

In the early morning, the new guard watched us gather ourselves together. I made plenty of coffee for the three of us, for it was a bit chilly after the rain. He told us that he was stationed down the road and that part of the regular duty was to stand watch at various posts around the town. He said the police force was small and there just weren't enough men to handle the job. We asked if there were much trouble. He shrugged. "Sometimes" was his non-commital answer. We ate our cereal and chatted about the weather.

There were two check points on the road to Panama City and the officials were more serious than any we had met before. But they were formally polite and our papers were in order and they let us though, without any trouble. A high bridge goes over the Panama Canal, just before the city. And down below it, on the right, we could see the Balboa Yacht Club - well kept buildings and neatly trimmed grass and a jetty, out into the water - with a dozen or more yachts anchored in front of it. And farther to the right, a ship heading out of the canal, into the Pacific Ocean. But we had to go to the other end of the canal, to meet the Rossini, so we turned left and followed the narrow, winding road across the isthmus (it is only 50 miles) to Colon.

The office of the Italian Line is on Roosevelt Avenue but when we got there, something was wrong. It was a street of old, run down houses in a residential district. So we made enquiries and found there were two Roosevelt Avenues, one in Colon and the other in Christobal. One Panamanian and one American. Though the two towns ran together, where they met there was a stark difference between them. In the width of a street, the scene changed from poverty to prosperity; from old, wooden buildings with peeling paint to modern, steel and concrete ones, gleaming white in the tropical sun. And in such a building we found the office of the Italian

Line. A man behind a long, polished wooden counter told us, in good English, that we must hand our car in to the authorities on Friday morning (in two days' time). Then we could board the Rossini ourselves on the Saturday morning and the ship was due to sail that afternoon. Meanwhile he would prepare our shipping documents, which we must pick up and take with us. Otherwise we would not be able to get our car back, in Peru.

In Guatemala we had been given the address of the Notts, an American couple who sailed all through the South Pacific in their 40 foot yacht, before settling in Panama. They lived at Gatun, in the Canal Zone, where he had a job maintaining the equipment at a lock, so we went to see them. The place looked like a suburban development, with paved streets curving around small hills. And many houses, each on a trim lawn. But all the houses were painted olive green.

Not a blade of grass out of place. The curves of the street were graceful. The sidewalks were level and swept clean. Cars, travelling at even speeds, would turn gently into driveways and stop under discreet shelters. All the buildings, some different from others, managed to radiate the same feeling of quiet comfort, each painted in the sun-faded olive. Even the land had been organized. Not too steep, not too flat, but interestingly rolling toward the canal and locks and lakes on one side and to the high wire fence that kept out the country of Panama on the other. Feeling like children sneaking a short cut through a cemetery, we lowered our voices and followed the regulation paths, trying not to attract any attention. We felt very out of place.

Inside, their house was comfortable, in an old fashioned way and they were glad to see anyone from the States. But soon the conversation turned to the Panama Canal. He told us the machinery at the locks was 50 years old and had to be maintained all the time. But the Panamanians would never do that and it would soon break down, if they had charge of it. He also said the United States had not got its investment back - maybe two thirds of it - and three quarters of the cargoes going through were bound to or from the States. He agreed that the U.S. military presence, which was causing half the trouble, was not necessary. But as things were, Panama was getting a good cut of the take, with no effort.

It was still daylight when we left the Notts, so we went to the Yacht Club in Cristobal, which is not as grand as the one in Balboa but very practical for people with boats. Set back from the road, in its own grounds, is a group of low buildings, looking more like a boat yard than a club, with a slipway and workshops and a place to do your laundry - just the things you need, when you come in from the sea - and they face a backwater of the port, well sheltered in any weather, so that yachts can lie alongside the dock. From the veranda of the club house, we could look down at the people working on their boats - drying their bedding after a passage and preparing their gear for the next one   for that is a major stopping place for cruising people. One yacht, a black yawl from Rhodesia, had spent four years in the San Blas Islands and there were two small ones with the self steering gear that is the mark of the long distance voyager.

We would have to prepare Minim for shipment, so we needed somewhere to stay, until we could go aboard the Rossini, and the only place that was reccommended was the old Washington Hotel, a big white building on the beach in Colon. Going there, we passed through a very poor district, even by Panamanian standards, but the parking lot was guarded (and we had no choice) so we moved in. Soon Lil Nott phoned, to say that we could dry our tent and wash our clothes at her house. And our room overlooked the Caribbean, so that we could see the lights of ships at anchor, in the outer harbor. And the clouds were low and gray and the wind was whistling in the bending, fluttering palm trees and it was a great night to be ashore.

Long rows of high palms shaded the cars in the huge garden in front of the hotel. A portico of white stone columns formed an impressive entry into a rather dowdy lobby. We were escorted down long, carpeted halls to our room; definitely inner-city used in decor. One look at the dreary, pretentious dining room and we headed for the neat, plastic coffee shop. Next morning, finding myself covered with itching red bites, I asked the desk clerk what they charged for a room without fleas? We were moved to another floor, much the same, but smelling of Lysol.

In the morning, we could make out five ships, through the driving rain.

And as each storm cell went by, they would swing to their anchors, until they were all facing the wind. Clearly the weather was not going to improve, so we drove to the Notts' house, which had an open space underneath it. And there we spent the day, preparing Minim for shipment. First we put up the tent and left it to dry. Then we took off the mirrors and hubcaps and stowed them, with the compass, altimeter and tachometer, in the lockers under the bed. When our laundry was dry, we put aside what we would need in the Rossini and stowed the rest in Minim with the tent. Then we screwed down the lids of all the lockers and filled the holes, over the screws, with plastic wood, so that it did not seem possible to get into the lockers, from inside the car.

It rained hard all day and we could see a long flight of steps, from someone's lawn to the road, down which the water was rushing, like a waterfall. But Jean Nott said it was unusual. In the dry season, it rained so little that the grass turned brown. And in the wet season, it rained from 3 until 5 each afternoon but everything dried out, as soon as it stopped. We asked about the Darien Gap and he said it was a swamp, sometimes 20 feet under water in places, so that a road through it would have to be a causeway, on piers. But there was nothing firm to put the piers on, so they would have to float in the mud and the cost of building the road would be so high that he did not expect it to happen, for many years. Two motorcycles once made it through the gap, at the end of the dry season. But they had all kinds of help, including air drops of supplies, and it took them a whole month. So the only practical way of taking one's own vehicle to South America. in the foreseeable future, would be by ship.

As we left their house, we were struck by the luxury of their big Ford car and the boat on its trailer, parked outside. They were ordinary enough, by American standards, but in Panama they stood out, as symbols of great wealth. And we wondered how such things affected the situation there. Back at the hotel, we telephoned the Italian Line. The Panamanian Customs office would open at eight o'clock on Friday morning and we must hand our car in to them before three in the afternoon. But the Rossini had been delayed one day by the storm and we could not go aboard her until 5:00 PM on Sunday. The Notts came to dinner, that night and Jean mentioned that the machinery at the locks was wearing out much faster than it used to, because bigger ships were going through. Some of them were amost as big as the lock and had to go full ahead to force their way in, while the water rushed back in the small space left, on each side. And the 'mules' had to heave and strain, to control them. So the ships that had been built to take advantage of the canal were destroying it.

We decided to have dinner on the narrow veranda facing the Caribbean. A few tables had been set with white linen. Candles spurted and flamed valiantly, trying to keep alight as the storm clouds flew overhead. Occasionally we would adjust a chair to move its occupant away from the splattering rain. Lightning would streak across the black sky, illuminating the gardens of palm and hibiscus that led down to the sea. It began to turn cold but we stayed. It was so much more cheerful and interesting there than in the dowdy dining hall. And we were not alone. Other diners came and went. The casino at the far end of the hotel was just beginning to come alive. Evidently the nightly gambling was what kept the old hotel going.

It took all morning to hand Minim in for shipment. First we had to get clearance from the Panamanian Customs, for her to leave Panama. Then we had to go to the Canal Zone Customs and get clearance for her to enter the Zone, where she would remain until she was loaded aboard the Rossini. Then we left her in a big parking lot, inside a chain link fence. We had not been able to find room in the lockers for the carpet, that we used in the tent, so we left it behind the seats, in its brown bag, and hoped it would not be stolen. Then we gave the officials the ignition key, which also opened the doors, but kept the other one, that opened the tailgate.

It was hot and sunny, that day, so we walked to the YMCA and had a lunch far better than dinner at the hotel, for a third of the cost. It was good to be in clean, modern surroundings and we stayed to chat with the manager, who confirmed what Jean Nott told us about the temperament of the Panamanians. They had insisted on taking over the garbage collection in Colon, so the Americans gave them the trucks. But within two years, they all broke down for lack of maintenance. He advised us never to walk in the streets near the hotel, for things were calm then, but they were not always. So we took a taxi and the driver told us that attacks on people took place by day and night in the area around the Washington Hotel. We found a guide book which said adventure for ladies in Colon was shopping and for gentlemen it was nightclubbing. What rot. Walking the streets would be a real kick. So we sat around, resting and watching Armed Forces television programs.

On Saturday morning, we picked up Minim's Original Bill of Lading from the Italian Line and found a stamp on it which said they could unload our car at any port they chose, keep our money and not be responsible for anything. That was the first we heard of any such condition, though they had taken our money for the passage in full 2 months ago. And we were paying $86 extra for the increased price of fuel. But there was nothing we could do about it then. The man behind the counter did not know what pier the Rossini would use and the office would be closed on Sunday. But he said it would be all over soon, the business was dying. And he warned us to stay out of 'Little Viet Nam' beyond 8th Street in Colon, where our hotel was.

Ordinarily we would have walked from the hotel to the shopping section of town to wander around and see the sights but after the warning about Little Viet Nam we took a cab whenever we left the hotel. I was sure it was all a myth, to keep the cab fares high. But the drivers swore it was dangerous even to ride through those few short blocks. So we didn't take any chances. On our one brief tour of the shops, we decided it wasn't worth all the fuss anyway. Just another port town with the standard tourist souvenirs. I had truly wanted to buy a Panama hat, though. Then Patrick pointed out the MADE IN HONG KONG label inside one that I had taken ten minutes to choose. So we put it back on the shelf, much to the disgust of the clerk.

At the Yacht Club, there was a trimaran from New Zealand, on her way around the world. But the rain was pouring down, out of a gray, overcast sky and the people were below decks, out of sight. So we went back to the hotel to wait. In the morning, we tried to find out if the ship was in but the desk clerk did not know how to do it, so we phoned the Port Office. The Rossini was due at 1430 at Pier Benjamin. By 1:30 we were peering through dirty windows at the gray sea and about 20 minutes later, we saw a white ship. As she came closer, we could see that she was a passenger vessel and when she entered the harbor, we could read her name: Rossini. They said she would not load passengers until 7:00 PM so we waited two more hours in the lobby of the hotel, then took a taxi to the pier and sat on our luggage in the great, high shed, among the packing cases and vehicles and waiting people.

Before six, a line formed at a gangway and joining it, we went aboard the ship, where three officers in white uniforms sat behind trestle tables in a crowded passage. We did not speak Italian and they only spoke a few words of English, enough to order us to hand over our passports and health cards (which they kept) and give us the number of our cabin. Carrying our luggage, we worked our way through the crowd of people down two flights of stairs and a narrow passage to the door, which opened into a tiny cabin with no porthole. And June, who suffers from seasickness, flatly refused to stay there. So back we went, to negotiate for something better.

How could there be a porthole? We were below the water line. There were already people in the cabin. Were we expected to share that miserable space with strangers? There wasn't enough air for one person. The throbbing vibrations of nearby engines were deafening and the ship hadn't even left the dock. I'd swim the Darien Gap before I'd tolerate five minutes in that hole. Patrick never listens to anything I say. So I left. Maybe, seeing me standing on the pier, he'd realize that I meant business.

I explained our problem to the three officers in English, French and Spanish but they just stared at me. Then they made it clear that whatever cabin we had was all we were going to get. So June walked off the ship and stood on the dock, in the rain, until the Chief of Cabins broke into fluent English and promised to do something about it. He was not specific but we should have dinner and come and see him, about nine o'clock. The ship was old and run down (not nearly as nice as the Guaymas ferry) but we found a bar where an elderly waiter served good, cheap drinks. And at dinner, we shared a table with a friendly Peruvian who told us, in rapid Spanish, that there might be political problems in Chile but they should not affect us. He had been aboard the Rossini for 17 days since boarding her in Nice, and he said that the sea was very rough on the last day, coming from Colombia to Panama.

I have nothing against old, run-down things. In fact, at my age I've come to find a certain charm in things beyond their prime. But the Rossini was filthy. There was nothing you wanted to touch. Our dinner companion said the food was exceptionally good that night. Perhaps because a new group of tourists had just come aboard? The napkins and table cloths were clean. Food was hot and the wine decanter was never empty. Maybe I was being a bit too fussy. If everyone else could stand it, so could I. Just another half glass of wine, please.

At nine o'clock we saw the Chief of Cabins and he led us to a cabin with a porthole and four berths, that we could have to ourselves. I offered to pay the diference between it and the small one but he suggested I give him something, instead. So I gave him twenty dollars and off he went. The airconditioning did not seem to be working but I managed to get the port-hole open - using a hairbrush as a lever - and soon we were settled in, for the voyage to South America. At ten, the loading of cargo stopped and all was quiet on the pier. We remembered a story we had heard, of how someone's car had been left behind and when he got back, it had vanished. So we tried to find out if Minim was aboard but nobody seemed to know (or care) and we just had to hope she was. We must have slept lightly, because the vibration of the ship's propellors woke us at 4:00 AM, when she left the pier. And sitting on the upper berth, we watched through our porthole as she approached the locks at Gatun.

A red navigation buoy slid past, below us, and there were fluorescent strip lights, standing on piles in the water, that lit up the trees and grasses along the bank, until the dark wall of the first lock came across and blocked our view. As the lock filled with water, we rose above the wall and saw a spare 'mule' being repaired. It was an electric winch, the size and shape of a locomotive, with motors to turn big reels of steel cable and others to move it along its track. It took four 'mules' to handle the Rossini - one on each side, at each end - and by keeping tension on the cables, they held her in the center of the lock, until it was full. Then they moved forward with her, to the next one and before dawn, she had gone through all three. But she had to wait there, so she anchored just beyond the locks, at the side of the channel.

After breakfast, we went up on deck and found two other ships anchored nearby. But soon our anchor came rattling up out of the mud and off we went, across Gatun Lake. That was the largest man-made lake in the world, until the Russians created a bigger one, and it was made by flooding a valley which had many small hills in it, so that their tops are now islands in the lake, all of them covered with green trees, except for occasional patches of red earth. And the ship channel, between the islands, is clearly marked by aids to navigation - buoys, beacons and ranges - just like those in the Chesapeake & Delaware Canal in the United States.

In the lake, we met three ships, coming the other way. Two of them were freighters, piled high with cargo, and the other one was a white passenger ship of the Italian Line, so there was much waving and cheering as she passed by. Then the lake narrowed into a winding canal and after a while, we came to the locks at the far end. As the Rossini entered the first one, lines snaked down from her decks to the concrete walls and pulled up steel cables from the 'mules', which were made fast to the ship. And moving along with her, the 'mules' took up the strain, until she came to a stop in the middle of the lock. When the gates behind her were closed, the water went down. Then the ones in front of her opened, to let her into the next lock. And when the last gates opened, she cast off the cables and steamed out, past the Balboa Yacht Club, into the Paciic Ocean.

It was raining steadily out of a gray, overcast sky when she cleared the offlying islands and headed for her next port of call, which was Buenavenura in Colombia. But the sea was calm and below decks, it was hard to detect any motion. Our cabin was long and narow, with two bunks - one above the other - along one side and two more across the end, where the porthole was. And the decor was Early Railroad Sleeping Car, with many light switches, some of which worked. But there was a desk to write at and we could be alone there. The bathroom, across the passage, was a minor Hell Hole, always steaming hot and dripping with damp. But the Italian Line was the cheapest. And we were in the Tourist Class which was also the cheapest.

In the dining room, roaches wandered across the ceiling and the food, handed out by bored waiters in gray uniforms, was about as uninteresting as could be imagined. But there was good bread and plenty of wine and chatting with our fast-talking Peruvian friend was good for our Spanish. He was an agronomist but he said it was hard to get ahead of the demand for food, because of the population explosion and because much of the land in Peru was unsuitable for mechanized production of it, so that with a population density of 14 people per square mile, they had 15 meatless days a month.

As Tourist Class passengers, we were restricted to the stern of the ship but we had enough deck space to walk around on. And it was fun trying to figure out what the notices said, about lifeboats and such, in Italian. But the announcements that came over the loudspeakers were repeated in German, French, Spanish and English. And it was soon clear that the ship's officers spoke all of those languages, though they pretended not to, when it suited them not to understand a passenger. But the old waiter in the bar was nice enough and sitting there, we heard two young couples speaking English.

They turned out to be a Chilean, going home with his new American wife and her girl friend, travelling with an Italian called Tony, who was on his way to see his parents in Chile. They had driven from California to Panama in a gray car that was now in the ship and one of the girls clearly remembered seeing Minim put aboard, which was a great relief to us, for it was the first time we had any evidence that she was there. Tony had made the trip before and while waiting in Colon for the ship, they stayed in an hotel that charged one third of what we paid, for airconditioned rooms. He said that the mood toward Americans was okay in Chile but less so in Peru, where we could only cash our travellers' checks at the National Bank and would have to account for all our money, because they had strict curency control. And he told us that we could go and see Minim, in the ship's hold, if we asked the right officer.

On Tuesday morning, the rain stopped and the sky cleared a little and there was land, gray in the distance, on the port beam. Strolling on deck, we met an elderly Australian woman in a big hat, who told us firmly that the Rossini was a migrant ship. She had put off about 200 of them in Venezula. But she only had about two more years of service left. And after lunch, she docked (rather sloppily) at Buenaventura. But we decided not to go ashore there, for the sun had come out and the dirty old town was sweltering in the heat of the flat, low lying coast and we had been warned that it was a place where you did not take your watch, or it would surely be stolen. So we went down to the cool of our cabin.

Toward evening, the passengers who had been ashore came back along the quay, walking in groups and clutching brown paper bags containing duty free liquor and perfume. But by then, the sky had clouded over and it was cool - though we were near the Equator - and we were on deck, leaning over the rail to watch things being unloaded from the ship. Three cars were put ashore, and some crates of machinery. Then they started unloading cartons of glasses, from Italy. The ones from the forward hatches were set on wooden pallets and as they swung clear of the ship, they were lowered gently to the dock. But from number five hatch, the steel cable would bring up a whole bundle of the long, narrow cartons, cinched together in the middle, with a loud noise of breaking glass. The ship's winches were operated by Colombians from the port, while others were in the holds, sending up the cartons and evidently there was some disagreement between that crew and the ship's officers, who waved and shouted sporadically from various points of vantage, but with no discernable effect.

Perhaps the problem was that the ship's captain insisted on having the unloading completed that evening and most of the glasses were in that hold, for as time went on, ways were found to increase the percentage of glasses broken. Two or three bundles of cartons would be hoisted out of the hold at once and dropped firmly on the dock, with a tinkling crash. Then a fork lift truck would flip each bundle on its side a couple of times, before taking it away.

We watched in disbelief. There was not the least attempt made to keep the glasses from bouncing on the dock. The crews shouted at each other for a while, but the stevedores, between shouts, giggled and winked. Like us, our fellow passengers watched in surprise, then shock, then disgust and slowly, singly or in groups, headed below decks. It was too much.

Altogether, they were probably breaking 75 percent of the glasses in each carton. And they were still doing it, when we gave up watching and went to bed. But in the morning, we were at sea, bound for Guayaquil in Ecuador. We were told there would be police checks in Peru, where we would be stopped and required to give all the details of our car and its contents and ourselves (age, marital status, reason for travelling, etcetera) so we borrowed our passports from the ship's officers and typed out six Information Sheets, in Spanish, to hand over when we came to the check points. Then we went with Tony and his friends, to see Minim in the ship's hold. We had tried to get permission the day before, without success, so we asked Tony (who was Italian) to make the arrangements, for us as well as for himself. And he assured us it would be no trouble. So we reported to the Purser's office at the appointed time and were told that it was very dangerous to visit cars, that were in the hold. But after a long argument in Italian, Tony switched to English and told us that we could definitely see them at nine o'clock the next morning.

We would need some money when we arrived in Callao (the seaport for Lima, in Peru) and there was a money changing office in the First Class lobby, which the Tourist Class passengers could visit at five in the evening. Of course there was no one there at five but after a while, the officer came bustling in and told us he was not allowed to cash our traveller's checks, because Italy had currency control. However, we might be able to cash one in Guayaquil, though it would probably be for Ecuadorian currency, not American dollars. He was clearly indignant, that we should have asked him for dollars, which would be illegal for him to handle. But while he was talking, he opened a drawer of his desk and we saw a fat bundle of new-looking American dollars there. So we guessed that they were probably counterfeit and refrained from offering him a premium, to get some. And we took the opportunity to have a look at the First Class accommodations, on the way back. They were more spacious than the Tourist Class ones - the passages were wider - and the public areas were less drab. But when we found a cabin with its door open and looked inside, it was scarcely different from ours, though we were told that the

First Class fare was very much higher.

Probably for another twenty dollars could have switched to First Class. But it was less objectionable to stay where we were than to deal more than absolutely necessary with the crew. All conversations should have been started with a few dollar bills in sight. But we have never lived that way and would just as soon not.

At dinner, June got her second cockroach. He was walking across the ceiling and lost his grip (in a patch of grease) and fell staight down, onto her head. And there was a small fuss until she dislodged him from her hair and he fell down onto the floor and went off, under someone else's table. The first time it happened, we mentioned it to the waiter but he seemed incredulous and by the time we got his attention, the cockroach had gone, so we dropped the matter. But this being the second time, we called loudly for him and suggested he do something about it. In fact, the ceiling was low enough, so that he could have reached up and taken down the various cockroaches that were going in different directions across it. But he did not seem to feel that it was his job and glancing up, he made us understand that it was no big deal. Probably there were far more cockroaches, back in the kitchen.

There were roaches wherever we went. Floors, ceilings, everywhere. No wonder. The cloths on the serving table in the dining room had not been changed since the day we stepped aboard. There was not even an attempt made to shake off the crumbs. I wondered briefly, what the crew's quarters must be like, then stopped myself. Only a couple more days until Lima. Have another glass of wine.

Our Peruvian friend laughed politely when the cockroach fell on June's head but he did not seem to have a sense of humor, as we know it. And he did not think that a few cockroaches on the ceiling of the dining room were anything to talk about. But the fourth chair at our table was empty and a constant stream of girls - one every few minutes - would come and sit down and have a few words with him, then get up and go away.

He never really laughed. More of a snort, followd by a giggle. It didn't seem to bother the young girls who visited our table throughout each meal. They did most of the talking. Like subjects gaining the ear of the king, the girls came one by one to pay their respects. And the king remained aloof. There was a feeling of arrogance, of hardness about him that put us off. He was always polite - barely. He gave us his address in Cuzco, the center of Incan Archaeology. Perhaps we would call on our way to Macchu Picchu. In his own country, away from the adoring entourage, he might relax and become a little more real.

There were stars overhead, that night, and the moon was reflected in an almost calm sea, as we neared the equator. But we were asleep in bed when we crossed the Line.

Some time after midnight there was a lot of noise in the passage. Then pounding on our door. Of course, the Equator. Visions of old movies flashed before me. King Neptune. Dancing. Music. Come on Patrick..... He whispered something very final like "I'll kill you if you answer that" It really didn't matter. Seeing a bit of South America was the important thing. I'd written off the Romantic Cruise long ago.

In the morning, there was a slight swell under a gray sky and we had breakfast with a young couple - he was Bolivian and she was French - who had spent four years in Paris. They told us that we could camp anywhere in Bolivia, even by the side of the road, and it was not too cold at Lake Titicaca. Also there was no currency control in Ecuador and we should be able to change our traveller's checks into dollars there. And so, a little at a time, we gathered the information we needed, about the conditions that lay ahead of us. I was interested to see if the water really did go down a drain turning the other way in the Southern Hemisphere. But my tests were inconclusive. Probably we would have to wait until we were farther south to see the effect clearly.

While Patrick watched water run down the drain, I read everything we had brought aboard. Including one bit of Rossini literature that listed the ship's library among her attractions. Each time we asked, we were given a perfectly good reason for it being closed. It never opened on Thursdays. Wednesday was the librarian's day off. On Monday and Tuesday it opened between 11:30 PM and midnight. One really couldn't expect it to be open on Saturday or Sunday, could one? After all! But on Friday, between four and five, there should be someone there.

We started searching for it early so that we wouldn't miss the short time permitted. Thank heavens. For it took us several hours to realize that the delapidated glass fronted bookcase we had passed a thousand times was in fact the library. Some time after four o'clock, a sour faced man, seeing us leaning against the case, pulled a key from his pocket and unlocked the door. There must have been at least seven books in English - three of which were the Gideon Bible. I took one of the others.

By nine o'clock, we were at the Purser's office with Tony and his friends. And ten minutes later, a seaman arrived. When he was told to take us to our cars, he resisted but after an argument, the Purser threw up his hands in a gesture of helplessness and reluctantly the seaman led us away. Tony's car was outside, on an upper deck, and we found a large, new dent in one fender. It was not insured and Tony said some things in Italian but the seaman made it clear, even to us, that it was a minor matter, of no importance. Then he led us to a lower deck and unlocked a steel door off a passageway and turned on some lights. The door opened into one side of a hold - a huge, empty space - and below us, near the far side of it, was Minim. The only way to get down to her from where we were was by stepping through the doorway, over a clear drop, onto a vertical ladder beside it. And the seaman said it would be very dangerous for us to try that. But Minim appeared to be in good shape, with no dents that we coud see, and we were relieved to know that she was still aboard the ship, so we thanked him for his trouble and left.

By then, the motion of the ship had changed. Her slight heaving and rolling had stopped, though she was still under way. And going on deck, we found that she was heading up the winding, muddy river toward Guayaquil, 40 miles ahead. The land was low on either side, with palm trees among the mangroves along the shore. But it was cool, under the gray sky, and the river looked like the Waccamaw, in South Carolina, with American style fish boats in the deep water and the same kind of fish traps - mazes of poles with nets between them - in the shallow water at the sides. At lunch, there were fancy menus - perhaps because we were coming into port and some people might be leaving the ship that day - but the food was as bad as ever. The boiled potatoes and pasta had just been given new, elegant names.

Our friend at the table said it was usually cloudy and cool in Lima. But in the southern part of Peru, it was always sunny and in some places it never rained. At the purser's office, landing cards were being given out to anyone who wanted to go ashore. But I would need my passport, to cash a traveller's check, and I had to make quite a fuss to get it. Finally the Purser produced it but he made me sign for it (though he had never given me a receipt for it) and promise to give it back to him that evening.

Farther up the river, there were dugout canoes, most of them drifting along under sails made from old sacks and some piled high with goods - the people perched wherever they could - just as they were in the Caribbean 20 years before. But the docks at Guayaquil were new and when the ship was secured, we joined the people going ashore. It felt strange and rather grand to be standing on the continent of South America, after so many years of preparation to get there. And soon we were rattling toward the city in a rickety old bus. Guayaquil had been destroyed many times by fires, pirate attacks, earthquakes, even swarms of termites. But there had been much rebuilding in the past five years, in concrete, using earthquake proof techniques from Japan. And the outer suburbs, of two story houses, looked neat and clean. The bus went very slowly and when it came to a big, new monument, it stopped altogether and the passengers from the ship dutifully got out and photographed it. I forget what it was about but it was a huge figure, maybe 80 feet high, of a man with his hands above his head, like the victim of a holdup.

But we were anxious to get to a bank before they closed, and when the bus stopped in the city, we dashed off on foot asking directions of passing strangers to the nearest one that handled foreign exchange transactions. Inside, it again reminded us of the Caribbean islands of 20 years before, with its high ceilings and slowly turning fans. And we were introduced to a senior official - a polite, elderly gentleman - who first had $ 200 worth of our traveller's checks changed into local currency, then had that changed into dollars, all for a modest $ 3 service charge.

The transaction cost little but time. Over two hours later we were back wandering around the city streets. The bank had been jammed while we were there. Each transaction had to be recorded in several places. Typists sat before ancient typewriters filling out a different form for each different proceedure, I'd watch a man join one line, appear later at the head of another line, then at the tail of another, and then I'd lose track. Perhaps he'd gone to the second floor. There was an endless stream of people coming and going on the stairs in front of us. Certainly all those forms would have to be burned every night, just to make room for the next day's output.

Somehow we fetched up with a few dollars worth of local currency (sucres) so we bought some things we needed in the busy downtown area, which was much like any other city, except that the policemen on traffic duty wore steel helmets. But along the river, there was a nice malecon (promenade) with shade trees and across the road from it were shops which sold corrugated iron. And old buildings - some with sides made of it laid vertically, and some of wood - remained, between the more modern concrete ones.

Guayaquil's architecture had a quality of theatrical impermanence about it. The several-storied buildings of wood or corrugated metal were painted in now faded, peeling colors. Huge, small paned windows were set into the walls. And doors, with no porches in front of them, opened into the air, thirty feet above the ground. What a place to be in an earthquake or a fire. Yet those buildings had been there for years. You could tell the new ones. All concrete and sheet glass. Even the shops had a temporary feel about them. They all sold the same things. Bits of plastic, this and that. Sometimes there would be a specialty shop. Gear wheels only. We began to wonder if this were really the center of town. But the park along the river was pleasant. We roamed through it for a while.

Across the river, the land was low and undeveloped. The only hill that we could see, on the same side as the city, was covered with poor looking houses. And occasionally, along the malecon, we came to wooden docks, with fish boats tied up to them. But at one dock, we saw several fine yachts, including a modern schooner and a well equipped sport fisherman. Though the sky was gray and overcast all day, it was hot and sweaty, walking. And arriving at the Humboldt Hotel, we went inside for a drink.

The barman never smiled and the drinks were small and expensive but we used up the last of our sucres and met a man, from Ecuador, who had just been robbed. He was in his late thirties, with a neat black mustache, and looked like a businessman. He had gone into a bad section of the city, to get something for his car, but a man hit him on the head with a piece of metal and took his wallet. So he was having a drink and wanted someone to talk to. As he recovered his composure, he remembered we were foreigners and explained that it was really his fault, for going there. Without saying it, he implied that the city was a perfectly civilized place, like any other. But he had just made an obvious mistake and of course he had been robbed. But that was over now and we should enjoy our visit.

Walking back, along the malecon, we noticed that the new cars, which were displayed for sale, were all very small. And those in use, on the road, were mostly old and dented. Where we were supposed to meet the bus, back to the ship, there was a bench under the trees. And as we waited there, four schoolgirls came along the sidewalk, their brown faces contrasting with their clean white uniforms, and stopped to try out the English they had learned on us. They were delighted to find that we could understand them - each said a few words, while the rest giggled - and they were still with us, when the bus came. There were two busses for the ship's passengers but they could not stop for more than a moment in that traffic, so they went around the block and tried again. We got onto one, the first time it stopped, with the girls saying goodbye through the open window. And the next time it stopped, they were still there, waving and calling to us. But some of the passengers tried to catch the busses by chasing them around the block.

They would almost make it, when the bus was held up in a jam or stopped at an intersection. Then off it would go, leaving them behind. Some of them were First Class passengers, who were very old, and we expected them to drop dead at any moment, after galloping around in that heat. But none of them did, so far as I know, and eventually the busses set off toward the ship. That was the only time we came in contact with any First Class passengers - I can not say we met them - and they seemed a curious lot, to us. Mostly they spoke English, among themselves, and we gathered that they were going around the world on some kind of package tour. When the ship got to Valparaiso (the port for Santiago, in Chile) they would fly on, toward Australia. But they were not outgoing, at all. And we were glad that we were travelling (at half the price) in the Tourist Class section, with the younger people, most of whom spoke Spanish.

Beyond the center of the city, we went through a poor section and inched our way through a crowded market, with stalls selling plastic Christmas tree ornaments. But in the suburbs, our old bus went very fast, bouncing along, often on the wrong side of the road, all the way to the dock. Getting off, we saw a car which had been unloaded from the ship. It had big, fresh dents in one fender and people were standing around it, filling out forms. As it got dark, a dugout canoe came alongside the Rossini, near her stern, and six cartons were passed down to the men in it, from the ship. Then one man slid down a rope, into the canoe, and they left. Probably the cartons contained food of some kind and most likely they got it from the ship's crew.

We watched the exchange with others. Both passengers and uniformed crewmen stood quietly along the railings. No one moved. No one commented. No one gave any indication that some action should be taken. We had all learned that there was nothing we could do. We were captive. Someone else was in charge and wanted nothing from us.

Then the ship left the dock, with the aid of three tugs, and started down the river, toward the sea. For a while, the Port Captain's new boat roared along beside her, but in spite of the loud noise it made, it was quite slow and as the Rossini speeded up, it dropped behind her and turned back. Later, before going to bed, we sat on the top berth in our cabin and watched though our porthole as the ship went on down the river, now much wider but still calm, past lights along a curving shore, like those we had sat and watched so many times on night passages in small boats down Chesapeake Bay. In the morning, I plugged my razor into an outlet marked 220 V (after setting it to that voltage) but it turned out to be DC instead of AC. Quickly I unplugged it and there was no smoke, so I tried the 110 volt socket and it was fine. And as I shaved, a large cockroach watched me, from the mirror.

Going on deck, we noticed that the Rossini was steaming very slowly, though the sea was calm and the weather was clear. And seeing Tony, we asked him what was going on. Probably she was doing it to save fuel, he thought. For she was losing money and the Italian government only kept her running to honor a contract they had with Chile, by which they could buy copper at a special low price. But the contract was due to run out soon and meanwhile, the crew deliberately tried to discourage passengers from sailing in her. The members of the crew were lowly paid, so they had to engage in smuggling, to make a living. Which meant that they had to pay off the officials in the ports. So they had to do more smuggling, to cover their expenses. And they really did not have time to cope with a bunch of passengers.

When Tony explained it, with his warm, friendly smile, it all seemed to be perfectly reasonable.

We mentioned the dent in Tony's car but he said he was going to Arica, in northern Chile, where labor was cheap - it only cost $ 80 to have an engine overhauled - and he would sell the car, when he got there, so it was no problem. But we should stop and see him in Arica, which was the first town across the border from Peru and had a far nicer climate than Lima. And he said there were camp grounds in the lake district of southern Chile. We could get the details from the automobile club, on our way though Santiago.

Any time we got confirmation that camping really was possible in the places ahead of us, we were encouraged. For if we could not use the tent most of the time, we would run out of money before completing the trip we hoped to make.

Then we met the young Bolivian and his wife from Paris, who told us the rains were so heavy that the roads from Peru to Bolivia were impassible, at that time of the year (the AAA knew nothing of it) but they would be okay in April. Which confirmed that our plan to go quickly south on the west side of the Andes, then come slowly back north on the east side of them, would give us the best chance of getting through. They also said that 'll', which was pronounced 'y' in Central America, would be like 'ly' in Peru. So Callao, which we had been calling Cayao, was really Calyao. But among the people on the wrong side of the tracks, it would be Cajao.

That afternoon, there was a movie under a forward hatch, where folding chairs had been set out in the empty cargo space, between two decks. And watching David Niven in Casino Royale, we forgot the ship for a while. But later, strolling on deck in perfect weather - a calm sea under a clear sky, filled with stars - we were both anxious to get off her and back to the freedom of life ashore, after 5 days aboard. Saturday morning was also clear and the ship steamed over a sunlit sea, so calm that we could hardly feel any motion. But our ETA was now 1530, instead of 1400 that day. And though it had been an interesting experiment, we would never again travel by ship if we could help it. It was far too slow and confining to suit our temperament.

Near Callao, the ship ran into fog and slowed right down but some officials came aboard and we filed past trestle tables in the Red Room to have our papers examined. All the officials were abrupt and rude and we saw a man go around, quite openly, giving each of them a carton of cigarettes. As the Rossini entered the harbor, the fog lifted and we could see cranes and sheds across the still water. And when she was secured, we took our luggage and pushed our way through the crowd of people, down a gangway onto the dock.

And we did push. Shoved, stumbled, slid down the gangway and off the ship once and for all. No matter that there were high fences wherever we turned. No matter that rain had begun to fall and wet us through. We would soon be free. That voyage was the kind of thing we would remember for minutes.

There, in a big new building, the Customs officers made everyone wait for more than an hour, until the last passenger's luggage was ready to be inspected. Then they went quickly along the counters, making a brief check of a few items, and suddenly we were free to go. So we went outside and stood by our luggage, waiting for Minim to be unloaded. At six o'clock, a black steel cable drew her up from the hold and when a second cable took up the strain, she swung out from the ship, rotating slowly in the air. As she came down, I went forward (probably shouting) and three men helped me steady her before she landed, quite gently, on the pavement.

Examining her, we found a dent in the right rear fender, with white paint on it. And since she had not touched the side of the ship, coming off, it must have happened when she was put aboard in Panama. Which accounted for the fuss, when we wanted to inspect her, aboard the ship. But now it was too late to make a claim against the company - the ship was due to sail for Arica that night - and otherwise she was in good shape. A piece of chromed stripping on one side had nearly come of but we put that back. And the knob of the light switch had been pulled off but it was lying on the floor and I knew how to fix it, so that was no problem. The carpet for the tent was in its bag, down behind the seats. And all the cushions were still there, so we considered ourselves lucky. But when we asked if the Customs officers would like to inspect her, we were told they had gone home. All cars from the Rossini would be held in bond until Monday.

The official we asked also told us we would have to pay $ 60 for unloading her, plus $ 50 in landing fees before we could take her away. And he tried to persuade me to give him my dollars, in exchange for Peruvian soles. When I said that would be illegal, he told me to lie to the currency control offcers - telling them the dollars had been stolen and when I refused to do so, he first pleaded with me, saying he needed the money for his wife and children, then finally gave up with a sneer. Tony's gray car was on the dock and he confirmed that we would have to leave Minim in bond until Monday, so we drove her into the fenced enclosure, locked her and took the key. Then we helped Tony push his car, which would not start, to the same enclosure. And as we watched, the gates were closed and locked, with the two cars secure (we hoped) inside.

The thought of getting off the ship and into Minim and driving into the sunset was a bit unrealistic . We should have guessed this would happen. It was so like the Rossini to mess things up. But at least we would have the car back on Monday and in the meantime we had two whole days to see Lima. Knowing Patrick, he would have headed straight for the hills and I would never get another chance at the city.

By then, it was nine o'clock and few people were left on the dock. A soldier with a gun came by, cadging cigarettes. And a young French couple, who had found a taxi, agreed to share it with us for the ride into Lima, about 15 miles away. Tony's friends were going on to Arica in the Rossini, so he was alone. And we had nowhere in mind to stay, that night. But the other couple had reservations at a German pension, which they said was not expensive, so we all got out there. It was an old house, set back a little from a tree lined boulevard, and the manageress was a short, thin woman with long black hair, who spoke quickly and sharply. Of course she had a room for us. But first we must fill out the form, required by the Government. With our passport numbers, in the proper places. It would be $ 13 for two people, with breakfast. Taking a key, she led us down a hall and threw open a door. The room was large and comfortable, with modern furniture and indirect lighting. And walking across it, we found a nice bathroom and a door which opened into a small, floodlit garden. We expressed our approval and she left. After six days in the Rossini, it was hard to adjust to the space and cleanliness and luxury. But we had not eaten yet, so we contacted Tony and went out with him for dinner.

That part of Lima, called Miraflores, looked like Paris but there were palm trees, here and there, among the others. And strolling down the boulevard, we had to watch out, for the driving was worse than in Mexico City and the parking was free form. Cars were left on the sidewalk, at intersections, anywhere. But a few bloks away, we came to a glass fronted restaurant and after a short wait, we got a table. It was expensive, by our standards - about $ 12.00 each, with drinks - but the meal was good and we were glad to be back in the real world. And in conversation, Tony said that when he took a car into Chile, he did not get a bond for it. Instead, he got a temporary permit, to take it into the country for two weeks, and sold it for twice what he paid for it in California. But he made the buyer give him a letter, saying that he would be responsible for paying the import duty on it, which made it quite legal, from Tony's point of view. Of course the buyer did not pay the full duty of 100 percent. He made a deal with the official for a much lower rate and gave him a little on the side and everyone was happy. Then, going back, Tony would buy a car so old that it was cheap in Chile and sell it in California as an antique.

It was nearly midnight as we left the restaurant, feeling better and more civilized than we had in weeks. And Tony said we were quite safe, walking back to the house. But I did not sleep well, for worrying that our gear (which we needed, to get to Cape Horn) might be stolen from Minim, on the dock. Breakfast was in another house, a few doors away. There were separate tables in a plain room, whose windows faced a walled garden. And the people were all young and quiet - much more so, than in an hotel - but they came from many countries and each of them spoke several languages. Then we saw the manageress of the pension about a place to keep Minim. And she showed us a one car garage, under a house nearby, which we could rent for two nights.

There was nothing else of a practical nature that we could do on Sunday, so we took a taxi to the Gold Museum, which was said to be one of the finest in the world. But it was far out in the suburbs and when we got there, it was closed. So we walked to the end of the bus line - where they turned around - and took the next one, into the center of Lima. We had been told there was some anti-American feeling in Peru but we never saw it, that day. The people on the busses we took were very nice. Though we did not know where we wanted to go, the drivers sold us suitable tickets and the passengers told us where to get off, with polite enthusiasm. Even the shoe shine boys in the ecntral plaza were more civil than usual.

A cascading fountain was the center of attraction in the old Plaza de Armas. Pigeons fluttered and splashed around the heads of various water sprites and gargoyles. Children jumped and splashed at their feet. Others, sitting on the steps of the fountain or on benches around, watched the activity. It was nearly Christmas and the plaza was crowded. There was a small enclave of amusements in one area. Pony rides, wheels of fortune and, if you could gather your family together, a big camera on a tripod for a souvenir picture. The massive, solid government buildings around two sides of the plaza were locked and guarded. But on the other sides shops were open and busy. We went into one and could barely find our way through the crowd. All of Lima was Christmas shopping. At every street corner vendors offered boxes of their traditional sweet fruit bread. It came in two sizes: huge and outlandish. After all the pasta and potatoes aboard ship and days of sitting, we passed it up. Everyone seemed to be happy.

We walked for miles, then reluctantly found a bus that would take us back to Miraflores.

Back at the pension, we met Tony and went out with him, to have dinner at a sidewalk restaurant. And at eight o'clock on Monday morning, we took a taxi with him, to the docks. He said we would need an agent, to get our car out of bond, in Callao. And since he was experienced in such matters, we agreed to share one with him. So he found a slippery little man with a fixed smile and off we went, from one grimy offce to another, each located in a more unlikely corner of the vast area of docks and warehouses and crumbling old brick buildings. The proceedure was the same, in each offce. The agent would greet the thin, birdlike minor officials like old friends and give them a little money to prepare a document. Then, after a while, he would lead us into a back room, where a big man like a well fed bear sat behind a large desk. And as we stood in silence, the agent would make supplicating noises, while slipping a larger sum of money under the pile of papers on the desk. Then the official would take out a rubber stamp and apply it to our documents and sign it and we would all leave, with expressions of gratitude, and go running off toward the next office. What each document was for, I do not remember but one of the officials was a police officer and in due course, another (probably customs) took us to the fenced enclosure and inspected our cars. He was mainly interested in the serial numbers but we were relieved to find our gear, still in Minim.

Altogether, we paid $ 90 in landing and unloading charges (not counting the bribes) which were based on the weight of our truck. Then we were told we needed a paper from the Italian Line, to prove that we came in the same ship, with it. So off we went, in a taxi. But the only girl on duty at the Italian Line took one look at us and went out to a pharmacy. With the taxi ticking up charges outside, we waited for a long time until she came back. Then, reluctantly, she typed out the paper but refused to take it in to her boss, to be signed, on the grounds that it would interfere with his routine. So June picked the paper out of her tray and went in with it.

All this nonsense was getting to me. We had been patient and polite for hours. Yet anyone connected in any way with the Italian Line seemed deter-

mined to make life miserable. By that time I was in a rage. If the man hadn't signed the paper, I might well have throttled him. Perhaps he guessed. He did look a bit startled but said nothing. He made his mark in the proper place and ceremoniously bowed as he handed it back.

The girl was smouldering at her desk and when I said our truck had been dented, she told me with great authority that the Italian Line took no responsibiliy for such things. But we had no time to waste, arguing about it, and when June came back, we went off to find our agent, on the docks. At noon, the officials all left, so we followed the agent though some offices and up a steel stairway, onto the roof of an old building, where a crude lunch counter sold things we preferred not to investigate. But the fish soup looked as it it had been boiled, at one time, so we had some of that, with a package of crackers and a bottle of nameless soda.

Bits of flour sacking formed a shade over the wooden tables and chairs. After a taste of soup, I advised Patrick not to eat too much. It had overtones of Lima Bay. The soda was interesting. A little watery to our taste but cool. And what a relief to get out of those grubby offices.

It was hot, up there, but we had a fine view of the ships at the various docks. Many of them were Russian freighters, big and clean and well kept, unloading cargo. And there was an empty space, where we had last seen the Rossini. Predictably, the officials came back late, after lunch. And waiting, we tried to make a telephone call. But not a single public phone, that we tried, would work at all. So back we went, to the task of satisfying all the regulations. One of them said we could not use our Carnet de Passage en Douane without first going to Lima and having it stamped by the Touring Club. But that would have meant another day's delay, so we switched signals and (for a slightly higher bribe) got a 15 day permit to land Minim in Peru without it.

And so it went on, though the afternoon. But the enclosure where our cars were being held would be locked for the night at five o'clock. And it was almost that, before we finished with the last authority. So June went ahead, to make sure they did not close it, until we got there.

People must have thought I was mad. In all that heat I ran the quarter of a mile or so to the pound. The gates were open so I went to Minim and unlocked her. The guard saw me but did nothing. Since I had a key and made no attempt to move the car, they saw no reason to interfere. Besides, they were helping someone else get his car started. I wondered how long it had been sitting there. No battery power left at all.

Still Patrick didn't come and the guards were looking my way more frequently now. It must have been five o'clock for two of the men headed my way. I sat behind the wheel, holding on firmly, one window open, for the heat was unbearable. They told me it was time to leave. And I told them I was waiting for my husband. We exchanged a few words. They were getting more and more firm but so was I. They were speaking so rapidly I could no longer understand them. And I had resorted to English and kept repeating: "Over my dead body will you keep this car another night". We had reached our impasse when Patrick came running and shouting through the gate. The poor guards looked every bit as relieved as I was.

At the end, all the documents were taken away and I was given a slip of paper. But that made the men let our car go and we parked outside the gates, where I sat and guarded it, while June went off with Tony to pay the agent.

He wanted $ 30 for each car but Tony settled for $ 48 for the two (which was a week's salary for a teacher).

While I was there, a young soldier came by, his gun over his shoulder, and wanted to buy our sewing machine. We did not have one, in the truck, but he could not believe it and all the time June was gone, the soldier went on asking, quietly but very insistently, how much we wanted for our sewing machine. Then we drove to the gates of the dock, where we had to put our cars on the scales, to make sure that they did not weigh more than we had paid for. And ours was all right, because I had been generous in my estimate. But Tony's was overweight. That meant he had to hire a lawyer (who was conveniently available) and pay another bribe. But Tony said he could handle it - they would take a check - so we went out, into the streets of Callao, looking for gasoline. Our tank was almost empty (as required, in a ship) but we soon found a station which had two kinds: 85 octane for 30 cents a gallon and 95 octane for 60 cents. We bought a little of the 30 cent kind and drove around the block but Minim was not happy with it and her motor would not stop, when I turned it off. So we faced the facts and filled her up with the 60 cent kind. Then off we went, into Lima, though the rush hour traffic. But with a driver and a navigator, we made it without any incidents (that I was aware of) and before long, Minim was safely locked up, in the garage that we had rented.

The breakfast at the pension had been good and dinner was available for much less than we were paying in the restaurants, so we tried it that night and the food was dull. But we met an elderly couple who were missionaries in the upper part of the Amazon Basiin, beyond the Andes. And a young couple, just arrived from Germany, who were looking for an apartment. They found one, in a development, but to get to it, they had to cross a barrio (neighborhood) which was so dangerous that a taxi driver wanted $ 4.00 extra to go 600 meters across it. However, they would find another one, soon. And they gave us an address in Lima, so that we could find them and stay with them, on our way back from Tierra del Fuego. But we only had two more nights in Lima, before living in our tent for a while, so we went out to a cafe for dessert. The strawberries and cream were fresh and good, and the Pisco Sours - the national drink of Peru - were similar to whisky sours but we liked them better. The boulevard looked like Paris in the 30's, when there were few Americans and those were young. And sitting there, we saw an Anti Meter Maid at work. She was a young woman, wearing a dark colored dress, with the strap of a leather handbag over her shoulder. And in the bag was a supply of coins, which she fed into the meters in front of her clients' cars, whenever they were needed.

Between times, she would stand back against a building, almost like a lady of the evening. But no one accosted her and she was constantly glancing from one to another of the dozen or so cars in her care, as though she were protecting them from thieves, as well as from the police. Before each car left, the driver would pay her. And when the space was again filled - almost immediately - the new driver would nod briefly to her, as he walked away, evidently authorizing her to look after his car until he came back. Later that evening, Tony came to our room at the pension. He had succeeded in getting his car off the dock but he had run out of money, with all the charges and bribes and fees. And his friends had gone on to Arica in the Rossini. He would need gas, to drive down there, and something for emergencies, along the way, so we lent him $ 90.00 and he gave us a check for it, that we could cash at his father's store, when we got to Arica. Then he left, that night, to drive straight through.

Tony asked for just enough for gas but we thought it better to give him more in case of a breakdown. Besides, he really should eat and perhaps sleep a night in a motel, if he hoped to make a safe journey. We did wonder about getting it back. But as Patrick said, he'd rather trust a smuggler than a government official anywhere.

In the morning, we went to the Touring Club. It was not at the address in the phone book, or the one we were sent to, from there. But on the third try, we found it. The people there could not tell us anything we wanted to know, about routes or weather or insurance. And I decided it would be safer not to let them stamp our Carnet, in case they did it wrong. Then we went to the business district, in the center of the city, to buy car insurance for our trip around South America. The people at the Fenix company (one of the largest) were polite and quite understood what we wanted but unfortunately it was not possible, because all insurance was government controlled and none of it would be valid outside Peru. So we tried another company (Pacifico) and they said exactly the same. They would be glad to sell us car insurance, valid only in Peru, for $ 100 a month but the policy would take 24 hours to prepare. So we declined their offer with thanks and went back to the pension.

Backing Minim out of the garage, we unscrewed the lids of the lockers - the plastic wood was still over the screw heads - and put the hubcaps and mirrors back in place. Then we installed the tachometer and compass and she was back to normal. Tom Follett, the captain of the Sol Reefer, had advised us to look up her agents in Callao and arrange to keep in touch with them, in the spring, in case he could give us a ride home in his ship. Which would save us a great deal of money, as well as being more fun, so we drove to their address. But they had moved to Lima, so we drove back. And while June kept an eye on the truck, I went up in an elevator to their office. The man I spoke to was an Englishman, born in Cuba, and he confirmed that it was impossible to buy insurance in Peru, for other countries, since the industry was nationalized. But we could go ahead without it and try again in Chile.

Coming back, in the spring, we should call him from La Paz in Bolivia on the Telex - he had a machine in his office - and be at the pension in Lima at least three working days before the ship sailed, to give him time to prepare the documents that would be needed before Minim and we could go aboard. If we could not meet the Sol Reefer, he might be able to get us aboard a Polish ship to Cristobal in Panama. But that was all he could think of, apart from the Italian Line. And he had a letter for us, from June's mother in Michigan.

Back at the rented garage, we sorted the gear in Minim. And after changing into our travelling clothes, we packed our good ones, for we would not need them, living in the tent. It was hot, in the afternoon, and I was sunburned (already). But we were very glad to have our truck again. And to be leaving, in the morning, for the desert of southern Peru.

Packing Minim is always a hassle. I seem to spend hours deciding what to put where. For once something is in the bottom of a locker, it is best forgotten. I certainly could get along without high heels for the next part of the trip. Also the Indian neckace I had brought with me. It had been worn only once so far. We'd heard so many stories about jewelry being ripped off in broad daylight that I'd kept it in my handbag, But then at the pension we were told stories of handbags being slashed open on the crowded streets and thieves catching the spilling loot and disappearing in the confusion. So the necklace was tucked away in a suitcase and locked in a closet. At least in the car we had no worries. The only problem was finding somehing when you wanted it. And beside our clothing, it was now necessary to refurbish the cooking department for we would be camping again. The time for decisions had come. What to pack, what to wear, what to buy and where to put it. And you know before you start that nothing will work out quite right.

But first we must go to the National Bank, to get money for Christmas week. And the manageress of the pension told us we would have to wait until the morning for that. So we went out early for dinner. And walking past the National Bank, we noticed that it was open. But presumably not for transactions involving foreign exchange. Dinner at a small Italian style restaurant - Antipasto, Canneloni, Strawberries and Cream, Espresso - was not cheap but very good. And we decided that the Peruvians were nice people. Those we had spoken with seemed to approve of our camping, so we were in bed by nine, anxious to get on with it.

6 - THE LAND OF TWICE CAFE

By nine o'clock in the morning, we had packed our things, paid our bill at the pension and walked to the bank. And though the proceedure for cashing traveller's checks was complex, with various forms to be typed and signed, it did not take long.

Earlier, while Patrick was dressing, I went out into the front hall, where the manageress of the pension sat at a large desk. We figured the number of days we had been there and the meals we'd had. She added the totals on the back of an old envelope and I gave her cash. For some reason I asked for a receipt. The woman stared coldly at me. It was just for my records. You see, I like to keep accounts. It helps to know how much you're spending on a long trip like this. She became quite hostile. Said flatly that she did not give receipts. Besides, she had no paper to write on. I produced a clean white sheet from my bag. This seemed to annoy her even more. It was odd to have seen her so friendly, then suddenly to become so belligerent over a little thing like a receipt. Was she cheating us or the owner of the pension? It really didn't matter. The charges to us were not unreasonable. And today was a big day. South America lay ahead. A hostile desk clerk was the least of my worries.

As we put our bags in the truck, at the garage, a man in Air Force blue uniform - all smiles and charm - took away from the house a very unhappy man, while his children cried. What he had done, we never knew. Obviously, he was being arrested. And clearly the official taking him away did not want us to think badly of Peru. But before we had time to gather any more, they went off in a black, unmarked car.

Our immdiate concern was to back Minim out of the narrow driveway, into the quickly moving traffic and find our way out of Lima to the south.

But in the suburbs, the driving was less hectic and finding a supermarket, we stopped to buy ice and food (we already had water) for the next few days. There we found fish and French bread and vegetables. But each apple or other fruit was separtely marked, its individual price written on it with a black felt pen.

The supermarket was in an ordinary shopping plaza. Lots of shops and lots of parking. And all around were housing tracts. New - few trees yet. Unlike the old residential section of Miraflores with some very beautiful homes set in well tended gardens. And very unlike the old Spanish towns where what wealth there is, is hidden behind high walls. Just ordinary, middle class, admitedly ugly, tract housing. But no worse than the ugliness of the barrios that surrounded so much of Lima. The developments stretched for miles. To the northeast toward the foothills of the Andes and to the southeast along the bay. We found the ring road, a modern highway that passed over busy intersections and led us southward.

At the edge of the city, the road ran straight out, into a desert surprisingly bare, after the lush green of Miraflores - and an hour later, we came to our first control point: A small building, beside the road, full of policemen. While June watched the truck, I took our documents inside and gave the Inspector a copy of the Information Sheet (in Spanish) that we had typed in the Rossini. He seemed glad to have it and after checking a few of the numbers on it, against those in the documents, he allowed us to proceed. Then we drove more than 200 miles though a fine desert, all sand and stones - no cactus - with oases and towns every now and then. Where it says Tunel on that road, you watch out, for it is one lane wide and dark, inside. And to pass a truck, you drive on the dirt shoulder. It was Christmas Eve and there were taxis, each with six men in it, going home for the holiday. And late in the afternoon, we arrived at Nasca.

We knew the men in the taxis were going home, because they were all holding gift wrapped packages.

A mile or so beyond the town, on our right, we saw bushes with tire tracks leading to them, among which ours would hardly be noticed. So we turned off the road and worked our way between the bushes, until we were behind the farthest ones, a quarter of a mile from the road. And there we

SOUTH AMERICA

PERU

LIMA

BOLIVIA

BRAZIL

PARAGUAY

PACIFIC OCEAN

ARGENTINA

CHILE

URUGUAY

ATLANTIC OCEAN

PUERTO
MONTT

USHUAIA

set up our tent, on firm sand, with a clear view across the vast, level desert. While June cooked supper on the tailgate of Minim, I went around, checking our security. And though the bushes were not at all dense, it was impossible to see the tent or the truck - both light brown - from the road. But I could see far enough, through the nearest bushes, to observe anyone coming that way. It was good to be back in the tent again. The door flaps were mildewed a little, from being damp when we folded it, back in Panama. But otherwise, it was the same as ever. Just the view had changed, to the drama of southern Peru. We were far from people but warm and dry - there was a light breeze, under a clear sky - and with the carpet, the tent was very comfortable. And with dinner and wine on the table, it felt as much like home as anywhere I know. As we finished our meal - with fresh melon - the sun went down and the stars came out and the breeze turned cool and there were lights of the town, low in the distance, to our right. And after closing up the truck, we went to bed.

When you are past fifty, you often have to get up in the night. Some time between midnight and dawn, you wake up and at first you resist, because it is warm in bed. But soon you know you will have to go and when camping in a desert, it presents a problem. For if you shine a light, to warn the snakes that you are leaving the tent, it may attract unwanted attention. So you forget the light and step outside, but carefully - if I were a snake, after a plump mose, and some ass stepped on my tail, I would certainly bite his damned leg - and when you feel sure there are none around, you walk a few paces from the tent. Staying well away from shadows, of course. There, you can relieve the situation, though it makes a great deal of noise in the still, desert night. And afterward, you hardly want to go back to bed, because you are wide awake - watching for snakes - and it is so lovely, out there. That is how it was on Christmas morning. But as often happens, the chill drove me back into the tent. And when I woke again, the sun's first rays were lighting up the sky. We had both slept well and got up at once. It was still cool, in the early dawn, and the tent was damp with dew. But there were no bugs, so we set the breakfast table outside. And as we ate in silence, a man passed by.

He was far off - maybe two hundred yards - walking from right to left, across our view an old man, slightly stooped and all in black, - with a white sack over his shouler and his dog going in front of him. Somehow, it seemed, he made a living in that place. But how? He was not after firewood, the sack was too small. Perhaps small mammals, with the dog? We never found out. But people had lived there many years ago, for there were lines aross the desert, we had read, so long they could only be seen from the air, laid out with great precision by an ancient civilization. And maybe the man we saw that morning was descended from those people.

As the sun rose, the desert warmed up quickly. And by the time we had done our chores - June washing the dishes, while I checked the engine - it was hot. But after folding the tent and stowing our gear, we headed back to the road. And with the airconditioner going, we were soon cool again. The road went south to the coast, then southeast along it, climbing over rocky headlands and dropping down to run along the beaches between them. At the headlands, it would wind and twist, often with a sheer unguarded drop on one side. And along the beaches, there were drifts of sand on it. In some places, it was beach sand, blown onto the road by the wind. But in other places, there were great hills of sand, hundreds of feet high, on the other side. And some of that slid down, onto the road. Where the sand was shallow, it was no problem. But where it was deeper, we had to go faster to get through a drift. Then Minim would slip and slide across the road and back, until her tires bit down through it again.

Lunch was on a high bluff, overlooking the Pacific Ocean - the wind was less, up there - and later, we stopped to buy gas in a small town where they advertised Inca Cola. When in Peru, you drink what the Peruvians do. Once. But it was really horrible, to our taste. So we washed it down with locally made Coca Cola and continued on our way. At the end of a long curving beach the road goes up a hill - through a town that appears to be deserted - then northeast, climbing up into a high desert. And an hour or so later, we dropped down into a bright green oasis. It was in a valley, between bare hills, and there was a village, where the road crossed it. But the time had come to find a camp site, so we turned off the road, to the right, and followed a track used by farmers, along a sharp, clear line between lush green vegetation and barren desert.

But the track ended at a farm, so we came back to a place, as far as we could get from anyone's house, where it ran along a sandy ledge, overlooking the oasis. And there we set up our tent, where the ledge curved out, above the green vegetation, but the track took a shorter route across the corner. There was no question of not being seen there. But since the track only led to farm land, it should only be used by farm people, who would be unlikely to bother us, for one night. Besides, it was Christmas. People went past, behind our tent, whistling or carrying radios playing music. And there was one man, quite drunk, who waved his arms like an amateur tight rope walker. But he was still on the track when he disappeared around a corner.

It seemed odd that no one spoke to us. We would nod or wave when someone walked by but no one stopped. They might be afraid or perhaps simply not interested. The few houses clinging to the side of the oasis were plain mud squares with roofs of thatch made from the tall grasses growing along the ditches. Some of the buildings had been whitewashed once. There were small barns and corrals made of unfinished planks or rough tree trunks. A chicken or two, a tired old mule, a skinny dog. In the yards were big clay urns - four or five feet high - used to bake the family bread. But the houses were quiet. There were few signs of activity. And the young people walking by   high cheek bones, bronze skin   looked shabbily dressed. They were Indians but not at all like those we knew in Central America. These people, in their shoddy European dress with their cheap transistor radios, looked beaten.

Soon it was dark and I rigged a light over Minim's tailgate, for June to cook supper. And when we went to bed, the only sound was of rushing water, somewhere below us. Before dawn, several people went by, including one with a yappy dog that disapproved of our tent. And by five thirty, the sky was clear and blue overhead. Small birds sang in the bushes near us. And farther away, we could see fields of corn and rice, with tall trees like poplars between them. Near the tent, the ledge we were on dropped straight down to the rushing stream we had heard in the night. And peering over it, I could see that the firm white sand was only six inches thick. Then the land turned to soft, brown rock. But it was cool that early, at 3,500 feet. And we had some problems. June's stomach was giving trouble after the fine meals in Lima. I had been chewed by sand flies. And when I started Minims engine, it sounded rough. So we were anxious to move on, and left right after breakfast.

But there was a junction ahead, where one road went southeast toward Arica and another went northeast to Arequipa - the White City - which they said was very fine. We might not be back that way and it was only 35 miles from the junction, so we told the customs officer at the control point we would like to see it. And he asked us to take a police officer with us. He was a slim young man in civilian clothes - probably a lieutenant of detectives - quiet, polite and highly intelligent. He chatted easily, telling us how things were improvinmg for the ordinary man, in Peru. And in due course, he asked - with equal enthusiasm - what we were doing. By then I had decided that he was either being completely open with us - relaxing, on holiday - or he was a brilliant interrogator. So I played it both ways, telling him of our travels but stressing the hope that our work as writers might lead to a better understanding between his people and ours.

The accent of southern Peru is a bit different from others and I had trouble following the rapid conversation. He talked proudly of new collective farms - they were working out well in his area. That would explain some of the agricultural areas we had just driven through, where houses were of good quality and neat. And there were schools and clinics along the road and signs of expensive irrigation systems. But much farm land, he said, was still in the hands of a few companies. There the labor lived poorly, he claimed. His city of Arequipa was traditionally progressive. He said little about Lima, except that it was too big and too dirty and too conservative. But he had hope and was a happy man.

Arequipa is indeed a fine city, built of white rock from the snow-capped volcano Misti, on whose shoulder it stands, some 7,500 feet above sea level. As we approached, it gleamed in the desert sunlight ahead of us. And when we got there, our friend the policeman insisted on showing us around. There were many narrow, interesting strets. And a convent for Franciscan monks and nuns who never speak. And in the middle, a large Plaza de Armas (literally Parade Ground but in fact a public square) with

green lawns and palm trees and neat pathways. And along its sides were
buildings with rows of arches. I wanted to take a picture of the square,
from the second floor of a building. And a policeman in uniform, standing
there, told me it was forbidden. But our friend the detective went over to
him and said a few quiet words in his ear and led me through the building,
clear up onto the roof, to take my picture. Then he gave me his home
address and told us to look him up if we came back to Arequipa and took
his leave. And since we wanted to be in Arica that night, we drove out of
the city, back to the junction and off down the road to the southeast.

*While Patrick gazed at the White City, I guarded the car. Happily, a
family stopped to chat. They noticed the license plate and wanted to know
how in the world we had managed to get an American car into Peru. Their
son was going to school in Chicago. If only there were some way for him
to bring back a car. They asked us to lunch with them but Patrick had told
Tony we would be in Arica to collect the loan and was determined to
charge ahead. The next several miles of road wound through deep gorges
and craggy hills left by centuries of Misti's volcanic eruptions. The land
was nearly worthless. There were occasional ranches tucked in gullies. But
little sign of life, until we passed some working mines, then planted fields.*

It was nearly five in the afternoon when we came to the border, after
going through two control points. And the Peruvian officials demanded 5
copies of a Passenger List for our vehicle, on a printed form. But they had
no such forms available. And of course we could not proceed, without
them. Probably they just wanted a bribe but we did not know how much
it should be or who to give it to. And while I was trying to figure that out,
the driver of another car walked in. He was Peruvian and had plenty of the
forms with him, so he kindly gave me some and we were cleared to leave
the country. The Chilean offcials were not looking for bribes, so far as we
could tell. And they took their time, inspecting us. They carefully recorded
the serial numbers of our typewriter and electric heater (worth $ 15.00
new, five years ago). Also, there was an hour's time change at the border.
And by the time we were free to go, it was eight o'clock at night. A
couple of miles from the border we found a track down to the beach. But
there were poor-looking shacks nearby and we thought it unwise to camp

there, so we headed into Arica   it was not far away - and went looking
for Tony.

But with no street map, we had trouble finding his house. We would ask
a passer-by for directions and perhaps because our Spanish was quite good,
he would rattle off a stream on instructions, like: "Go down to the second
corner - no, the third one - and turn left and follow that road - No, there's
a shorter way   Listen, go back to the second corner, behind you   "
When we found the street, it went through a quiet suburb of small, neat
houses and ran into another one, at an angle. But we still had not come to
the number he gave us. And that was the end of the street. We drove
around, looking for a continuation of it, but did not find one. Perhaps there
was no such number. I knocked on the door of a house near the end.

The lady who answered listened to my story and smiled a distant smile
and went to the phone, in her living room. And a moment later, she was
back. Tony would be right over. As I walked back to Minim, he came
across the road - his father's house was on the curve, where the two streets
joined   and when we explained our problem, he offered to show us a
place to camp, on the beach. Or take us to a motel, in the valley. It took
June about three microseonds to choose the motel and soon we were
following his gray car across town.

The valley is an oasis, running inland from the sea, with tall trees and
many houses, for Arica is a resort. And the Motel Azapa, set well back
from the road, looked very nice. They had new, deluxe units for $ 22.00
a day and older cabins for $ 8.00 but nothing in between, so we took a
cabin and it was fine. There was a paved, secure parking place for the
truck and from it, we walked along a winding path, through the trees, to
a small, wooden building   just a bedroom and bath and behind it, a
covered porch - in a garden of flowering shrubs.

*The accommodations were marginal but the setting was lovely. A
perfect summer's night. Surrounded by hibiscus, orchids dripping from the
trees, so much green after days of sand and rock. I could have stayed on
the porch all night. But Patrick was hungry and it was nearly midnight by
then.*

The restaurant had an open patio, where they were still serving drinks and omelets, under the bright stars. And when Tony left, we went to bed, glad to be in Chile. We had come a thousand miles from Lima, so I was up early in the morning, while it was still cool, to check Minim's engine. But that day, it refused to start. I changed the spark plugs and the fuel filter (the two most likely things) but still it was no go. And since we were in a town, I decided to let someone else find the trouble, rather than get any dirtier. Soon Tony came by, with the money we had lent him, and asked if there was anything we wanted. Insurance for the truck was one thing, so he took us in his car, to get some. And his three friends - the man and two girls from the Rossini - were with him, so they came along for the ride. But one insurance agent was away, in the south of Chile. And the next one had not been seen in his office for three days. The Auomobile Club was closed on Saturdays. And Lloyds' agent only adjusted claims. By the time we left him, it was noon and all offices were closed until Monday, so we gave up.

At least we were able to see a little of Arica while we chased after non-existent insurance men. Tony claimed that no one bought insurance, anyway. It was much too expensive. And by that time we were getting less and less interested. Driving was certainly not as hazardous, so far, as it had been in Mexico or Central America. Or in the States, for that matter. The roads were two lanes. There were relatively few cars and almost no pedestrians except in the middle of towns. We seldom drove at night and were too interested in looking out of the window to speed. An accident would be just bad luck.

But we had a fine breakfast of fruit juices and empanadas (small pies) in an open fronted shop, all of us sitting in a row on stools, facing a long counter where the juices were made. There were all kids of fruit, stacked behind the counter, and whatever you wanted was put in a blender - one of several which whirred away, while the pies were getting hot. We caused a slight stir, because we were the only people around who spoke English. But chattering among ourselves, we were regarded with friendly curiosity - like strange, harmless birds - by the local people. Arica is an old sea port - there is still a fort on the hill, overlooking the harbor - but more recently, it has become a vacation spot for the people of northern

Chile. And it was a pleasant place to be. But we had things to do. First I found an adaptor plug, so that I could charge the batteries in my electric razor. Then we went looking for a mechanic friend of Tony's, to fix Minim's engine. He was not at his garage, so we drove around, asking various people where he might be, until we passed him in the street, going the other way.

After a brief chase, we caught up with him. Of course he was in the middle of a job and had two more waiting but he could spare a moment to take a look at our truck and when we got there, he found the trouble. The rotor in the distributor had worn out and damaged the cap. Luckily I had both parts in stock, so he changed them and the engine ran as smoothly as ever. But before I could stop him, he took a screwdriver and altered the mixture of the carburettor. Which was a pain in the ass, because I had it just right. It was my own stupid fault, for not checking the rotor myself. And nearly always, if you let a mechanic fix something, he puts something else out of whack, so I should have been ready for it. Now there was nothing I could do but watch the engine for a few days, check its fuel consumption and figure how much he had altered it, so that I could correct it.

While he watched the machanic work, another friend of Tony's dropped by. His name was Colin Smith-Hughes or something like that and very English. Be was blond, blue eyed, thin and pale. Yet he spoke not a word of English, nor had anyone in his family for several genetations.

Lunch at the motel was good and we thought it cheap, at the rate of exchange we got for our dollars. But the restaurant was almost empty and Tony explained that things were difficult in Chile, just then. The cost of living had gone up 340 percent in a year. And the owner of the motel, whom he knew, could only survive because his mortgage was paid off.

But it was hot and sunny. And birds were singing, in the trees. And there was classial music, at the restaurant. And to get coffee, you had to ask or it twice. If you said cafe', they would give you instant coffee. But if you wanted real coffee,you had to say cafe' cafe'. And so, for us, Chile became the Land of Twice Cafe'

Tony also told us that the barrio on the coast, between Arica and the border of Peru, would soon be a port for Bolivia, with a road and railroad leading to it. But there would be a special system, so that people goimg from Peru to Chile would not have to pass through four frontiers in a row. Then he and his friends left, while June and I went off to get things ready for the journey south, through Chile.

We took Minim to a garage, where they cleaned her, inside and out - including the engine - and greased her old joints and changed her oil and its filter. And when they finished, she felt (and looked) a great deal better. Then we filled our red ice box and went to a supermarket, to buy food.

We saw a sign for a supermarket and rushed to it. It was a market but less than super. Then we toured the crude shelves of rusted and dusty cans and began to spot interesting things. There were locally grown and cured olives that had a very different and good taste. Which, of course, Patrick refused to touch. But he did find a huge bottle of fruit juice concentrate. And then the best part: Bottles of Tia Maria, Gand Marnier and Mumm's Champaagne, all for prices like a dollar. The labels were exactly like the ones we knew, except that the fine print was in Spanish. What luck! We found some canned fish. Vegeables were dead or non-existant. There were saltines. The rest really didn't matter. You can feed Patrick anything as long as there is a final course of Tia Maria.

Back at the motel, we stowed the food in Minim. And apart from the suitcases in our unit, she was ready to go. But we were invited to have dinner with Tony and his friends, that night, so we changed into our good 'shore going' clothes. The wind sighed in the casuarina trees and palms rustled and doves cooed outside our cabin, that evening. But we had been bitten by mosquitoes, for they too like oases.

This would have been a good night to wear my Indian necklace but I couldn't put my hand on it. Had I tucked it into a sock? Or was it just folded into a blouse? In all the hurry in Lima, I hadn't noticed it. And again we were in a rush. I'd have to sort things out in the morning.

Dinner was at the casino, by the sea, which was owned and run by the government and though I would not usually have left Minim in an open paking lot at night, she was quite safe there. For the place was crawling with tough-looking types, each with a prominent bulge - doubtless a gun - under his gray suit. And as we went up the stone steps, three of them checked us out, their eyes staring at us out of hard, unsmiling faces. But we were not interested in gambling and though it was past eight o'clock, there was a table for us in the dining room.

Tony's friend (Mario) was from Arica and had degrees in mathematics and business administration but found he could only get menial jobs in the United States. So he came back, with his wife - a thin girl in a blonde wig - whom he met there. And Karen, a friend of hers, was travelling with Tony. But those two would be going to California again soon, with an old Mercedes and an old desk, to sell as antiques. I asked Mario about the passage from Lima to Arica in the Rossini and he said it was rough. So it seems that we were lucky, not to have been aboard her. For the slow, lumberinmg motion of a ship like that would surely have upset June.

By eleven, the dining room was full, so we moved to the night club in the casino, to drink Pisco and Coke and listen to a rock and roll band. June does not dance - what kind of woman would agree to go backwards? - and I had not done it for thirty years, so we sat there, like tourists in a boiler factory, while the four young people danced.

I danced once with Patrick when we were first married. That was a time somewhere between the jitterbug and the twist. It didn't work out.

Being very polite, they invited us to join them. And not having the slightest idea what to do, to that kind of music, we declined their offers, with suitable thanks. But after a while, Karen came and stood beside me, insisting that I give it a try, while her friends backed her up. And before I could think of a way to get out of it, we were on the dance floor. I glanced around, to find out what the score was. Most people seemed to be scooching bugs into the floor with both feet at once, so I did something similar and looked up, to see what Karen was doing. But she was out of sight. A man was facing me, a few feet away, bobbing up and down. And as he drifted off, to my left, I saw Karen behind him. Evidently one did not dance close to one's partner but I tried to keep her in sight, while the noise continued. Tony went by, smiling happily around him, but I did not see his partner. And a couple of times, I got a clear view of Karen, who seemed to be enjoying herself. But when it was over, she thanked me earnestly for the dance and suddenly I felt a hundred years old.

At midnight, the floor show started. A man stood in the middle of the dance floor, with spotlights on him, and made the audience sing (in Spanish) "Arica is a city with a spring-like climate" ... over and over, for maybe half an hour. Then another man did tricks with two tambourines, for a while. And finally, a young man with a guitar came on, with a tall blonde girl. Backed up by the band, they sang popular songs, some in Spanish, some in English. And between the songs, the girl would freeze, staring down at the young man with a fixed smile, while he told long off-color jokes, made clear by gestures, grimaces and appropriate (?) sounds. The audience liked them, for they applauded each joke and chattered among themselves, after it. But at 1:30 AM, the entertainment finished and people went back to dancing.

There was a curfew in Chile, so I asked Tony about going home so late. At first he laughed it off, saying it was more to get people to go to bed, than anything else. And it had been put back to 3:00 AM on Saturday nights in Arica, so we would have no trouble, getting back to our motel. But then he told me quietly to be careful, going south. Usually the curfew started at nine in the evening and if we were out after that, we stood a chance of being shot by some over-zealous young soldier. With which sobering thought, we said goodbye and left the young people to their dancing, while we went back to bed.

It was late when we awoke, to the sound of a man sweeping the yard, outside our cabin, with a broom made of sticks. And as we packed our things, June discovered that her necklace - the only thing of value she had brought with her - was missing from a small purse which was locked in her suitcase. Carefully we searched, all through her clothes, around the cabin, all through the truck. But it was not there. It was one of her nicest things, made by American Indians of abalone and coral and torquoise and silver. And as we came to realize that it was indeed gone, we were both very sad.

We believed it was stolen by the manageress of the German pension in Lima who tried not to give me a receipt for our bill and was angry when I insisted on it. And who told us we had to go to the bank, the morning we were leaving, which gave her an excellent opportunity to search through our belongings.

We reported the loss of June's necklace to the manager of the motel, who made some enquiries about it. But none of his peole had seen it - and we were pretty sure it was stolen in Lima - so we gave him our address, in case it should turn up later. And it was after midday when we headed south, out of Arica. Soon the road turned inland and went winding through the foothills, between the Andes and the Pacific, following valleys of sand with mountains of rock on either side. Tony had told us that the 'real' desert started south of Arica. And after going through southern Peru, we thought he was being provincial. But he was not. The desert of northern Chile was far more bleak and barren than anything we had seen before. In some places, rain had never been recorded. And as far a we could tell, nothing - animal or vegetable - lived there.

We left Arica with half a tank of gas, because there was a town on the map, about 120 miles away. But when we got there, it was just a control point and a restaurant, beside the road in a narrow pass. And rather than go back, we bought a few gallons (at a high price) from a man there. But it was windy in the pass and as he poured the gas from a can, not all of it went into our tank, though a fair amount of sand did.

What a day. The necklace business really upset us. And now we had done another stupid thing. We just wanted to leave and had not taken the time to search for gasoline. There are always stations on the outskirts of towns. We had both agreed there was no sense in turning back when we didn't find one. And now to find that the town marked on the map was nothing more than half a dozen shacks housing a few army guards and a ramshackle restaurant. I went into the restaurant to ask for gas, just in case. They had nothing. Not even a customer. Not even the smell of rancid fat. I bought a soda. It was warm. There was no refrigeration, either.

Outside the wind blew steadily. You had to shield your face. You didn't dare open your eyes or your mouth. The poor soldiers stationed there looked truly miserable. They also weren't very helpful. And it took a great deal of tact on Patrick's part to get enough gasoline to move on. We asked if the wind always blew like that. The guards nodded yes. They figured out exactly how much we would need to get to the next station and didn't pour

164

an ounce more than necessary. At that price and with the sand content, we didn't care. All that mattered was that we didn't have to go back.

Beyond the pass, the road ran straight through the desert and after a while, we came to a gas station. Then on we went, at fifty miles an hour, for the road was paved and smooth. Which seemed odd, in that desolate place, until we saw that there were side roads, now and then, leading to copper mines.

There was even less traffic here. An occasional truck. And no development along the road. Not a house, not a corral, not a fence, not a sign of vegetation that might support life.

About seven in the evening, we came to an army control point at a small oasis. And when they had finished checking us, I asked the officer in charge if we could camp for the night under some trees, a quarter of a mile ahead. He was a big, fat man and after breathing heavily a couple of times, he said: "Why not? Go ahead". So we went to the place I had indicated. It was a small hollow, between the main road and one that forked off, toward a village. And under the trees was a level spot, with some bushes to break the wind, where we set up our tent, with Minim close to it on the other side.

Before we finished, a Chinese gentleman called Thomas Loo came by. I had spoken briefly with him at the control point and knew that he ws going south, with his two nephews. But he was concerned about our camping there - he said it would be windy and cold and there would be bugs - and offered us a room at his house, in the next town. Finally we assured him that we were all right and he drove on, after warning us to get gas at the next station ahead, to take us as far as Antofagasta.

As Mr. Loo drove off, he said: "Please tell people in America not to think too badly of us. Tell them we are trying to do what is right." And I regretted having refused his invitation. He seemed to want to tell us more but couldn't, not with the soldiers nearby.

When the tent was furnished, June looked in all our socks for her necklace. But it was not in any of them. And we decided that we must face its loss and forget it. Otherwise, it would be on our minds and spoil the fine trip we were having. Then she cooked dinner, while I made a really bad drink, of Pisco and lemon concentrate, that we drank, anyway.

By nine o'clock, when the curfew started, it was dark but the sky was clear, with many stars. Gusts of wind swept though the small oasis, now and then, but in the hollow with the trees and bushes around us, we were protected from it. I have a note, written that night, which says 'Tenting has a charm of its own that nothing else can equal. The sudden house in a lonely corner. The privacy and peace. The wind and stars and cozy shelter'. And well content, we went to bed.

It was four in the morning when I woke up. The time had come to go outside. I put on some clothes, unzipped the tent and stepped out, into a beautiful, calm desert night. What I had in mind would make less noise, against a tree. And there was one close by - its branches outlined by the stars - so I started toward it. Then I heard a dull, metallic thud.

The only thing I know which makes that noise is a machine gun being set on the ground, ready to fire at someone. And the soldiers would doubtless get points toward promotion, for shooting a curfew breaker. Quickly and quietly, I went back.

As I zipped up the tent - slowly, not to make a noise - I saw the yellow beam of a Chilean Army flashlight, beyond the tree. But lying on the ground, in our hollow, we were below the line of fire of a machine gun, sited over there. So we were safe enough, in bed, even if they did fire a burst of bullets at some fleeting shadow. And after convincing myself that I did not need to go out, I fell asleep.

When we woke again, the curfew was over. And outside the tent, it was cool and clear and sunny and still. We had both had a fine night's sleep, so we set about making breakfast. Soon a breeze came through the oasis, moving the branches of a tree beside Minim. And the dry, hard twigs made a squeaky grating sound the kind that sets your teeth on edge - against the metal. But by using clothes pegs, we found we could hold the branches back, without damaging them. And as we packed up to go, the air was still cool but the sun was already hot.

An hour later, we picked up a hitch hiker an Indian boy, standing alone beside the road - in the middle of a vast, empty desert. June made a seat of boxes and cushions, between the two regular ones, and moved over, to let him in. His Spanish was hard for us to understand but we gathered that he was a student, 16 years old, going home for the holidays.

Patrick thought he was Indian, but I didn't. Probably more Spanish than anything. His name was certainly Spanish, for he showed us his travel documents. One was a much folded piece of greenish paper giving all the dates, names and places pertinent to his existence. The other was a letter written by his father, saying that the son was a good boy, had no police record, and asking that he be granted a safe passage. Both had been heavily and officially stamped. He guarded them carefully for without them he could not leave his home town. He claimed to be one of the lucky few to have such papers.

At noon, we hit a rough section of highway and had to slow down to 25 miles an hour. But after a while, it improved and soon we came to the turnoff to Antofagasta. There, at the control point, we left the boy off - hoping that he would find another lift - and went down to the coast, to the big, sprawling city, all the same drab color as the desert, where the copper from the mines is shipped out. All the shops were shut for the siesta but we bought some fruit from a cart on the street and went back into the mountains, to join the highway at another control point, south of the city. And there was our Indian boy, waiting for a ride.

That was a problem, for we only had two seats and when June rigged a temporary one, between them, she had to use it - putting her legs around the gear lever and being careful not to hit the instruments - which was uncomfortable. Also, I had to drive all the way, instead of our taking turns, and we felt that we had to make polite conversation (in Spanish). So while we were glad to give someone a lift to the next town, we did not want to take him with us for hundreds of miles. But the boy came toward us with a big smile and we could hardly turn him away. When the soldiers had inspected everything in our truck and checked all our papers, they allowed us to proceed. And once again, he was in the right hand seat.

The road went up to 7,000 feet above sea level - over a vast, open desert running parallel to the coast, far inland. And as we hummed along, we gave the boy a peach. He thanked us politely and bit a tiny piece out of it, which he turned over in his mouth - staring thoughtfully out of the window - until it was gone. Then he took another tiny bite and did the same thing. He must have taken an hour, to finish it. But he never spilled a drop of the juice. And when he was done, the pit was bare.

Our passenger's luggage consisted of a paper bag that held little more than a magazine. He read when the conversation lulled from what looked like a sporting monthly printed with vividly colored ink that came off on everything. When we asked what he did about eating and sleeping along the way, he showed little interest. Evidently the game was to move during all the daylight hours. Since you could not travel at night, you slept by the road or wherever chance left you and ate when there was something to eat. Oh to be sixteen.

There was no shelter in the desert, from wind or view. But toward evening, the highway came near the coast, on the map. So we decided to go down there, for the night. As we approached the junction, we passed two trucks. And we dropped the boy off, ahead of them, hoping that one of them would give him a lift. But if they did not, he could wait there, by a posada (inn) and a gas station, for another one. When he got out, we said "Hasta la vista" (see you) and walking away, he waved and said "Good bye" But I am pretty sure that those were the only two words of English he knew. Then we took the side road, toward the coast. Winding down through a canyon, we looked for camp sites but found none where we could get out of sight. And the town of Taltal, by the sea, was drab and poor. So we went along the old road, one lane wide, that clings to the side of the coastal mountains.

Six miles later, it cut across a tiny headland, leaving a ledge below it that we could get to, with the truck. And between the road and the ledge, at the corner, was a wall of rock. There were no people, in either direction, so we pulled off the road - our tires left no tracks on the hard, brown rock - and I walked along the ledge, while June followed in Minim, until we were out of sight, behind the high, jagged wall.

We had crossed the Tropic of Capricorn that day and were beyond the tropics, in the southern temperate zone. But we might have been on another planet, in that dismal place. On our right, brown, forbidding mountains swept up into the sky. On our left, the ocean - silvery and glinting   lay far below us. And between them, everything was barren rock. The wind was off the ocean but it was less strong, in front of the mountains (a fact which is easier to prove than to believe) so we pitched our tent. And there was a rowboat, near the shore - though we did not see anyone in it - so we had our dinner before darkness came, to avoid using a light. One truck came rattling along the road, behind us. And a few sea birds looked us over. Otherwise, we saw no sign of life. But there were holes in the rocks near us - some of them large - and we wondered what might live inside them.

At nightfall, a dark cloud came slowly down the mountains. And the wind died. The whole scene was dramatic and ominous, like something out of a horror movie. But the tent, by magic, made even that place seem like home. Inside it, we were among familiar things - our stools and cushions and clothes - and in our warm bed, we went peacefully to sleep.

Thank heavens for night. We could no longer see that tower of brown rock piled precariously above us or the sharp rim of our narow ledge so close to the tent. We had seen no shore directly beneath us. Could it be that our ledge was in fact jutted out over the sea? In the darkness, the only sound was from the waves. And you close your eyes and remember that nice State Park on Lake Erie with its yellow sand and soft pine needles and the attendants who locked the gates at ten o'clock. And you go to sleep.

We awoke to a cool, misty dawn. Everything around us was gray and still, with just the rumble of waves on the rocks below. The rowboat had gone, so the curfew was over and we could leave. But the place felt less menacing, at the beginning of a new day - or perhaps we were getting used to it - so there was no hurry. And after breakfast, June did our accounts. We were spending more, per day, than we had planned. But the cost of gasoline was high and the distances were great. Even bad gas was more than a dollar a gallon, in Chile. And South America is large - Brazil alone is bigger than the whole United States - so we would have to be careful. I figured our gas consumption and reset Minim's carburettor to the most economical mixture. Then I adjusted the speed at which the engine idled and we packed up to go.

We did not meet any trucks on the old coast road, which was a relief, for we would have had to pass them on the outside, going south. But there were several grinding up the long hill, from Taltal to the high desert. And near the control point, on the main road, we may have seen our passenger again. The soldiers who inspected us were curt and abrupt and no civilians were hanging around, near them. But as we drove off, there was a group of people, standing well back from the road, a short distance ahead. And among them, I thought I saw the Indian boy. I was driving, at the time, and June did not think it was him, so I continued to accelerate. If it was him I told myself - he would get a lift soon. In any case, he was no worse off than the others, waiting there. And probably it was not him - he should be far ahead of us - but I could not be sure, And I worried that we might have disappointed him. as we drove across the wide desert.

Later that morning, we came to an agricultural inspection point. We were getting quite used to police checks and thought we had all the information they wanted ready for them when we stopped. But this time the official asked to see our food locker. And he took all the fruit I had bought in Antofagasta. Shades of Arizona. I was furious. And he was just as sympathetic as the Arizona border people. I was welcome to sit right there and eat every bit of it. So into the refuse bin went several beautiful oranges. As we drove off, the man stood gazing thoughtfully down the highway, while a couple of little vagabonds retrieved the fruit.

Then the road went down to the sea and we had lunch by a group of small wooden houses on a sandy beach. They were painted various colors and looked like vacation homes but they seemed to be empty, though it was summer there. And we wondered where people who could afford such things would come from. At the town of Caldera, the road went inland again, up a long, steep hill. And an old man was pushing a heavily laden cart up it, with a young boy. So we stopped to help them. The cart had four wheels, though it was rather top heavy, so we got out our nylon line and took it in tow. And as I drove Minim slowly up the hill, June helped them balance it.

That was slow? We all thought the cart and its load would surely disintegrate. It leapt like a startled jackrabbit in every conceivable direction with the most pitiful groans and screams I've ever heard. Its owner and I

*looked at each other with panic on our faces and raced up the hill after the
car. The youngster with him reached the top first. He stood with Patrick
next to the cart, grinning happily, while the old man and I panted and
sweated up the hill. I think Patrick offered to tow it a bit farther, but the
gentleman wisely declined.*

The desert was changing, now - becoming more like those in the United
States, with enough vegetation to support animals - and we passed the
Carnegie Institute observatory (a sign said so) white against the blue sky,
high on a distant hill, with a dirt road leading across a valley toward it.
We thought of going to see the people, there. But we had not come all that
way to talk to Americans, so we kept on going. And late in the afternoon,
we came to a control point, where the corporal in charge was rude and
angry, because our license plates said 'MINIM' instead of having proper
numbers. It was time we found a place to camp, for the night. But though
we tried, we did not find anywhere that looked safe. And twenty minutes
later, we came to another control point, where a fat, jolly sereant quickly
checked our papers. When I showed him the kitchen in the back of our
truck, he said (in English) "beautiful". We were welcome to Chile. There
were two 'campings' (campgrounds) ahead of us, one nearby in La Serena
and the other on a beach, 22 miles away.

*We were overjoyed. Instead of stealing off the road at last light and
packing up hurriedly at dawn, we wold be able to pitch the tent in a
campground and relax. There would be toilets, perhaps even showers. And
fellow campers. For the guard assured us that camping was an acceptable
sport in Chile.*

La Serena is a pleasant town, with shady boulevards and stone statues
and a fine old tourist hotel, looking down toward the sea. It had no tourists at that time, but the market was busy - there were fresh figs or sale -
and in the small shops, we found wine, Pisco, ginger ale and food.

*I had never tasted a fresh fig before. The fresh fruit and a Fig Newton
have absolutely nothing in common. We shopped from the street stalls first
and then crossed the street to stores where we found mostly canned goods.
There was no fresh fish or meat in sight, so we stocked up on crackers and
canned mackerel. At least we wouldn't go hungry.*

It was a relief, after being in the desert, to stroll along the sidewalk, from shop to shop. And the people were nice. In one place, I was teasing June in Spanish when I noticed the young girl who was waiting on us. She was standing quite still, looking away, pretending not to hear us. But making a purchase was complicated, because of their system. First you decide what you want and tell the sales girl, who adds up the cost of the items and gives you the paper tape, from the machine. Then you go to the cashier, who takes your money and gives you a receipt for it. Then you go back to the girl, who exchanges the receipt for your purchases. So the owner of the shop can check the goods taken from stock (by the sales girl) against the tapes (which the cashier has). Then he can check the tapes against the receipts (that the girl has) and the receipts against the cash (from the cashier). Which must be a lot of work but evidently he feels he has to do it, to prevent anyone from stealing from him.

When our shopping was done, we went down to the 'camping' (they use the English word to mean a campground) which was in a grove of shady trees, off the main road, toward the beach. There were plenty of spaces but no people around and in the middle was a low house, probably the owner's, with a large black dog lying beside the doorstep. As I left the truck, the dog growled, so I growled back - I always talk to dogs - but evidently I said the wrong thing, for he got slowly to his feet, as though he were about to stroll over and bite me. And I went back into the truck.

If Pattrick would stop trying to talk to dogs in their own language, he wouldn'y get into so much trouble. A two-legged growler unnerves even the most gentle canine.

Then a tall, thin, fair haired man came out of the house. Indeed he was the owner - the dog went back to his place - and we were welcome. There were showers in a hut behind his house and he would light the gas in the water heater, so that we could use them in half an hour. He only had a two month season and it had hardly started yet, so there were no other campers. But he grew things and sold insurance and it all worked out. And after five minutes' conversation, he switched to English.

It took them quite a while to discover that they were both Englishmen. They had both left England about the same time, too. Shortly after the war,

Mr. Holloway had been in the British navy. His ship docked briefly in a Chilean port and after the war, he returned to marry and stay.

Soon his daughter - young and blonde - came by and when he introduced us, she answered in English, with no accent. Then he asked us to take any site we liked and went off. Before dark, out tent was set up and June was cooking dinner. We were clean and had everything we needed and there was a light breeze coming through the door of the tent. The tree, over the tent, had round leaves and long, thin ones on the same branch. And at nine o'clock, we went to bed. It was eight in the morning when we woke up. That is a long time to sleep (eleven hours) but we must have relaxed, in the safety of the campground, after the tension - which we had not acknowledged, at the time - of camping in the desert.

After breakfast, I was reading the manual on the Scout II and discovered that it must not be towed unless the engine is running, or in neutral. So we should not go down a mountain with the engine off, as we had done in Costa Rica. And we had driven it 115,000 miles before we found that out. The problem is that those manuals say so much. And the good stuff, like 'How to avoid ruining the transmission', is all mixed up with the boring stuff, like 'How to change gear'. So it takes a real effort of will to plow though it all. But I ran through the details of the Great Descent - that we had made in Costa Rica - in my mind. And I was fairly certain that it had not done any harm to the transmission. Certainly it was not apparent, from the truck's behaviour. So I decided not to worry about the past, but to be careful not to get into a situation like that again if we could help it.

The sky was overcast and it was cool but there were bugs around our camp site, under the trees. And the ground was black dirt, which tracked into our tent, onto the red carpet. So we decided to try the other campground, down the coast. But after folding our tent, we first drove into La Serena. It was New Year's Eve, the banks were closed and the manager of the tourist hotel said he would not have enough money to cash a $ 20 travellers check until 8:00 PM. So we bought the essentials - fish, fruit, a note book and bread in the small shops, around the market.

We found the central market. A steel and glass skylighted structure that must have covered two city blocks. A parking place was harder to locate but we did find one along a side of the building. Then ensued the standard argument about the safety of the car. This time I won. A substantial looking gray haired man standing near the car agreed with me. Besides, he would be right there and keep an eye on it for us. He was selling bread from huge baskets. When the contents of one seemed low, a stack of shelves on wheels came thundering down the sidewalk from the nearby bakery and the basket was refilled. He would evidently be there for some time. So we bought a couple of loaves and left him in charge.

Inside, the shoppers walked along the center aisle. On each side were stalls, neat and clean. I was sorry that we had bought so much stuff the day before. But our space was limited so that I had to content myself with some fresh meat and fish. The meat was kept in walk-in refrigerators with fine, varnished wood doors. And the fish, in tubs of ice, was cleaned for us and then wrapped in newspaper to carry home. Patrick would periodically disappear through a side door to check on Minim. All was well in the street too. Reluctantly, we returned to the car with our few purchases.

About a block from the market, on a quiet side street, Patrick remembered that he needed another note book. He parked quickly and dashed around the corner back to the market, leaving the keys in the ignition and his window half open. Doors and windows were shuttered on this street. Perhaps it was a section of offices that were closed for New Year's Eve. Some young boys ran by, laughing and calling to a couple of women behind them. The women didn't respond and as they neared the car, I saw they were dressed in gypsy garb: Bright peasant skirts, gathered blouses and gold chains around their necks. They saw me and headed for the car.

The taller of the two stuck her head in the window and said "Gimme Money", in English. Patrick had all the small change with him. And I wasn't going to admit to having a purse, anyway. I just kept smiling and saying that I didn't understand. She tried to open the car door, but I had locked my side. Then her friend started around the car to the other door. A man walked by and they both turned to him. He kept on walking, but the diversion gave me enough time to drop the keys on the floor and lock the other door. By the time the girls returned to me, the other window was fully closed, too. Now only one side to defend.

Both girls returned to my window and tried to reach the glove compart-
ment. By that time, I had stopped being polite and had nearly caught their
arms in the closing window, when a couple of healthy, happy young men
appeared. The girls withdrew their arms and laughing at me went off to
follow more pleasurable pastimes, I presume, just as Patrick rounded the
corner. Poor dear, he missed all the fun.

Then we filled up with gas (another essential) and headed southwest,
down the coast. And just outside La Serena was a tool booth, the first one
we saw in South America. The road ahead was no different and there was
no other way to go but the fee was only 35 cents, so it hardly mattered.
Still, we wondered why they suddenly decided to charge a toll. And soon
we came to the other campground, which was among white sand dunes,
between the road and the Pacific Ocean. Down in a hollow was a wooden
building, with toilets and showers and a dining room which was being
prepared for their New Year's Eve party. People were standing on chairs,
hanging paper streamers across the ceiling. And the walls had been decorated with large posters, one of them a photograph of a well developed girl,
naked to the waist. Which seemed odd, in a family-oriented place in a
Catholic country. But the children running between the tables did not seem
to notice. And getting down off a chair, the manager told us politely to
camp wherever we liked.

Camping was a new and expensive sport, in Chile. The few people who
could afford it came in luxury cars - mostly Mercedes - and had fine, new
tents in bright colors (red, blue, orange or yellow) each with two or three
rooms in it. But there were very few trailers and those were all the same
size and shape, like a slice of a small Quonset hut - going sideways - with
the door in the middle and bunks at either end. And there were no facilities - that I cold see - in the tents or the trailers. So the people must have
eaten most of their meals in the restaurant. Perhaps there were twenty
families altogether, and many of them were camped along a low ridge of
sand, facing the sea. So we set up our tent beside the others - at one end -
and had a fine view of the magnificent, white sand beach that swept in a
gentle curve, clear out of sight in either direction. The ocean was dark
blue, under a pale blue sky, with one line of breakers following the curve

of the beach. And inland   well back from the sand dunes - were brown mountains with white, soft clouds, here and there, floating beside them.

There was no one on the beach, after lunch, so we walked for a while, along the firm sand near the water. And the whole thing is so big that while the tents behind us got smaller, the far end seemed no nearer. But we came upon a flock of seagulls   large ones, with curved beaks guarding their young. There were dozens of chicks on the beach, with some adult birds among them and others standing like sentries, around them, a little way off. And as we came closer, the whole flock took to the air at once, as though on a signal. But the chicks flew low and far - keeping close together - and when they landed, the older birds set up their defensive pattern again.

Back in the tent, I wrote to the manageress of the German pension in Lima, saying that June had lost her necklace and we would pay a reward of $ 55 to whoever found it, on our way back. That was more than twice what I figured a 'fence' would give her and even if she had already sold it (which was likely) she would at least be mad at having taken so much less for it. Then I sketched a design and worked out the details of a boat (a 45 foot, single screw motor yacht) that we might one day build for ourselves. For when I have a day off, with nothing to do, I always start planning something new.

Two people, slightly younger than us, arrived in a Volkswagen camper and parked it beside our tent, so we invited them over for drinks. She was Chilean and he was French but had been in Chile for 18 years and worked for the United Nations, out of their local office in Santiago. Both of them were intelligent and interested in everything, so we had a fine time. And during the evening, we learned more about Chile. The economy of the country was based solely on copper, so it varied with the price of copper, in the world market. And we really should be careful of the soldiers, who would shoot anyone they saw outside, during the hours of curfew. In fact, if we were going to camp 'out" (in the open) we shoould first get permission from the nearest control point. There were plenty of them.

The Auto Club had a list of 'campings' south of Santiago, that we should pick up. It was just one typewritten page but it would help. Our friends said that the lake district of southern Chile was very beautiful and they showed us routes, on the map, to take through it. But it would get cold, as we went south, and we might even be able to ski at Punta Arenas, which is on the Straits of Magellan, just before Tierra del Fuego.

The conversation was going splendidly, in a mixture of Spanish, French and English, when we ran out of Pisco sours, in our tent. So we all moved over to their camper, where there was a good supply of whisky. And when we got there, the first thing they showed us - with great pride - was a chemical toilet they had installed, which they said made them autonomous.

We mentioned having seen some gypsies. Oh yes, we were told, there were many gypsies in that area. They were sweet, gentle country people who came into town for the holiday. I wanted to disagree, but perhaps I was in the wrong. Anyway, next time I would have some money handy.

When we went to bed, it was late but most of the people in the campground were still at the party in the restaurant. And where we were, the only sound was of the surf on the beach. But we woke with slight hangovers, to a gray dawn. And when we were ready to leave, we found that Minim's wheels were buried deep in the soft, white sand at the end of the ridge. Before getting out the winch, I went to the restaurant, where I had noticed a red tractor. And soon I found the driver - a friendly man - who cranked it up and went rattling off. By the time I had run back - over a sand dune - to our camp site and got out the tow line, he was there. And a minute later, Minim was back on firm ground. I offered to pay him but he assured me it was no trouble, so I insisted that he take a dollar for the gas, which seemed to please him. And as he went about his business, we checked out of the campground and headed south again.

Evidently everyone gets stuck in the sand, so the campground provides a free towing-out service. And I was happy not to have to dig out the winch. We had used it only once, more than four years before. It was now buried in the most inaccessible spot. Of course, if we had four wheel drive, there would have been no problem. On the other hand, so far, Minim had been able to drive out of almost everything we had gotten into. We still felt that keeping the car as simple as possible had been the right decision.

Soon the road left the coast, to go through the foothills, parallel with the ocean. The land was still desert - brown and dry but now there were many small bushes, all the same bright green, scattered across it. And outside a small town, we picked up a boy with a can full of gasoline. He was English and a few miles down the road, his parents were waiting in an old pickup truck. While he put in the gas and started the motor, they thanked us and said they had two houses, one in Argentina and one in Chile. They were going to Argentina, just then, but if we would like to use the one in Chile, we were quite welcome. The servant would let us in.

It seemed odd to hear those people - dressed in dirty, old clothes and standing by their dirty, old pickup truck - talking about their houses and servants. But probably it was wise not to look too prosperous, going through the mountains. The house was by a small lake called Vichuquen, near the coast, south of Santiago. But we would not feel comfortable, in someone else's house, and we declined their offer. So they told us there were two campgrounds beside the lake, which was quite beautiful, and suggested that we go there.

Just north of Santiago, there is a road over the Andes to Argentina and near the pass, on the Chilean side, is the famous ski resort of Portillo. It would not be open, for it was summer there, but we went to see it, anyway. Climbing out of the foothills, we came to a long, narrow, winding valley, with high mountains rising steeply on each side of it. At first, the road followed the valley floor but as that narrowed and petered out, it clung to the side of the mountains, climbing steadily up toward the pass at the top. Near the summit, it made a series of switchbacks and there was the Hotel Portillo, a modern, six story building, with a ski lift going up into a narrow bowl above it and another going down, over the switch-backs, below it. In winter, when everything is covered with snow, the scene may be quite beautiful. But when we were there, it was bleak and barren. Grim, gray mountains glowered down at us from every side and a small lake - Laguna del Inca, dark and deep - lay trapped between them, its banks the mountain slopes. Two doormen outside the hotel stirred and walked around, as such people do when a customer appears, in a quiet time. And we sympathized with them but the hotel was not for us. Nor was there any place, that would be sheltered from the wind, where we

178

could camp. And I had a feeling we should go. So back we went, down the switchbacks, to the valley below.

I couldn't understand why Patrick refused to even step inside the hotel door. It might be perfectly nice. But from the outside, I had to agree, it was the most uninviting place I could remember seeing. You had the feeling that the mountain peaks were about to move together and crush the miserable little place. It just didn't belong there. The old sailor seemed to know instinctively that something was about to happen. He wanted off that mountain and he wanted off right now. So we turned tha car around and raced down to more compatible land. Darkness comes suddenly to a narrow valley like that and we had little time left to find a place for the night.

The mountains, which were gray at the top, were brown and less forbidding, farther down. Between them, there was soon a widening strip of green grass, with dark bushes along its sides, clinging to the lower slopes. And at Guardia Vieja (a few houses, scattered down the valley) there was a restaurant, with a small, fenced meadow across the road from it.

Tall white daisies catching bits of the fleeting sun shimmered in the green field. Far back was a split rail fence and beyond it cows were grazing. It was all so peaceful after the ominous gloom of Portillo. Even Patrick began to relax. We felt we could handle whatever might happem there.

That would be a fine place to camp but we did not like to ask permission to do so, without buying something, so we went inside and ordered drinks and asked the waiter if we could have dinner there and sleep in our tent, across the road. He was a fat, jolly man and he said "Of course", as though ut were quite a normal thing to do. But I don't think anyone had done it before, because he stood and watched us putting up the tent, with great interest. And when some girls came by, he said "These are Northamericans", which explained everything.

When he saw that we had a capet and a table in our tent, he got into the spirit of the thing and said he would bring our dinner to us and serve it there - which would have been rather grand, since he was dressed formally, in black and white - but we insisted on eating in the restaurant, where we were the only customers in the big, high ceilinged room. From the windows at one end, there was a fine view of the mountains, as the valley filled with darkness. And the waiter hung a Coleman lamp hissing to itself - on a cluster of electric lights overhead, which did not work because the generator had broken down (he did not say when) and since it was made in Czechoslovakia, it was not possible to get parts for it. There was a parrot, on a perch, by the bar. And the coffee after dinner was a can of Nescafe, brought to the table in a fitted basket. There were many cats, in the dark shadows of the big room, and when we left, some important dogs saw us off. But they did not go far, from the building. And back in our tent, it was calm and peaceful as we went to sleep.

When I woke up, it was dark. And a strong wind was rushing down the valley, pulling and tugging at our tent. So hard that it might tear it or break something at any moment. I felt for a flashlight and shading it (because of the curfew) I looked at my watch. It was one in the morning. I lay back down. Perhaps it was a gust of wind, that would quickly die. In a moment, it did. But soon it came back, stronger than ever. June was awake, too. And after fifteen minutes, we decided it was time to let the tent down, onto the ground.

There was no need to be quiet, in that wind. But we had to be careful, not to get shot by the carabineri (soldiers with carbines) for going outside during the hours of curfew. We stayed low and worked quickly, releasing the aluminum poles and letting the canvas down, into the tall grass. Then we burrowed back inside the tent - between the floor and the rest of it - and slipped into bed. But we could not sleep, with the canvas flapping, close to our faces. And soon the alarm in Minim started blowing the horn, as she swayed in the wind. It was not loud, at first. but it was getting louder. And we did not want to attract the carabineri. So it seemed better to take the chance if going from the tent to Minim, turning off the alarm and sleeping there, for the rest of the night.

It was just a few yards. And Minim was between us and the road, giving us cover. We took the essentials - bed and bedding, flashlights and documents - and moved into the truck. In spite of the wind and the creaking of Minim's springs as she swayed in the gusts, we slept quite well. And when we woke up, it was daylight. The tent, lying flat in the tall grass, was unharmed. And as we folded it, a large dog came by. He ran through a ditch, on his way to us, and left muddy footprints on the tent. Then he jumped up at us, in greeting. But when we asked him (not unkindly) to go away, he wimpered and his tail went down and he ran away, afraid of us.

We wondered how the wind had been in Portillo. It was probably just as well that we hadn't stayed in the hotel there. Patrick wouldn't have slept at all and we certainly couldn't have driven down in that gale.

While we were packing up, the waiter came and apologized for the wind. It had never happened before. His outside chairs had been scattered and his glass-topped table had been picked up and broken. We assured him that we were all right and went to the restaurant for breakfast.

It had never happened before! The exact words used in Belice the night we were nearly washed out into the Caribbean, tent and all. I'd had about enough of these 'first time ever' experiences. But at least this time our gear wasn't soaked with muddy water and covered with leeches.

As we ate, a bus load of young people - mostly men - came in but after a brief stop, they continued east, over the pass into Argentina. And when I started Minim's engine, one cylinder was misfiring but I hoped it would clear itself as we went down the valley - into the foothills - to Los Andes. That was a nice old city, with a central square, and quite busy. The National Bank could not cash our traveller's checks but a commercial bank nearby did, so we went shopping

Los Andes isn't a country town. Many of the women on the streets were well and fashionably dressed. Men wore business suits. We were nearing Santiago and Los Andes looked like a rather chic suburb.

The butcher we went to was rather mean and muttered "Go back to Argentina" when he gave us our meat. But a thin, blonde woman I spoke to in the market - asking where to find something - answered in English and when I expresed surprise, she said "Everything here speaks English" She had always lived in Los Andes but it was taught in the schools, there. At the Auto Club, on a side street, we were given the list of 'campings' but there were only a few and none of them seemed to be on our route south. And farther out, we found an ice plant, where a helpful young man cut a piece to fit our box.

As he worked, I asked how things were, in Chile. His smile faded and he looked wistful as he said quietly "Life is difficult. It is a political thing". And I felt it was all he could safely tell me. For with inflation over 300 percent a year, the ordinary man could barely get by. And the tight military control left him little freedon, as we know it. Yet all the people we met in Chile, wih few exceptions, were cheerful and kind.

When we left Los Andes, the truck was still running badly, so we stopped by the road to clean the distributor. But there was not much improvement and I had to nurse her through Santiago, to prevent her from stalling in the city traffic.

We were both so busy trying to keep Minim alive and at the same time follow the twisting road to the south that we had passed through Santiago before we realized it. A wide boulevard from the north crossed the Mapocho river into a sudden surge of rushing, pushy traffic. Our route ran along the river bank for a very short distance, then veered south through narrow, snaking one-way streets and suddenly we were back on a wide, ugly boulevard, congesteed with everyday commercial traffic, and then into the country. Beautiful Santiago. What I had glipsed between squinting from map to street sign and prayers to the heavens to keep the car from dying in six lanes of speeding traffic is not worth mentioning. Patrick muttered something about turning arond, if I insisted. We might have had a lovely time: Patrick tearing apart the engine in an area equivalent to Fifth Avenue and 42nd Street while I strolled around, shopping. Some other time.

The road leading south, from the city, was four lanes wide - almost a superhighway - for a few miles but then it reverted to two lanes and after a while, we came to a control point. That meant stopping Minim's engine, while our papers were examined and all our gear was inspected. But when we were cleared to proceed, it would not start, so the officials helped us push the truck into the shade of a tree. And since there were no other vehicles for them to inspect, they watched us fix it. In the engine compartment, there was a strong smell of gasoline, so we guessed what the trouble was. A piece of dirt had stuck in the needle valve, where the fuel line goes into the carburettor. So we took off the line and cleaned the valve and soon the engine was running again. The officials were pleased, when it started and as we left, they went back to their post.

They were more relieved than pleased. One of the senior officials seemed to consider us a threat. He thought we should be towed away. Was he concerned because his men found the event entertaining, or did he think we were some sort of planned distraction before an attack? We were all a bit tense by the time the car finally started.

Just south of San Fernando, we turned off the highway and headed west, toward Lake Vichuquen. It was too small to be on the AAA map of South America but we found it in a map of Chile - put out by Esso - where the English people said it was.

They hadn't given us any specific directions and the map showed a fairly straight road between the highway and the lake. We should be there well before dark.

At Santa Cruz, the pavement ended. Beyond the town, there was a gravel road - passing through more villages than we could account for - and we were nearly hit by a blue truck. Then the gravel turned to dirt. In one place, a cowboy stopped us, to ask if we had seen a cow (we had not). In another, we almost sank in deep sand. And as the light began to fade, we started looking for a safe place to spend the night, since we did not seem to be anywhere near a lake. Probably we had missed it.

The roads were narrow dirt tracks. When the man asked us if we had seen a cow, we honestly couldn't remember. At each hill, around every bend we looked for the lake and everything else along the way was ignored. We would have turned back but there had been so many turns since leaving the highway that we were completely lost. We should have asked the cowboy for directions. But it was dark and he was dressed in dusty black, hat and all, with two pistols belted to his hips. We weren't at all certain about looking for him either.

Then there was a sign, small and hand painted, beside the road. It said 'Camping Elvenwald' and with the carabineri around, we had better go there. We followed the arrow and after a while, there was another sign, so we kept on going - winding over steep hills - for several miles. Then we saw the lake, down below. A sign sent us down a very steep trail through tall pine trees - and at the bottom, we found a house beside the water. A young woman came to greet us and led us along a trail - between the lake and a steep, wooded hill - to a fine camp site, with a weeping willow for shade and high, dense reeds on either side of our own private dock, on the lake. There was beer in her storeroom, and freshly baked bread. And a girl would come in the morning to pick up our laundry.

That last hill down to the campground had been so long and steep and rugged that we wondered about ever getting back up. Not that it mattered any more. We might just stay there forever.

The campground was run by the young woman and her husband, who was of German descent, and the facilities were simple but very well done. There were 25 sites, each with its own dock, and though it was their second year of operation, only six or seven sites were taken for the long New Year's weekend. When our tent was set up, we walked along the trail past the other sites. All the camping equipment we saw was newer and better than ours. And there were a few boats - a sailfish and two inflatable ones - but most of the people were sitting around in groups, near their tents, engaged in conversation. By ten o'clock, the campground was still and quiet, but for the sounds of children and crickets and faint, distant music. And we were indeed glad to have found our way there.

We gathered pine cones from the hill above for a fire. A little snake slid across the dock and into the lake, making the reeds flex and the water lap softly against the shore. But nothing could disturb our peace. The worries of the day, the car, the heat, the suspecting police, all became unreal.

December through March is summer in southern Chile but it was cool and pleasant, the next morning, eating breakfast on our dock beside the lake. There had been a few mosquitoes, the night before but we did not see any, in the day time. One could easily fall off the path to the John, it was so narrow and went so steeply up, into the trees. And the building was made of wood from the forest - straight, round poles and roughly sawn planks - and ten penny nails. The wash basin was installed with two poles and four nails, altogether. And the roof was thatched with reeds, taken from the lake. The other buildings, including the owners' house, were made in the same way. And their child had his own small play house, like them. Nearby were a court for ball games and things to climb on but the children - even quite small ones - did not seem to use them. Rather, they would call by for a polite chat and take their leave, saying "Ciao"

I spent the morning on the truck (oiling the carburettor and distributor, cleaning the plugs, changing the condenser and coil) and while I was working, two men came by. Evidently their children had told them about us and our travels. Both spoke perfect English, one with an American accent and the other with an English one, which he had picked up at an English school in Chile. Both were interested in sailing and one got the leaflets put out by our publisher, so he would look for our book Wind Song, when it came out. He had spent two years as a lieutenant in the Chilean navy, servicing lighthouses, out of Puerto Montt. The other worked for Schlumberger in oil and had a business on the side, cleaning houses - down to the bare metal - with water under high pressure. The equipment to do it was made in England and he hired men to operate it.

They said there were only ten million people in Chile and plenty of copper but the Allende regime had ruined the economy and now they were paying for it. The Chief of Tourism was an attractive woman - we should go and see her. But they were worried about their image in the world outside (Fascist). In fact, they were a gentle people, who smiled and laughed easily.

Or pehaps only mesmeized, as we were, by the tranquility of Vichuquen. Certainly they were as aware of the constant military presence as we were. An indication, if nothing else, that not everyone in the country was so content.

When I finished working, the truck seemed to start and run all right, so we went to the owner's house to buy Coke and ginger ale and eggs - all different sizes and one of them green - which she said were from farm bred (not nursery raised) chickens. It was a bright, sunny afternoon with a light breeze and she had an outboard engined boat for rent, so we took it for a run around the lake. The scene was like summer on any small lake in the United States - sailboats and water skiers, houses in the pine woods, along the shore and one light airplane circling overhead - but such things were for the wealthy few, in Chile, not for the ordinary people.

Back ashore, we were invited for drinks with the men we had met that morning, their families and friends. Everyone said that things were much better, under the new government, though there might not be any elections for years. At least things were quiet and there was no fear of being killed now. Everything was under control. The military people had saved the day. But those were the wealthy few.

The women gave me a recipe for Pastele de Choclo, which they claimed is the national dish. It's a combination of beef and chicken, hot spices and sweet corn. But only fresh corn would do. A waste of time to make it with anything but fresh. The corn crop would be ready in a few weeks. Then all of Chile would sit down to eat the Pastele. And by that time, we should be well on our way through Argentina. I have tried to make it but so far my attempts have produced a curious mixture of flavors, somehow lacking the depth and character that I would associate with a National Dish. Perhaps I misunderstood some proportions.

When the sun set - about nine o'clock - June was cooking supper at our camp site, over a fire of pine cones. And on Sunday morning, we took our time, getting organized. The tent was remarkably flexible, making a bedroom. dining room, office or bathroom as needed. All with full standing headroom. And the water bags we got in Texas, hung on the car, were very convenient. The owners of the campground served lunch that day, at a long table, under the trees near their house. His German was very good and when June sang a few bars of 'Die Lorelei', he congratulated her politely. Another man, a friend of theirs who worked in the local post office, also spoke German but we found it was easier to get along with everyone in Spanish.

These people, about a generation younger than our friends of the evening before, voiced very nearly the same feelings. They wanted to do their work, raise their families, live their lives without interference. They weren't quite as adamant about all being better now. You could note a bit of hesitation in their responses. Perhaps they were closer to the needy majority. At least they could see some merit on both sides. But in the last analysis, to live their lives and be left alone. Social problems were of little interest.

They said there were red-faced, black-necked swans on a lake, not far away. And when I mentioned the cows, grazing in lush grass nearby, they

186

told us that Lake Vichuquen rose nine feet, during the winter rains. And their whole campground was under water for several weeks each year. We had promised ourselves a walk to the top of the hill, for the exercise but we found a nice level road along the shore of the lake and took that, instead. We went past a military post - just a small building, all closed up - and saw a man standing in the lake, waist deep in water, cutting reeds for a roof. And walking back, we met our friends leaving.

By late afternoon, all the campers had gone and while June chatted with the young woman, I walked along the trail, past the empty sites. Each one had been left very clean, with all the garbage stacked neatly in the middle. And it was quiet and sunny and still. And I met two snakes - one green and one brown - who froze when they saw me and then poured under a dock. When darkness came, there was a new moon and as we sat on our dock, some people in a rowboat offered us a ride. But we declined with thanks and went to bed. A speedboat went slowly by, playing classical music. And later, the rowboat came back, with a splashing of oars in the calm water and people quietly singing - mostly 'la la la" and laughter and happy sounds. But such things can not last. Too soon, it was daylight and we were leaving that place   probably forever.

Climbing the steep trail, we left the pine trees behind and took the dirt road south, over more hills - the soil between the green bushes was hard and dry, like desert sand - until we came over a ridge, into the valley of the Rio Mataquito. Below, the land beside the river was laid out in a patchwork of green fields, scattered with white houses. And there we found a firm gravel road, that took us eastward - up the valley to the main, paved highway down the length of Chile. As we went south, that day, the countryside changed from semi-desert to rolling farm land, with rich brown soil. Between the farms were forests of mixed trees, such as you see in North America. And toward evening, we came to Laja Falls.

That was a tourist attraction, with a small, modern hotel and since there was nowhere to pitch our tent, I went inside. The dining room had long windows, overlooking the modest falls, and was full of wealthy people. But a room would be $ 20, plus meals - the sleek girl leaned back in her chair, confident that we could not afford it - so we tried the cabins nearby.

Those were $ 8 a night but after seeing inside one, June suggested (rather firmly) that we continue down the road. Fifteen miles south, the road passed close by the city of Los Angeles. There we found the Motel Majorca, a row of single-storey units, with a restaurant at one end. And for $ 6 a night, we were given a perfectly nice room, with our own bath. June had a problem with the shower, for each room had its own water heater, which was set at a lower temperature than she liked, and she ran the whole ten gallons down the drain, waiting for it to get hotter. But the highway was quiet in the evening, and the back window looked onto a cool meadow. The restaurant was simple, with plain chairs and tables and a TV on a stand, to one side. But the waiter was dressed formally and brought us Pisco Sours and white wine with our meal (chicken, tomato salad, fresh raspberries and cream and Nescafe, in a ceremonial can) while we watched an old epsode of Star Trek in Spanish on the television.

In the dining room were two families - the children were quiet and well behaved - a single man (perhaps a salesman) and an old couple with a Thermos jug on their table.

The next morning was bright and sunny, so I went out to work on the truck, that was still not running properly. And two other guests were working on their cars, outside the motel. It was nice to be doing the same thing as the local travellers.

He worked in his old clothes, then changed and we went to the pleasant little dining room for breakfast. The food was so good. Even the orange juice was fresh. And no packets of plastic jam. Everything was perfect until the Nescafe appeared. Didn't anyone ever drink real coffee? I asked he waiter for cafe cafe. There was none. But as we drove away, we saw volcanoes, far off to our left, in the clear morning light.

At that point, Chile is about 120 miles wide from the border of Argentina, high in the Andes, to the Pacific Ocean - and the main road goes south, down the middle. The famous Lake District starts at Lake Villarrica, between the highway and the Andes, and goes on for about 200 miles, to Puerto Montt. So we turned off at Freire and went southwest, toward it. The road followed the Rio Tolten through a countryside of grass and trees, with many spring flowers and sometimes a whole, big field of blue ones. The river was a darker blue and the sky was more pale, with white clouds. And when we stopped for lunch, by the river, there was a white-topped volcano in the distance. The sun was hot but the breeze was cool and there was a feeling of summer in the air, which was quite unlike the 'false summer' of the tropics. This was the real thing.

Lake Villarrica - about 8 miles wide and twice as long - was calm and clear and blue, with gray-blue mountains around it and the white-topped volcano beyond. Where the river flowed out of the lake, it was wide and people were standing in the shallow water, fishing. Beside the lake among green trees and between tall poplars - were the red tiled roofs of the old resort town, also called Villarrica. And there we stopped to buy food in some nice, new shops before heading eastward, along the south side of the lake, looking for a place to stay. Beyond the town, there were young people hitch-hiking and along the shore, there were several camp-grounds but only one seemed busy - with many tents and blaring music - so we made a note to avoid that. And at the end of the lake was the village of Pucon, with an old hotel for fishermen.

It loooked charming to me. It was a big old clapboard house with screen porches all around and shutters at the windows. There were some small outbuildings, perhaps cottages, all clustered around a huge green lawn under towering old oak trees. It had been raining and the moss covered branches looked sodden. The only sign of life was a bit of smoke coming from a chimney. Somewhere inside was a cheery fire. Patrick would have none of it.

But there was nowhere to camp in Pucon, so we went back to the best looking campground, called Millaray, and set up our tent under a large tree, facing north across the lake. The beach was of back sand - volcanic lava - but it was not so fine as to be dirty. In fact, it ran through your fingers like a handful of tiny stones, leaving nothing behind. But it was hot to touch, in the sun. And the wide, sweeping crescent of dark gray looked odd, between the trees and the lake. There were toilets and showers in a red and white hut on the beach and a few people around so we were in good shape. But our life was very high key. Everything changed from day to day, requiring constant attention. Travelling and shopping, keeping the truck going and finding places to sleep was a full time job, leaving us little time for relaxation, except over drinks and supper at the end of the day. Our main worry, just then, was that our money might not last the trip back to the United States. With all the different currencies and the high rates of inflation, it was hard to tell. But we decided it probably would.

The sun was in the north at noon, which bothered me, but it set in the west, as it should. And when it rose again, it was in the east, which was reassuring. The sky was gray and the lake was calm, as I went to work on the truck (changing the plugs and adjusting the fuel level in the carburettor) but later, the sky cleared and a man - walking along the beach   stopped by to sell us a kilogram of sweet grapes for 18 cents.

By mid afternoon, the engine was still not running as it should and I was pretty sure that the ignition timing had slipped, so I asked someone in the campground and he sent us to the Garage Maynard in Villarrica. It was just a small place, set back from the street, but inside it was very clean and a crochety old German mechanic firmly took charge of our truck. The timing was indeed far from its proper setting   he muttered something about people who let things get like that - and the points in the distributor were too close but he soon had everything set correctly and the engine ran as smoothly as ever.

Back at the campground, a small trailer had arrived and two little girls were singing and chattering, near our tent. It was a quiet, pleasant sound and the evening was serene, until a house behind us, across the road, began broadcasting rock and roll music, so loud that we could hardly think. But soon it was turned down (perhaps there was a grownup in the house) until we could only hear a thumping noise, like a sewage pump.

As the daylight faded, electric lights came on, in the campground. Each light was on a tall pole, which had an outlet on it, about five feet from the ground. So I plugged my razor into the nearest one, leaving it tied to the pole with string, and by morning it had charged its batteries. For in that part of the world - unlike Central America - you could leave such a thing out all night, with no fear of it being stolen.

That's not quite true. He waited until it was dark, before tying his razor to the pole. And he took it off at dawn.

There was a strong northwest wind, under a gray sky and much noise of surf, along the shore of the lake. Our tent was all right, under the tree, but the wind was increasing and we should leave right away. Putting our things in Minim, I noticed a package which said (in Spanish) 'OMO is a total detergent'. And a half empty bottle of 40 cent wine, which had tasted fine. As we folded the tent, heavy rain swept across the lake but the tree sheltered us long enough to get going. Heading south, out of Villarrica, we took the gravel road to Lican-Ray on Lake Calafquen. But there was little to see, in the driving rain - just a few houses, among the trees, along the shore - and we turned west, to go around the lake.

The road looked, on the map, as though it followed the shore and would be quite level. But soon it went inland, though rolling farm country. And the dirt surface was already deep mud. So we rushed down into each hollow, slipping and sliding from side to side, to keep up enough speed to get over the next rise. Sometimes we doubted we would make it. But the farther we went, the less attractive was the idea of turning back. And suddenly we came to the gravel road that went to Panguipulli.

There was no way to tell from the map which roads were travelled by automobiles and which were merely wagon trails. For miles, through thick black mud, the only other wheels we saw were on oxcarts. And it was such a wet day that few of those were in sight. If there had been a bit of sunshine we wouldn't have been so worried. But the rain and mud increased through the day. Occasionally a farmer would watch us pass but for the most part the little, mud splattered houses looked deserted. There was no use in asking for directions, either. You seldom found anyone who had been beyond his own village.

But as the rain continued, even the gravel roads became slippery, so we gave up the idea of visiting every lake and took the paved road from Los Lagos to the main highway. Going south, we left the storm behind us. Gradually the rain eased off and the sky cleared. And by mid afternoon, it was warm and sunny, as we came into Puerto Montt. That was the end of the highway, in Chile. Beyond it were sheltered waterways, between the mainland and countless islands, all the way to Tierra del Fuego. But no through roads. And we wanted to go there in Minim, not in a ship. So we must cross the Andes into Argentina, before going farther south.

According to our map, we could go north to Puerto Varas, then northeast to Lake Todos Los Santos (All Saints) where a car ferry would take us to the far end. Then there was a road over a mountain pass, into Argentina, where another ferry would take us across Lake Nahuel Huapi to the far shore. But first we ought to see Puerto Montt, after driving toward it for so long.

We arrived late on a Saturday afternoon. There was no activity. The city had grown from the water's edge, over a series of low hills to a high plateau. There were no cruise ships tied to the docks. The shops were closed. Most of the buildings looked temporary. Of corrugated metal or wood, they had once been painted bright colors. Outside the walls of the heavily guarded shipyard were an area of rusty railroad tracks and the remains of an outdoor market. The stalls were being dismantled. Time to go home. It was an old town, and it looked tired that day. Perhaps the season hadn't yet begun.

The city campground was at Chiquique, about six miles to the southwest, on a bluff overlooking the sea. And there we set up our tent, on a grassy site, sheltered by tall trees. Several other campers were there, but it was not crowded. And going for a walk, we came to a graveyard. It was a small one, with many graves in it, and between them, the grass grew wild. Most of them had fences, freshly painted in white or gray or blue. And every one was neatly kept - many had flowers, growing in the ground - as if the people of that village were very independent.

The sea below was the Gulf of Ancud, the first of the sheltered waterways that went south from Puerto Montt. Though it was clear and blue, there was no swell to it. And along the shore were low hills some covered with trees, some cleared for farming - with bay after bay, into the gray distance. Down to our left, in the nearest one, was a boat yard on the beach, with the masts of a big sailing boat above it. So we scrambled down the bluff and over the rocks at the bottom, onto the beach and went along the white gravel, toward it. As we came closer, we could see that the big sailing boat was a yacht, quite new but built in an old fashioned style. And beside her were two smaller, more modern ones. Inside a big shed, two men were building a motor launch, to carry passengers to the nearby islands - there was a good smell of freshly worked wood - and they said they had built the big yacht there, to plans which had been sent from the United States. Going through the boatyard, we came out on the road, so we walked up the hill - the easy way - to our tent on the bluff. It was odd to think that we had finished another stage of our journey. Puerto Montt had always seemed as distant as a star. Now we were there and in the morning we would be leaving, to see if we could really get though Argentina, down to Cape Horn.

7 - CAPE HORN

It rained hard and was windy, in the night but we were warm and dry in our tent, protected by the trees. And backing the truck up to our tent, I rigged a shelter between them, so that June could stand in the dry to cook breakfast.

Very decent of him. And actually it was better than trying to find a restaurant, in that downpour. But I had to rearrange the top part now and then, for it would fill up with water, then burst like a dike, all over the stove.

The guardian of the campground - a tall, lean, tanned, graying farmer with a mustache and a flashing smile - came by, so I asked him when the rain might be expected to stop. And he said (in good Spanish) that it rained a lot, there, at any time of the day. Then he looked off into the distance, still smiling and I concluded that the conversation had ended.

Eventually there came a momentary break in the downpour and I made a resolute dash for the facilities: A row of wooden huts, perched over the bluff. They seemed to be unisexed and the door of one stood open, so I pulled the door shut behind me, but there was no latch. So holding it firmly, I arranged myself as well as possible. Then someone tried the door. I pulled hard but he pulled harder. I sat there in the half light, sputtering aloud. I don't remember what I said, except that it was not very ladylike. He backed away, apologising in flawless English. Thank heavens our paths didn't cross again.

Leaving the tent, in the hope that it might dry, we went to a bank in Puerto Montt, to get some Argentine money. They did not have any - it was hard to get   but they said we would have no problem, we could change our dollars at the border. When we got back to the campground, the rain had stopped and our tent was half way dry, so we folded it quickly and left, ahead of the next rain squall, for Puerto Varas. That was a resort town, like Villarrica, in the southwest corner of Lake Lanquihue. But the lake was much larger - more than 20 miles across - and in that weather, we could not see the far side, as we went northeast along the shore road. Beyond Lake Llanquihue, the paved road ended but a dirt road went on, over the lower slopes of the volcano Osorno. In several places there were big signs, saying that the ground was hot. And often the way ahead led across a wide river of lava. But it was black and firm and we kept up our speed, so that our tires would not catch fire. And at the end of the road was Lake Todos Los Santos, with a ferry dock and a hostel.

Pictures of Osorno decorated every place we went. We looked forward to seeing the volcano ourselves. It must be a wonderful sight: The snow capped cone towering over the lakes, reflected in the still waters, and the occasional bursts of smoke and fire. If only the rain would stop and the clouds would lift.

The lake was narrow - though the map showed that it was long and winding - and its wooded banks went steeply up into mountains, on either side. But the low clouds cut off the view and below them, in the rain, the water was pale green. The office of the ferry dock was locked, so we went ino the hostel, where we found a girl selling coffee and sandwiches. And she told us that the ferry ran every day, for people to see the lake. But if we wanted to transport a car on it, we must go to Puerto Varas and make the arrangements. That was 40 miles but we might as well get on with it, so back we went, over the rivers of hot lava and along the shore of Lake Llanquihue, to the old resort town. Looking around, we noticed many tourists and some beggars (the first we had seen in Chile) and when we stopped, a man came up to us - saying that he was a sailor - and asked us to change thirty dollars worth of US quarters into Chilean money. That was rather a lot but I offered to change five dollars worth for him and he went off, saying he was not interested.

Puerto Varas was a pretty little town, with small gardens and old hotels scattered along the edge of the lake. But for the first time, we were under siege by the local beggars.

It was after five o'clock and the ferry compamy's office would probably be shut but we saw a travel agency, so I went in to ask about transporting the car. There was one girl, sitting behind a desk, and she was explaining some coupons to her client, a tall, well dressed man standing in front of her. Evidently he and his family were going to take a trip on Lake Todos Los Santos the next day. There were coupons for each person, for a tourist bus to the lake. Then there were coupons for each person, for the ferry boat, there and back. And coupons for lunch and coupons for the ride back to Puerto Varas, in the bus. And there were spaces where other coupons - for things he did not want - had been taken out. All this she explained to him, with the air of a school mistress (though she looked more like the other kind) and when she finished, he thanked her profusely, saying that everything was quite perfect. As he left, she looked at me and I asked her about taking our car on the ferry. Quite sharply, as though I were some kind of idiot, she said that the car ferry had not run for a year but cars passed every day to Argentina on the road from Osorno. And it was clear that I had wasted enough of her time.

So that was it. A new road over the Andes had been opened and the old ferry service had beeen discontinued. Back in the car, we studied our maps. The AAA one of South America showed a road going east from the city of Osorno but after 25 miles, it turned to dirt of the lowest class (ungraded earth negotiable only in dry weather). The map of Chile showed the same road, but turning to gravel at that point and ending at the pass, with a projected section beyond that. But evidently the road went through now, in some form or another, and that was the way to go.

Osorno was 90 miles north of Puerto Varas and it was too late to start out that day, so we went northeast to a campground we had noticed, on the shore of Lake Llanquihue. It was quite primitive - just a place in a field to set up a tent, with two outhouses in a corner - but there were some trees for shelter and though it was still windy, we were able to dry our tent and its carpet a little, in the lulls between rain squalls. There were sheep in the field and some baby chicks came to see us, in the charge of a small girl from the owner's house. And the only other campers were a group of Boy Scouts. They had no vehicle and we wondered how they got there. Then we remembered seeing young men and boys camping all through southern Chile, with no transportation. Probably they hitch-hiked or went by bus, from one campground to another.

That gave us another chance to see the volcano. Driving over the lava flows was a bit unnerving and when you're that close, you can't see the top, anyway. Certainly the weather must break soon and then we would get a glimpse of her. But even when the sun did appear, the clouds kept the peak well hidden.

Toward evening, the sun came out and the wind died and it was peaceful there with the sound of surf along the shore of the lake and birds singing in the trees and few bugs around. And when darkness came, we were soon asleep. Before midnight, we were awakened by voices, calling to us though the tent. Men's voices. When I opened the door, I was looking at two Chilean Army flashlights, their yellow beams showing white holsters on the men's hips. With guns in them. That was a good sign. And the voices were not harsh. June gave me our passports, which I handed to the soldiers - telling them, in a quiet voice, that we were tourists, on our way through - and politely, they explained out of the darkness that we should have registered with them, before camping there. So I said that I was sorry, I did not know the regulations. And they said it was all right but they had a job to do and must get our details, for their records. If we would come in the morning to their post, they would complete the formalities. I assured them that we would and after giving me back our passports, they wished us 'good night' and went away.

We must have passed the check point three times and not seen it. And evidently the soldiers weren't too concened, or they would have hailed us down. It seemed odd that they would seek us out in the middle of the night and then go away, trusting us to stop in the morning. Trying to analyze the minds of the Chilean soldiers was enough to put us both back to sleep.

It rained steadily all night but by dawn it had stopped, though the sky was gray and the wind was strong. Soon it looked like rain again, so we packed up quickly and left. The soldiers' post was a gray and white house, beside the road, not far away. And it did not take them long to record all the details of our visit, in their book. Then we went southwest, along the shore of the lake, to Puerto Varas.

We left Puerto Varas reluctantly. It was stil gray and overcast. There was no chance of seeing the volcano. We talked about staying longer, but it would be days before the weather changed and there was so much more ahead.

From there we went north to the city of Osorno, where we stopped to buy food and ice. As I took out our red ice box, to fill it, I knocked a milk bottle off Minim's tailgate, into the street. So I took our dustpan and broom and swept up the broken glass and went into the shop, looking for somewhere to put it. And an old man inside showed a metal bucket, saying sternly that I must be sure to clean up all of the glass, so that it would not damage the tires of any cars, coming to his shop.

We did not buy any fruit or vegetables, for we were told they would be taken away from us at the border.

Going east from Osorno, we passed a small sign on a tall post, saying International Road. And it was still paved, along the shore of Lake Puyehue. But as it went up into the mountains, the surface changed to gravel and soon we came to the buildings on the Chilean side of the border, where we cleared with all the authorities - Customs, Immigration, Health and Police. Then the road climbed up into the Andes, winding through dramatic scenery of rocks and trees and steep-sided valleys, and over a pass at 4,000 feet, with snow beside it - in mid summer - and down to the Argentine side of the border.

For once the AAA map was correct. There was no road. Only a wide trail of brown mud. And more traffic than we had seen for days. Both cars and fairly big trucks. All churning up the slime. We were up to our hub-caps before we knew it, veering from side to side, looking or high spots and trying to keep the speed up, before we were drowned by the splatter from passing traffic. It was a race for the last spot in the line at the border.

The officials there were formally polite and handled our papers with brusque efficiency. But ahead of us were a young man and a girl, travel-lng together. And although the officials let them pass through - evidently they had no reason not to - they took their time and made it very clear that they did not approve of such behaviour by unmarried people.

The gravel road went down to Lake Nahuel Huapi, where it joined a paved one, going southeast along the shore, through a forest of tall trees - with no branches, low down, so that they looked like brown poles, supporting a high, green roof. Between them, on our right, was the blue lake and beyond it were high, jagged mountains. The whole scene was more dramatic than the lake district of southern Chile. The colors were brighter, the outlines more sharply defined. And the air was much colder. The lake is about 50 miles long and at the end we crossed the river flowing out of it, then turned west along the southern shore, which had no trees - just grass, dotted with small, green bushes, bending and swaying in the wind, that was making white-capped waves, far across the water.

Ahead was San Carlos de Bariloche, a big, modern resort town on the hills by the lake, with many signs and pushy traffic and no place to park. But here and there, incongruously, a dirt road. The atmosphere was German or Swiss, with billboards advertising a ski lift and several chocolate shops and a money shop, where we changed some dollars at a good rate. The town was full of tourists, though none of them spoke English, and everyone we dealt with was friendly and polite. But the idea of camping in that strong, cold wind was not inviting (even if we could find a place to do it) so we went out looking for a modest hotel.

Near the edge of town, we found the Huemul Hotel - built of logs, with a stone basement, between the road and the lake - and went down the steep driveway to it. Outside the front door, displayed on brackets above a trimmed hedge, was an old dugout canoe. And inside, it looked clean and well run. As the manager wrote down the details from our passports, people came scurrying in, all wrapped up in warm clothes, chattering about the cold outside. But our room had double windows, like the old Swiss hotels, and a steam radiator that clanked and bonked and hissed to itself but gave off plenty of heat. The people in the dining room looked like vacationers on package tours - all families and groups of single girls, clearly unhappy because there were no spare men, except two young blond boys with their parents. But the dinner was fine.

We were offered the package dinner that we saw other guests ladeling out of huge tureens but we decided to order from the menu and chose a local fish. It was very fresh and good.

Back in our room, we went to bed, with the sound of surf under our window, glad to be in Argentina. And at nine o'clock the next morning, we were the first ones in the dining oom, so we took the best table, with a view of the lake. And far in the distance, under a white cloud, was a small rainbow. But we must get going. Driving into Bariloche, we found ice and bought food for the next few days - and 'common' wine (very cheap) to try - then left town, heading south.

We found a couple of stores next to each other. One was a delicatessen and meat market with good bread and cheeses. From the other we bought staples: sugar, paper napkins, etcetera. I was just beginning to understand the currency, I thought. But instead of the change I expected, the cashier handed me several pieces of hard candy. I didn't want candy, I wanted my change. But she explained that the rate of inflation was so fierce that they had stopped trying to make small change. It was so worthless, they decided to give the customers candy instead.

Ten minutes later, we came around a curve and found the road blocked by soldiers - their trucks forming a barrier, guns at the ready - and lined up to be inspected by a tall, heavily built officer with a loud voice and a commanding manner. After checking our passports, he waved us on, so we presumed that he was looking for people who might have entered the country illegally. But the whole scene was more serious and military than we had been used to in Chile. Then the way south was through a national park, on a gravel road - barely wide enough for one car - that clung to the edge of a long, narrow lake between steep mountains, then wandered through a forest to another, and another.

At times the forest was at least two feet above the water and at times it was several inches below but nothing seemed to slow down the local drivers. They would zip around the blind corners as if they were on one way streets. Every few hundred yards, there was a wide spot where we would pull off and let others pass, from behind or in front. It was a relief to leave the lake's edge, for wider roads through the trees.

A sign by the road said 'Auto Camping' but there were no facilities, except a table in the woods, a place to build a fire and - at the end of a short path - a shrine. And all through the park, it rained steadily out of low, gray clouds.

A shrine where the traveller gave thanks for having made it this far? We wondered of the roads were worse, ahead.

Then we went up into the mountains and down into valleys beyond them and slowly we drove out of the rain, into an open, bleak area of blue sky and high wind and coarse grass, where the road was wide and made of large gravel. There we saw two cars, going the other way, with plastic guards over their windshields. And soon we came to one, across the road, with the glass broken and its owner cleaning up the mess. We stopped to help but he was all right, thank you. The wheel of a passing car had flung up a rock, that was all. It often happened, on those roads. His passengers, sitting in the car, smiled in polite agreement. He thanked us again for stopping and we had the decency not to mention that it was raining, ahead of them, all the way to Bariloche.

That could be a problem for us. We needed the shelter of our truck and there was no hope of finding a new windshield for it. But long ago, when we bought Minim, we refused to consider any truck with a curved one. So we could make do, if we had to, with almost any flat piece of safety glass.

After a while, the road dipped down into a hollow, past a clump of bushes, so we went around to the lee side and set up our tent, to dry - spreading our red carpet on the ground - then sat on the tailgate, to wait. But it was warm in the sun, out of the wind, and soon we were under way again. At El Maiten, a small town with dirt streets, we stopped for gas. There were two kinds in Argentina, called Common and Super. So we bought the Super when there was any and the Common if we had to - as we did there. And Minim's engine seemed to be happy enough with the resulting mixture.

Often at a gas station, even in an out-of-the-way place, there would be an outpost of the Automovil Club Argentino - just a room, in the same building - where you could get information and maps. But there were eight maps, for different parts of the country, and the one for the part you were in was usually out of stock. So the trick was to keep looking, at each ACA post, and buy the maps you expected to need later on.

It was difficult to anticipate the journey ahead, from our map. Large cities were shown in large print, medium sized towns in medium sized print. But those names in small print might be anything. Sometimes we would find an actual community with a few small houses, a church and even a gas station. At other times we would find an intersection with not a building or body in sight. Our road ran down the center of a broad, high plain rimmed by distant mountains. Crevices in the foothills, where the water collected, looked greener than the brownish grasses around us. There were often large trees in those gullies and the sun would sometimes reflect off a metal roof or a whitewashed wall. The evidences of man would correspond roughly with a name in small print on our map. If we should need help, we could either sit by the road and wait for another vehicle or go the five or fifteen miles, off to he side, to a ranch. The air was so clear and the visibility so good that distance was difficult to judge. But knowing that something - no matter how poorly defined on our map - lay ahead was a comfort in that barren section. We paid close attention to our fuel and food consumption and water supply, making sure to restock them at every opportunity. There was no way of telling how many miles of that sort of country we must cross, before more would be available.

Beyond El Maiten, the road surface changed from gravel to pavement and we went humming along, with no fear of flying rocks. But we would need a place to camp, for the night. Somewhere out of the strong, cold wind. And out of sight, from the road. Which might be hard to fnd, in that bleak, open landscape.

And there were other considerations. It was our first night of open camping in Argentina. We weren't quite sure of the score. Was it an acceptable thing to do or did we run the risk of trouble from thieves? We would be perfectly safe and probably welcome at a ranch or in one of the tiny towns. But we did like a bit of privacy. We hadn't quite gotten around to the custom of performing our toilet in an open field or against a wall in full view of the passing world. Besides, the few people we had seen didn't seem to have the relaxed air of acceptance you often find in a country people. These people seemed tense. There were few smiles. We would rather not impose ourselves on them.

But toward evening, we came into the lee of a long hill, curving beside the road. And across from it, down to our left, was a winding stream, with two good-sized willows together on its near bank and dense bushes around them. It was not hard to get Minim down to the bank and nose her in between the bushes. And inside, there was a perfect camp site, sheltered from wind and view but looking out across the stream. Someone had been there, before. There were marks, on the bank of the stream, where he sat, probably fishing. But now the only occupants were a family of Golden Eagles. We know little of birds, so we could not be sure but they were the right size - more than six feet, across the wings - and the right color golden brown, with white markings. The habitat was right for Golden Eagles and their calls - rapid, sharp chips - were loud and clear, as we put up the tent. Clearly they disapproved of us and soon we found they had young (scrawny, awkward chicks) to protect. So their nest was in the bushes, nearby. But we also needed shelter for the night and they would simply have to put up with us.

It is a curious fact that a tent, which may be no thicker than your shirt, not only makes the people inside feel safe from anything outside, but also the other way around. Once we were in our tent, the urgent chipping noises subsided and it was quiet, except for the wind in the trees and the noise of the stream and an occasional, brief comment by an eagle. There were scattered, white clouds in the blue sky and we tried the 'common' wine, from Bariloche, with our dinner. It was perfectly adequate, we thought. And a note in our log of the trip says: 'So here we are, open camping in the Andes, about five days' driving from Cape Horn (Hic').

When we were planning the trip, from Vermont to Cape Horn and back, we had used the AAA map of South America, which showed two roads through Patagonia: Route 40, going down the west side of Argentina and Route 3, along the east side. So we had chosen to go south on Route 40 and come back on Route 3. But now we had the ACA maps, which were more detailed. And studying them in our tent, we found that Route 40 did not go through. There was a gap, more than 50 miles wide, at the Plateau of Death - between Las Horquetas and Tres Lagos - where no road had ever been built. To get around it, we would have to go east, almost to Route 3 and back again, to rejoin Route 40. Which would hardly be worth the time and trouble. But there was another road - not shown on the AAA map - which left Route 40 about 100 miles ahead and went southeast to Route 3. It was called Route 20 and according to the ACA map, it was in better shape than any other (much of it was paved and the rest was gravel). So that was the best way to go.

When darkness came, we put away our maps, for it would be unwise to show a light in that place. And it was cold, in the night but we were warm and slept well, in our double bag. As the sun came up, it quickly warmed our tent, which was facing east. And over breakfast, at our table looking out across the stream, we were inclined to linger, it was so pleasant there. But the eagles chattered loudly, letting us know that we did not really belong. And taking the hint, we left.

After an hour or so, the pavement ended and we went rattling over large gravel, past yellow machines that were about to improve the highway, when they got around to it. And coming to a fork in the road, we took the more likely direction. But soon we were going down into a small valley, on a narrow trail of deep, loose dirt. And ahead were 6 or 8 wild ostriches. They were brown and hard to see, among scattered bushes. And when we spooked them, they ran off. But they were about six feet tall and looked like elderly chorus girls, with big eyes and sharp features and long, skinny necks. And feathers, around the middle. And those long, tapering legs. Evidently we had taken the wrong way, for the trail ahead was no better than the part we were on. So we turned around. But going back, up the valley, was ticklish. If we used too much power in that deep, loose dirt, our wheels would slip and bite down into it. And we could spend a happy day, winching the truck out. So we kind of tiptoed up the hill, as gently as possible, to the level ground above.

And very glad too that we had made a wrong turn, for to see the flock of ostriches - or Rheas as they are called in the bird books - was exciting. We never again saw one that close. They kept their distance from the main roads.

Back at the junction we found a yellow machine with its engine running and the man on it assured me - when I climbed up to him - that the other road was the one we wanted. So off we went, that way. And soon the rough gravel changed to fine, new pavement, going straight ahead over land so wide and level that we could easily see the curvature of the earth. The gray, stony ground was covered with coarse yellow grass. And in the distance were a few scattered bushes. But the main features of the landscape were the shadows cast by small clouds. And the only inhabitants we saw were shiny black horses, wandering freely over the vast pampas. Until we came to an old man, standing beside the road.

He waved for a lift so we stopped and I piled the pillows into the space between the seats and slid onto them. The man wasn't really old, just weather beaten. We asked him a few questions but he seemed afraid of us. He answered in a few words. Perhaps he didn't really understand our accents. We certainly found his difficult. I think he was a ranch hand and just had a few days off in town, for there was a slight smell of alcohol and sweat. Except for his ragged shirt, everything he wore was black leather. He called our eagles Condors and thought it strange that we thought Rheas were strange. I don't think he knew anything about the world outside his own, for he showed not the slightest interest when we said we were from North America. Perhaps he just had a hangover.

At the town of Facundo, beside the road, our passenger got out, thanking us formally for the ride, and we continued on our way to Sarmiento, between two lakes, where there was a campground that was highly reccommended by the ACA. It was in an oasis of lush, green grass and tall trees - their tops waving in the wind - that must have been impressive to anyone who lived in the vast, treeless pampas. But the campground was not very nice, so we decided to move on. And in the town, on a dirt street, we came to a general store. The counters were widely spaced on the gray wooden floor and we wandered arond, picking things up - four small bottles of orange juice, a package of margarine and a bottle of the 'common' wine - and the bill for the lot was 56 cents.

Then we went east, across the pampa del Castillo, to the city of Comodoro Rivadavia, on the Gulf of San Jorge. And there we drove around, looking for somewhere to stay. The motels were all at gas stations, in poor neighborhoods and the hotels were in the center of town, with nowhere safe to leave Minim. But we found a Tourist Information Office in a big building and a girl said there was a campground at Rada Tilly.

As we had neared the coast that day, the pampas had turned into rolling hills and oil wells. It is always strange to come upon high technology, after hundreds of miles of open country. And of course the police checks began again - also traffic and people. I'm sure any hotel would have looked after the car but we weren't quite prepared to return to civilization. Another night in the tent in a quiet campground would help. Perhaps tomorrow we would be ready to adjust to this world.

'Rada' is a nautical term, meaning 'anchorage' and about nine miles south of the city, there was a wide bay and set back from the beach, under a barren hill, was the campground. It was run by the ACA and so new that their own maps did not show it but the guardian encouraged us to set up our tent in the lee of the white and yellow hut which would one day contain a restaurant and other facilities. For the moment, there were toilets and cold showers, that he assured us we were welcome to use. And as soon as our tent was up, it filled with children. There were several other campers, some in small vehicles but most in tents, and the children wandered around in a group, discreetly tailed by one of the mothers. As foreigners, we were quite an attraction but when each one had asked a few questions and examined our posessions, they left.

Though it was nearly mid summer, it was cold in the night on that windy beach. But by morning, the barometer was rising - we use our altimeter as a barometer - and it looked like being a nice, warm day for travelling. But first we stopped to chat with the people in the other vehicles there. Next to us was a young couple with a small trailer, down from northern Argentina on vacation. And out in the parking lot, alone and aloof, were some people in a gray Mercedes motorhome, not large but very fancy (they barely spoke to us peasants). But the surprise was a red Volkswagen camper, with an elderly couple in it from Seattle, Washington.

We saw very few people from the United States, in all of South America, but the husband had worked for a big company and spent some time in Argentina. And when he retired, they decided to stay and look around, before going home. They said that if we changed our money at the banks, we would be given the official rate of 80 pesos to the dolar. But in the Parallel Market (what a lovely term) we could get 120 or 140 and it was not even illegal. All we had to do was go into a money shop and demand the best rate. And they told us about a hotel, in the middle of Buenos Aires, that had a garage next to it, where we could safely leave Minim.

After missing Santiago, there was no way that I would bypass Buenos Aires. And now with a safe place for Minim known well in advance, even Patrick would have to reconcile himself to a few days in a city. It is hard to believe that he was born in London. I thanked them profusely.

Shopping in Comodoro Rivadavia, we noticed a great deal of prosperity, from the oil found there. And at a junction, outside the city, we saw a monument to a dead driver. It looked like a shrine, beside the road. But there were rows of empty bottles, on each side of it. And old tires at the corners of a barren plot, outlined by white stones. And a sign, on two tall posts, saying 'Dead Driver' Freshly cut flowers in tin cans stood among the bottles, though the monument did not look new. And wreaths of artificial flowers, gleaming white, hung on fence posts. We could not tell if it were all for one driver, or in memory of everyone who had died at that intersection. Probably the latter.

Beyond the junction, there were two control points, a few miles apart. One was run by the immigration authorities and the other by the police but at each one, we had to go through the same proceedure, submitting all our documents for inspection and answering the usual questions: Age? Marital Status? Reason for Travelling? And so on and so on. We still found the Argentine officials more serious and abrupt than the ones in Chile but as each inspection progressed, finding nothing out of order, their attitude softened a little. As we left, the police lieutenant said there was a campground 14 miles west of of Ushuaia, on the far side of Tierra del Fuego. And he told us to come back on Route 40, to see the woods and lakes, and the glaciers at the foot of the Andes.

Every check point seemed a little different from the last, so we were never quite sure what to expect. But usually Patrick would take care of the paper work, so that if it were necesdary to leave the car, he would get out and deal with the officials, while I stayed in my seat and watched our belongings. I would have offered to go with him but it seemed a bit rude - if not downright suspicious - for both of us to get out and then lock the car. So mutual distrust dictated our routine. But Patrick was showing signs of impatience. A moan when still another road block appeared in front of us. Less cheerful when I asked him about his talks with the officials. Maybe, when we reached more travelled routes, there would be fewer mandatory stops.

Then we drove off, along the dramatic, sweeping coast of the Bay of San Jorge, to the village of Caleta Olivia (on the map) which turned out to be a busy new town with a huge statue - in the middle of the road - of an oil worker in a hard hat, turning a wheel to open a valve in a pipe. There Route 3 left the coast and when lunch time came, we pulled off the road, behind a bush, to get out of the wind (two horses who were there moved to the next one). While June put out the food, I crawled under Minim, to investigate a new noise - an intermittent bonking - and found that the bracket which held the front end of the muffler in place had broken. The next village, called Fitz Roy, had nothing but gas stations, so we turned off the highway and went nine miles down a gravel road to Jaramillo - just a few houses, with dirt streets - where we saw two gas pumps, beside a gray house. And behind it was an old fashioned garage, complete with a picture of a naked girl pinned to a wall but clean and well equipped. Its owner, the mechanic, could not repair our bracket, for it was an assembly of rubber and metal, bonded together. But we suggested that perhaps he could contrive something out of an old piece of rubber hose, lying in a box of junk. And soon he made a fine, new bracket, better than the original one.

We helped him search for bits of wood and metal, in the piles of trash, inside the garage and out in the yard behind it. There was plenty to sort through. And for good reason. We were getting farther and farther from any source of supply. You could stand in the middle of that dusty road and except for a few houses around you, there was nothing in sight. A railroad track ran to the east of the village and there were poles along it but it did not seem to connect to anything. A train did pass while we were there. One car only. Coming out of nowhere and going no place. It didn't even stop where we were and it was so far away that we barely heard it, over the sound of the wind. I had a very distinct feeling that it didn't really exist, or maybe we didn't exist. But back to the piles of useless things which were about to become useful again. We were full of suggestions, inventing all sorts of rigs from the materials available, but the mechanic denied them all, until just the right thing turned up. Then he performed a miracle, as people who live in places like that do, almost every day.

As he worked, the wind whistled in the roof of his garage, rattling the corrugated iron. And I checked our latitude, on the map. It was about 47 degrees South. That made sense. We were in the Roaring Forties, that part of the world where the wind blows hard out of the west, all around the earth. His bill for the job was less than a dollar, so we bought some gas - he had Super, which was surprising, in that place - and went down the street, to the local control point. It was a clean, white hut - just one bare room - and the policeman inside it was very friendly. He showed us the silver pipe though which he drank his tea (as we do, in Patagonia) and the cup - made from a small gourd, decorated with silver - out of which he drank it. But while he was writing down the details of our documents, I wandered over to the far corner of the hut, to admire his loaded sub-machine gun. hanging on the wall. And June thought he became quite nervous, for a moment.

The policeman spoke of his mate' with firm reverence. He drank it at mid morning and mid afternoon. And only from that cup. It had been his father's and was now his. It was carefully rinsed out after each use and locked away in a wooden case. It was used only for mate' and now, after so many years, imparted a distinct flavor of the drink. Mate' from any other cup was not the same. Was mate' more than an ordinary tea? I was told that it had nothing to do with the tea women drink. Did he make it in the hut? No, his wife or child delivered it to him twice a day. That was their job. He seemed pleased let me know that women and children in his world had things to do and didn't waste the time of important people by asking silly questions. If Patrick hadn't admired his machine gun, our conversation might have gone beyond basics. But the atmospehere seemed to be getting strained, so we shook hands and parted.

It was too late to go much farther, so we went southeast - the land was flat and windy and bleak and empty, with nothing but short grass and tiny bushes, a few inches high - to Puerto Deseado, a small seaport on the Rio Deseado, where it flows into the Atlantic Ocean. Driving around, we found a sign which said 'Municipal Offices' and going inside to ask for information, we were taken in to see the Mayor of the town. Ships no longer called at the port, so he was trying to develop a tourist trade, based on the fact that penquins could be seen on some islands in the river. They had already built a Municipal Hotel, overlooking the Penguin Islands. And they had a campground for people like us. Sending for his assistant, he told him to show us all the facilities.

The mayor was a handsome young man with thick black hair and a very businesslike manner. He did want us to enjoy our stay and was quite disappointed when we insisted that our visit was just an overnight stop. And even more disappointed when we asked about a campground and spurned his new hotel. If we had stayed a few days in the hotel, I'm sure a banquet would have been arranged in our honor. At least, he gave us the distinct impresion that we were the most important happening in town. His assistant politely took charge and led us in his truck to the campground, at the edge of the town. But it looked more like a city park and there were piles of empty beer bottles - a bad sign.

The campground was in a small ravine, well sheltered from the wind but with no facilities (though he said that they would have a new one, with hot showers, soon) and there were no other people there, at all. June thought it would be unsafe, at night, so close to the town, and I was inclined to agree. Any Bad Guys could knock you off at their leisure, there. So we took a room at the hotel, a small, modern building on a hill. Down to the left was the port, just a few docks along one side of the narrow river, near the sea. And to the right were the islands, farther upstream. But we could not see any penguins from there, so we drove down to the bank of the river. On the shore of the nearest island, there were many large seagulls, wandering around. And among them were some penguins. But they were small and hard to distinguish from the gulls, at a distance, except by the way they waddled, when they moved.

In the town, there was quite a lot of activity, in spite of its having 3,000 people and no industry. But it was the only place that big for 100 miles around. And it must have been the commercial (and social) center for all the people living in the lonely ranches, out on the vast, bleak pampas. The Municipal Hotel was laid out like a small gas station, with the reception desk, a bar, a gift shop and the restuarant, all in one big room. We saw no other tourists, that evening but some of the local people came in for a drink   it was doubtless the nicest place in town - and a few stayed for dinner.

Our waiter spoke English and much better than I could speak Spanish. He had been a waiter in New York and dozens of other places. I had forgotten that Rio Deseado was a port. It provided one of the few jobs available to a young man - that of a sailor. He had joined a ship's crew when he finished school and sailed aboard freighters for several years. But this was his home, where all his family lived, so he had come back. Our dinner arrived. I had ordered the local fish. It was light and fresh. But Patrick had fried chicken. Everything on his plate was the same color and he complained of indigestion before he finished eating. The waiter returned and beamed when we said we were enjoying our dinner. He was advising the kitchen on what was popular with tourists, since he had travelled so widely. And the chicken dish was his recommendation.

Minim was parked outside our room and when I went to check her in the morning, I found a tire flat. The problem was a nail, so I took off the wheel and marked the place. Then I asked the manager of the hotel about getting it fixed. And he insisted on taking it down into the town, in his own truck. While he was gone, I checked the spark plugs. They were foul, after seven days' use - which was not unusual, in South America - so I changed them for clean ones (checking the gaps, with a gauge, to be sure they were properly set). But the new bracket, holding the muffler in place, was fine. When he came back, I rotated the tires (it was that time) then checked their pressures. And the one that had just been fixed had 45 pounds in it, instead of 30. Of course, the man in town did not know what pressure we wanted, so he gave us plenty. But if we had left it like that, we would probably have had a blowout before long. If you did not check such things for yourself, you could get into trouble, in those parts.

The AAA map of South America showed a highway (number 282) going southwest from a point just outside Puerto Deseado. But it did not exist, in real life, so we had to go back 75 miles, over the route by which we came, to Jaramillo. There were several llamas grazing, along the way. In the distance, they looked like deer but some were quite close to the road and we could see them clearly. June tried to get a picture but each time she aimed the camera, they would turn away and she fetched up with a fine selection of llamas' rear ends.

We hadn't seen llamas until now. I think they are very much a cold weather animal and we had been in relatively warm areas. In fact, we hadn't seen much livestock so far. Wild, or perhaps just loose, horses but few range animals. But now llamas began to appear, grazing by the road. It was very exciting.

As we neared Jamarillo, it was windy, as usual. We could see several twisters, full of sand, working their way over the arid landscape. They moved slowly and we soon tired of watching them. We were making good speed on the flat, gravel road. But quite suddenly the sky turned beige, then brown. We couldn't see the road ahead of us. We stopped and watched the sand beat against the windshield. It was sand, not dust. The surface of the car didn't suffer much but the windshield was evenly pitted. And our visibility was cut considerably, from then on.

At Jaramillo, we got lost on an airfield, trying to find our way out of town. The runways were like the roads, just paths bulldozed flat, over the stony ground. And there were no signs or marks, to show which was what. But eventually we found Route 3 and headed south again, over coarse gravel. The only feature on the map in the next 100 miles was a gas station at Tres Cerros (Three Hills) beside the highway, in the middle of nowhere. So we stopped to fill our tank. But the young attendant did not know about narrow fill pipes, such as a Scout has. He stuck in the nozzle and opened the valve all the way and before long, it shut itself off. Then he set the meter back to zero. But the tank was nowhere near full and you do not leave a place like that without plenty of gas.

When I told him about it, his first reaction was to brush me off, as clearly ignorant. That was the way to pump gas. There was no other way. Of course the tank was full. And there was nothing he could do, now. The sale was completed. But I held my ground and explained that the fill pipe on our truck was too small - it was a fault in the manufacture - so that it could not be filled in the proper way. It was necessary to put the gas in very slowly. If he would be kind enough to try it, he would see for himself that it was indeed so. Still he resisted but we did not move the truck and I kept on talking, quietly but firmly, until he gave up and filled our tank. But if we had not been able to speak Spanish well enough to argue with him - which means thinking in Spanish, because you can not carry on an argument, translating back and forth in your head - we would have had to leave there with less fuel.

Then on we went, through the afternoon, rattling over the gravel in the strong wind   the sky clouding over and looking rather threatening - to another control point. And down a short side road to the town of San Julian. It was on a fine, sheltered harbor but seemed to be more residential than commercial, probably because it was the nicest place to be, for many miles around but there were few people in the surrounding countryside to come and buy anything. There was nowhere to camp and we saw no sign of a hotel but the old town dock was quiet in the evening and we found a spot, behind a large shed, where we could get out of the wind. A man in uniform came by in a car, so I stopped him and asked if we could spend the night there. He was rather offhand, like "Why not?" But he had a gun, so I decided we had the blessing of the authorities.

After picking up various nails and pieces of glass, we parked Minim alongside the shed, as close as possible, with her tailgate away from the road. Then we set up the table behind her and sat down to enjoy our dinner, with a fine view of the harbor. It was a wide, natural inlet, winding in from the sea, with lighthouses and ranges but no ships. Just two small boats and an old barge, white with black trim (and a tall privy, all the way aft) on the foreshore. There is something about such scenes that is beyond time or place. The iron sheds and coarse grasses and the low salt marshes beyond. We had seen them all so many times, before. And we were at home, there.

There were few people about in the town. An occasional car passed and once a group of young boys ran by, shouting at each other. But they did not seem to notice us, or care that we were there. The wind never ceased and soon a threat of rain hung over us. It was cold and damp and the evening took on a steel gray light. I was glad to pack things up and get Minim ready for our night's sleep. Even the gulls took refuge after a while.

It is useful when travelling like that to have a sense of danger, a little bird that whispers in your ear when it's time to run like hell. And we both have it, thank goodness. But there was no feeling of impending trouble, there. Still, you can't be too careful. A town that size cold have a few Bad Guys and one of them might find us. So we slept in the truck, with the doors locked and the ignition key in place. I could have slipped out of bed, into the driver's seat and started the engine, in seconds. And then Minim would be no easier to rob than an irate rhinoceros.

It was still windy, in the morning (I cleaned my electric razor, just by holding it up in the air) and the barometer was very low but the sky was clear, with few clouds and it was hot, in the sun - we had to wear sunglasses, eating breakfast at the table behind Minim - but the town was still quiet. As we drove up the road, toward the highway, we were overtaken by a police jeep. The sergeant was rushing to get to the control point ahead of us, to make sure that his men dealt with our papers properly. And he balled one out for not recognizing our license plates, which was unfair. For none of them, including the sergeant, cold understand a word of English. Yet they insisted on seeing our passports and both of our driver's licenses and all the truck's papers, which they stared at, singly and in groups, and passed to and fro and put down on desks and covered up with other papers, while June guarded the truck and I tried to keep track of all our documents, so that I could get them back when the charade was over.

The highway, going southwest, had a good gravel surface and the professional drivers would slow down and move over to the side of the road, when they saw an oncoming vehicle, to avoid breaking any windshields. But the hot shot amateurs - the gung-ho, gas can outside set - would barrel through, in the middle of the road. And we would stop altogether, as far over to the side as possible, as they went roaring past.

The wind was so strtong, in that section, that small birds would often take off straight up - climbing vertically, because their airspeed was no greater than the speed of the wind - then turn off, to go on their way. And the countryside was very dry, until we came to Piedra Buena, a small town in an oasis on the Santa Cruz river, down off the highway. There was a control point, as always, at the turnoff and we went through the usual proceedure, presenting our documents for inspection and answering questions about our ages, marital status, reasons for travelling, etcetera before we were allowed to go into the town. But between the highway and the town - it was only a mile, we passed a race track. It was nade by a bulldozer, over the gently rolling land, in an elaborate layout of left and right hand turns, some very sharp, some more gentle, with a straightaway past a grandstand. And it could only be for cars, or possibly trucks.

At the edge of town was a campground - tents on the grass, under tall trees, beside the wide, green river - and on the main street, there was a cooperative store, with everything we needed but wine. For that, we went down a dirt street, to the far end and into a small, dark shop where an old man did not believe us, when we asked for 'common wine', then explained that he only had it in rose' and filled our bottle from a wooden barrel.

It was nice to be in a town that looked alive. Perhaps because it was still early in the day and the wind hadn't come up to its full strength yet. People bustled along the streets, doing their errands. I fully expected the race track to draw a crowd, at any moment. But probably we'd have had to wait for a weekend - or maybe even longer - for that.

Leaving town, we stopped by the police at the control point and were made to go through the whole proceedure, of presenting our documents and answering the same questions again. And I told the sergeant that we had no control points, in our country. He was a nice man - otherwise I would not have said it - and he seemed genuinely surprised. He waved his hands from side to side in the air and said "You can't have people driving around without any control" I tried to assure him that it was true - that people went wherever they wanted to, whenever they felt like it - and it did not create any problems. But the idea was beyond belief to him, so I gave up. Clearly no man wants to believe that his job - his whole career - is unecessary. And we know that for generations, those people were ruled by Spain, though such controls. But they have forgotten that their lives were ordered for Spain's benefit, not theirs. The idea was to make them serve as masters, across the Atlantic Ocean. Now Spain no longer has that power, but the system remains. Why? It provides good, respected jobs for many people, who in turn have some influence on their communities. It is sanctioned and hallowed by long existence, so that those whose activities it limits would hardly dare suggest that it be done away with. And it is convenient for those in power. Of course, it has great disadvantages. It slows down the movement of goods and people, so that commerce as we know it is scarcely practical. The sheer drag of all that paper work must be enormous. And it leaves the poor people at the mercy of the bureaucrats who issue the travel permits. But it is unlikely to change for a long time.

The highway south of Piedra Buena was paved. And a note in our log says: 1310 - Cloud 9/10 cu. Speed 50. Wind W fce 6. Vis good. Road smooth. Engine running well at 2,800 RPM but a little rough at idle. We are both tired from too much travelling by now and should rest in a motel tonight, if we can. The land was less arid, now - occasionally we would see a ranch house, always with white walls and a red roof, set back from the road - and at four in the afternoon, we arrived in Rio Gallegos, our last stop on the mainland of South America before crossing the Straits of Magellan to Tierra del Fuego.

At a gas station, on the edge of town, we asked about the ferry across the straits, And the attendant said it went twice a day, at 6 AM and 6 PM but according to the map, it was 80 miles away, in Chilean territory and we would have to cross a border, to get there. So we went into the drab, sprawling city   mostly low, commercial buildings   to find out about hotels.   The girl in the Tourist Office was sleek and well dressed and spoke flawless English. She said the ferry ran from 8 AM to 8 PM on a continious basis - you had to wait for maybe an hour - until the 29th of the month, when it could not operate, because the tide would be too low. It was then the 15th of January, so we could make it, there and back, before the 29th. But she also said we needed a paper from the police, to get on it. So off we went, to the police headquarters, across town.

They do not let you park in their block, so June stayed to guard Minim, while I took my shoulder bag, with all our papers, and went up the steps into the red brick building. And a soldier with a machine gun - guarding the police, I suppose - ordered me to leave it on the floor in the hallway, beside him, then go and stand in line at an office at the end of a corridoor. I opened the bag and showed him there was nothing in it, except papers and money, but he would not let me take it with me. So I walked to the truck and left it with June, then went back with just the essential papers, in my hand. And the soldier had left. If I had obeyed his orders, the bag - containing money and papers and the Carnet, worth several thousand dollars - would have been left unguarded, in a hallway full of people. But those expensive papers were required by the authorities. And if they had been stolen, we might never have been able to take our truck home to the United States, through all those countries.

The line was not long, at the office where the permits to visit Tierra del Fuego were issued, and the whole thing only took a few minutes. But when I got back to the truck, neither of us could remember the names of the hotels that the girl in the Tourist Office had recommended. So back we went to ask her. And this time, her attitude was quite different. Before, she had welcomed me as a visitor to Argentina and treated me as an equal - she was probably the wife of someone important, who had been given the job - but when I walked in the second time, I knew immediately that I was not welcome. She stared at me, across the room, as though I had farted in church, and demanded - quite sharply - to know what she could do for me. There was no doubt that I had had all the service I was entitled to and any further questions would be a serious imposition on her goodwill. With suitable apologies, I admitted that I had forgotten the names of the hotels and she said "Try the Covadonga, on Roca Street" And thanking her, I went back to the truck, repeating the name, over and over.

In fact, the hotel was fine - an old, low building in the Spanish style, gray with white trim and more important, there was a safe place for Minim, in the enclosed yard beside it. The room we were given had a window facing the yard and we were able to park her so close to it that I passed our things in to June, through the window. We could keep an eye on her, there.

The room was small, just big enough for two narrow beds covered with pale, faded cotton spreads. But we had our own toilet and shower, with hot water. We washed ourselves and our hair and then I did some laundry in the hot water that was left. It was always a struggle to keep ahead, in the laundry department. Probably the clothes would not be dry by morning, hanging in the damp bedroom, but it was worth a try.

As soon as we were organized, we went out on foot, with a set of spark plugs, and had them cleaned by a mechanic in a small workshop, down the street. He was friendly and obliging and had a sandblasting machine, specially for that. Back at the hotel, we cleaned our water bags, which had collected some unidentified goo inside them. The sky was overcast and it rained, now and then, quite hard. We were too tired to go out for dinner, so we ate cheese and crackers in our room and drank the last of the wine and went to sleep. Before dawn, I woke up and looked out of the window, to be sure that Minim was safe. Then I was asleep immediately.

When we got up, it was a dull, gray day. There was a small dining room in the hotel, for breakfast and soon we were on our way. Driving across town, we passed an army barracks - huts set back from the road, on well kept grass - and there were notices, maybe thirty feet high, saying that the soldiers would shoot any vehicle that stopped. And there were soldiers with machine guns, who looked as though they certainly would.

You didn't have to read, to know what those signs meant. The black silhouette of a soldier aiming a gun was all that was necessary. I'd hate to have a tire blow out there.

Beyond the city, there was a police control point, then a gravel road to the frontier, where we cleared out of Argentina, into Chile. Then the road went on, to a junction where you turn left, to go down to the ferry. And at noon we came to the East Lighthouse, where the road went down into the water. The lighthouse, with a small cluster of buildings and two tall radio towers, guards the eastern end of the First Narrows in the Straits of Magellan, which are about 10 miles long and 3 miles across (the Second Narrows, farther west, are much wider) and beside it were a few cars and trucks, waiting to cross. So we took our place in line and sat looking across the calm sea - for there was little wind - in light rain under a gray sky, at the low shoreline of Tierra del Fuego.

We chatted with the family in front of us. They were from a town in the north and had come to see Tierra del Fuego for a holiday. There were five children. The youngest rode with his parents in the cab of their pickup truck but the older ones sat on crude benches in a homemade camper on the truck bed. It must have been a very rough ride for them. Still they were every bit as excited as we were to see what lay ahead.

With our binoculars, we could see that the ferry - an old landing craft, painted pale green - was on the far shore. But for nearly an hour, there was no activity. She did not move and no vehicles went aboard. Probably it was lunch time. Then we saw trucks moving, on the shore and soon she was heading our way. Thin sunlight was coming through the overcast, now and we could see white foam at her bow. As she approached, it subsided - she was slowing down - and when her bow grated on the gravel shore, the ramp rattled down, revealing 4 cars and 2 trucks, which came up the steep foreshore. Beside us was a big commercial truck - 34 wheels, in all, with its trailer - but a man from the ferry told the others to go aboard and there were six, including us. Near the water, we turned arond and backed up the ramp (so as to drive off, at the other side, forward) and when we stopped, the ramp went up. Going astern, the captain swung his vessel around and soon she was rumbling on her way, across the straits.

So the poor truck driver had to wait for the next crossing. He seemed rather resigned about the whole thing. It had probably happened before. And at least he was assured of space - he would have the whole ferry to himself.

The old landing craft had not been altered since she was built, except that high sides had been added, to keep out some of the spray in rough weather. And the atmosphere was casual - people wandered into the pilot house - but the fare was rather steep (@ 12.00 each way, if you paid in Chilean money, more in Argentine currency) for the twenty minute trip. Still it was fun to drive Minim up onto Tierra del Fuego (the Land of Fire) after so much effort to get there, And to go rattling south again, over the rough gravel road. At first the land was flat but there were patches of green grass and healthy little bushes and big clumps of white flowers, here and there. And well fed llamas with thick coats - brown and white - were grazing among them, unconcerned about us. The sky cleared and the sun came out and soon there were more mirages than you can imagine. Time after time, great lakes of shimmering water would appear and quickly vanish.

And sheep. Millions of them. I had no idea there were so many in the world. The road was very narrow, often no more than a pair of ruts through the mud. And every few miles, we would pass through an even narrower gate affair - a pit over which crude planks or sometimes poles had been placed to keep the herds of sheep from crossing into another ranch or pasture.

Then the land became gently rolling and we arrived at the second frontier - a collection of small wooden buildings that might have been an old ranch - where we cleared out of Chile, into Argentina (the island is divided into roughly equal parts) and from there, the road was paved. Along the east coast there were high, green hills and big, level meadows where hundreds of sheep grazed. The grass was lush and the sheep looked fat, they had so much wool on them. But the ranches were very large, for the houses were far apart, set well back from the road and surrounded by trees. And late in the afternoon, we came into Rio Grande, which looked like any small seaside town in northern England.

We could have camped on the grass, between the gas station and the beach - one enthusiast already had an orange tent set up there - but it was rather windy and the ACA had a hotel, called Los Yaganos, on a slight hill, overlooking the ocean. And things were so cheap in Argentina that we might as well be comfortable. They had one room left (though they had lost the key) and dinner would be served in their restaurant at nine o'clock.

The road ran between the town on one side and some docks on the other. There were big metal warehouses along the docks but no signs of activity - no ships in port that day. In fact, the hotel looked like the only open business in town. Cars were parked near it, while the other streets looked deserted. Like so many other towns we had passed. The one story buildings, all much the same, with cracked plaster, faded paint, curtained windows, huddled close together. Perhaps there were people inside, it was impossible to tell. And this was their summer! There were so many months when they couldn't go outdoors, they must have forgotten that in this month they could.

The hotel also had a bar and a bowling alley but no parking, except on the main street, by the front entrance. But other cars were parked there and the town was quiet, with few people around. And if anyone stole a car there, he would still have the problem of getting it off the island, without its papers. So we took the room, which was very nice, and wandered downstairs. In the lobby, we found maps and literature which indicated that the southern part of Tierra del Fuego was a vacation area. There were four ACA hotels (though each only had about 15 rooms) spread out along the last 75 miles of road, before the end. And a town called Ushuaia, where we could get supplies.

So we were evidently not the only ones going to the end of the road. But surely we must be the only ones who had not booked rooms and were expecting to camp, down at Cape Horn.

At eight o'clock that night, it was a bright, clear day. Outside the hotel was an exhaust fan, from the kitchen, dripping with grease. And upstairs, from our window, we could see down into an enclosed yard, where a side of beef was hanging against a wall and some fish was lying on a stainless steel tray, beside some old tires but quite far from the garbage. So for dinner, we had fish and it was good, fresh salmon. There was not much wind, in the night - far less than we expected - and in the morning, it was cloudy bright and still, with no wind at all. As we left, the manager of the hotel asked us to deliver two letters and a door spring to ACA hotels down the line. And at the edge of town, the road changed to gravel, going southeast along the shore for a while, then heading inland and climbing steadily up into lovely mountains.

First there were large bushes and small trees, beside the road and horses, with foals, taking their ease in the roadway, many of them lying down - then larger trees and a logging camp, with logs floating in a pond and big iron sheds and beyond them in a clearing, many small huts for the loggers. They were all the same size and shape, with a pitched roof and a door in the middle of the long side, facing the road, and a small window on each side of the door. But they were scattered unevenly through the clearing and painted different colors. as though it were important to the men who lived in such a place to express their individuality.

There was a pole near each hut, strung with wire, so they must have had electricity. A man sat on the steps in front of one, the doorway open behind him. And he stared, as we drove by - the vacant stare of a very tired man.

Farther south was Lake Fagnano - about 5 miles wide and 60 miles long - going through the mountains, from east to west. And near its eastern end, we found the ACA hotel called Kaiken (a neo-Bavarian structure of stone and wood) where we delivered the door spring. A tour bus was there and the line for the women's john went clear across the dining room, from the stone fireplace to the windows overlooking the view. It was a relief to walk away from that scene, back to the truck and go westward for a while, beside the lake and eat our bread and cheese on the tailgate, among the trees. Then the road turned southwest, over more mountains, with dark green trees to a certain altitude, then pale green grass, then gray rock, streaked with snow. And we passed a high, level meadow with jagged, snow-capped mountains behind it and dropped down to the south shore of Tierra del Fuego.

On our left was the Beagle Channel (discovered by HMS Beagle) and beyond it were many islands, reaching out to the Isla de Hornos (the Island of Ovens) whose eastern tip is Cabo de Hornos, which we call, in English, Cape Horn. And ahead of us, below the mountains on a sheltered bay, was the town of Ushuaia (The 'h' is silent, so it sounds like 'Use-WY-er'). The frame houses and small buildings, along the shore and scattered up the slopes, were painted white or pink or blue. And coming closer, we could see that many of them were covered with corrugated iron. Between them were gardens, full of vegetables and bright flowers - sometimes rows of tall lupins - and in one of them, we found the Telegraph Office.

Inside, it was all varnished wood, with blank forms on a counter. And taking one, I wrote a message to June's mother in Benton Harbor, Michigan, saying: ARRIVED CAPE HORN ALL WELL WRITING

222

LOVE PATRICK AND JUNE. The fee for sending it was modest but there was a second fee for sending it in a foreign language (English) and another if you wanted it sent correctly, plus taxes, which the man behind the counter started figuring on the back of an envelope. So I took out our calculator, to help him. And he was fascinated by it. He had never seen one before. Then I asked how long it would take the telegram, to get there. And he said (in colloquial Spanish) "Let me see   It'll go by microwave to Buenos Aires ... Then by satellite to Chicago... Would you believe ten minutes?

Down the road, there was a shop for tourists - full of fur rugs and gift items - where we bought postcards of Ushuaia which said, in four Languages: 'The World's Southest Town' Another shop had Cinzano (made in Argentina) for 50 cents a bottle. And on a side street, we found a delicatessen - with all kinds of good things to eat - run by a friendly Italian who made us taste his spaghetti sauce (to go, yet).

It was a treat just to walk into a shop where you could smell the food. Everything looked so good and it was difficult to decide what to buy. We chose marinated fish, seviche, and some chicken that was done about the same way. There was good bread, too and some gooey cake that looked much better than it tasted. And a selection of cheeses. But we had to stop. No room in our icebox for all that food, or in our stomachs, either. We had been making do with bits of canned fish and cheese and biscuits for so long that anything more was too much.

In the middle of town was an ACA hotel, with a lounge on the second floor, where we had tea and cakes in front of a long window, looking across the street (and over three pink busses) at the Eagle Channel and the islands beyond it.

A good thing we arrived on a day with no cruise ship in port. We were able to get a table at the hotel and to stroll through the shops at our leisure. What a difference the tourist trade had made to that remote town. For the first time in hundreds of miles, there were flower gardens around the houses and signs of fresh paint. There were smiles on the shopkeepers' faces. People looked alive. Even the sun managed to shine through holes in the clouds that ran endlessly across the sky.

Then we went to the docks, to buy fish. The port policeman let us in, when we told him what we wanted, and there were two fish boats at the dock. But it was Saturday and I could not find anyone on them, though I went aboard. The crew's quarters were bare - a few chipped mugs in the galley and little to cook with - but in each pilot house, there was a full complement of modern electronic equipment. Probably they needed it, there. Nearby, a bearded sailor was taking pictures of seagulls with an expensive camera, so we spoke to him in English. Sure enough, he was American, from the Research Vessel Hero (like a big offshore fisherman, with a red steadying sail and a high pilot house, well aft) working the Antarctic.

He told us there was usually someone selling fish, but not on Saturday or Sunday. We had missed the market day. It didn't really matter, since we had overstocked at the deli. And in spite of the sun, it was so cold and windy, standing out there on the dock, that I no longer cared. I climbed back into Minim and waited for Patrick.

From the dock - out in the water - we had a good view of the town. The pastel colored houses did not go far up the green foothills and close behind them were gray mountains, with snow on their upper parts. Patches of blue sky showed, now and then, between the clouds that passed rapidly overhead. And it looked as though a storm might come up at any time. But the main road stayed in the lowlands, near the shore, and it was only 12 miles to the end, where a sign said we were entering the National Park of Tierra del Fuego. There we found a campground, with a few tents in it, but it was in an open, windy place. Then we came to an ACA hotel, in a small meadow. And another campground, in a forest of tall trees, with many tents (but few vehicles) under them.

On the far side was a clear, level spot, near the end of a lake, where we set up our tent. It was a perfect site, there was no wind in the forest and we were sheltered from any storm, yet we could see out, through the trees, across the lake. And that was the End of the Line. We could go no farther south. It was cool, in the tent, as we ate our dinner. And there were children, running and laughing in the woods. But I did not recognize the trees. At eight thirty, it was still daylight but getting cold, so we went to bed and were soon asleep.

We might have been warmer in the truck, But most of the other people were in tents and if they could stand it, so could we. I wondered where they all came from. We hadn't seen many cars along the road. Or had they flown into the little airport near Ushuaia, with their pup tents and fishing poles? Like many campers in remote spots, they kept pretty much to themselves, so we did too. Somehow I felt let down, to have come so far and then found a campground at Cape Horn. But the beauty around us made up for that - all the clear colors, in the mountains and the lake and the huge green forest. Even if we did die of pneumonia, the trip would have been worth while.

About midnight, some people in a motorhome started thir diesel generator, which made a loud noise and woke us up. We were snug and warm in bed - just our noses were cold - and we lay there, angry at them for being so inconsiderate. But others were awake, too. After a while, a delegation with flashlights banged on their door and made them turn it off - we hoped they would freeze, without it - then the campground was silent, but for quiet chatter and a flute playing. It rained lightly, for a while, in the night. But when we woke up, it was a glorious morning - blue sky and white, fleecy clouds and sunlight, through the trees - and we went for a walk beside the lake, with snow-capped mountains around it - and one fisherman, standing quietly in the distance.

Then back to our tent, for breakfast. The campground was silent and there were many brown rabbits in the forest. For so long, we had only been concerned with going south. Now we were far from home - very far - and must find a way to get there. But on the way, we should see more of South America and its many countries, while we had the chance.

And the rush was over. We could take time to look around us. To stop and rest now and then. Not there, in that cold, but farther north, in warmer summers. There was so much to see   Lake Titicaca, Macchu Picchu and of course Buenos Aires. Only a thousand miles of gravel roads and another thousand of pavement and we would be in the big city. I was ready to start as soon as we finished breakfast and folded our tent.

8 - WANDERING DAYS

While our tent dried in the sun, I checked Minim's oil and so on. Birds were singing, in the forest but otherwise, we could hear the silence. Everyone must still be sleeping. As we left. we saw the red Volkswagen from Rada Tilly and stopped to speak to our friends. And on the way out of the park, we passed a new wooden building, where toilets and showers (with hot water) were being installed, for the campers.

The people in the Volkswagen were going to stay a few days. They liked fishing and for an angler there could not have been a more beautiful spot. And too, the van was probably quite pleasant at times, with the stove going. But Patrick wouldn't let me take our stove inside the tent.

Driving into Ushuaia, we noticed that the Hero had left already. And when we stopped for gas, the attendant was drunk - a thing we rarely saw, in South America but then it was Sunday morning. Perhaps he had overdone his Saturday night. The Beagle Channel was dramatically beautiful - shimmering blue, in the sunlight, with dark green trees, along the shore - and the islands beyond it looked like mountain tops in the water, gray-blue in the distance, with snow on their crests. But soon we turned away from them, to go up into the mountains and an hour later, we came across an accident.

A gray pickup with a camper shell had arrived just before us, from the same direction, and a small boy was being sick out of the back. And beyond it were two wrecked cars. Both were small sedans - a family in a blue one and some young boys in a red one - and in a long, straight stretch of good gravel road, they had collided head-on. The wreckage told the story: As they approached, the red car swerved across the road, in front of the other one. Probably the driver was going too fast, applied the brakes and lost control. Several people were hurt, so June gave them first aid, on the grass, while I got out Minim's towline and dragged the cars off the road. When I asked the blue car's owner what to do with it, he looked at me in disgust and said "Push it down the bank, it's no more use" And turning, he walked away. Soon a small, open truck came along and the people from both cars piled into it, with their posessions. A big woman sat in front, weeping and the driver of the red car lay in the back, on the steel bed. Someone gave him a drink of 7-up and off they went, rattling down the gravel road.

I could not help them much. A small child from the front seat of one car had a good bit of glass around his eyes. And they all had cuts and bruises but were not bleeding a lot. The boy driving the red car seemed pretty badly hurt but the men managed to get him out of it and into the passing truck. Sometimes I wonder if he got to a hospital alive.

There was no more we could do, since both cars had been abandoned, so we continued on our way. And in the afternoon, we ran into snow, freshly fallen since the day before. It was wet and not heavy (maybe two inches thick) but in theory, the 20th of January should have been the hottest day of the year and that was the 18th. The overall timing of our visit to Tierra del Fuego was just about right. But it seems that the weather is unreliable, even in mid summer, there. As we dropped down, out of the mountains, we left the snow behind and at Rio Grande, there was no sign of it. But the ACA hotel was full and the others were not very nice, so we got gas and went on, in rain now, to the frontier of Chile. When we finished clearing with all the authorities on both sides of the border, we asked permission to camp nearby. But the soldiers would not allow us to do that, so we drove on, looking for somewhere to spend the night, where the carabineri would not shoot us for being out, during the hours of curfew.

We really never knew what would happen next. We thought, when there was no room in Rio Grande, that if nothing else, the soldiers at the border would let us camp near them. It did seem logical. They could keep an eye on us, if they thought we were suspect. Now it was dusk and we were very tired but we didn't dare stop in sight of them.

Going north, the land was low and bleak, with no shelter. And as the sun went down, we were getting anxious, when we saw a gravel pit, beside the highway, that would do nicely. It was just a small one, for gravel for the road, but our tire tracks would not show, among the others leading to it. And inside it, we were out of sight, from the highway. Around us, the sides were about 20 feet high, so we were sheltered from the wind. And the rain water would drain down, through the stones. Surely the carabineri would not suspect that anyone would spend a night there. But in fact, it was fine, for us. After eating our dinner in Minim, we made up the bed and put up the curtains and slept all night, undisturbed. In the morning, I used my electric razor and we put on clean clothes and by eight o'clock, we were on our way, refreshed and looking like ordinary, middle class people on vacation.

There were signs, by the road, for Punta Espora, which we took to be the ferry ramp. But when we go there, we found that it was no longer used, since there had been an oil spill from a supertanker. So we went on to Bahia Azul, where we found a line of vehicles, waiting to go across to the mainland. Standing there, we spoke with a scientist from Texas, who was studying the oil spill. He showed us Polaroid pictures of it - like an airplane runway, about 4 inches thick, along the shore near the old ferry ramp - and he said that such spills are bound to happen, now and then, for economic reasons. A big tanker like that only has one engine and if it ever breaks down, she is uncontrollable, until a tug reaches her. She is very long and hard to steeer, in narrow waters. And so heavy that it takes her a long way to stop, even when everything is working. Yet she routinely goes through narrow channels at full speed, in any weather, without adequate visibility. For it is cheaper to pay lawyers to haggle with the victims of accidents than to build and operate such ships any other way. And to their owners, the bottom line is all that matters.

At noon, it was our turn to go aboard the ferry. She was called (in Spanish) the Southern Cross. The day was cold and sunny, with a strong west wind, but the sea was quite calm in the Straits of Magellan, except for a slight tide rip near the middle, where the current was running at nearly 10 knots. The air was so clear we could see every detail on the far shore. And going across, we met a Chilean engineer.

We were introduced to his daughter, a girl of about twelve. She seemed embarrassed that her own father would speak to strangers but he was enjoying the conversation. His eyes danced and he laughed easily, while she stood silently looking away.

When we said we would be travelling north through Argentina, he told us about a man, with his wife and children, who had been stopped by bandits near Cordoba, the year before. They had used a woman, with a child, as bait - standing by the road, as though needing a lift - and when the car stopped, the came out of the bushes, took eveything of value, including the car (which was not insured) and drove off.

But we did no take such stories too seriously, when they were about things that happened to somebody else.

As the ferry slowed down, the engineer invited us to join him for lunch there was a restaurant at the junction, about 10 miles away - so we followed his car and when we got there, he went across the main road and down a driveway, to a white house (with no signs on it) surrounded by tall trees. Inside there were tables in the main room (formerly the living room) and a long passage went from it, past other rooms. So we sat down at a vacant table and while June and the others were chatting, I looked over her shoulder. An elderly Patagonian waitress came down the passage - her hips swaying, from side to side - in an emerald green miniskirt, with a bouffant hairdo and a great, big leer. Quickly I glanced around the room. There were eight other customers - all men - but none of them seemed to be interested. Probably they had seen it before. And she was looking at me. We must be in a Full Service Establishment. I decided to pretend I didn't notice her and looked the other way. She came up beside me and I joined in the talk of food, as the engineer gave our order. Then relaxing, when she left, I saw the green miniskirt go back down the passage.

I wanted to wash up and was directed down the passage, past the kitchen. There were several closed doors but the one to the lavatory stood open. A few minutes later - as I emerged - a door just beyond opened and out came our waitress. I could hear male voices in some of the rooms and then a call for service came from the end of the hall. We both ignored it. She hurried into the kitchen and I returned to our table. Our food must be ready.

When she brought our lunches, the waitress seemed faintly amused but did not persue the matter. And as we ate, our friends at the table gave June a recipe for making Choclo.

The recipe seemed identical with the one we had been given in Vichu-quen. But I copied it down, anyway. We tried to include the daughter in the conversation but she would have none of it. Finally she told her father that she couldn't understand our Castilliano. He became quite annoyed and told her that she wasn't trying. But we could not blame her. She had, after all, lived most of her life on Tierra del Fuego. A stranger was a rarity in her world. And she coped with this rarity by turning away. We had met her on their first day of travel. After three weeks visiting the mainland, with all the new experiences, she would probably return a very different child.

The engineer was working for an oil company, out of Punta Arenas - about 80 miles southwest, on the Straits of Magellan - which had a booming trade in sheep, plus new activity from oil found in that area. When the bill came, he insisted on paying for our lunch and as we parted, outside the restaurant, he said "Think well of Chile" It sounded like a plea. At the frontier, we cleared out of Chile, into Argentina. And outside Rio Gallegos, we were inspected by the police. Then we went to the same hotel as before and since it was early, we gave them our laundry, to be ready in the morning. It rained hard, now and then, out of low, gray clouds and we were too tired to go wandering around the drab city, so we slept until seven and walked to a nearby restaurant for dinner.

The waiter suggested a mixed grill and pointed out that most of the people, at the other tables, had them - small iron stands, enamelled white, each with charcoal in the lower part and bits of meat and such in an open tray, above. So we ordered one and it was awful. The chunks of grilled mutton were almost impossible to chew - I found no way of separating the gray meat from the yellow fat - and the other items seemed to come from parts of a sheep that I would prefer not to know about. But two girls at the next table were having a great time, spearing choice items with their forks, chatting happily and looking around them, with the air of people enjoying something special. So we told the waiter it was fine - just too much - and went back, between rain squalls, to the hotel.

That meal became the low mark on our gauge of dining experiences in South America. It was worse than the fish stew at the docks in Lima. It couldn't be compared with the lunch at the restaurant cum brothel. Heaven help us if things got worse. It wasn't the meal itself that was so bad. The bad part was the memory of it. It would not go away. And the nagging feeling that it might happen again.

As we left in the morning, we took Route 40 northwest toward the Glacier National Park. For a while the gravel road went straight across beak, level pampas, where we saw many mirages. Then it climbed into rolling hills, with now and then a ranch house - and sheep pens - in a hollow. And dropped down to the Rio Bote, where we stopped to clean Minim's galley. It was hot and sunny, with a light wind and snow-covered, jagged mountains in the distance. How quickly the climate had changed. There were few cars on the road but the people in them were all on vacation. And when we got to the small resort town of Calafate, no accommodations were available until March. So we bought food and went west, on a very bad road along the south side of Lake Argentina, to the park.

There was an efficient police check as we drove into Calafate. They were used to tourists but there were a couple of cars ahead of us, waiting to get through. Patrick went into the hut when called and since there were people standing arond the car in front of us, I got out to chat with them. I'd grumbled about the five police checks we had to pass though that day and one of the women said she thought it wonderful that there were only five police checks for them, that day, too. The government was much more relaxed about travel than it had been.

At the end of the lake is a high, wooded peninsula, with narrow arms of water on its north, west and south sides. And a glacier, more than a mile wide, coming down from the Andes, at its southwest corner. The road went west, along the south side of the peninsula and in the trees, down by the water, we saw a campground, with many tents in it. So we found a good spot and made our camp there, for the night. There were no facilities but we got water from a mountain stream, a few inches wide, across the road. Anything else would have to wait, until after dark. Most of the tents had families, in and around them, quietly enjoying themselves. But a group of young boys arrived and started blasting the area with their music - the bang and shout kind. We did not feel that we could say anything, since it was their country, but it seemed a shame that the people who had come so far to spend an evening in the woods should be forced to listen to it. In that society, only the children of the very rich could afford cars, while they were still young. And probably they were used to the privilege of doing what they liked. I do not think that any of those boys even considered whether their music might bother anyone. It did not matter, either way. No one complained, perhaps because it was not wise to do so. Money and power went together. Someone's daddy might be the Chief of Police.

While I was fixing our dinner, one of the young men came over and asked to borrow some parsley. We had none but he saw the fresh tomatoes on our table and took one of those instead. We wondered what he was preparing, that he could use tomato as a substitute for parsley. But when he left us, he headed for another campsite, then another. I'll bet they had a thick, hot soup for their dinner, that didn't cost a thing.

At ten o'clock, it was still daylight. The water below us was calm but a light northwest wind was bringing very cold air down from the Andes. A whole Swiss family - we did not ask their name - went into a tent like ours but smaller and closed it for the night. At eleven, the boys turned off their music and in the stillness of the woods, we soon fell asleep.

At five in the morning, the young boys started their car, zipped the engine for fifteen minutes, banged the doors and drove off   badly honking the horn.

There was no sense in getting up so early. It was cold but not the icy cold of Ushuaia. So we stayed under the covers and soon got back to sleep again.

It was still cold at eight, so we folded the tent and set out for the end of the road, near the glacier, where the ACA had a hostel. On the way, we passed a better campground, down in a hollow. And at the hostel, there was breakfast.

A heavy set Germanic type was drinking from a gourd cup at the bar.

232

Evidently he was the innkeeper. He was very friendly when we qestioned him about the mate' and even offered Patrick a sip. He also said that women don't drink mate' It was too strong. Was it narcotic? Patrick couldn't tell from the taste he had. It wasn't a distinctive flavor.

Nearby was an open headland, beyond the trees, facing the glacier - a great river of ice, gleaming white in the sun - that came straight from the top of the Andes, fifteen miles away. On either side of it were high mountains, white in the distance and on their tops but green with trees, lower down. Where it hit the headland, the glacier piled up on the shore. And on each side of the headland, it was flowing down into the water. Though the glacier was level, from one side to the other, its surface was not smooth. It was all jagged peaks and hollows, with deep crevasses every few feet. Where it ended in the water, near us, a vertical cliff of ice - scarred with crevasses - went across to the far shore. And every few minutes, a huge chunk of it would fall into the water, with a thundering roar. As they drifted away from the icy cliff, the chunks would melt slowly into the water of the lake. And one day, find their way down the Rio Santa Cruz to the Atlantic Ocean.

We must have stood there in the shivering cold for nearly an hour, watching the glacier move. The ice had a green or turquoise tint in the hollows between its peaks. The movement was too slow to detect until the last second, when there would be a resounding crack and - as if in slow motion - a huge chunk would fall into the water, Then a sheet of spray would fly ino the air, splashing rainbows over the ice.

Two other people were on the headland, a French couple who had spent the night at the other campground. They told us that a climbing party had waited three months that year for the rain to stop, before going on the glacier. In fact the fine weather we were having was most unusual. So we headed back, the way we came, to be out of there before it changed. At the control point beyond Calafate, the man on duty did not believe that our passports were documents. Evidently he had never seen American ones before. He glanced at them, flipped a few pages and handed them back, ·ing "Not those, I want your documents" Clearly he thought I was up ·mething. So I told him that we were from a foreign country, far away, where proper documents were not yet issued. And with great misgivings, after much hesitation, he allowed us to proceed.

The road from Calafate to the junction with Route 40 was called Route 0 (Zero) on the map. We checked the insert that covered the area around the Glacier National Park. Sure enough, it was Route 0. You might as well use all the numbers. On route 40, we went north and at the village of Charles Fuhr, a few miles away, there was a ferry across the Rio Santa Cruz. A large sign said OFFICIAL FERRY - FREE SERVICE DAILY HOURS FROM SUN TO SUN - MAXIMUM LOAD 10 TONS. And a small one said: Road Closed from 1300 to 1400 hours.

The river carries all the water from Lake Argentina, down to the sea, and there is a strong current in it. A steel cable hung across the river and a pulley, on the bow of a boat, ran freely along it. So when the boat was turned at an angle to the current, it drifted slowly across to our side. It was a narrow boat, made of steel and painted gray, with just enough room for two vehicles, one behind the other. But the bow was pointed, so they had to go on and off by a ramp, lowered down from the stern of the boat to the gravel shore.

The ferry's name was the Fifth of October. But we never did find out what great event happened on that day.

A pickup and a tank truck came off, all right, but a truck going our way could not get on. The angle between the ramp and the shore was so sharp that its wheels got stuck in the rushing water. After a few tries, it came back, so we turned Minim round and took a run at it in reverse, and went bouncing up onto the ferry. Then four boys in a small Citroen came up, going forward, and the ferry drifted across to the other bank. When the boys tried to back their car off the ferry, they got stuck in the river, at the bottom of the ramp. So three of them took off their shoes and waded ashore to take their weight off the car, and the driver backed it up the gravel. But going forward, we had no trouble in Minim and went past them with the shy, diffident smiles of the totally smug.

Ten miles later, there was another ferry, across the Rio La Leona (Lioness River) and since a lone man was operating it, I helped him. Then the road continued north beside the river, which carries the water of Lake

Viedma down to Lake Argentina. But the land was so bleak and barren that the occasional clump of yellow flowers seemed out of place.

The ferry's name was the Ninth of July. On that day   in 1816 Argentina declared her independence from Spain.

The third ferry, near lake Viedma, had been replaced by a bridge. And east of the lake, the road turned northeast, toward Tres Lagos. But then Route 40 doubled back, to the northwest - to end at the Plateau of Death - while we took Route 288, which went east across the pampas, toward Piedra Buena. At eight o'clock that night, we were driving across vast, open plains, when we saw a lamb, beside the road. So we went up a driveway, to an estancia, to tell someone. It was a plain, white frame house on a slight rise, with a few small outbuildings and some large bushes, to break the wind. When I knocked on the door, an old woman let me in. She and her husband looked English and all the funishings in the house were like those I had seen in northern England. But they spoke only Spanish and lived alone, in that remote place. I told them about the lamb and they thanked me and I left.

We wondered if they would really care about the lamb at that time of night. But the poor thing had been struggling to stand up. Maybe, if they wanted, they could save it.

At nine, we were under dark clouds   there were puddles of water, beside the road - with the sun golden behind us and a big rainbow on either side. The Rio Chalia was down in the valley to our right and we were going well, on smooth gravel but there was nowhere in sight (or on the map) to spend the night.

At times, the land would fall away on both sides and we seemed to be on a high, endless ridge. Each mile of road looked just like the last one: Straight, gravel, not a tree, nothing to give us a sense of size or perspective. And there were rainbows ahead - all the colors in vivid, distinct arcs - touching the earth at both ends. Our speed was good over that empty road but there was no feeling of it. For mile after mile, nothing changed.

An hour later we came to an oasis of level farm land, with a long row of poplars beside the road, secluding a fine estate. And across the road was a patch of gravel, in the lee of some dense bushes, so we stopped to check it. Going east, we had hardly noticed the rising westerly wind and by then, it was strong. But close to the bushes, we would be shelered from it. Though not from the road. Anyone passing could see us. We thought about that. There was no curfew in Agentina, so the soldiers would not shoot us, but there might be some Bad Guys out at night, We could go into the estate and ask for permission to camp there. But most likely, the owners would be away and the foreman would say no. Then we would just have attracted attention to ourselves. And if the owners were there, they would feel obliged to invite us into their house, which would never do. It was better to be travellers, outside the gate, and take our chances. But it would be stupid not to minimize them. So we parked the truck in the farthest corner, where people driving east would have little chance of seeing us and those going west would not catch us in their headlights, for the road was quite straight there. It was warm, out of the wind and although a few vehicles passed in the night, no one bothered us.

There were pieces of trash on the bare ground. So we weren't the first travellers to make use of that little bit of shelter. And we slept in the truck, that night. Neither of us felt comfortable in those surroundings.

Going on, in the morning, we passed an even finer estate, with six rows of poplars on all sides. And at the junction near Piedras Buenas, the ACA had a small restaurant at a gas station, where they served breakfast. Then we went north on Route 3 (the way we came) past San Julian and Tres Cerros. It was clear and sunny but very windy (as it was before) all across that bleak, empty country. And there was a line of vehicles waiting for gas at Tres Cerros. But we had enough, so we went on to Fitz Roy, where there was no line but they would only sell us 3 gallons. Still, that took us to Caleta Olivia, where there was plenty, of both kinds. Thank goodness we had a car that went a long way on a gallon of gas. Approaching Comodoro Rivadavia, we were questioned and had our papers examined and everything in our car inspected at three control points. One was manned by police, another by immigration officers and the last by customs inspectors. But they all looked at the same things and asked the same questions.

Patrick became increasingly impatient with the questioning and we wondered if they were being more thorough because we were coming back into the area of oil fields.

When we got to the campgrojund at Rada Tilly, it was very windy and some other people were camped in the lee of the white and yellow hut (the only sheltered place) so we went up on the hill behind, a little way and slept in Minim. But not much, for she rocked on her springs in the wind all night. As we packed up to go, a small girl in a white blouse and pink slacks climbed 45 wooden steps up a steep bank to a water tank nearby, then slid down the dirt bank to the bottom - again and again - with a happy smile and cries of "Hola" Then we went northeast on Route 3, recently paved, and it was 260 miles, straight across bleak, level country to the city of Rawson, where there was no gas of any kind.

A government town, it felt like a cross between a resort and an asylum. But it had a hotel, called he Provincial - a modern building, on legs - and there was one room left. Things were so cheap in Argentina, we did not have to ask the price, so we took it and the girl at the front desk said a friend of hers would tell us when the gas truck came. The interior of the hotel was done in Early Bus Station, with tiled floors and a booming radio and tall windows, with venetian blinds. But the dinner, at nine oclock, was nice and the wine bottle was marked Tourist Selection.

We always liked to end a meal with flan, the baked custard so prevalent in South America. At least it was prevalent on the menus, if not in fact. For often when we asked for flan, we were told "No hay" (there is none) and given an alternate. But that night, there was plenty. So will all dessert lovers please note that in Rawson, Argentina, half way between Buenos Aires and the Straits of Magellan, "hay flan".

After dark, we went outside to see the Southern Cross - the constellation in the southern sky, equivalent to our Great Bear and Pole Star, in the north - but we were not sure if the one we were looking at was the False Cross or the real one. So we asked a well dressed man passing by and he had no idea. In fact, he was not aware that there were two of them. Breakfast was served in the bar. Few people (and no customers) were up by 9 AM. And there was still no gas in the city, except at one garage, where a long line of cars was waiting. So we went to Trelew - an ordinary town - ten miles away It was a Saturday and the streets were jammed but we needed to change some money, so June looked after Minim, while I asked about a money shop. But there were none, in that town.

Patrick thought Trelew ordinary because it was like most U.S. farming towns on a busy Saturday. Everyone and his brother was there to get things together for the week ahead. We had to wait and then fight for a parking lot. The hardware shops, the grocery stores, the auto parts places were all full. We would double park - waiting for a slot - until a policeman came down the street and then drive two or three times round the block, waiting for him to get out of sight, before we dared to double park again.

Passing an air cargo office, I went inside, with the idea that anyone engaged in that sort of business might know about a money shop. And a customer standing there offered to change our dollars for us. He owned an ice cream store, so we followed his car there and he emptied the till. But it was not enough, so he went off to get more, from various friends.

To entertain us while he collected funds, we were served huge ice cream cones from the shop. The ice cream was made there and he was very proud of it. The best in all of Trelew.

Then we bought groceries and went to the ice plant, which was closed. But they let us in and sold us some, anyway. There was no gas in Trelew but someone told us to try at Puerto Madryn - another town with a Welsh name - about 40 miles north. And there we found plenty, even super.

The government was in charge of the petroleum industry and controlled its distribution, which they had not as yet mastered. There seemed to be no set schedule for delivery. It came when it came and if it didn't come you waited until it did. Which amounted to a very simple plan of distribution.

That was a seaside resort, with a road along the shore of a bay and many shops, full of people. A few miles to the southeast lay Punta Loma, famous for its seals but they had all gone south. And it was too windy for tenting on the beach beyond the sand dunes, so we headed north again.

The town was full of tourists and the beaches were crowded. We passed a camping area that was packed to capacity with brightly colored tents. And we had been told that the Valdes Peninsula, which lay to the northwest of there, was a 'must' to see. But we just couldn't face the mobs, so we passed it up.

238

The highway ran straight across bleak, empty plains, with nothing but short grass and tiny bushes. The surface turned to gravel and we came upon a green truck, full of men, broken down in the road. So we towed it, up a gentle hill, to a gas station at Sierra Grande   the men were surprised but happy - and went on to San Antonio Oeste, a small town with dirt streets.

And found a small store open. It was at the end of a block and the doorway was cut out of the corner. Across the open door hung a curtain of beads, commonly used to keep out the flies. Inside, young women stood behind glass counters and wrote down, on scraps of paper, everything we asked for. Some of the goods were stacked on stands, on our side of the counters. And other things (the more expensive items) were on shelves behind the girls. We found boxes of mate', right out in the open, where anyone, even women and children, could help themselves.

Each clerk worked a very specific area and when we asked for something outside her realm, we had to go to another - and no argument about it. Finally, we were given chits, which we took to the cashier - near the door - who tallied them up and asked for payment in full. Only then, after the money changed hands, did we receive our purchases. To get them, we had to go back to the clerks and present the stamped receipts. It was all very time consuming. And considering how small the shop was, and that each girl could see and hear the whole process, it seemed a waste of time. However, we did now own a box of mate'

Southwest of the town, there was a watering place called Las Grutas - cottages along a beach and campgrounds (inside a chain link fence) on a rise, above them - and there we set up our tent, to the great interest of the other campers. Though there were many tents, we were the only foreigners. And people did not expect us to speak Spanish, so they would try to translate each word. When we said "Carpa" (tent) they would say Carpa? - then pause, and think, and say "Carpa!" - as if it were the last thing they expected to hear. But soon they began speaking more easily and told us to visit Mendoza, in the wine country, but to beware of bandits in Cordoba.

They were mostly teenagers and young married couples. The youngest ones ignored us, but the others crowded around, asking questions. They wanted to know if it was true that the standard of living was higher in the U.S. The yardstick seemed to be the number of electric appliances we had.

We could not sleep, that night, because some boys in the next tent kept shouting - they were having a party - until dawn, when two cars blazed off, racing their engines. Then the rest of the boys turned in but we were wide awake and frustrated, so we gave up trying to sleep and drove away from that place.

We didn't belong with the surfing, swinging set.

From there, it would only be two days' drive northeast to Buenos Aires. But we wanted to see more of Argentina, before we left, so we headed north toward Santa Rosa.

The coast, between Bahia Blanca and Buenos Aires, promised to be a tourist alley. We weren't interested, so we went inland, across the pampas, toward the wine country.

At Rio Colorado, there was a campground (the sign said a Camping Park) down by the river, with tall trees for shade, so we stopped by for lunch - sitting on Minim's tailgate - and it was very nice. But though there were plenty of sites, few were occupied. All the campers seemed to be at the beaches. At that point we were on Route 22, going east toward the city of Bahia Blanca, and we wanted to be on Route 35, going northwest from the city. So it would pay us to cut the corner. And Route 2 went north, between the other two. It was just a narrow, dirt road but went straight across the rolling country and the weather was fine, so we took it. The land on each side was less arid than before more like Texas, with mesquite trees and cattle - and there were ranches, now and then. But the soil was dry and after a while, we ran into deep, loose sand to which Minim objected, so we turned back. Ten miles east along Route 22, there was another road to the north and though it was not on the map, the surface looked better, so we tried it. And after bumping over washboard for a long time, we came to Route 35, paved and smooth.

We drove though fields of grass, tall and green in the sun. And for many miles along the way, white and yellow butterflies accompanied us. Pests, I know they are, killers of grain crops. But lovely to our eyes, after our round trip through Patagonia. At lunch by the roadside, under cottonwood trees and still among the butterflies, a flock of parrots, about the size of our blue jays but bright green, chattered in the branches as we ate. I suppose they are pests, too.

By then, we were unlikely to reach Santa Rosa before dark and we were wondering what to do when we came to a sign, beside the road, saying (in Sanish) Camping Permitted. It was just a small place, with room for a few travellers to park and some bushes for shelter. But no one else was there, so we set up our tent behind two bushes, looking across the dry land, where a slight dust storm was in progress. A sign warned about fires but there were few trees around. And it was good to be camping in the pampas, even if we were dirty. At sundown, the wind died and the sky filled with stars - it was a superb night - and we went out to admire the Southern Cross, before turning in for a good, long sleep.

After breakfast, I worked on Minim (changing the air filter and fixing a door) but there was a faint tapping noise, in the engine, that I did not like. And when we left, it was warm and sunny, with a light breeze and scattered clouds. About noon we arrived in Santa Rosa, a nice old ranching town. A Tourist Office was being set up, in the central square, but it was not open yet. And at the edge of town, on Route 5, was an ACA motel, set back in a garden, with a carport beside each unit and a small restaurant. They even had all the maps we had been trying to get. And we had been on the road for 19 days in a row, so we decided to stop and get organized again. First we had Minim cleaned - it made it easier to work on her - then found a laundry and a barber shop. There had been no rain for 3 months and many forest fires. And back at the motel, there was pleasant Spanish music on the radio.

At breakfast we had trouble pronouncing 'naranjo' (orange) to the satisfaction of the waitress. And many Spanish nouns had changed, as we went from country to country. 'Quarto' (room) had become 'habitation', 'finito' (finished) was 'terminado'. and 'Espanol' (Spanish) had changed to 'Castillano' (Castilian). Asking about a mechanic to investigate the tapping noise in Minim's engine, we were referred to a garage by the monument to Mate' So off we went across town, looking for a statue of a general (most of the statues in South America were of generals) but in fact, it was a huge mate' cup, with a 'straw' in it maybe 40 feet high. And across the road was the garage.

The small white building only had room for one car, with a workshop along the side, but the mechanic was formally polite and seemed to be competent and after listening to the noise, he thought it was a 'big end' bearing, beginning to go. That was very serious. The engine would have to be taken out and torn down, to replace the bearing. And the chances of getting a new one were slim. We had not seen a vehicle made by International for months. And it was illegal to import parts into Argentina, at that time. But if we did not get our truck out of South America, we were liable to lose it (and our gear) and forfeit our three thousand dollar bond.

The mechanic sensed our concern and suggested that we get a second opinion, from an expert on engines. His boy would show us the the way. And off we went, across town again. The expert - a slim, youngish man with a mustache and a grave expression - came out of a machine shop on a busy street and listened to the engine with a stethescope as he took the leads off the spark plugs, one at a time. And finally he said "No, it must be a valve lifter, or a loose tappet" That was wonderful. Those parts are much easier to get at than 'big end' bearings and could probably be fixed. We thanked him and asked what we owed him. But he said "Nothing, it was no trouble" and left. So we went to the garage and arranged to see the machanic at 4:00 PM, after the siesta.

As we left, the car stalled. But it was just dirt in the carburettor, so I fixed it myself. At the motel, I did some odd jobs, like cleaning the battery terminals. And we were back at the garage early, to wait for the mechanic. He arrived 40 minutes late - in a clean white shirt - and took off the valve cover. With the engine running, we could see that # 1 lifter was making the tapping noise. But it should not do any harm, so he put the cover back. I thought it might clear itself if the oil were changed, so he did that.

Then we went looking for a money shop but there were none in that town. And we were warned about the National Bank, which would not only give us half the right price for our dollars but also take hours and probably lose our papers. Back at the motel, we found we had to say "Gin and Tonic and Gin" if we wanted a Gin and Tonic. For "Gin and Tonic" meant the tonic, alone. It was that kind of day.

There was a wind storm in the night that left sand lying in the streets, all over town - drifts of it, several inches deep and many yards long - and when we asked for directions, we got them at full speed in Castilian (proper Spanish) but Grand Marnier and Tia Maria were 90 cents a bottle. The manager of the motel changed our traveller's checks - he was glad to - so we bought gas and had a set of spark plugs cleaned. But the bossy little boy who did it set the gaps too close, so I had to reset them, before putting them in Minim. Then I changed the fuel filter and checked the engine and the tapping noise had gone. We were ready to move on.

Waiting for someone else to do something is the most frustrating thing I know. Perhaps we were overprotective of Minim but we did feel that the car and our belongings should be in sight if at all possible. So hour after hour was wasted waiting - first for work to begin, then for work to be finished. Then for the next day to come, so that we could start waiting again. There were lots of handshakes and smiles at the garages and the motel, when we finally drove off. We were all glad that it was over.

That evening, we went to a cafe on the square for drinks. The waiter left the bottles on the table, for us to help ourselves and seemed to know what we had taken, when we asked for the bill. And in the morning we left town, first heading north to Realico, then west toward the Andes and Mendoza. It was a long, dull drive across the pampas. Most of the journey through South America had been like voyaging in a small boat, where the islands - with their people and activity - are separated by vast stretches of nothing much.

Estaciones - ranches, or stations - were much closer together on the northern pampas. Much more good grazing land. And instead of tucking the buildings into crevices at the feet of mountains, here the ranches were set back from the road and surrounded by trees, just as they are on our prairies, to protect the occupants from the incessant wind. Driveways to the main houses were lined with Lombardy poplars or sometimes tall pines. Grasses were high, in the fields and the horizon seemed closer. Things were on a more normal scale than they had been in Patagonia.

Late in the afternoon, we were in San Rafael but a man at the ACA post said there was a good hotel in the next town, so we went on going northwest, now - and the countryside changed until it looked like northern California, with eucalyptus trees and poplars and vineyards beside the paved road. But the hotel was on the main street of the busy town of San Carlos, so we went on again - heading north - over high, bare foothills and through a thunderstorm, with a fine view of the Andes to our left, between the dark clouds. Then down into a valley, where we were stopped by the police. There were several of them, in the road, with machine guns and flak vests. And a very rude young man ordered us out of our car. But he was quite incompetent to serch us or to question us and he wanted to know what the car cost, so I did not give him a straight answer and eventually he let us proceed.

This bunch made us nervous. There were more men than usual and they carried more machine guns. We began to wonder if we had made the right decision, to carry on into the city.

It was dark when we arrived in Mendoza, a big city on the main road from Santiago to Buenos Aires (via the pass over the Andes at Portillo). So we went into the center, looking for a safe place to leave Minim. The man at the first garage we tried wanted us to leave the keys and from the look in his eye, that would be expensive. But later, we found an ACA one and left her there, on the second floor. The man in charge wanted a key, to move her but we kept the other one, for the tailgate. Throwing some things into a green duffel bag and an open string one, we set out on foot, to find a room for the night.

Driving around the city in intermittent rain squalls was unpleasant. At first, Patrick would not go into the center of town, where we knew there would be hotels. He tried to find one in a residential section but didn't. And after the last police check, we avoided the city limits. It seemed like hours before he finally gave up and drove into the center.

Nearby was a middle class hotel - the lobby was full of salesmen - but they did not have a room left. So we went around a corner, to another one. And though the girl behnd the desk was polite, there was no room for us. Of course, it was already ten o'clock at night. Maybe they were full. Or maybe our dirty old clothes and lack of luggage had something to do with it. We were advised to try a different one, on a back street. That was not nearly so nice but we were tired and hungry, so we asked for a room. The old man behind the counter demanded our passports and examining them, he became quite rude. It took us a while to disover the problem: June's said 'June Ellam', instead of 'June de Ellam' and he assumed she was my sister. He made it clear that it was not that kind of hotel, at some length and with a good volume of sound. So we explained that in our country, the names of married women were written in that way. And grumbling, he set about filling out the forms, to check us into a room just for one night. He spoke no English, so we could confer between ourselves without his understanding what we said. So we agreed on a plan. We waited until he finished and held out the key to us, then we walked out, leaving it dangling from his hand.

That old man must have been the grandfather of the police. We had not met anyone so unpleasant, in months of travel. He seemed to loathe us, as foreigners and we must admit that we did nothing to soothe his hate.

But we needed somewhere to sleep and it was getting late, so we went into the next hotel we found - a flea bag, where no questions were asked - and in the dirtty little room, we put on clean clothes, then took our valuables and went off toward the bright lights, looking for something to eat.

It was a disappointment to have to check into such a firetrap when we could have well afforded a decent room. And we were worried about carrying our valuables with us but we didn't dare leave them behind. We both wished we were back in Minim and out of that terrible place. But hunger drove us on. I wouldn't even consider eating cheese and crackers there. From the looks of the sheets, someone already had.

Though it was nearly midnight, the Avenida San Martin was busy. Cars were driving around, the shops were lit up and along the wide sidewalk, people were taking an evening stroll. At one place, there were tables, across the sidewalk from a restaurant the people went between - and when we sat down, a waiter came over. He was young, competent and nice. Certainly we could have dinner. He brought us steak and salad and good red wine.

We sat in the warm night air, with the noise of the city all around us, cars and busses, people laughing as they strolled along the sidewalk, the waiters joking amiably with us, with other diners, as they brought trays of food from the kitchen. Everything tasted so good. The meat was delicious. The bread was warm and crisp. Perhaps Mendoza wasn't such a terrible place, after all.

Then back we went to the shabby hotel and soon after dawn we were at the garage. The men there had not been able to start Minin, because they did not know how to operate the key and the steering lock. So they had pushed her a few feet to let another car out but otherwise they did not seem to have interfered with her. And with great relief, we drove off.

Safe and sound in Minim and on the road out of town, we had time to muse over the events of the evening, the hostility of the hotel clerk. As the crow flies, we were less than ninety miles from Los Andes, Chile where many thousands of miles ago a butcher had told us to go back to Argentina, where we belonged. On each side of the pass, we had been mistaken for the enemy. We had thought of going up the Argentine side, to see the huge statue of Christ, placed on the border years ago to help hold the peace between the two nations. But we decided not to risk it.

Heading north on Route 40, we picked up a young policeman who was hitch-hiking, with the thought that his presence in our truck might make things easier, at the check points. But it did not seem to help much, at the two we passed through. The police were still quite rude and our passenger explained why. A policeman had been shot recently, which accounted for the machine guns and flak jackets, the day before. Also, a general and a colonel were killed, not long ago. But that was political and did not concern us. At San Juan he got out and to the north was a desert, with views of the Andes and many signs saying 'baden' (gully), which marked fords, full of water and mud. Beside the road was a railway, with stations and platforms and signals, just like those in England. But no trains. And we stopped to help a businessman - alone in the desert - who was fixing the distributor of his car. But he was just changing the points, thank you.

When we stopped for lunch, we found the back of the truck unlocked. We thought it had been opened in the ACA garage during the night. But nothing was missing, that we could find. And if the men in the garage could open the back without a key, they could surely have made the engine run, with the key. More likely it had been opened by the police in Mendoza, checking up on us.

Near San Jose del Jachal a boy was trying to start his Jeep and wanted us to give his battery a boost, so I asked if it were a 12 volt one, like ours, and he assured me that it was. Then I took a look and found that it was a 6 volt one. If I had hooked ours up to it, I could easily have damaged our battery, as well as his. But the boy was indifferent to the whole matter. So I made his friends push him, to start his engine. Then the road became gravel and headed northeast, winding over dramatic mountains - all red rock and green bushes - where we drove through a flock of parrots and saw huge, black spiders, as big as your hand, and crossed 'vados' (fords) and arrived, late in the evening, at Chilecito.

Again we gave the police all our details, then drove into the town - once a mining one, now a vacation place where people came to escape the heat of summer - to an ACA hotel, where they had a room for us, for one night only. But we changed into clean clothes for dinner and in the morning, the manager said he had a room for us, for another night, after all. It was a cool, sunny morning in the pretty, quiet valley. Strolling around the town, we found many small shops, hotels and rooming houses, catering to people on vacation. There was a Tourist Office where a girl told us about a campground, above the town but when we got there, it had no facilities, just a place to park. And beyond it was a crude road - more a track, over big stones, following a large water pipe, no longer used - past many goats and some big cacti in bloom. They were tall saguaros with several branches and near the top of each branch was a cluster of big, white flowers with pale yellow centers, contrasting sharply with the harsh and defensive appearance of the spiny, green cactus.

Farther up was an aerial tramway, leading to an old mine but looking quite modern, as though it had been built and used and abandoned, all in a short space of time. And farther still, in the mountain village of Vellecita, a school was being built of wooden boards, brought up the road from the valley. In the afternoon, we took another unlikely road it went straight up a river, in one place - to the Indian village of Famatima, a cluster of houses on dirt streets, with tall trees for shade, where the ACA had bult a small motel. And on the way back, we found the ruins of Copayan   some adobe buildings which once had pitched roofs - among palo verde trees, in a desert like the one near Casa Grande, Arizona.

Behind the ACA hotel in Chilecito, the garbage men were lying on the ground, around their truck, listening to a radio. Our room had no shower curtaiun (or rail) and no toilet paper. The toilet seat was broken and the airconditioner did not work. There was no hot water, anywhere. The stair carpets were worn out. The girl at the desk downstairs was in curlers by day and primped up at night, smoking a cigarette and reading. But the other guests did not seem to notice anything out of the ordinary and it was not for us to complain, as foreigners in their country. Evidently their standards were different from ours. Things we thought important were of little interest to them. And vice versa. We would do better to see things from their point of view - if we could.

At dinner, we asked the waiter to bring a wine that was typical of the area. We were still in wine country, there were vineyards to be seen, to the south of the town. He brought a bottle of what he assured us was the one preferred by the knowledgeable. It was an Argentine version of Retsina - turpentine and all. We bravely toasted the good taste of the locals. The staff seemed quite pleased when we left some for them to enjoy later on. Or had they planned it that way?

Many things in Argentina were like America in the 1940's - wooden doored refrigerators and cars with loudspeakers in the streets, advertising things - but there were very loud speakers in shops, here and there, that dominated the whole block. On the road, the next day, the police were rude - one of them said "All right, who's the chick driving? Let me see her license. Get everything out of that car"   but mostly they were just stupid and could not understand the documents they stared at. Still, they seemed to have an almost absolute authority, so we were polite and diplomatic. But being nice to them began to please us less, with each encounter.

We had to go southeast, to Route 38, before heading north and about noon we came upon a car, parked beside the road in a desert. A young, pretty woman hailed us for help, while several other people stood in the shade of a tree. But they looked like a family, rather than bandits, so we stopped. And they were out of gas. We had little, ourselves and anyway, you can not get it out of Minim's tank, because of a right-angled bend in the fill pipe, so we could not give them any. But they assured us that a car would come along soon, as we drove off. They told us there was no gas in the town ahead but we had just enough to reach La Rioja, so we went on - slowly, to eke it out - and made it there. And by the pump was a little girl, with a pacifier in her mouth, on a Lambretta with her father.

She sat behind him, straddling the seat, with no visible ties to keep her from falling. As they left the station and sped back into the highway, her tiny hands grabbed his belt, the pacifier still bouncing up and down in her mouth.

It was so hot that we were glad of the airconditioner in Minim (we used it often, on that whole expedition and it never gave us any trouble) but at lunch, in the shade of a tree, with a light breeze, it was surprisingly cool. Six large stones had been arranged in a circle, to sit on but there was no trash on the ground, at the simple wayside stopping place. Farther along, we passed a shrine to a dead driver, much like the one at Comodoro Rivadavia, with rows of empty bottles, and stones painted white, and wreaths hung on fence posts. But it was on a straight stretch of road and seemed more likely to be for the victims of one accident, than of several.

The policemen who stopped us as we entered Catamarca were polite and chatty but took their time, with us. Some old ladies in the car ahead got into the spirit of the thing and made tea, while they waited but their car was blocking the road and after a while, an exasperated policeman moved them on. Then we passed through the city and took the road to La Vina, which one of the policemen recommended. But the narrow, gravel road was winding and dangerous. A car coming toward us narrowly mssed a cow and veered across the road, nearly hitting us. Then the road went up over a pass and down into a plain - lovely country with lots of proper trees and green grass - that reminded June of France. La Vina was just a tiny village, so we went down to the lake nearby, looking for somewhere to camp but the road went down into the water, with a fence on each side of it, as though the land had been recently flooded.

Back at La Vina, there was a village inn, like the French ones of 40 years ago. Inside, the decor was red, white and blue and three youngish men were sitting around a table - surveyors, from their conversation - so we ordered two beers and asked the owner if we could camp anywhere, for the night. The inn was next to the post office, which had a patch of rough grass in front of it, and he assured us that we could camp there. No one would bother us. It would be quite all right. And the land was level. So we thanked him and set up our tent there. But in the morning, the postmaster arrived on a bicycle and did not seem to hear June say "Good morning". In fact, he seemed to ignore us rather pointedly, as he swept out the office. Taking the hint, we folded our tent and went to the inn, for breakfast. Which was coffee and ladyfingers. And the owner showed us the skin of a boa constrictor, caught nearby.

Not wanting to leave behind an offended postmaster, we wrote a couple of letters and then, when he had finished sweeping, we made a handsome purchase of postage stamps. It took a while to sort though various volumes, to be sure the charges were correct. Then, of course, weighing the letters was a very exacting proceedure. And we had to decide which of several possible combinations of stamps we preferred. But, at last, he seemed confident that all parties involved in the transaction hand been faithfully served, so we shook hands and left.

Then we headed north and came to a military check point, with machine guns and a man lying in the grass with a radio and men covering the bridge ahead, in case we made a run for it. But the soldiers, who were rather dark skinned, were very friendly. They admitted that they had a problem with subersives but said we should be okay. So we went on again. Further north, there was another military check point - by then, it was very hot, indeed - and at noon we arrived in Tucuman, just as the shops shut, so we drove though the city and headed south on Route 9, toward Cordoba.

We stopped at an ACA service station to try to get maps for the section ahead but there were none. They were very busy. Tucuman was large and industrial and dreary. Too large for us. And with all the shops shut, there was no color - just drab, gray buildings, row after row, along straight paved streets. We saw no reason to stay.

The going was easy, on a paved road, and in the evening we went into the village of Ojo de Agua (Spring) for ice. But there was none. And nobody we asked knew of any camp site nearby, so we headed south again. The land on both sides of the road had been cleared, in that section, and there was no shelter from the strong wind. Or the bandits. As we drove into the dusk, we each scanned our side, for a place to spend the night. Then we found a gully, down beside the road, between an embankment and a field beyond. It was deep and wooded, with a path angling down into it and since there was no one in sight, we followed the path in Minim. As we came into the trees, the path made a couple of turns and a wire fence blocked the way. But already we were sheltered, from wind and view. And unless the bandits came down there for their own reasons, they would never find us. It seemed like a good place to camp.

Getting out of the truck, we looked around - taking care not to be seen, from the road - checking lines of sight, escape routes and so on. There was only one way out for Minim, so we turned her around, ready for a quick getaway. But otherwise, it was a fine place to spend the night. A stranger might have been surprised to find two elderly Americans, casually discussing details of survival. But the trouble was, we liked that life. The need to be wary and take a real, immediate interest in what was going on around us made everything seem sharp and clear. And we were much happier, in our tent, than cooped up in a hotel.

We set up the tent behind Minim and furnished it, with the carpet and table and stools, for dinner. And by nine thirty, we were in bed, for the night was clear and starry and it was cold in the sandy hollow. But when the sun came up, it was warm and pleasant outside, with few bugs around. And many red, while and blue flowers. So we took our time over breakfast and while June did our accounts, I checked the truck again. The locking gas cap had broken, so I put on the other one. And there was oil on the engine - I keep it clean, so that I can spot a leak, right away - due to a loose bolt on the valve cover, but otherwise it was okay. It needed constant small maintenance but then we did long runs, nearly every day. We had already gone about 9,000 miles since leaving Lima. It was almost noon when we packed up, to go south again and at the village of Jesus Maria, we turned off the highway   just before the city of Cordoba   to take a back road (past a nice, small resort in the woods) to Salsiburdes. Then we went west - on a winding, gravel road - over high, moorland hills, with stone hedges, like those in northern California.

It was cool and windy, with huge white clouds blowing across the sky. We could see patches of dark green woods on distant hills and clumps of gray, grazing sheep moved along the upper slopes. But later, the hilltops disappeared into mist and it began to rain.

As we ate lunch, beside the road, a car stopped and a man got out, to tell us it was dangerous on the roads near Cordoba, because of bandits. Then we dropped down from the hills - under gray clouds - into the busy tourist town of Falta. We were short of money, so we just bought bread and fruit and ice. Then we found a travel agent, who changed 200 dollars for us at 190 pesos each. That was up 60 percent (from 125) in two weeks. No wonder the manager of the ACA motel in Santa Rosa was glad to change them at the old rate. We went straight out to buy wine and Grand Marnier, then headed south on a road like Route 100 in Vermont, with wooded hills on either side and facilities for tourists strung out along it.

After a while, we saw a campground - across a stream from the road - with one trailer and many tents in it, so we stopped there, for the night. It was large, relatively quiet and only a year old but dirty and full of flies. Horses wandered through it, attracting the flies. And when I went to the water tap, to fill our plastic cans, an old woman blew a whistle, to call her boss (a blond, correct German type) in case - as she seemed to suspect - I was not entitled to take it. All the tents were brightly colored (most had orange top flies) and some had tall, narrow tents near them, which were obviously toilets. A little boy said ours was ugly (his mother took him away) and it was indeed drab, compared with theirs. But it was good for not being seen, especially in desert areas, and thus more practical for our kind of travelling.

Next morning, the old woman would not let June close the door of the john. Then a black cloud appeared, moving fast, so we left, heading south again. Half an hour later, we came into the big, modern resort town of

Carlos Paz (which was much like the Ozarks) and just beyond it we found an ACA campground, huge but clean and with all kinds of facilities. Near the middle of it was a restaurant, under a high metal roof. And distrusting the weather, we stopped there for coffee. Soon the rain started, then it turned to large hail, rattling on the roof, so we gave up the idea of camping for a day and found a clean, modern motel - like a Californian one. Of course there were differences. The shower was over the toilet, with no curtain but they provided a squeegee, to mop up the mess. And there was a bidet - when I turned it on, a jet of water got me under the chin . The airconditioner was eight cents an hour extra and was switched on at the front desk (you phoned for it). And when you looked closely, the whole building lacked real thought, as though designed by an interior decorator, with no practical experience. But outside, it was raining hard, from a gray sky, lit by occasional flashes of lightning.

A notice in the room said we should be quiet from 1400 to 1700 and from 2300 onward - from 2 PM to 5 PM (for the siesta) and from 11 PM onward. But the houses and buildings and names of people around there were often Germanic, and there were many blondes. So the German immigrants had adapted to Spanish hours, but were quite precise about spelling them out. We had hardly met anyone who spoke English for weeks, by then, and we kept reading the dials of our car in Spanish. We would be driving along and glance down at a gauge and think (in Spanish) "What does that word 'fuel' mean?"

Since leaving home, we had averaged $ 11.57 for Transportation, $ 6.06 for Food, $ 3.03 for Lodging and $ 1.30 for other things, making a total of $ 21.96 a day for 2 people and the car, which was not bad. But we were talking about taking a break when we got back to Vermont. Toward evening the rain stopped, so we went shopping. The town was a mad house - very busy - and a man on stilts strode through the crowd, with a megaphone in one hand and a clipboard in the other, calling out advertisements. Two shop keepers we met spoke English. One had worked in the United States before settling in Carlos Paz. Then we went out to a restaurant for Dubonnet and dinner. The owner put some Louis Armstrong records on the hi-fi in our honor - the other customers seemed to approve - and as we left, the sky was clear. Tomorrow we could go camping. The scheme by which we used the tent most of the time and motels when necessary sleeping in the truck, as a last resort - was really very good. It left us free to go where we pleased, when we felt like it, and kept the cost of living down (our food and lodging came to $ 4.55 a person a day).

When the sun came up, the land began drying out - it was cool and pleasant after the rain but we seemed to weary easily with all that travelling. Probably we should ease up for a few days. So we went to the campground and piched our tent in a quiet corner of the vast area. It was quite level, with brown dirt roads winding through proper park land - lush, green grass, dotted with trees - and between the trees, everywhere you looked, were brightly colored tents. Here and there were 'pilas' (places to wash your clothes) and near the middle, clustered around the restaurant, were stands selling fruit and beer and such.

The beer came in quart bottles, with no labels, for twenty cents (plus deposit) and was quite good, as I remember.

The whole place was fenced off and the gate was guarded, so it was safe to leave the tent and we went to a car wash, in town, where we met various well-to-do types. They all said the government was to blame for their financial problens. One - a career Army officer, who now ran an inn - said that Mrs. Peron did nothing for a year and things went to hell. A year before, one Argentine peso would buy one Brazilian cruziero. Now it took six of them. But all the people were polite and friendly and admired Minim. And they said there was a bridge over the river above Buenos Aires, which we could take to Uruguay, instead of the ferry steamer across the River Plate. Back at the tent, some other campers came by to chat. And they expressed the same views. Also, credit was too expensive - interest was one percent a day. And there was none to buy a car, though they cost far more than in the USA because no insurance (that was any good) was available. And traffic accidents were matters for civil suits, the police were not interested in them (so just don't hit a lawyer). But everyone said bandits were no problem in Argentina, though there were robbers in the cities. Maybe those people did not use the back roads.

The evening was cool, with a clear blue sky, and there was a general noise in the campground, but few specific ones. Birds sang nearby, as June cooked dinner. And at dawn, a big old cock started crowing - intermittently - outside our tent. Being a sailor (not a farmer) I was surprised to find that he crowed before laying a hen, not after. And the hen went on eating. If she stepped aside, he missed and came to a stop, some distance off, and stood there, looking bewildered. All that day, I worked on the notes for this book, typing them from my daily log, to send back to Vermont in case bandits or police took the originals, before we got home. And now, as I write my part, I am trying to keep the words I used at the time, to preserve the flavor. Which may account for the weird grammar and the curious little observations, now and then.

And I spent my day at the pila, with all of the other women, trying to keep up with the family laundry. There were four cement tubs, each with a faucet and you had to stand in line for your turn. The accepted proceure was one soaping and two rinses. Then off to find a tree to hang things on. I was slower than the others and surprised to learn that hand washing was a daily chore for them. There were no machines - or laundries, even - at home. But it was a pleasant enough time at the camp, standing in the open, under a warm sun and gossiping with each new arrival.

Oil was still leaking between Minim's engine and the valve cover, because the man in Santa Rosa had not tightened the bolts evenly. So we got out a spare gasket and went into town, where a mechanic put it on. But he was a 'hot shot' type and while doing it, he broke a vent pipe and bent the fuel line. By then it was evening, so we went off to explore the town but the throttle cable stuck, in the heavy traffic (he must have kicked the guide) so we limped back to the campground. Each mechanic seemed to fix one thing and break at least one other thing, as often as not. But the younger men - like the 'hot shot' type - were worse and the answer was not to let anyone under 45 touch the car, if at all possile.

For the second night, there were very loud cars revving up their engines from about 2 until 4 AM, so we could only sleep before and after that. But it was remarkably quiet there, in the day time. The campground bordered on a large lake, in the back, and probably most people were there during the day, So sleep was no problem, if you scheduled it correctly.

I worked all morning on Minim, adjusting the bolts on the valve cover, straightening the guide for the throttle cable, lubricating the cable and fixing the broken vent pipe. Then she seemed to be okay, for the moment. And as I finished, June came back from the pila with more clean laundry. A German couple dropped by, that afternoon - he was an expert on perm- anent magnets - and they said that Mrs. Peron was okay but the people around her were crooks, who looted the country and sent the money away to Switzerland and Spain. And later a girl teacher came by. She wanted to live and work abroad but she had no idea whether it was possible or not.

It was noticeable how we slowed down, when the pressure to move ahead was off. And the heat seemed to contribute to a feeling of laziness. Orion was bright and clear, that night - it was as easy to find there, as it is in the northern sky - and when I woke up, a wasp-type insect was drag- ging a huge, dead beetle out of our tent, so I opened the door for him.

Two of the men we had met at the car wash were spending their vaca- tions in the campground. They looked like successful businessmen and they were well dressed, in a sporting sort of way. But their wives looked like Southern Belles. Each morning, one of them came across the grass, from her tent to the bathroom - in a long dressing gown - with a covered chamber pot and a bright, social smile. And she always spoke to us slowly and clearly, syllable by syllable. That day, one of the husbands came by, in a Datsun pickup truck, with the two wives in the back - on the ribbed steel bed - made up and dressed like big, talking dolls.

We saw none of the rugged, unshaven, he-man type campers even in the most out-of-the-way places. Rather, the people seemed bent to the opposite extreem. We wondered if the women dressed and made-up every day at home, too. Probably not. Perhaps that is what made camping a vacation for them.

Three small boys, clean and neat, came to see Minim, so I opened her up for them. And when they left, the oldest took his leave, with formal expressions of respect. But the sky had been darkening and in the evening, it started to rain. All the next day it rained, out of a gray, overcast sky. Each tent in the campground seemed to be filled to capacity, with whole families - from old ladies to young children - and like us, they sat inside, waiting for it to stop. The tents were nearly all wall types but some were quite elaborate. The campground had a capacity of 500, with a beach on the lake, but no spaces were marked off and most people had picked a tree to camp under, for the shade. A third of all the cars were diesels and another third were ultra midgets, like Fiat 600's and Citroen 3 CV's. And we both felt flat, by then, after the long rest in one place.

Next morning, the rain was hard and steady. All the tents were wet, now. Most of them had low headroom and some had people digging trenches around them, to drain off the water. The whole scene reminded me of summer in Jolly Old England. At midday, it was cold and damp, in our tent. The sky was dark gray and it was raining harder than ever. So we went into town, where all the streets were running with water, for there were no drains, to take it away. But in the afternoon, the rain eased up and toward evening, it stopped altogether.

We walked to a delicatesen near the gates of the campground. It did seem good to get out and stretch our legs, even if we had to jump puddles and skirt patches of mud. In the store we found pans of cold marinated chicken, meat roasts, breads and cakes and a good local cheese. We returned to our wet tent laden with food and feeling much more cheerful about life in soggy Argentina.

After dinner, we sat on Minim's tailgate, discussing the problem of old age. Spanish speaking families keep their old people around. A gray haired lady was knitting outside a tent, not far away. And we had seen them minding babies, while the young people were down at the lake. They still had a place in the family and something useful to do. Which seemed better, to us, than sending them off to an instiution. And we agreed that there were few material things, if any, that we really wanted - perhaps a house, but a small one - and South America was now real to us, which it was not, before. But we had now had all the relaxation we could face.

There was no rain that night and though the sky was overcast in the morning, our tent began to dry. Checking the truck, I found the right rear tire was down to 11 pounds, so we pumped it up and took it to a tire place. As we waited there, several people came to look at Minim, so we opened the hood and windows for them - those people would not take anything - and when our turn came, the man soon found the trouble. The rim of the wheel had spilt, for maybe 15 inches. Leaving the tire there, we took the rim to a welder, who said we could have it at 5 PM, and back at the campground, everyone was drying things out. The sun was coming through the clouds and it was nice to sit on the tailgate, dangling our feet, while our tent and carpet and bedding dried. There was laundry hung out, all over the campground but it was not offensive. And an economist came by - he was going to study in Kentucky, next year. Travelling as we were was a good way to meet the middle class people, who go camping and run shops and the like, on an equal basis. People would ask where we were from and say "How nice" when we told them. Everyone was interested and helpful - 9 times out of 10 - all through Argentina.

We got to the welder's place a quarter of an hour early but he already had our rim finished. It was a fine job, welded on both sides, smoothed down and painted. And there was a 'go kart' for sale, outside. His son raced them and now that he was 13 years old, he was getting a new one. All the shops were open until 10 PM, so we went to the tire place, where the man put our tire back on he wheel. We decided to use a tube now, since we had two with us, then he balanced the wheel. And the cost for the whole job, including the welding, was about $ 3.20.

For us, due to the rate of exchange. But for a local person, the price was about what we would expect at home.

On the map, the campgrpund was 4 blocks wide and 8 blocks deep, from the highway, down to the lake. Most people - men and women wore blue jeans and were stocky, blondish German types, though we met one Italian immigrant. And a woman told us the tap water was not dirty but had earth in it from turbulence in the rivers (there were no filters). The sky was clearing, now. Our tent (which was under five eucalyptus trees) was dry. Crickets were chirping in the trees. There was one airplane, high up. And the sounds of children, in the distance. It was time for us to move on. But after staying so long in one place, it took us more time than usual to pack up and it was ten in the morning when we headed west, toward the city of Cordoba.

Again, we managed to arrive in Cordoba just as the siesta began. We

*had planned on a few hours of wandering around but now everything was
shut. We would have to wait until evening and then have to spend the night
there too. We had been held back too long in Carlos Paz and wanted only
to keep moving, so we followed the highway signs through the outskirts and
headed into open country.*

All through that section the AAA map of South America was of little
use. It showed small villages but did not mention big towns like Carlos
Paz. Or the superhighway that went southeast, from Cordoba to Rosario.
But the maps put out by the Automobile Club of Argentina were fine, so
we found it. Then it was a long drive, down into farm land. And about 10
miles from Rosario, we were stopped by two policemen, under a bridge.
They had a red Jeep, parked beside the road, and appeared to be making
a spot check of travellers, so we gave them our licenses and the car's
registration, as asked. Then one of them said we must pay a fine of 6,000
pesos. Which was about $ 32 for us but a lot more for a local person. And
he wanted us to give it to him in cash, then and there.

When I asked why, he said that June (who was driving) was in the left
hand lane. But there were two eastbound lanes, then a median divider. And
she was passing a car, which had stopped in the right hand lane. And there
was no other traffic in sight. So that hardly made sense and I said so.

Then the two men went a short distance away and talked in low voices
for a while and the other one came over, to tell us that there was a very
serious discrepancy in our documents, for which the 6,000 peso fine
would be very lenient. When I asked to see it, he showed me a digit in the
car's registration, which had been inked over by another Argentine
policeman, long ago - to make it more clear. So I told him that and said
he could hardly blame us for it. And back he went, to confer with the
other police man again.

Then the first one came over, with another approach. He understood that
what I said might indeed be so but rules were rules and we would have to
pay the fine, anyway. Otherwise he could not let us leave. We must stay
there. By then it was evening, so I told him that we had no cash on us -
I pulled a few small bills and some change from my pocket, to show him -
but we could stay there for the night, in our tent and if he would go with

us to the National Bank in the morning, we would get the money for him.

We had money tucked away in various corners of the truck. And I had some in my bag. But they accepted the contents of Patrick's pocket as being all we had. Thank goodness. For they both carried machine guns, as well as the revolvers on their belts. It isn't much fun lying to a man with a gun.

That called for another conference between the policemen and when the second one came over - they were taking turns - his tone was quite different. He did not want to put us to all that trouble. We were visitors in his country and he would like to be friendly. If we could spare a small gift for them, he would overlook the whole matter. He wanted Minim's compass but I vetoed that, so he chose the altimeter. I was equally friendly and agreed that his sugestion was reasonable. But unfortunately we would need the altimeter, to get over the Andes, back to North America. However, if he would give me his address, I would send him one. So he wrote it down and we drove off - the two policemen waving as we left - with his name and address. But I do not believe that he kept any record of ours.

Toward the end, I think they were looking for a way to let us go, without losing face. Our polite determination may have given them the idea that we had 'pull' somewhere.

In case there might be more clowns like that, down the line, we left the superhighway at the next exit and circled round the city, on back roads, before heading southeast again. We had been told, often enough, that the police in Argentina made no effort to enforce traffic laws. So the whole thing was a scam but at first we had almost believed it.

It was dark when we came to San Nicolas and Route 9 went through the sprawling, commercial town and somehow we got lost. But we found a police station, on a narrow, empty street, with barriers half way across it, at either end. So we drove around the one nearest to us and stopped at the front door to ask for directions. And the effect was dramatic. A policeman came around behind us, swinging his machine gun into position to fire and calling for help. Another came out of the station, saw us and went back in. There were shouts and the sounds of men running, inside the building. Then several policemen came rushing out, cocking their machine guns as they surrounded us and backed off, covering us.

I saw some people, who were sitting in the shadows near a doorway across the street, get up and go inside.

We stayed in Minim, rolled down the windows and said it was all right, we just wanted directions. The men were panting and looked frightened. If one of them fired his gun, it would be a mess. The others would fire, too. They did not seem to be interested in what we might have to say. Then a heavily built man   an officer   came out of the building and ordered me out of the car. Laughing, I said there was no problem, we just wanted directions. He told me to turn off the headlight but as I reached for the switch, he became even more nervous and ordered me not to touch anything. I told him, with a casual smile, that I would have to use the switch to turn off the lights. So he okayed that and I did.

Something had gone right - nothing blew up when I touched the switch - and the officer collected himself. In a loud, clear voice, he ordered me to get out of the car. I protested, saying that it really was no problem, we just wanted directions. But he waved his gun impatiently, so we got out. Someone pushed me against the car from behind and frisked me (not very thoroughly) and glancing over my shoulder, I saw an officer close behind me, his gun in my back. It looked like a Colt.45 automatic, a gun I had in World War II. The whole thing struck me as being funny and I laughed, quite loudly, as I told them we were just tourists, passing through his town, who were lost and had stopped to ask for directions.

On my side, more or less the same thing was happening. I remember being grabbed by one of the men. He tried to pull me away from the truck but I kept protesting, in English, that I would not leave without my purse. When things get out of hand, I usually start issuing orders in a clear, loud voice. The men seemed to understand. At least they stepped back, let me get my purse and didn't shoot me.

The officer relaxed a little. He lowered his gun and told me to show him our documents. His men, sensing that there was no danger, made important, agressive gestures. But they were no longer dangerous. Carefully, so as not to alarm anyone, I took my bag of papers from the car and showed them to him. But he was not interested, really. We had some documents, which was good enough. With a short, harsh laugh, he turned away and went into the building. And his men lowered their guns. So we got back in Minim and drove off, down the street.

By that time, we were a bit shaky. All we wanted was to get out of town but we had no idea which way to go.

We still had no directions, so we went straight ahead - turning on our headlights at a discreet distance   through the red light district. The buildings were dark but now and then a thin girl stood silent in a doorway. Going southeast, as best we could, we found our way out of town, onto Route 9. And about an hour later, we came to a motel, by a gas station. The long, low building was set back from the road, with grass and trees around it. And the room we were given was fine but the restaurant, which had big windows on three sides, was closed. However, if steak and salad and wine would do? At that moment, it would do nicely. thank you.

Before leaving the motel, we repacked Minim, putting our city clothes in suitcases and stowing or camping gear in the lockers. Then we screwed down the lids of the lockers and went on our way, down Route 9 toward Buenos Aires. It was rather grand to be driving into the city, having come from Vermont by way of Cape Horn. And the traffic was not as bad as we had expected. But the sun was hot, before noon. Maybe everyone (who was anyone) was out of town. We found the Hotel Castellar, which we had learned about at Rada Tilly. And more important, we found the garage, on a narrow street behind it, where Minim would be safe from thieves.

The garage was the whole floor of a small building and it was not full. Between the narrow pillars going up to the high ceiling were maybe two dozen cars. But the door was always locked and it was run by a family, so we left Minim. And across the street was the back entrance to the Castel-lar. That was an old hotel in the Spanish style, with a large restaurant on a wide, busy street. And though we had not made a reservation, there was a room for us. It was second rate and the airconditioner was noisy but it was not expensive. And it was located right in the middle of the city. There was a ladies' hairdresser, down in the basement - where men could not go and after being there for two hours, June came up, looking remodelled and reddish.

Men weren't allowed because, beside the hairdresser, there was a steam bath. The old fashioned type where you were clamped into a box, with nothing but your sweating head showing. Towel wrapped ladies with orange hair were being pushed into and dragged out of the machines. I settled for a shampoo and a set. But the beautician asked if I didn't want a bit of color. too. In my most exacting Spanish, I consented to a touch of something that looked close to my natural brown.

Although the area was airconditioned, the equipment was unable to compete with the adjoining bath house. Exposed pipes running along the ceiling dripped rusty water onto the brown, painted cement floor. Reading material consisted of tattered movie magazines but I really needed no other entertaiment than the endless stream of bodies, shuffling to the baths and back to the beautician entrusted with the final attempt to transform the sweating mass of flesh into a lady for another week of society.

When my turn came for the finishing touches, I was seated in front of a mirror covered with drops of hardened hair spray. My orange curls were combed out and arranged to the satiafaction of the operator. She beamed with pride.

On the sidewalk near the front door was a news stand, where we got a copy of Time magazine - our first international news in many weeks - and read that there had been a severe earthquake in Guatemala. We wondered how all our friends had fared but there was no practical way to find out. Farther along the sidewalk was a shoe shine man - middle aged and very European - in a sport shirt (with no collar) and light blue slacks, sitting on a low stool with his brushes and cans and bottles of polish laid out in neat rows on newspaper, beside him. In front of him - also on newspaper - was a stand to put your shoe on while he worked. And on the other side was a chair which he provided for his customer's friends to sit on while they waited. As he did my shoes, he laughed and chatted easily with June, and I had the feeling that he was accustomed to being treated as an established tradesman. The shop keepers we spoke to - looking for small gifts to take home - were much the same. And one of them told us that the police sation in San Nicolas had been attacked recently. The terrorists arrived by car and had a woman with them, to divert suspicion. Then they tossed a bomb into the building, through a door. No wonder the policemen were nervous, when we pulled up in front of their door in Minim, the night before.

Back at the hotel, it was cold in our room and there was no way to control the airconditioner, except by telephoning the desk downstairs and having it turned off. But the location, in the center of the city, was very convenient. Later, we took a taxi to a movie house. The driver said that the city had gone down badly and become very dirty in the past four years, though it looked clean to us. And we saw 'The Godfather' (part II) in English and Italian, with sub-titles in Spanish, which was confusing. But it was pleaant to walk back, along the wide streets, in the cool of the night and at 1:30 AM, when we reached our hotel, the big dining room was full of people drinking beer and eating sandwiches, so we did the same.

Fans droned above us, on the high ceiling of the restaurant. Between the clatter of dishes, the wire soda fountain chairs scraping across the marble floor and the chatter of the diners around us, there was no sense in trying to talk. Traffic beyond the big plate glass windows increased with the night. People, mostly men, strolled in, joined friends or sat alone and read a newspaper over a glass of beer. There was no urgency or excitement in their behaviour. This must be the way they spend every Friday night. But Patrick and I were not used to such hours. About 2:30 in the morning, we left the crowds below and returned to our little room tucked in a corner, high above the street. It was very quiet there.

That was Saturday the 14th of February and at breakfast the newspaper said there might be a strike on Monday - not of workers but shop keepers - to protest the inflation, which they blamed on the government. And in Argentina a strike like that might be hard to distinguish from a war. So we decided to leave for Uruguay on Sunday and went to the United States Embassy, to get our mail and any information they might have about the strike. But they had neither for us, so we took a taxi (he overcharged us) to the office of the ACA and were told we would have to be at the dock by 6 AM to catch the 8 AM steamer for Montevideo. But they confirmed that there was a bridge over the river at Paysandu and we could go around that way, by road, at any time of the day.

Having an afternoon to spend in Buenos Aires, we went to a museum but it was shut, that month - as we had guessed, most people were out of town, because of the heat - so we strolled around a nice residential section and went back to the hotel, to tell that we would be leaving on Sunday. But they said that would be impossible. The garage in which our truck was locked would not open until Monday. And there was no way that anyone could reach the man in charge of it.

That meant we could not leave until after the strike had started. And then it might not be safe, on the roads - or even possible for us to get through to Uruguay.

So I went down the narrow street behind the hotel, asking questions of the people leaning against doors and following up leads - quietly, politely - and soon I was talking to the wife of the man in charge of the garage. He would be glad to open it for me on Sunday. It would be no trouble at all.

For our last night in the city, we went to the opera house - a fine, old building but not airconditioned, as advertised - where a symphony was well but uninterestingly played, until in a moment of silence, a man dropped one cymbal on top of another - the conductor was less than pleased - and in an aisle near us, a woman was sick on the carpet. But it was really hot and jackets were required, so we left at the intermission and walked back to a restaurant near our hotel, for dinner.

A man followed us for a while, through the crowded streets. We both noticed him. His behaviour was a bit too obvious for a trained policeman, so we assumed he was probably interested in our billfolds. We made it quite clear that we were aware of his presence. Every few yards, we would turn and watch him. At first he would stare hurriedly in a shop window, then he finally gave up and disappeared down a side street. How did he know we were tourists? I had thought my orange hair made me look like one of the local girls.

Inside, the restaurant was like the kind in New York City where businessmen go for lunch - with elderly waiters, always in a hurry, pushing between the crowded tables. And the fish we had was not very good - the people in those parts did not seem to be interested in it, even near the sea. But soon we would be heading north again, into Uruguay and Brazil.

9 - LOOKING FOR SPIES

The streets of Buenos Aires were quiet on Sunday morning - there was no indication of the impending strike - as we went out to the northwest, into the level countryside. And an hour later, we were stopped by a policeman, who said we were speeding. We still believed that the Argentine police made no effort to enforce traffic laws but we might have been going faster than the posted limit and this man seemed to be serious, as though he really meant it and was not just looking for a bribe. So we pretended not to understand his Spanish. I let him go through his whole speech, about our sins, and smiling politely, I explained in slow, halting heavily accented Spanish that we were tourists from North America. If he would be kind enough to start at the beginning and speak very slowly, and clearly, I might be able to understand what he said.

He was really very good. He went though it again, slower at first but faster as he warmed to his theme. And as he got to the good part, I stopped him. I was very sorry but I just could not understand him. He was going too fast. He did not believe me, but he could not be sure. He stood back and stared at me, for a moment, then waved us on - turning toward his partner in the Jeep, across the road. And as we left he said quietly (in Spanish) "Congratulations"

For a moment, I felt guilty but it soon wore off. We had had enough guff from the Argentine police to last for a while. Surely it was our turn to be tiresome. And at Campana we found the ferry that went across the Parana River. At least, it tried to but it broke down. Luckily it was near the dock and someone threw a line ashore, for there was a strong current in the brown water, down toward the sea. And as it swung from the line, a mechanic fixed it. Then came a second ferry, from an island in the middle, to the far shore. Beyond, the road was gravel - the paved one on the AAA map did not exist - and the cars waiting there had windshield protectors, made of wire netting, held away from the glass by many corks. A small boy tried to sell me one and got mad when I pretended not to understand him. It was hot and sweaty and tropical - with green trees, down to the water's edge - but soon we were across the river and rattling along the straight road to the north.

At Gualeguaychu - a farming town - we found a nice, small delicatessen with tables for lunch (Yogurt, empanadas and strawberry ice cream). Several men with deep, loud voices were there and we heard that every business in Argentina would be shut, on Monday, for the strike against the government. As we left, June turned in the doorway to say "Good luck, tomorrow". And all the men looked up, surprised and pleased. The road north went through farm land, beside the Uruguay River, and near the town of Conception was the new International Bridge, with buildings housing the Customs, Immigration, Health and Police authorities, at either end. It was dark, by the time we finished with them all. But we were out of Argentina, before the strike started - presumably at midnight.

Down off the bridge were the outskirts of Paysandu and on a wide, tree lined street we found the Hotel Bolivar - a small, modern building with rooms upstairs and a restaurant (more like a coffee shop) below. The only place for Minim was in a garage, next door and they wanted the key, to move her. But they seemed like nice people - they had quite different accents from any we had heard before and spoke loudly, when we failed to understand them, as if we were deaf - so we gave it to them.

For a reason we couldn't fathom, everything seemed quite different on this side of the border. The officials at the crossing had been friendly and jovial, compared to their Argentina counterparts. The small town appeared neat and organized, as we drove though the cobbled streets, looking for a hotel. And now the young man and woman in charge of the garage were easy and open with us. The tense air that had engulfed us for weeks, in Argentina, suddenly disappeared. We felt very safe.

It was hot and sweaty, in our room but we had a fine view of the street from a long window. And the restaurant was closed but since we had no local currency to go out and eat, the waitress made sandwiches for us. Then we went for a walk. It was a nice, quiet town with real policemen - strolling along the sidewalk - who looked as though they were there to protect the people, not to enforce the will of a central government. After breakfast, we went to the garage and explained that we would need our truck, to go and get money to pay them. But it was no problem, at all. So we drove into the town and parked it on a busy street - a friendly police-man offered to keep an eye on it - while we went into a bank. The rate of exchange was not nearly so favorable as in Argentina and gas would cost us about $ 2.00 a gallon. But luckily the distances were not great in Uruguay, so it hardly mattered.

Food was expensive, too. We did a little light shopping: bread, cheese, fruit - things that would last in the heat - in scrubbed clean, bare floored stores. No one hurried. It took most of the morning to complete our few errands.

The main roads were numbered from left to right, as they fanned out from Montevideo, so we chose to go in on Route 3 to see the countryside and then take Route 9 from the capital, to see the Atlantic coast on our way to Brazil. Outside the town was a check point, where the police were quick and polite. But the customs officer at the bridge had put a big sticker - several inches square - on our windshield, with 'Temporary Importation Permit. Do Not Remove.' on it, so that we could not see forward, from the passenger's seat. Once again we were victims of mindless bureaucracy. Obviously an official had ordered that they be put there, for the conveni-ence of his minions. And the question of whether it might be inconvenient, or even dangerous to the occupants of the vehicle was not even considered. For a bureaucrat does not have to account to the people he orders around.

The road went southeast, through rolling country - mostly cleared for farming, with a small wood, here and there - and soon it was hot outside. But at lunch time, we found a clump of thick trees and it was cool in their shade. Few cars went by on the road, and there were green parrots on the telephone wires overhead. They flew strongly and could carry twigs as big as themselves, to build their nests in the trees. In the afternoon there were thunderstorms, moving across the country, with heavy rain beneath them.

And toward evening, we came into Monevideo. It was large and sprawling, less modern than Buenos Aires but probably a better place to live, with old houses on green lawns, set back from wide streets. We had no map of the city, so we asked a well dressed man the way out to the east. And he firmly directed us to the Rambla.

What a pity to miss Montevideo. Unfortunately, we arrived at the beginning of a rush hour. Everyone in town with a car was going some place in a great hurry. That was enough for Patrick. We skirted the center and headed out. But some day, we will go back. Even the little we saw made us think the city must be a special place.

That was a fine road along the coast, with wide beaches of yellow sand, curving between grassy headlands. No wonder he was proud of it. And across the road, between the older houses. were modern apartment buildings, looking out to sea. Just beyond the city was a Tourist Information booth, run by two policemen, who were friendly and helpful. When we asked about a campground, they directed us to Atlantical at Kilometer 45 on the coastal road. And before dark, we camped on a bluff, high above a beach, with some trees for shelter.

The tents were older and not so fancy as those we had seen in Argentina. And there were no facilities, except a store which sold beer and Coke. When I asked about water, the store keeper - a tall, thin man - said "Help yourself, it's in the kitchen" and went off to see about something. It was nice to be treated as an ordinary, responsible person in a strange land. But our tent gave us away, as foreigners. And three lots of campers came by to say "hello" that evening. They did not see many people from outside South America in the campground, so naturally they had questions to ask. And they were different from the people of Argentina - they seemed to be more European, somehow, in their outlook and thinking.

It had been a pleasant evening, chatting with these friendly strangers. Finally, when everyone left, we dug out the box of mate' This might be a good spot to try it. We were certainly not in any danger, on that sandy slope above the sea. I heated water on the stove, prepared the cups and made a light brew. Hesitant to use much mate' the first time, I crumbled a few dried leaves into each cup. It tasted like slightly 'off' water, so we added more leaves. The aroma was of green tea. After much discussion and many sips, we decided it really was green tea. It was the ceremony, not the drink, that had made addicts of the Argentinians.

There was a huge full moon, when we went to bed. And it was cool, with a light breeze. And there was no noise at all, in the night. But when the sun came up, it began to get hot. The bluff was not sheer but steeply sloping, with trees on it and a flight of steps, down to the beach. And in the distance was a headland, across a wide bay. Atlantical was an old fashioned seaside town, with a few guest houses for summer visitors but more vacation homes, some quite substantial, for people from the city. The shops were on a narrow road, winding through the trees, and there we changed a $ 20 bill into pesos. Then we bought 15 gallons of gas (that cost thirty dollars) and headed northeast.

An hour later, there was a toll booth (the second one we found, in all of South America) which cost 60 cents, leaving us with just 15 cents in pesos. Suddenly we were poor, after many weeks in Argentina, where we hardly thought of money. The road was inland, parallel to the coast and though it was paved, the quality varied. But the countryside was pretty, with rolling hills and small woods and farms. And in the afternoon, we came to the frontier of Brazil. The customs officer in Uruguay was not interested in the sticker on our windshield. He had all the details, in the documents. We could have taken it off and seen where we were going, for all he cared. But we did not know that.

It really wasn't that much of a problem. Patrick had unstuck a corner and pulled the bottom edge up, so he could see perfectly well. I had no trouble, since I'm a head shorter and sit closer to the wheel, anyway.

White waiting, we bought $ 5 worth of cruzieros from the owner of another car. He said the rate changed every two weeks but always in our favor, so we were lucky. The Brazilian officials were slow but cheerful and gave us leaflets, a calendar and colorful stickers to put in the windows of our truck. Then we continued northeast, across low flat land, with big rice paddies on either side.

Patrick objected to the used luggage look so after each border crossing he would stop and scrape off the labels from the previous country.

Beside the road, on the right was a small river - or a big ditch - and in one place a hand operated ferry went across it to someone's house. But there were few villages in that section and three hours later, we ran out of gas. We had one plastic can of gas, in reserve (the others we used for naptha, for cooking) so we put that in the tank and it took us to the outskirts of Rio Grande, where we found some policemen, at an intersection. They were nice people - relaxed and friendly - but they spoke Portuguese. In every other country of South America, the people speak Spanish. And Portuguese is quite different. For the first time in years, we could not converse easily. But they understood that we were looking for a campground and directed us to one at Cassino beach, nearby.

The border, where everyone was bilingual, had been deceptive. Now, just a few miles into Brazil, we were having trouble, communicating with people. But most of them were patient with us and able to make out what we wanted.

The campground was set back from the beach - out of the wind, in some tall trees - and it was dark when we got there. We asked a man in Spanish where we might pitch our tent and he said in Portuguese that it would be all right, anywhere, so we found a clear space near a low building which contained a restaurant and toilets for both sexes. There were many tents - of high quality and good design - between the trees. And a few had families in them, watching television. Someone played 'Taps' on a bugle. Then here were sounds of tree frogs and voices in the dark, around us. The man we had spoken to came by, to see that we were all right - his tent was not far away - so we asked where we should go, to pay. But he said there was no charge. Which was lucky, because we just had enough money for gas to get to a bank. And already we were adjusting to Portuguese, which was not hard to read or understand, though difficult to speak.

Patrick may have been adjusting to it. I couldn't understand a word.

It was cool and breezy, in the morning. And ladies were fetching water in buckets from the restaurant to their tents. Two small girls visited us and spoke Spanish, which must be taught in the schools as a second language.

The children and I had about the same Spanish vocabulary. We could talk about clothes, school, hair, food and home. They were fascinated by our cooking arrangements on the truck's tailgate. I had to show them all our gadgets, from peelers to can openers, each just a tiny bit different from the ones they were used to.

In daylight, we could see that the campground was a mess - there was litter everywhere - but the toilets were clean and most of the tents were nicer than ours, though a few were old. And there was one trailer, among the tents. As we packed up to go, we had to pry loose the two small girls and all their friends. But it was not far to Rio Grande, which had cobbled streets and old houses, like those in France 40 years ago. And new, shiny cars and braless chicks in jeans, strolling along the narrow sidewalks. There were no money shops and the rate of exchange was the same, at all the banks, so we cashed a traveller's check at the nearest one, then went to buy gas. And ran out, beside the pump. It was a Texaco station, just like the ones in North America and they even gave away maps. But the gas was $ 1.75 a gallon, so we had to rethink our plans for seeing Brazil.

We had intended to go northeast to Rio de Janiero, then northwest to Brazilia and southwest into Paraguay (there were no roads into Bolivia, passable at that time of year, farther on) but that would be about 3,000 miles. And we had been told that the roads near Sao Paulo and on to Rio de Janiero were always full of commercial traffic. So we decided to go northeast as far as Curitiba, then head west, for the falls at Iguacu - the largest in the world - where we could cross into Paraguay. Which would cut our journey through Brazil down to about 1,000 miles altogether.

From Rio Grande, Route 471 went northwest to Pelotas, then Route 116 headed northeast - the main highway to Rio de Janiero. But though paved, it was just two lanes wide and at Porto Alegre we got lost in a drab, commercial section (like New Jersey) with many cars and trucks and pushy traffic. It was raining steadily out of a gray, overcast sky when we found our way out of town and went northeast into the lush, green hills of the Sierra Gaucha but we were told it was one of the most attractive parts of Brazil, so we turned off the main road, to the east, and took a back road - not shown on the AAA map - toward the State Park at Caracol Falls.

At the top of a hill was a small village of neat, tidy houses, where we stopped to buy food. The prices were high by our standards but the people were nice and some of them were black - the first ones we had seen, since Panama. At the State Park, a sign by a gate said 'Camping Club' Inside were several tents - all better than ours - and a few trailers, scattered across a wide expanse of well-kept grass, with tall trees for shade. It was dark, when we got there, so we pitched our tent under a lone tree. Then it was quiet, all around us - with light, intermittent rain.

But by morning, it had stopped and while our tent dried in the warm sun, we looked around. The tents were of various designs, some V-shaped, some like square boxes with several rooms and two front doors, but all of them were new and very fancy. Clearly camping was for the rich in Brazil. The grass between the tents showed no signs of use, for the campground was exclusive, for members of the Camping Club only. There was a restaurant, with a veranda, near the main gate which was guarded by a watchman - and all around the green, grassy area was a black and white fence, with woods beyond it.

The toilets and showers were rustic - almost primitive - but clean. Even the laundry, hanging out to dry, did not seem offensive, in that setting. And the campers - mostly families, with quiet, well behaved children looked European. Some of them came by to see us, including a doctor, who was working on the problem of alcoholism, which accounted for fifty percent of all the hospital admisions (he said gas was $ 3.00 a gallon in Paraguay) and a woman from Rio de Janiero, who was vacationing in the campground with her family because it was so hot in the city, at that time of the year.

Several of the people from Rio spoke English. It was fun to be able to talk without great effort on my part for a change. We were assured too, that while Rio was a fascinating city, it was no place to be in the summer. Anybody who was anybody had left town. We would probably have enjoyed the relative emptiness but certainly not the heat. And definitely not the expense. There were other more important things to see. We would leave Brazil soon, as planned and without regrets.

The town nearby looked like a Bavarian resort - very neat and clean, with big eaves on the houses - except for the palm trees, here and there. The Bank of Brazil could not cash an American Express traveller's check but one of the hotels did   at ten percent discount. On the main street, there were lots of flowers and at a sidewalk cafe, lunch was a big hamburger, with ham and eggs, lettuce and tomato. And good beer.

That was a hamburger with everything. Patrick thought the waiter hadn't understood his Portuguese but people around us were eating the same thing. Probably just a local custom. Anyway, it was delicious.

Back in the woods, the campground was silent, except that a young couple in the tent nearest to ours had their car radio blaring. So while June took our laundry to the pila, I took our tent down and moved it to a flat, shady spot at the far end of the grassy area, where we could not even hear the music. For we were sensitive about noise, living in the tent but it was easy to get away from it, if there was somewhere else to go.

Though the Camping Club was for members only, the man at the gate had authority to admit foreigners like us, if they seemed okay to him. But he would probably have rejected anyone who looked groungy - or young men with beards. The falls at Caracol, a short walk from the campground, were quite dramatic. A small river came along and fell over a sheer cliff, dropping about four hundred feet, straight down. It was good to relax for a day, in the woods. And very peaceful in our tent, at its new location

After dinner, we sat on Minim's tailgate - with our Tia Maria - under the stars that shone between the trees, listening to the news from the BBC in London, on our short wave radio. But when it came to the part about the crisis in Argentina, it was blanked out by a jamming signal (a roaring noise and quite effective). Then the station was clear again. Evidently they did not want us to know about the crisis - probably the 'strike' we had been expecting - but even that much information was helpful, for we would have to go though Argentina, to get to Bolivia and back to Peru.

Before breakfast, I rotated the trucks tires and checked it out. The oil was okay, with no serious leaks and soon it was ready to go again. Cars hummed in the distance and birds sang nearby, while we packed up. Then it started raining, as we went back to the main highway and headed northeast. All day we drove on the two lane road, with much traffic and many hills and corners, in heavy rain. For lunch we stopped at a truckers' rest area, by a deep gorge (it had no edge, so if your brakes failed, you would go over) and by the afternoon, it was very tiring, with the slow trucks and fast cars and the commercial establishments, beside the road.

It was costing about $ 5.00 an hour to drive the car. All the calculating was depressing. Or was it the rain and mud, that made the countryside so dreary, that depressed us?

When darkness came, we parked in a gravel pit, near the highway - for that was not bandit country - and with the sound of rain on the roof, we went to bed in the truck. Because we were so tired, we slept quite well and awoke feeling fresh. The rain had stopped but the sky was gray. While June was making breakfast, I shaved - then we left. Driving in Brazil was no fun because of the high traffic density, on the few paved roads. In the towns, there were many large cars but between them, most of the ones that we saw were Volkswagens. And all day it rained, on and off.

Near Curitiba, there was much industrial development and west of the city on Route 277 was a campground but it was open to the wind, so we carried on. The trucks belched black smoke, going uphill and streamed white smoke from their brakes, going downhill. And all the cars were brown with mud. But as we went up to 3,000 feet, past tree farms and big fields of crops, the countryside became green and open and flat. There was nowhere to pitch our tent, out of the wind and the mud, so we kept on going, long after dark. And came to the busy tourist town of Iguacu Falls. Beyond the hotels and motels, we found a Camping Club sign and turned in. The man at the gate asked for our membership card, so we gave him out AAA one (from Vermont) and that was fine. The campground was quite full but we found a good site, on the grass, under a lone tree and since the rain had stopped, we set up the tent.

After two days of hard going, it was a relief to be back in the tent, like being back home again. Everything was damp and we tracked light brown mud wherever we went. But tomorrow would be better. Perhaps we would have time to clean up.

Early the next day, it was cool and clear and sunny, with no clouds and a light breeze and some bugs, but not many (we had been told they would be bad, there). It had rained, the day before but now the land was drying out. And our truck was full of mud, so I set about cleaning inside it.

The campground was larger than the one at Caracol Falls and had dirt roads (mostly outlined by black and white posts} dividing it into several areas. But some of the tents, on the well-kept grass, were very fancy - one even had a TV antenna on a tall tower, beside it - and again the people were mostly families with children, friendly and nice. But they did not seem to do much cooking, if any at all. The restaurant served breakfast and a big lunch (for $ 1.50 a head) and the campers either went out for dinner, in the town nearby, or had sandwiches in their tents.

Minim was coated with mud and looked old and ratty, now. But everything in Brazil - cars, roads, steps, the lower parts of houses - was covered with red dust, which was mud when it rained. A man told us it was the best kind of dirt for growing things (how parochial can you get?). And it seemed that after two days' run, we had to get organized again. We had 12 gallons of gas, plus $ 30.00 worth of cruzieros, so we could just about afford food, ice and gas to get across Paraguay to Argentina. Premium gas was called Azul (blue) and cost $ 2.00 a gallon, versus $ 1.50 for Comun, but we figured that half and half would be an adequate mix.

Foz do Iguacu was a big, modern town, not unlike Niagara Falls. And the ice was $ 2.50 (to fill our red box) so we went back to the campground and I washed Minim by hand. By noon it was hot and small cumulus clouds moved slowly across the sky. A woman nearby was trying to explain to her child that June could not understand her, though she was grown up. And a man who came by tried to persuade us to leave our car there and fly to Rio, though it was as hot as that - I was pouring with sweat, in swim trunks. After lunch we took a siesta - it was too hot and sweaty for anything else - and later we tried the showers, which were quite exciting, because the cold water was heated right at the shower head. There was a gadget on the pipe, with a wire going into it, and a lever that said 'Summer - Off - Winter' When I moved the lever, there was a boiling noise and immediately the water was hot. Clearly the chances of being electrocuted there were quite high. And reaching a wet hand up, to turn the thing off, was the kind of moment that one remembers.

Then off we went, to see the famous falls - the Largest in the World - a short drive away. But they are not very dramatic, because the Parana

River, coming from the north, flows over flat country, covered with trees and there are many falls, instead of one big one. Wherever you look, there is water, coming between the trees and dropping to a lower level, with white spray rising above it. And the scene nearby was very commercial. The nicest thing was an old tourist hotel - pink, with red roofs and white trim - with arches along the front and green lawns, dotted with palm trees, down toward the falls. And a flag on a pole, above a tower, in the middle. On the lawn of the hotel was a helicopter with a big sign offering rides for $ 27.50 per person, for 4 minutes. And not far away was a hot dog stand, beside an elevator that went down toward the bottom of the nearest falls.

The view down there was quite impessive, with the water rushing past, a few yards away. But there was a line of people waiting, to go back up. So a man and a girl edged their way to the head of the line and the other people told the operator of the elevator about it. But the man and girl stood there, lying quite blatantly, until the operator let them in. And when they reached the top, they strolled off, grinning. They were not in a hurry, they just liked to win, any way they could.

But the hot dog stand was interesting. It was octagonal, with a counter all around it and a central core, supporting an octagonal roof. And it had a crank by which the operator could lower the roof at the end of the day, to close the whole thing up. Then it was protected from rain, wind or theft. All in one smooth operation. Which gave us an idea of the mind of the man (presumably Chilean) who had designed it.

Back at the campground, it was cool and buggy. A family slowly took apart a big tent and stowed it in a Volkswagen, a piece at a time. And five young people came by to chat. They were from Sao Paulo and spoke a little Spanish and told us it was a big, industrial city we would not want to visit. Now we had enough money to pay our camping fees ($ 4.00 a night, for two people) and buy gas. But that was it.

We were hesitant about returning to Argentina but at this point, there was little choice. Our money wouldn't last if we kept spending at this rate. And we certainly weren't being extravagant. Going northeast to Rio would be a dead end. Going back the way we had come would be senseless. We might as well head for Paraguay where we would find roads leading into northern Argentina and from there over the Andes to Peru.

The morning was fine and clear, with heavy dew. And soon we were under way. There was no premium gas in town, so we filled up with Comun and went to the bridge over the Parana River. Crossing the frontier was fast and easy, with no paper work at all, on either side. But the town of President Stroessner just had more hotels and shops for the tourists. So we headed west, on the paved road across Paraguay, toward Asunchion.

Young timber edged the road for miles. Sometimes there were clearings and you could see cattle grazing. In one clearing, where hardly a bush remained, were tall mounds of mud, perhaps four or five feet high. Castles to a termite. And we wondered if the insects had eaten all the trees around. Later, we passed a row of man made mounds, ovens, most likely for charcoal production. There were no trees left near those, either.

The countryside was level for a while, then we came into rolling hills. But the main impression was of emptiness - or maybe lack of development. The houses we saw were nice enough, but there were few of them, even near the main road. And the land itself seemed little used, as though the country were run by one large family, that wanted no change. It was only 200 miles across Paraguay, at that point and there was very little traffic on the two lane road, except for a few busses. About half way, there was a rest area and beyond it we passed a large house, with white walls and red roofs, on a hill. But nearer the capital, there were smaller houses, by the road, with displays of lace work for sale.

The lace mats and table cloths had been stretched on nails along crude wooden frames. They were like gigantic spider webs, hanging rigidly from trees or propped up against houses. There were reds and yellows and some darker colors but most were white or soft ecru.

As we came into Asuncion, there were signs for the ferry across the Paraguay River to Argentina, so I followed them and we missed the city, whih was fine with me. For all cities are much the same - just change the style of architecture and give the old man on a horse a new name - and unless you want to buy something or do business, why put up with the fuss? Though we were well over a thousand miles from the sea, the water of the wide river was green - even blue - and there were many small boats, tied to a dock. The immigration and customs people took their time with our papers, and the ferry waited for a full load, then went off stern first, for she had a bus on her bow and would have been impossible to steer, going the other way. The paperwork was slow on the other side, with one overworked official handling everything, in that heat. But finally, we were cleared into Argentina and went southwest on Route 11.

We still had no idea of the political situation in Argentina. It was not wise to ask questions at the borders. But people seemed to be moving as freely as ever, between the two countries. We had just stood in line and in due course we were back in Argentina.

Three times in the first half hour we were stopped by the police, who checked ou papers. But they were cheerful and they thought we must be rich, to be travelling like that. We said we were, once but not any more. And they laughed.

Whatever the crisis had been, it did not seem to have an upper hand in that part of Argentina.

Just before Formosa, we found a roadside park, with a small tree for shade and a stream along its far side. The only other people were a businesman and a girl in a white car, so I asked if we could spend the night there. From the look on his face, I gathered that we had just upset his plans for the evening but he was very polite   the girl remained smilingly neutral - and assured us that it would be quite all right. So we set up our tent at a discreet distance   facing the other way - but quite soon, they drove off. I felt guilty, of course but then it was too late to do anything. And the mosquitoes, from the stream, started biting as the sun went down, so we zipped up the tent.

It was a calm, clear night and there was some traffic on the road at first but none, later. Once a man went by, singing a melody in the dark. Then it was time to get up. Minim had used a quart of oil in the last thousand miles, so maybe there was a leak. We would have to watch it. And the police at the control point, outside Formosa, were competent but rude. However, the town itself was pleasant. At the hotel on the main square, we ordered coffee, as an excuse to use their facilities (I was brought up to believe that you did not do it, without first becoming a customer) then we bought food nearby. In a money shop, we were told the rate of exchange was 254 pesos to the dollar (twice as much as in Bariloche) but the man who changed money was coming back on the 4:00 PM flight from Buenos Aires, so we did not wait.

It was a pretty town. Big trees lined the streets. There were plenty of open shops along the fronts of two and three storied buildings. I spotted a nice looking grocery and after a bit of searching Patrick found a parking space. The minute we stopped, sirens sounded and we heard shouts and men running. Oh Lord, we'd parked in front of another police station. Being old hands at this sort of thing, we drove off smartly. The sirens stopped. We decided that I'd shop, while Patrick drove around and around the block. Inside was absolutely everything I had wanted for weeks. Because we had spent so much time in the country, I recognized the brands. It was like getting back to Campbell Kraft land. The shopkeeper was chatty - we did have a good time. I kept glancing out the window, watching for Minim to round the corner. Finally I exhausted my vocabulary and went out to search the streets. Patrick was pacing the next block. He'd found a parking place but then he couldn't remember where I was.

At a gas station we waited in line while a man fixed the pump. But for an oil filter, we were sent to a specialist, who recognized the Rambler engine in Minim and gave us the numbers of equivalent filters, of three different makes - such numbers were very good to have, for any part of the truck. Route 81, northwest from Formosa, was dirt for the first 300 miles and would be mud, if it rained, so we went southwest to Resistencia, where we tried to buy some pesos. But the girl travel agent (in the main hotel) would only give us 200 to the dollar - evidently she thought we had no choice - so we let it go. Then we headed northwest on Route 16, that was now paved - we were assured - all the way to Salta.

Late in the afternoon, the pavement ended. The road ahead was dirt. But it went straight, between the trees, in the right direction. Perhaps it was just a gap in the pavement, which had not been completed. So we kept on going. As darkness came, we looked for somewhere to camp, beside the empty, featureless road. But there was nowhere that was any good at all. And on we went, into the dusk.

Then we came to a control post. The policemen said it was the frontier, between two States. And when they had checked our papers, we asked if we might camp there for the night. The two men were formally polite and the senior one gave us his permission but as we laid out our ground sheets, before erecting the tent, the other one came over to show us a better site, near their brown adobe hut. We thanked him and moved but he did not go away. He just stood there, watching us. And when we finished, he told us about the snakes. His accent was strange to us, so we had to listen closely to understand him and his reaction was to illustrate his speech with dramatic gestures. He twirled his right hand around, as if it were a snake, coiling to strike. Then he closed his fingers, to make a pointed head, swaying from side to side. And suddenly it darted forward, in the strike. Then he said " ..... not many, but some", and walked away.

We had nothing to fear. After all, our tent was snake proof. It said so, on the label.

Later, we went over to chat with them. They were farmers, born in that remote place (the nearest village was called Dead River) and were lucky to get the jobs. But there was no electricity, telephone or radio for communication and they needed a mantle for their lamp (so there was no light, except a candle). The one with no teeth who warned us about the snakes had never been to Salta but he said the paved road had ended. Now it was dirt, for the next 200 kilometers, that way.

Oh lucky us.

Meanwhile, it was hot and sweaty, with many bugs. And back in our tent, we tried to sleep. A radio played - very quietly, so as not to wake us - and one of the men coughed all night, in the dust. The dawn was gray, with a splatter of rain drops on the top fly of our tent. And the clouds were dark, to the west, so we packed up quickly and left. The two policemen saw us off - one was sweeping the dirt, near their hut, with a broom - and they looked sad. We would have liked to give them something but we had no Argentine money to spare, then.

As we went northwest, the dirt turned to mud but we kept on going, trying to beat the rains to the other end of the unpaved section. We passed through many small villages and as we left each one, there was a big sign, saying that you could not transit the next section of road, on rainy days. But the rains were intermittent - from dark clouds, moving across the land - and each time, we thought we could make one more.

After a while. we found a new highway being built, beside the old dirt road. It was not yet paved but firm gravel, so we got onto it and went rattling happily along. But the bridges or culverts had not been put in, so we had to get off and work our way through deep mud around each one.

Seven hours after we started, we reached the paved road. Now it could rain all it wanted. We parked and ate breakfast - it was the first time we dared to stop, in case we should get stuck in that dismal place for days.

The road continued northwest for some time, then curved into the southwest and came to Metan. There was a campground outside the town but it had no facilities, so we went north over excellent roads, though beautiful, hilly country - to Salta, a pretty city with many trees, in a valley between the hills. And beyond it on Route 9 was the Hotel Huaico.

There were several low units and a restaurant, set back in a garden. And after camping for ten days, it looked pretty good. So we checked in and took long showers, before strolling over to the restaurant for drinks and a leisurely dinner.

We could afford such things in Argentina. And the beef was so good, it was impossible to pass up a steak. We ordered it 'a la' the local region. It arrived with a slice of ham and a fried egg on top and surrounded with lettuces and tomatoes.

In the morning, we asked the desk clerk about a money shop but he told us to go to the National Bank, so we went into town and tried a travel agent, who said the official rate was now 225 and there were no money shops but the bank could indeed cash our traveller's checks (though the local people were not allowed to buy dollars) and the open rate was a little higher but not much. So we went to the bank and they cashed a $ 100 check for 225 less $ 2.00 commission. How quickly things had changed.

Everything we had learned, about avoiding the banks and changing money elsewhere, was no longer valid. One had to be constantly aware of the situation. as it varied.

Next, we had the oil in our truck changed for HD 40 weight (the only

HD kind available). It had gone 20,207 miles since we left Vermont and 126,500 miles altogether. Then we found a car wash, with a row of chairs for customers to sit in, while their cars were being cleaned. And there we met a young man who spoke English, which was very rare in those parts.

His English was so good. Then he explained that he taught school in the U.S., California, I think. His father had been a diplomat and since childhood he had travelled widely. But Salta would always be home.

As the sun finally came out, he mentioned that it does not rain much in northern Bolivia, though it does in the south - and gasoline was expensive, there. Then we asked about the troubles in Argentina and he said that the leaders of the resistance were sons of the wealthy classes. Which figured, for it must cost a great deal to equip even a small group of men with the machine guns and ammunition they needed to be effective.

He spoke guardedly, glancing around to see that no one was near. Our conversation seemed innocent enough to us but he assumed he was being watched - just as everyone he knew was - by the fearful government. And he didn't want to spend his short vacation in jail.

That afternoon, we went shopping in the city, for presents to take home. And bought a pasta machine - about the size of an office typewriter - for our restaurant in Vermont. We would have to take it thousands of miles, through many different countries but it was too good a bargain to miss.

The machines had been about $ 60.00 when we first noticed them displayed in a shop window in Buenos Aires. And now the price was about $ 30.00. In a few weeks, money had halved. Delightful for us but a tragedy for so many.

At the hotel, we met Mr. Sloane, an English scientist who was working for the United Nations. He had made a study of the feasibility of a glass factory in northern Argentina, but could not give any figures, in that economy, with interest at 600% a year. He said a workman's wage was 8 cents an hour but building costs had gone up more than inflation. There was plenty of the right kind of sand but whether it would be financially sound to put up a factory, he simply could not tell.

He was quite distinguished looking, with his almost white hair, and his dress - dignified but a bit rumpled - suited his occupation. He spoke quietly and with certainty - as much a diplomat as a scientist.

Over drinks on the patio, we were joined by a tall, lean Frenchman and his young Belgian assistant, also working for the United Nations, on irrigation. And in due course, we went into town with them - in one of their cars - for dinner. The conversation got around to the sins of writers and Dr. Sloane said that long ago, when he was doing research for a well known glass company, he saw an article in his newspaper, about a new kind of glass - that he had developed - for building houses. It was all very dramatic - they would be cheap and last forever - but it was not true. The whole thing had been cooked up by the public relaions people in London. And he was still getting inquiries about it, many years later.

They did the same thing to another scientist, in the same company. They wrote a story about a new kind of glass - that he had invented - which killed flies. It was all lies but they paid a columnist to print it. We asked about the proceedure for that and he said it was simple. You wrote a story of the right length to fit the column and handed it over, with the money. Which saved him the trouble of writing that day. And everyone was happy.

The large, barn like restaurant was crowded when we finally arrived. We drank good beer and of course ate beef. And told stories of meals, in strange places, that we hadn't been able to eat. The Frenchman claimed he had been served rat in Bolivia. He said it came baked whole in a crust. Very elegant, head and all, but he couldn't face it. We half believed him and swore to be on our guard in Bolivia.

After dinner, we went on to a night club, where we sat at a small table, listening to local singers. They had loud, clear voices, so they did not need a microphone. And about 1:30 AM we headed back toward the hotel, a few miles away. But before we got there, we came to a check point - new in the past few hours - where men with machine guns were stopping cars. The Frenchman was driving, with the young Belgian beside him, while June and I were in the back with Dr. Sloane. As we stopped, a man asked for our papers and the other three passed theirs out, through the window. But we had left ours in my bag - locked in Minim - back at the hotel.

We had wondered about taking them with us but decided they would be safest left in Minim at the hotel. We were concerned about pickpockets in town and never even thought about the police putting a roadblock between there and the hotel.

The man checked the passports, gave them back and asked for two more. So we explained that ours were at the hotel, not far away. He asked for them again, more sharply - his hand in the open window - and again we told him they were at the hotel. Then he ordered us to get out of the car. Our three companions got out with us, while more men with machine guns closed in, to cover us. And soon a man in civilian clothes came over. There was a bright light on a tall pole and I could see him clearly youngish, fit, surely with the Secret Police, probably a Captain - as he approached. The first man must have given him the details, because he came straight up to me and asked to see our papers. I explained that we had left them at the hotel, not thinking we would need them to go into town for dinner. But I would be happy to go and get them, for him to see. It was not far. He was equally polite but we could not leave, without our documents. That was not allowed. We must stay there.

Our three friends joined us and told him we had gone into town with them, from the hotel. They assured him that we were staying there and we must have papers to be doing so. Otherwise we could not have registered. The secret policeman was still polite but nothing seemed to matter, except that we had no documents with us now. And he could not allow us to leave, without them. So Dr. Sloane offered to get them. I gave him the keys of our truck and told him where to find my bag and what it looked like. The Frenchman said he would go, with him. And the two men were allowed to get back in their car.

The young Belgian stayed with us, as they drove off. But the secret policeman was only interested in me. Standing there, quite relaxed, he asked what we were doing in Argentina, where we had been and what places we had visited. Again and again he came back to the same questions like: "Where did you say you were, last Thursday?" - always with a smile. And I doubt if he missed a single word in my answers. The man was good. I did not want him to think we were worth questioning more thoroughly, for that was done with electricity in basements. So I was lighthearted and cheerful about the whole thing - if I had let myself become the least bit nervous, he would have known it immediately - and since I had nothing to hide, I told him with enthusiasm about the places we had seen. But I was careful not to look at the frightened people in the van with barred windows, who were waiting to be taken away.

I had difficulty following the conversation. Most questions were directed at Patrick and with cars starting and stopping and men shouting all around, I could not always hear the low, measured voice of the interrogator. They had forced us over by the van, its engine was running too. The light was brightest there but I didn't like standing so close to the van's occupants. Suppose someone started trouble and shooting broke out. We would be right in the midle of it. I kept edging away. But the Belgian, who was standing there, came over and pushed me back, under the light. He said to stay there, that we were safer where everyone could see us.

The questions went on for a long time, until the car came back. Then I gave him our passports (with some relief). But he asked for the other papers, too. And when he had checked all of them, he let us leave. But I had a feeling that he might put a tail on us, so we did not rush off. After a good sleep, we went into town and bought more small presents, to take home. That evening, we had drinks with our three friends and Dr. Sloane told us that the Argentine government thought the English had sent secret agents, to help the resistance people overthrow it. Then the new government would give back the railroads, which belonged to England before they were nationalized. And I was a former British agent, trained in that kind of thing (with an English accent in Spanish) which was embarrassing - but that was long ago and now I was American.

Before coming to Argentina, Dr. Sloane had worked in Ghana and three men had stolen about $ 50.00 (between them) from him. But when they were caught, he was told they would get five years in jail and would not expect to live through it. So he tried to get the charges dropped but it was no good. And he had a great deal of trouble, getting his money from the police, who often stopped cars and shook people down on phony charges, there. The Frenchman had worked with the resistance in World War Two (as I had) and he said there was another road, a secondary one, parallel to the one on which we were stopped. So if we had been up to something, we could easily have avoided the confrontation. In his view, the whole thing was silly. But it was also serious, of course. For since 1974, they had a law in Argentna, under which anyone could be held indefinitely, simply for being caught without the proper douments on him.

In the morning, I checked our truck and changed the plugs. It was a sunny day and there were two tents, in a small campground, beside the hotel. About eleven, we left for Jujuy (60 miles away) and followed the narrow, winding road over the mountains. There were two police controls but no problems, in full daylight. And beyond the town, still on Route 9, we found another Huaico Hotel - like the first one but older.

First we were shown a room in a basement area. The smell of mildew was overwhelming. There was mold on everything. The water taps leaked and the shower stall was covered with slime. We demanded something better and after receiving an o.k. from several levels of authority, we were taken to a new wing. On the second floor there was a clean, cared for room overlooking low, rolling hills. We settled in.

Then we went into town, to buy an air filter. The place was not as attractive as Salta - just a big farming town - but the people were nice. The stock man at the ACA garage did not have a filter the right size but let me take a few outside, to try. And I found one (for a Ford) that would do.

We were happy to be out of Salta. There was too much uneasiness there. Jujuy was much smaller, just a few main streets. A little boy, who cleaned the car's windows when we stopped for gas, was fascinated to speak to someone from the United States. He was studying geography in school and collected stamps. Would we please send him a card when we got back? I've often wondered if he ever did receive the card. We've never heard from any of the people we wrote to, when we returned.

Back at the hotel, I worked on Minim's engine - adjusting the carburettor and cleaning the ignition system - until it ran very well. And the next day, I started typing out the notes for this book, which I had taken since Carlos Paz. The hotel was 4,000 feet above sea level and the rooms had radiators but no airconditioners. Below our window was the top of a tall cactus - the kind with round 'paddles' but no spikes - and we could reach down to touch the yellow 'apples' on it. But the vegetation was very lush and varied. There were all kinds of trees, from firs to poplars to some that looked like aspens and we could barely see the red roofs of a couple of houses, between them, all the way to the tops of the neaby mountains. It was hot and breezy toward midday and the crickets were loud. For cooling, we had an old fashioned fan that went to and fro, as if looking for someone. But the room was pleasant, with the view, and we had the luxury of a table to work at.

Our trip would have cost much more (and we might have had to shorten it) if it were not for the very favorable rates of exchange in Argentina - four years ago, a dollar bought 2 pesos, now it bought 225 - which was one reason that we took the risk of staying there so long. And by not rushing off, we hoped to convince the secret police that we were not up to anything they might want to investigate, on the lonely road north.

Besides, it wasn't camping weather. The rain came and went throughout the day. And we needed a rest. We were both tired. It was time to sleep a lot and gather ourselves together. We would soon leave Argentina, to enter into the high Andes. Things would be very different there.

In my notes, I found that the Automobile Club had garages and motels all over Argentina. Probably there were no other satisfactory ones, in the remote areas, early on. But now they seemed to be in the large towns for purely commercial reasons and though their people were usually polite, their garages were not the best places to have a car fixed - in many cases - nor were their motels always clean. For the organization had become bureaucratic and the standards were mediocre. Another thing was that the guide book we took with us was of little value, in all of South America, except for historical background. For it was written strictly for tourists, arriving by air or sea, buying things, eating things and going away. But probably there were not enough people like us, wandering around on our own, to be worth writing for in such a book.

When it got dark, we brought bread, cheese and wine from the truck, for supper in our room. It rained hard, during the night, with thunder and lightning. And the next day was Monday the First of March, so we went into town for more typing paper and bought food, to head north again. There were two tents in a campground beside the motel and some others in the Municipal Autocamping area, across the road. But it rained lightly, all day and it was good to be warm and dry indoors.

As I typed my notes, it was clear that if we had not been clean and tidy and well dressed, that night in Salta - or if we had not seemed relaxed and amused   we might have fetched up in a basement, wired for sound which is a 'No No'. After the notes, I typed 13 data sheets for the controls ahead, giving all the details of Minim and ourselves. Then we had done all we could and were ready to leave, in the morning, for the high Andes of Bolivia and Peru.

10 - HIGH PLACES

As we carried our things from our room, down to Minim, a man said "Good bye" to June in English. He had the room next to ours, so undoubtedly he had been bugging us and we presumed he was with the secret police. But since he blew his cover, we were probably cleared to leave Argentina. And we should not worry too much about being stopped on the road out.

We had passed that man, with his attractive female companion, several times in the hall. They always seemed to be coming and going when we were. They hadn't been friendly, they hardly looked at us. I fact, no one had spoken to us, in all the time we had been there. I was very surprised when he spoke to me and in English, too.

In Jujuy, we went to get ice at a meat storage place and I was hit by a side of beef, hanging from a rail, that came up behind me like a man on a bicycle. Then we headed north on the same road (Route 9) toward the frontier of Bolivia. There were several police controls in the first hour but only one was serious. The rest were more interested in paper work. Then the pavement turned to gravel and we climbed up out of the lush forest, into bare, open copuntry with tiny bushes, evenly spaced on the rocky ground. The map said we just passed the Tropic of Capricorn but there were large herds of llamas, grazing with sheep or goats. The sky was pale blue, with small white clouds, and in the distance were more mountains. We gave a farmer - an Indian - a lift into a village. He spoke Spanish and was highly intelligent but he thought Bolivia was very far away (about 90 miles) and I doubt that he had any idea of the United States. He told us about vicuna - which were good eating - and the sand deposits, suitable for making glass. And he asked if we would go home by aviation.

The road ribboned into the distance, down the middle of a high, wide valley. The colors were pale, the greens so full of grey, the sky just barely tinged with blue. Grass fields fell away from the road and rose slowly higher and higher to far mountain peaks. Our speed must have been forty or fifty miles an hour over the gravel, yet nothing came near, the same scene was always ahead. Then on the right, flowing down a bare slope, so far away that we couldn't be sure we really saw anything, flecks of red appeared. A cloud would pass before the sun and the color would disappear, only to emerge again, a little farther down the mountain side. Soon we saw other lines, moving steadily down the slopes.

There was music, too. The rasping of bagpipes could be heard over the noise of the car on the road. Now, ahead of us we could see people gathering in a meadow and the lines of brightly dressed mountain people, their village musicians leading the way, descending ever more rapidly into the field of the festival. Some were dancing, the girls in bright red gathered skirts. They would swing their partners and the skirts flew wide. Others stood drinking beer, shouting, greeting new arrivals. Where had they all come from? There was no town in sight. From villages and outposts on the far side of the hills, from other villages where roads didn't pass, from valleys we would never see.

Above 13,000 feet the road levelled off, then went own a little - past a few lonely houses in small valleys, with stone corrals for sheep - to the town of Tres Cruces where the people were celebrating Carnival Week, before Easter. Though their faces were Indian, they wore European clothes - slacks and sweaters or jackets - in pastel colors and many of them were in a conga line, snaking down the street, behind a man with a flag. When he saw us, he swung over our way, dancing and singing. Then the line went past and the town was quiet - almost deserted   from the central square to the other side, where the road went out into the wide, open country again. Some of the llamas, along the way, had been decorated with ribbons, for the carnival. And when we arrived in La Quiaca, at the frontier of Bolivia, much celebration was going on. All the hotel rooms were taken and there was nowhere to camp, so we went to the ACA gas station. It had no gas but a tanker was due that night and we parked behind it, out of the wind. The sunlight was strong but there were thunder clouds, all around us. And a band was playing in the square, nearby.

Soon a gang of people came and poured beer on a white car and decorated it rather messily for an absent friend, to guitar music and with dancing. They said it was traditional. We could feel he thinness of the air at 12,000 feet but Minim had been doing fine all day - when we stopped for lunch, we did so on a hill - and the police seemed more relaxed, there at the frontier, than they were in Salta or Jujuy.

Probably they were all druunk. After all, it was the fiesta time, the start of Lent. We had heard rumors that the celebrating had been outlawed - the government was afraid the peasants would get out of hand. There was no sign of the people taking the least bit of notice. The police might as well have a good time, too. Besides, these high mountain people had little in common with Buenos Aires or even Salta. Their world was several thousand feet in the sky, cut off from the rest of Argentina, except for that one narrow road we had just driven.

The toilet at the garage fell apart, when June tried to use it, but a nice young man fixed it. Then the owner of the car which had been decorated came by. He did not seem pleased and giving orders for it to be cleaned, he left. The frontier was only half a mile away but it had closed for the day, so we sat there, tired, waiting to go to Bolivia. The clouds held off, while June cooked supper. But the lack of air made us feel edgy.Probably we would get used to it. And a loudspeaker was blaring, in the park. It was a man, making announcements, with a strong accent on the last syllable of each phrase ("   will be held at eight o'clock toNIGHT").

We wandered around a bit. There was a pretty park across the way. Lanterns had been strung through the trees and beneath them vendors sold food and souvenirs for the village people to take back into the hills. The streets were crowded, mostly with youngsters, racing and shouting. And there were drunks sleeping on benches. After all, the party had started early that morning. We didn't go far. With so many pranksters around it seemed wise to stay near Minim.

By eight, we were in bed, in the truck. And at nine, the band moved away   getting fainter as it went across town - and the loudspeaker had stopped and all was quiet. But we awoke with headaches (probably from the altitude) and at 7:00 AM some men came to board a steam train, which left silently, taking them to work somewhere. Soon it was a fine, sunny morning, so we sat on Minim's tailgate to eat breakfast. The man at the gas station said the tanker might not arrive that day and gas was $ 1.20 a gallon in Bolivia, so we packed up to go. But first we went to a shop and spent the last of our Argentine pesos on food. It was an old fashioned grocery store, with wide counters and rows of cans and boxes, on high shelves, behind them. So we put our money down, on the counter, and kept on asking the girl for one more thing - rearranging the money each time - until it was all accounted for, much to her amusement.

There were still crowds in the streets. But this morning women were shopping with baskets on their arms. Mothers were trying to keep the household running in spite of the fiesta.

We had to clear with the Argentine immigration people, at a building in town, before going to the frontier and crossing a bridge into Bolivia. The oficials there were friendly to us - as tourists - and gave us permission to stay for 90 days. But a young English couple, looking hippie (and probably not married) were only given 15 days. So it paid to conform to the standards of the country, if you wanted to stay around. The town across the border (Villazon) was quite different from La Quiaca so very much poorer, with dirt streets and old, crumbling buildings and brown dust everywhere - but the people were helpful. A money changer sent us to the bank, where we got 20 pesos to the dollar (against his rate of 18) and the customs officer took $ 1.75 or our papers, instead of $ 4.00, because we had it handy. But we could not get a map of Bolivia - we had already tried in La Quiaca - so we headed north, with just the general one of South America, put out by the AAA.

There was no sign of festivity on the Bolivian side. The curfew may have been taken more seriously there.

Outside the town, at a control point, a policeman told us we would need a Route Sheet. The system was that you applied for permission to make a journey, from one place to another, over a certain route, in a specified vehicle, within a limited time and with certain passengers. If that was authorized, you were issued a Route Sheet, which was a permit to do it (once only). Then at each control, along the way, you showed it to the police. And so long as the details matched, they let you proceed.

After examining our documents, the policeman said he would make a Route Sheet for us. But we must go back into town and get gas, or we would not make it. So back we went. And the only gas available was Comun - at 30 cents a gallon. When we got back to the control point, the policeman had left, without making our Route Sheet. But his replacement took one of the sheets I had typed in Jujuy - giving the details of our truck and ourselves - and put an Official Stamp on it "... so that the controls will not molest you"

The map showed two roads out of Villazon - a paved one to the east and a dirt one to the north - but in fact there was no paved road, at all - just a dirt one, going north. So we asked the policeman (who should know, since he talked to everyone who travelled those roads) which was was best. And he told us to go left at a junction, not far away. So we did. But after a while, the road dipped down to an oasis, with tall poplars and other trees. And at a control, in a village of adobe houses, a woman said we could not cross a river ahead of us, since the recent rains. So we went back to the junction and took the other road, hoping to find Route 1.

We saw wooden crosses scattered down the mountain side, glinting white in the pale sun. A bus or truck must have gone over the edge there, killing the passengers as it rolled down the mountain, into the canyon.

Going down, we could see fields of green crops, between the trees in the oasis. And later we could make out a village of adobe houses, with a two-steepled church, so much the same color as the dirt, we had not seen them before. Rocks and dirt had fallen down the mountain sides, over a long time, to give the canyon a narrow, level floor. And a wide river - now dry - meandered along it, with the green fields and trees on either side. And the road went along the edge, between the oasis and the mountain, just above the trees. Then we came under a dark cloud and for a while, we drove through sleet, wondering how we would get out of there. But the weather changes quickly in the high Andes and soon the sun came out again. When the road started up, it was already dry. And by late afternoon, we were back in the world above.

The trees were gone. Ahead stretched miles of nothing. Even the mountains no longer towered over us. It was inconceivable that anyone could live there.

Between the mountains, the land was gently rolling, with cacti and bushes in the dry soil. Then we picked up a farmer and gave him a lift to his house, near a big lake, in a huge, empty valley of coarse grass.

He had been in town for the celebrating. His family, a wife and several children, stayed home. The children were too young to travel. Anyway they couldn't all go. It was too expensive. His stone house, some distance from the road, looked bleak. Part of its thatched roof was gone, the understructure out against the sky. It was raining. He said he could not fix it until the grass was longer. We asked him why he lived there, so far from others. Couldn't he live nearer the town? He said he had always lived there. And his father and his grandfather, too. All of them had always lived there.

Then the road went gently down, to a control point (for customs) where we asked about Route 1 and the man said we were on it, which was fine. Now if we could find gas the next day, we would be in business. When we asked where we could camp, he said "Anywhere", so we drove for another hour and pulled off the road at a hairpin bend, to a fairly level spot maybe fifty yards away. The land was open, with grass and small bushes, so we did not use the tent. And there were thnderstorms around but they missed us. Two trucks gave us friendly toots, as they swept around the bend. And we settled in.

That type of travelling was much like ocean voyaging in a small boat. It required constant attention, leaving us little time for anything else. It was often uncomfortable, sometimes dangerous. But it gave us freedom and privacy, to see the world in our own way, which we valued very highly. The night was quiet and beautiful, with many stars and little wind, but we both woke up with headaches. The altitude was 11,000 feet, so it was probably mountain sickness. Maybe we should not have had wine with our dinner, so high up. And when the sun came up over a mountain, it was a lovely morning. One small bird and one huge fly came by, for breakfast. Then I checked the truck, while June cleaned up.

*Patrick had to force me to get out of bed. I could have slept for ever.
And when I stood up, the mountains spun around me. There was no horizon. Nothing was level. No matter which way I turned, the mountains
turned more. Only by crouching with my head falling between my knees
could I make the spinning slow down. At last there was only the light
headed feeling. But I was panting with every movement.*

The oil was okay but the brake fluid was down. I topped it up but we
should keep an eye on it, in those mountains. The battery was all right but
the fuel gauge had gone mad, so we would have to keep a fuel log, from
there on (unless it cured itself). And soon we were ready to leave. The
gravel road continued winding over open land, for a while, then it started
down a long, shallow valley, with trees and soon crops, in the middle but
still the grass and bushes, higher up the sides. Soon there were houses,
here and there - well built, with good roofs - and before long, there were
tall green poplars, beside a winding river.

*We felt less lightheaded now. Hopefully we were adjusting to the
altitude.*

About noon, we came to the town of Los Oertes, where we asked about
gas but no one had any to spare (they kept it in barrels) so we went on.
And when we stopped for lunch, beside the river, an Indian woman asked
for a lift. She was very intelligent and spoke Spanish and discussed the
weather, agriculture and so on, in detail. That was the rainy season, until
mid-April, but it had been a very dry year. And she warned us about the
people in the city of Potosi (ahead of us) who were self-centered and
unreliable.

*I didn't think she was Indian. More likely a mixture. She lived on a farm
we had passed, along the river, where she taught school to the laboror's
children. Her husband was a foreman on the farm, so it must have been
large. It hadn't looked that big, nestled in the narrow strip of land beside
the river, but all the work must be done by hand. The valleys were too
narrow and the hills too steep for machinery. Who owned the farm? People
from the city. They had always owned it. But they never lived thee. There
was a house for them, for sometimes they would come on business and stay
a day or two. We declined her offer of money for the ride. She seemed*

surprised that we wouldn't take the coins. Had we offended her?

She left us at a gas station in Camargo - a big town with many shops along its narrow streets - but the attendant was out for lunch, so we went to a bakery and when we got back, he sold us Extra (he had plenty) for 40 cents a gallon.

The streets were too narrow for Minim. They curved and cut canyons through the one- and two-storied stone buildings. Most of the doors and windows were shuttered. Were there gardens and open windows, in the back? We saw none. And it rained again. The misty rain that made the cobblestones slick and dangerous.

Again we went north, climbing out of the lush valley into high, barren country. In one place, a man was grazing a flock of goats on land so stony, we could hardly see a blade of grass every ten yards. Then we went down a little and the ground was covered with tiny bushes. But all through that section, the air was so thin that birds could scarcely fly. They went in little rushes   like flying fish - about two feet off the ground. And they were never airborne for more than 15 seconds at a time. If they came to a stone hedge, they would pull up over it, like crop dusters. And after they landed, they would rest awhile, before doing it again.

We saw no cars on that road but a few trucks with serious drivers (in face and manner) and one grader - smoothing out the gravel - whose operator moved over politely for June. In the evening, we looked out for a camping place but the wind was strong and there was no shelter from it, so we kept on going. And when darkness came, we were at 14,000 feet. But some kilometer posts indicated that we were near Potosi. And after a while, we dropped down into the city, which was at 13,000 feet, in a valley, with high mountains all around it.

These cobbled streets were wide enough for two cars and there were sidewalks. The streets were mostly straight, too, for the city was built on the smooth side of a hill. We entered at the top and drove down into the center of town. Some of the buildings were stone, others metal and there were open squares of flowers and trees.

Going in, we were charged a toll   for that road - and it was clearly no place to try camping, so we found the government tourist hotel, on a narrow street near the center. Inside was a room like a basketball court, with chairs and tables scattered across the varnished floor and railings, around a mezzanine, above. And more railings curving up a stairway, toward the bedrooms higher up. The manager came to greet us and when we told him about our truck, he took us to an open yard behind a high gate, with a watchman. Then he found us a room, on the third floor. And it was not easy for us to carry our luggage up the stairs, at that altitude, but we made it.

The floors slanted into the back wall of the building, toward the uphill side of town. Or maybe the wooden building was leaning down, away from the hill and the floor was really level. I was losing my horizon again.

The time had changed (back an hour) but it was too late to eat at the hotel, so we walked across town - uphill - to the Las Vegas restaurant, up a flight of stairs between two shops, which had a mural of Bugs Bunny holding a plate, with a chicken on it. There were just a few tables, over-looking the street, but it was probably the best in town. And the waiter asked if we would like a drink, so we ordered half a bottle of wine (we both had headaches, from the altitude, but moderation has its limits). But he had no half bottles, so he carefully poured half the wine out of a full one and brought us the remainder.

There were several small rooms where people were being served. Just a few groups and only one other table in our room was occupied. Two men sat there, I think they were faher and son. This might have been their weekly meal together. They talked about the family business in low, disinterested voices. It was more like a duty decreed ritual than a family meeting. Our meal of beef came. There was a piece of steak on the round, chippd plate, garnished with ham, fried eggs and some vegetables. It was good. The waiter had told us it was the house special.

Walking back was easier downhill and the old mining town had a certain charm, with its central square and narrow streets, all built on hills. But the stairs at the hotel were not easy to climb after dinner and the room was unusual. The pillows were hard, the sheets and blankets were almost un-bendable and a bare light bulb hung from the ceiling. But the stained wood floor was very clean. Much wood had been used to build it but there were no fire exits. Below the windows were a jumble of roofs, too far to jump onto. But it had a shower, with hot water and after a good night's sleep, we awoke with no headaches. And our breakfast was brought up (unasked for) and served at a table in the wide hallway, outside the room.

It was nice, sitting on the balcony, the light drifting in from a skylight above us, as long as you didn't look over the thin railing, down to the hall three floors below.

Driving across town to a gas station, we saw few cars. A mine whistle belew and there were people eveywhere, walking to work. And in daylight, the city was even more hilly.

We could see signs of mines on the hills around the city. It was surrounded by the industry. The people were all in a hurry. There had been mines operating for generations in Potosi. It was the first industrial city we had seen in a long time.

After showing our home made Route Sheet to the policemen at the control point, we were cleared to leave town and headed northwest, still on Route 1, toward La Paz. The hotel manager had said we could average 40 miles an hour but the gravel road followed the contours of the barren mountains, often doubling back in a sharp hairpin bend, so we took it slowly. And a big red truck nearly hit us in a narrow canyon - between high, rocky walls - as it roared past with its horn blaring

Our passenger from the day before had warned us about the people of Potosi. Were they really unreliable and self centered or just in a hurry to get to work?

Then we came out onto hillsides - between the mountains - with villages and small fields of crops, terraced up the slopes around them. The people of that area wore brown Derby hats and along the road, children held them out, begging for money. But in two different places, there were groups of people with flags and brass bands, holding religious ceremonies.

In the mist, in one barren, rocky section, we passed a woman, standing near a herd of llamas, wearing a tall, pointed witches hat. It was windy and she lent on a tall rod, her hair and long scarf billowing around her. An eerie sight, in a world all bleak and grey.

Later we dropped down to a vast swamp - with nothing but grass and water - by Lake Poopoo. When we stopped to show our Route Sheet to the police at Challapata, three soldiers wanted rides, so we took one a National Service type to his house down the road. There were many control points in that section but the people were nice and the police were delighted that we had given our spare change to the children.

They were glad too that we would give one a ride, although we thought we had little choice. The young man wanted to get home in time for the celebrating. This was to be the final night. He carried a blue serge suit on a metal hanger.

When we arrived at the city of Oruro, it was raining hard and the dirt streets had turned to mud, so we just stopped for gas. Then we gave the small boy who served us the change, which he took to show the man in charge. And they went off, down the street - the man's arm around the boy's shoulder - in the rain, with a second boy following behind them.

Oruro looked like a suddenly expanded city. There were lots of bright lights and wide muddy roads. Even the buildings along the mud avenue looked fairly new. But it is no place to visit during the rainy season.

Beyond the city, the highway was paved (though two lanes wide) and went straight across open, level country. There were two control points, twenty miles apart, and at the second one, the policemen hardly believed that June had a license to drive. When they let us go, it was nearly dark and half an hour later, we pulled off the road - just beyond the brow of a gentle hill - onto a wide, level area of grass, between the pavement and a cultivated field. And there we spent the night.

At the last control point a bus, headed the other waty, pulled up beside me. There was a wild rush by the occupants to get out. One woman, in a derby, shawl and red pleated skirt was particularly insistent. She dashed through an open gate into a fenced compound, pulling her skirt to the waist as she ran. Barely inside the gate, she squatted. A couple of the men she had pushed aside disappeared behind her, around the fence. After a moment they all returned to the bus, the men adjusting their flies and the woman smoothing her full skirt. They were all smiling and chatting now.

When we went to bed, the sky was overcast and everything was damp but it was no longer raining. And when we awoke after nine hours' sleep,

it was a bright, clear morning. As we sat on the tailgate, eating breakfast, the traffic was light and the trucks had mufflers and we could hear
voices in the field - but the people were out of sight, over the hill. Then
we left and before long we came to La Paz.

The city was in a deep, wide valley - like a huge bowl - and from the
rim, we could see tall buildings near the center, far below. Around them
were smaller buildings and houses, all across the valley and up the sides
amd spilling over the edge, onto the level land above. The road went down
the first steep part at an angle, through a poor section, then it levelled off
and went straight into the center, between the tall buildings. And there we
found a Tourist Information booth. While June guarded Minim, I went
inside and waiting there, I met two young men who were going south by
train. They told me about some English people who were arrested and tor-
tured with electroshock in Argentina - they were suspected of being spies -
so perhaps it was fortunate that we had American passports, when we were
held and questioned, that night in Salta.

The girl in the booth said that only the La Paz Hotel had parking facilities and those were nearby, not at the hotel. But there was a new place 20
minutes away in the mountains, so off we went (after having the truck
washed) to find it. That was not easy, for it was in a small, hidden valley,
below the rim of the main one. And it took far longer than she said, to get
there. But the valley was pretty with grass and pine trees and a brook,
running through it - and the motel had 'casitas' (little houses) each with a
bedroom and a living room, scattered around the main building. It was
new and architect designed and interior decorated and quite empty, except
for people in uniform - waiters and so on - standing around. Lunch was
ordinary but cost more than we expected. And in our casita, the rooms and
the water were very cold. So we telephoned the office and a girl called out
"Mama" and two men came. First they put a piece of thick copper wire in
the fuse box. Then they brought a butane heater.

It rained hard, that afternoon, so we stayed indoors and June took a
shower. But the butane heater only warmed one room (not much) and
when the water became tepid, a fuse blew and it went cold again. At which
point, she was soaped up and mad. So I got the two men back (it took 40

minutes) and after they had put more copper wire in the fuse box, the water became tepid again but the rooms were still very cold, so we went to bed at eight o'clock - without dinner - to get warmer.

In the morning, I put on old clothes and secured Minim's tailpipe, where a bracket was broken, with seizing wire. Then we got a Route Sheet - with no problem - from the local police and drove down a bad road (with several fords) for 60 miles, to the eastern shore of Lake Titicaca. The lake was beautiful - its clear water reflecting the pale blue sky and white clouds - with mountains far across it and tall reeds in the water, near the shore. Between the reeds and the shore, there was a calm lagoon and here and there a small sailing boat   not unlike those of the Bahamas - at anchor. Along the dirt road, beside the lake, were brown adobe houses with shining metal roofs, sheltered by tall eucalyptus trees. And in the village of Huatajata, behind a high wall, we found the Bolivian Yacht Club.

Inside was a long, low building in the local style, with many rooms - a bar, dining room, office etcetera - and beyond it were tables on a patio, looking out across the lake to the distant mountains. And down a grassy slope to a small, private harbor, made by clearing a gap in the reeds. It was full of yachts - mostly power boats, from 20 to 30 feet long - and beyond it, red buoys marked a channel through the reeds and shallows, into deep water. Since it was a Sunday, several of the members were there and when we asked for the Secretary, a lean man in his forties came over, wearing his yachting hat bent in the style that was favored by the British pilots of World War Two. Sure enough, he was a Royal Air Force type. His name was Vlastimil Reznecek - originally from Poland, now living in the city of La Paz - and he spoke flawless English.

At lunch on the patio, he told us about Lake Titicaca. It was 150 miles long, by 50 miles wide and went from southeast to northwest, between Bolivia and Peru   nearly 4,000 square miles of water, about 12,500 feet above sea level   very shallow near the edges but almost 1,000 feet deep in the middle. But it was divided by the narrow Straits of Tequina, into two parts, called the Big Lake and the Small Lake (nearer La Paz) and we were on the northeast side of that. All around the lake were villages and farms, where people in brown Derby hats tended their crops and grazed their llamas. And farther back were snow-capped mountains. But the air was so clear and the mountains were so high that the lake did not seem big, for we could easily see the land beyond it.

The Secretary had cruised about 7,000 miles on the lake - in 9 years and two boats - and the temperature of the water was always between 50 and 54 degrees fahrenheit. But the air would go from 68 in summer, down to 23 in winter, which was cold. A few of the members had sailing boats but usually there was either too little wind or too much and when it got up, the waves, though not very high, were quite steep. I asked how big they were and he said they could get as high as 10 feet on the Big Lake but no more than 6 feet on the small one. Looking out across the lake, we could see several of the small sailing boats used by the Indians for fishing. And they seemed to be moving along nicely, in a light breeze. But their owners did not have the option of motor boats.

The Secretary's yacht Kellua (Seagull in Aymara) was a 30 foot power boat, built locally, using ideas taken from Yachting Magazine but modified to suit the lake. Her beam of 8 feet made her narrow by our standards but enabled her to do 15 knots and outrun the Bolivian Navy with a single Chrysler engine. All the boats had outboard drives, which could be raised in the shallow harbors. And the single engine meant less fuel to bring from La Paz in his pickup truck, each time he used her. Otherwise, she was conventional - with 4 bunks, a toilet and galley below, an open cockpit aft and a sheltered steering position, between them and after showing us around, he asked us to join him for a short trip, out on the lake.

Two others came along - a friend of his and a woman who invited herself - and leaving the dock, we went slowly across the harbor and out through the gap in the reeds and down the marked channel, into deep water. Then he opened her up to her crising speed and handed her over to me. I asked where to go but he said "Anywhere you like" so I headed out, toward the middle, where there was nothing to hit. It was a fine day, with a gentle breeze and a slight chop, and though she had five people aboard, Kellua went very well. So I asked about the Bolivian Navy that she could outrun. It consisted of two gunboats, stationed at the Straits of Tequina, to guard the lake. And since Bolivia had no sea coast, it was all they needed.

But they had four admirals.

The gunboats were small and could only do about 12 knots, so Kellua was the fastest boat on the lake, except for a patrol boat which was used for chasing smugglers, who did a steady trade in flashlights and such with the people of Peru. They were mostly fishermen in sailing boats, out to augment their incomes, for the fishing was not good. Now and then, the Peruvians put fingerlings in the lake, but when they swam across, the Bolivians ate them. And all the fishermen used dynamite, so there were not many large fish left.

Though we were moving quickly, there was little change in the scene ahead of us. But when I turned to go back, we were a long way from the shore and for a moment I had trouble finding the yacht club. Then as we closed in, toward the narrow passage between the reeds, I gave Kellua back to her owner. Relaxing, I tasted the water and it was slightly brackish but he said it went down all right with whisky, though it was full of dead dogs and sewage from the villages around the lake. And the water level was up three feet that year, so he would have to get extra money from the members to fix the harbor. It sounded like all yacht clubs.

The club consisted of a couple of plain frame structures. There was a small bar in a corner of one dark room and an area of tables there but we sat at long picnic tables outside in the warm, bright sun. Sheltered from the light breeze off the snowy mountain peaks, it was quite warm. The resident dogs and cats begged for tidbits under the table. The slope to the water had been levelled into several tiers, with hedges and stone walls defining the rims, with a broad stairway cutting straight down the hillside to the docks. On one tier a tethered llama grazed. On another a tall, white flag pole had been erected. From it fluttered the Bolivian national flag and the club burgee. With the many boats gently tugging at their mooring lines below, it was a very pleasant picture.

Going back to La Paz, we came to a ford with deep mud in it and there was a line of vehicles - cars and trucks - trying to get through, one at a time. Ahead of us was a taxi, full of tourists, and when it got stuck (in the deepest part) they all had to get out and push, which seemed to surprise them. But it was the only reasonable thing to do, really.

And the driver stayed behind the wheel. Also a reasonable thing to do.

Of course, we could watch the whole thing with a cetain detatchment, for Minim went easily though the mud. And late in the afternoon, we were at the La Paz Hotel, looking for a safe place for our truck and a room. But they had none and the girl suggested we try the Hotel Libertador. If she telephoned them, the would never admit (to another hotel) that they had a room for us. But if we went there, they probably would. And they did. It was expensive, by our standards, but we had things to do in the city and there was no choice. They had no garage but let us park Minim on the narrow street, in front of their door, where she would be safe. And the room they gave us was clean and modern, for the hotel was quite new. It was not large but very tall, standing in the middle of the bowl-shaped valley. And from a bar on the top floor, we saw the lights come on, all across the city. The only other person, except the barman, looked like a house detective. But in the dining room, lower down, the food was good. And in the lobby we got a newspaper - our first city one for some time. The leading article was about a visit by Robert McNamara, from the United States, who was quoted with pride as saying that Bolivia was worthy of investment by the World Bank. And it seemed odd that a nation so large, with great resources, should allow anyone like that to pass judgement on it.

I woke up early, in the morning, worried about our truck, out on the street. So I went down and it was all right. Then I saw the stickers on our luggage - it had always been hard to believe that anyone would be so crass as to glue advertisements on other people's property - so I spent some time getting them off. Then we went to the United States Embassy, to see if there was any mail for us, or news of what lay ahead. But a girl there told us - rather huffily - to go to the Consulate, where we found two letters from June's mother (sent long ago) and that was all. So back we went, to the hotel. And in a small basement room, they had two Telex machines. The girl on duty was friendly and I said I could type, so she put me though to the shipping agents in Lima, who handled the Sol Reefer's business, and let me talk to them. Tom Follett was somewhere in the Caribbean and might be coming to Peru but he had not sent them an arrival date yet.

We would have to keep in touch with the agents. We didn't want to miss our ride back to the States. But if Tom didn't get as far as Lima, we might be able to drive farther north and see a little of Ecuador. That would be much more interesting.

It was fun using the Telex machine and rather eerie when it answered back - like a typewriter with a mind of its own - but the cost made me nervous, so I hit the wrong keys. And the girl did not approve of such sloppy work - she made clicking noises, with her tongue - so I gave it back to her and she signed off with 'BIBI' meaning 'End of Transmission'. Then we went to a bank, where a thousand dollars - sent from the United States - should have been waiting for us. But something had gone wrong and it was not there.

Everything closed for siesta, so we took Minim and drove through the quiet streets. All roads spiralled up from the city core, houses along the way perched one above the other, with terrifying drops to streets and roof tops below. We drove through a market with stalls of cheap plastic nicknacks, toys, balloons, wash tubs and bottles, tended by Indian women in bright skirts, dark shawls and Derby hats. There was little business, most of them were tending their napping babies or cooking some scraps of food over small charcoal stoves. They looked tired and dirty. There were few laughing faces. The mist became rain and a mother tucked a torn, dirty scrap of blanket around her child, sleeping on the sidewalk near a stall. A man urinated against the corner of a building while dogs fought in the gutter over a piece of flesh. Then the sun appeared and the brightly colored gadgets glistened.

After the siesta, we went back to the Consulate and asked them to forward any mail for us to the Sol Reefer's home office in Miami, Florida. Then we telexed Lima to say that we would be leaving the next day and would call again from Arequipa in Peru - which was on our way from La Paz to Lima.

We invited Vlastimil Reznecek and his wife to join us for dinner that evening. Patrick wanted to write an article about the yacht club and Vlastimil promised to bring some photographs he might be able to use.

Next we reached June's mother on the telephone - she was holding our reserve funds for us - and asked her to divert the thousand dollars from La

Paz to Lima. Then we went to a travel agent, who confirmed (as we had heard) that the roads to Cuzco were impassable, at that time of the year. June especially wanted to see Macchu Picchu, northeast of Cuzco, but he said we could fly from Arequipa to Cuzco and back for about $ 40 each. So we decided to do that. Minim was parked across the street from the hotel they needed the space near the front door for cars coming and going so I turned on the alarm and closed the gas valve under the passenger's seat. We only used those in cities but they were good to have. Then I got a haircut and soon the Secretary of the Yacht Club arrived with his wife.

Mrs. Reznecek, in her simply elegant silk blouse, diamond earrings and brooch, slipped off her fur coat and listened to our conversation. She had never been on her husband's boat. It was not the sort of thing she liked. But she was very tolerant about he whole thing. The talk was lively and we all enjoyed the evening very much, in spite of our different lives.

At dinner, he told us he was in the paint business, with a factory in La Paz. There was only one other manufacturer, so they got together and drew a line on a map, down the middle of the city, saying "That's your half and this is mine". Besides selling his paint in the city, he had dealers who came in from the country every six months or so, to place their orders. They were Indians and in that society the women handled business matters, while he men did the farming. So his dealers were little ladies, about five feet high, in Derby hats. The came by bus and since they could not write, they did their ordering verbally. But when one of them had finished, she could have ordered a couple of thousand dollars worth of paint, to be shipped to her store in the country.

On her back would be a baby, that had not been changed in weeks, and swinging it around to the front, she would lift it - the smell was awful - to uncover several thousand dollars worth of small bills, which she counted out. Then she would leave and he sent her the paint. She kept no records. But when first he gave the money to his bank, they would not take it - he could hardly blame them so he went to Miami, to buy a washer and dryer. And now each Friday he laundered the money from his dealers, before depositing it.

We sat around a white linen covered table with candles and silver. Bolivia, we were told, was trying to educate the people. Each village had a school and the brightest students were sent on to another school of higher learning away from their home. In due course to be returned to the village, where they then taught the younger students.

Then I asked about the club and he said it was founded in 1946. The first Commodore was American and another was English but now the 100 members were Bolivian and they had 30 yachts - 24 power boats and 6 sailboats   most of them built locally, of cedar on wood frames, with fiberglass coating. They were built by Nicolas and Max Catari, until the two brothers quarrelled over a woman and separated. Now each man had a shed of his own, on either side of the club. The members got their fastenings and such in La Paz but went to Miami for engines, depth finders and things like that. And they had to use propellers of finer pitch than usual, because the engines put out about 35% less power at that altitude.

The club held cruises on Holidays but now most of those had been abolished by government decree. Still they had one on October 12th - the Anniversary of the Club and Columbus Day - with a barbecue, and another one on June 23rd (the solstice) to call the sun back. Otherwise they cruised mostly to the Island of the Sun or to the first Peruvian island, where an Italian called Reviso was king and made spaghetti. Thor Heyerdahl's Ra - his reed boat - was built near there. The bad road from La Paz to the club would be paved in a year and there would be more activity on the lake. But so far, it was quite unspoiled. And he said the skiing - in the nearby mountains - was done at 18,000 feet in our winter, because the slopes were covered with ice in the dry season.

As we finished our coffee, long stemmed roses were laid on the table, in front of us.

They were very nice people and we would like to see them again, some day. But probably we never will. As they left, he said something to a porter and we were told we could bring our truck to the front door, where it would be safer.

He seemed to have some authority. But perhaps anyone well dressed and well spoken had, in that society.

It was raining in the morning and we could not park near any shops - though we got ice from an unmarked doorway - so we gave up the idea of buying food and went to a control point at the edge of the city, where we got a Route Sheet. The road to the yacht club was worse than before (it had numerous fords and mud holes) but as we approached Lake Titicaca, we left the rain behind and when we arrived, it was a fine day, with white clouds in a pale blue sky and a faint breeze. No members were there on a Monday but the club had an old launch for hire, so we took it out to make some pictures. Down the shore of the lake, a mile or so to the east, we came to the base from which the hydrofoil boats took tourists to the Island of the Sun. And a new one was being built, under a white shade, with its aluminum hull and upperworks side by side.

The hydrofoil boats were like the ones which used to go down the East River, from New York City to La Guardia Airport - all closed in, like a bus, with big windows - and it seemed a pity that the tourists could not travel in slower, quieter, open boats and really enjoy the fine lake. Going back, we saw two black faced gulls and noticed that the light was missing **from the navigation buoy which marked the entrance to the yacht club's harbor. It had been stolen.** But we could camp beside the lake. No one would bother us. As we set up our tent, three men watched us, asking what each thing cost, while two children ran quietly to and fro. It was rather windy, by then, but all right in the shelter of the trees. And soon we were alone, beside the dark water.

It was cold. In the damp and mist beside the lake, even our down sleeping bags couldn't cope. We shivered through the night, waiting for the morning sun to warm us.

At dawn there was no wind and the lake was calm. The sky was clear and pale blue, down toward the horizon but dark blue overhead. But soon small white clouds developed, over the land around the lake. A man came to work on a boat he was building, under a metal roof, beside the club - covering the wooden hull with fiberglass. He kept looking at a thermometer, for he had to adjust the mixture as the sun went in and out. Then the yacht club staff arrived - four boatmen, a cook, a gardener and an administrator (a woman) - so we made a formal picture of them, before leaving there. Going west along the shore, it was not far to the Straits of Tequina - a long, narrow strip of water - with the towns of San Pedro and San Pablo, on either side. At the end of the road was a crude ramp, made of large stones, with two wooden planks on them. And out on the water were many small ferry boats, each big enough to hold one truck or maybe two cars. Each boat was wide and low - curving to a blunt point at one end and squared off at the other, as if someone had built a double ended boat and sawn it in half - and had a big outboard engine at the pointed end but the other end was wide open.

When we got there, one of them came up to the ramp, so we drove onto it. Three other passengers stepped aboard and the young boy in charge of it backed away, the engine roaring like some huge egg beater as the boat swung around to head out. With Minin's weight near the stern, the open bow was well clear of the water (otherwise it would have scooped it up like a shovel) and we went slowly across the straits. And at the far side, there was another crude ramp, out in the water. But as we backed off - when we had two wheels on the boat and two on the ramp - the boat started drifting away. For a moment we thought we would drop into the lake, then we accelerated (instinctively) and since the drive wheels were on the ramp, that drew the boat back to it, and we went bouncing over the big stones, onto the land beyond it.

The landing was near an open, grassy square. There were some houses along its sides and a few buildings scattered up the hillside behind. Very few people were about.

Past the town, the road went along the side of a mountain, with fine views of the lake below. Then, beyond a headland, it went down beside a wide strip of level land, squared off into green fields, between the mountain and the weater. And there we saw a man in European clothes making a reed boat. Already he had cut his reeds and tied them in bundles, a foot or so across, which were stacked beside his house. Now he was puting them together, in the classic shape - much like a canoe - about 15 feet long. It seemed very practical, for they were fine little boats, ideal for inshore fishing, and did not cost anything but work. They would not last forever but could easily be patched or replaced, whenever needed. And all around Lake Titicaca, they were in common daily use.

Nearby was Copacabana, with large buildings two stories high but metal roofed - and a wide plaza, with a bandstand and ornamental trees, clipped in different shapes. On a small beach at the end of a side road were several outboard engined boats, to take people to the Island of the Sun. And the best hotel was the Ambassador, so we checked in there for the night. But the room was horrible, so we left our gear in the car and down at the beach, one man insisted in negotiating for all the boatmen. His price for the trip was $ 40 and the only other people were a couple from Uruguay who could not afford to share it with us, so we went to the hotel, had a bad lunch and walked back to the beach. By then, there were no other people and the man would not take a penny less, so we checked out of the hotel and went on to the frontier of Peru, a few miles away, where an official told us the right price for the boat trip as $ 1.50 a person or $ 20 for a whole boat full.

So we never saw the Island of the Sun, But really, we had to stand up for the Downtrodden Tourists.

The town of Puno was 60 miles away but the road was very bad, so we only did 15 miles an our. Toward evening, we looked for a place to stop but the land was flat and swampy, with many houses, so we kept going. And after dark, we came to a control point, where a policeman wanted to buy our folding seats, so we told him we would send him two from the USA. Then he allowed us to camp there for the night. But as we went to bed, we were sad because we would soon be leaving the fine lake.

But not sad to be leaving behind one more control point. We had witnesses another opressive scene. A woman asking permission to walk on to the next town, to visit an ailing relative. Permission was denied and she left, crying, to return to her village. We were certainly among the priveleged, to travel as we did.

We were near Puno, so for breakfast we went into town, to the Tourist Hotel, which was hard to find but much better then the one at Copacabana. A travel agent told us they had launches for hire, to take people to the nearby floating islands - made of reeds - but no yacht club. And the air fare from Arequipa to Cuzco would be $ 20 a person each way, as we had been told in La Paz, but now there were flights every day.

Puno was big, industrial, sprawling and very Indian. Street stalls were hung with brown and black ponchos, hats and sweaters made from the local wool. All earthy tones, matching the muddy streets and spattered building fronts. I wanted to stay but Patrick felt an urge to get out of the high Andes. The weather was so bad. It rained almost all the trime. The mud was getting worse. We really had no time to dally.

By nine thirty, we were through the control point beyond the town and for 25 miles, the road to the west was paved - as the AAA map said it was, all the way to Arequipa - but then it changed to bad gravel, with potholes and fords, and went over a pass, sixteen thousand feet high, with higher mountains each side. Beyond the pass, it dropped down, into grazing land and at lunch time we fed a sheep dog crackers, dipped in our soup, while his owner whistled for him. But the tension was too much and soon he went running off to work.

There were few people to be seen. So little vegetation for the sheep to graze on. The hills were mostly stone and we would see stone houses now and then, and small plots outlined with stone walls for gardens or corrals. The road passed a couple of reedy lakes, more gray than blue in the drizzling rain. There were dozens of bright pink flamingoes in one. A very strange sight indeed.

Later, the road narrowed to one lane and went down into a canyon, in thick fog - actually dark clouds - and steady rain. The potholes, full of water, looked like puddles but were steep sided and often deep. There were no guard rails, of course. And a precepice on one side, most of the time. But the mud, coming down the mounain on the other side, coated the gravel and made it very slippery, so that we had to keep up our speed, when we came to a dip, even if it had a sharp corner in it. In one such place, there was a steep dip and a very sharp corner - with a precepice on the outside - then a steep rise to climb up. So I took Minim down with enough speed to make it and as we started the turn, all four wheels let go. But she drifted very nicely, round the corner and as we went up the rise, June said "Nice going" in a suitably casual tone of voice, as though commenting on a halfway decent putt.

I couldn't think of anything else to say. The precepice was on my side. At one moment I'm sure there was nothing but air under Minim. When you're stunned, words are often hard to find.

Another inconvenience on that road was the bridges. They were usually at corners and made of concrete, just wide enough for one vehicle, with no markings or railings or curbs. Just a flat surface coated with mud, wide enough to cross if you took it on the right line. Otherwise you might drop a wheel off one side and then, of course you would go over the edge and fall - probably turning slowly - down into the clouds.

Patrick had to brake at one bridge and then reverse to aim the car over it. We could see no more than a few feet ahead. There wasn't time to speak in sentences. I would shout "Stop" or "Left" or "Truck ahead" the instant I saw a danger. Patrick had to oncentrate on the road beneath the wheels, I could peer into the mist for signs of headlights or precepices before us.

But that was the main road, the only passable road, from La Paz and Bolivia down to Arequipa and Lima and the coast. So there were trucks, driven skillfully and hard, going both ways, in the fog and we were glad when we came out below the clouds. But then it was nearly dark, so we pulled off the road, into a small gravel pit, cut out of the mountain side.

What a relief to pull into that gravel pit. We had been on the edges of our seats for hours, trying to see through the half light, knowing that the least slip might mean disaster. Still shaking, I poured a couple of good stiff gins and we sat on the tailgate trying to think of any drive in our thousands of miles of travel which compared to that day's route.

Soon the last truck went by and after a light supper, we went to bed, in the still dampness of the mountain. But when I got up, about 3:30 AM, it was a clear, calm, moonlight night and the morning was sunny, with few clouds. We were breathing more easily at 9,600 feet and after breakfast, I checked Minim out, adding brake fluid and putting in spare fuel. We had just changed time zones, so I put my watch forward an hour and when we left there, it was ten o'clock. That was a Friday and we had no idea how far it might be to Arequipa, so we worried about getting to a bank to cash a traveller's check before they closed. But half an hour later we came to a control point and the clock on the policemen's hut said 8:30. So I had set my watch the wrong way. Also we had just spent the night on the volcano Misti and were quite near Arequipa. Dropping down into the White City was like coming home to an old, familiar place, after a long time. Since we were there, we had driven thousands of miles - all over South America - and seen six other countries. Things had not always been easy - but now we were back on home ground and could relax.

And stare up at Misti, giving our thanks to it for not erupting, the day before.

After cashing the last of our checks, we went to a travel agent and bought tickets to Cuzco, with seats on the next day's flight, and asked to come back on Tuesday. Then we called Lima. There was no word from the Sol Reefer yet. But the phone call was cheaper and better - for us - than the Telex. The people we had met in Arequipa, the last time, gave us their address and now we went there, with the thought that they might know a safe place to leave Minim, while we flew to Cuzco. But they were away and would not be back for a week, so we went to the Government Tourist Hotel, which had a walled yard behind it for parking, and checked in there for one night. That was far from the center of the city, so we took a taxi back there and sent a telegram to David Humphreys, asking for news of the Sol Reefer. There were many nice shops but a roll of film would be twelve dollars, so we did not buy any - we had one left and it would have to do. Then we went to the travel agent, to get our tickets, and were told that Tuesday's flight back from Cuzco was already closed.

Since the airline was run by the government, we could not get a refund on our tickets, without a great deal of red tape. So the girl had us on standby to come back on Tuesday - but it might be later. And we must live on a tight budget, until then, so as to reach Lima before we ran out of money. The girl had tried to warn us not to pay for our tickets before we had reservations on the flight back. But we had not caught on - we did not realize the airline had special rules - so it was not her fault and the solution was for us to stay at a guest house in Cuzco, instead of an hotel. That evening we were charged $ 13 each for small, second rate dinners and decided that the Tourist Hotel was a ripoff. But Minim would be secure in the yard, while we were gone. And the next morning, we were off to the airport. It was a small place, with just one room, full of people. At a counter, an official told us we would take our bags with us, onto the plane. And on a bench in a corner, we met a young Canadian couple, who told us how to get seats.

They had done all their travelling in South America by public transport-ation, so they were very knowledgeable on the necessary proceedures.

Since we were new at this game, we went with them. That is, I ran with him to the plane and we each grabbed two seats - sitting between them, with a hand on each - while other men scrambled for the seats aound us. Then the wives came - with the luggage - and after a while, things calmed down.

After struggling aboard with the heavy cases, I wondered if that was really easier than getting the seats. But our friends assured us that a woman would be pushed aside by the eager men and was much more likely to be trampled to death, The other passengers thought twice about pushing our husbands around.

The airplane was a nice twin jet by Fokker and only took half an hour to get there. On the way, the Canadians said they would be staying at Leonard's Lodgings in Cuzco, so we decided to try it. Then we dipped down, out of the sunshine, into the white-topped clouds and through them and out into a gray world below and landed smoothly at Cuzco. And sharing a taxi to the guest house, we were welcomed by Leonard. He was an American, married to a local girl and had lost 50,000 acres in the land reform, recently. But she had three retired generals, among her relatives, so when anyone 'leaned' on him, he made a call to them. And he got by.

Sitting in the parlor, drinking pale coca tea, we listened to Leonard's stories of Cuzco. He loved living there. To him it was paradise. Not fancy, not pretentious but a simple life, in tune with the surroundings. The tea was warm and we were relaxed among friends.

The old house was clean and comfortable and he had a room for us upstairs, so we left our bags there and went out to look around. Just down the street, the trade unionists were having a protest meeting, across the way from the best hotel. And nearby was our travel agent's office, where they told us that we did indeed have reservations on Tuesday's flight. But of course there was a catch: We must leave our tickets there and get them on the day before the flight, properly validated. We had been warned not to stay at the mountain top hotel at Macchu Picchu - it was expensive and bad and we could get our own tickets to go there, so we thanked the agent and walked across town, toward the main plaza. Cuzco was once the center of the Inca Empire - a splendid city, in a wide valley, with palaces and gardens and statues of solid gold - but the Spaniards took the gold and destroyed most of the fine buildings, in the name of Christ. All that remained were the ruins. And tourists came to see them.

It was cold, at eleven thousand feet, and we walked hurriedly to keep warm. We passed an old man, sitting in a doorway, wrapping lengths of rugs around his feet. Children ran barefoot over cobblestoned streets, in and out of puddles of muddy water. They all chewed the coca leaf.

At lunch, in a snack bar, we were surrounded by American hippies, hanging out. And the three girls who ran it were quite the slowest I have ever seen. Just to make change took several minutes, with time out for reflection. It felt as though we had stepped into another world. But that was not South America, or even Peru. It was something different. Inside the train station, the ticket windows were closed but we could hear voices behind them, so we waited. And after an hour, a man opened one, to tell us we could not buy tickets for Macchu Picchu until 6:00 AM the next day. He said it with the air of superiority which people of low intelligence assume when they happen to know something you do not. But we found a copy of Time magazine and bought a book   for these notes - from a woman who overchaged us for it. So I gave her another, unused one I did not like. And left her looking baffled, which was rather satisfactory.

Then we went out with the Canadian couple to have dinner at a restaurant which specialized in chicken. It was run by a huge Yugoslav with flashing gold teeth (who spoke Spanish with the accent of his homeland) and since he liked us, there were chicken livers, for a start. Then there was chicken soup (June found a foot in hers) and after that, we had a choice: Half a chicken, or a quarter, or a whole one. We did not stick around for dessert. But there was a baby Jaguar, about three months old, wandering around the restaurant and he was superb. He had great big eyes and a strange voice   more a growl than a meow - and big feet, with strong claws. When he finished playing with the phone cord, he got into the cash box, pulling out the money. And we wanted so much to take him home. But that would be unwise - you could easily lose a finger.

Our Canadian friends, Joan and Steve, were as enchanted by him as we were. What a pity that he must soon grow up, probably to end as a skin nailed to the restauant wall.

The owner's loud, cheerful brother was there and said they imported things, like saw teeth, on the side. They would invest $ 4,000 in a shipment and when it got to Cuzco it would be worth $ 12,000. But he did not say how it came.

I think it would be cheaper to have it smuggled in, than to pay off all the officials in Callao.

The beds at Leonard's Lodgings were deep and squeaky and we were up at 5:20 but arriving early at the station, we had no problems, except that the seats we were given did not exist on the train and it was swarming with peddlers.

Since our seat numbers didn't exist, we felt free to choose those we liked best. There was little to choose. The old coaches were narow and dirty. We had to lace our knees between those of the people across from us.

As the train left the station, I wondered how it would get out of the valley, for there were high mountains all around and trains do not go well, up steep slopes. But someone had found an answer to the problem and it was quite simple. The track went through the city, toward he outskirts and as the land became steeper, it turned across the slope, to climb more gently. Then, when it came to an obstruction, it reversed. The rails came to an end and the train stopped and a man got off to throw a switch, beside the track. Then the train backed onto the next section, which angled up the hill, the other way. Until that ran out and we went forward on another section. And slowly we climbed up the mountain side, above the city.

Small boys grabbed onto hand holds as the slowly moving train climbed the steep hill. They would hang on for a section or two, getting a free ride for a short distance.

As the clouds moved across the sky, sunlight swept across Cuzco, down below. And the walls of houses shone white, between the brown roofs. And the fields beyond were green. Then we went over a pass and down a long, fertile valley, that got narrower and more steep sided all the time, with soon a small river - the Urubamba, which flows into the Amazon - in it and suddenly we came to Macchu Picchu. There was just a small station, with a few houses nearby and no sign of the ruins. But that was a hiding place, for the Inca Virgins of the Sun, and it was built between the mountain tops, far above. In fact it was unknown for hundreds of years, until an American called Hiram Brigham found it. Now a narrow road - all hairpin turns - went up the steep mountain side and at the station, there were many small busses, to take people there. But first there was a fuss about tickets. Officials waved and shouted orders, making sure that no one got on any bus until the number of his ticket was recorded. However there was plenty of room and when they had finished, the busses went roaring up the road to the hidden city.

The mountain tops were like huge towers, drifting through gray clouds, and much of the city was built on a narrow saddle, between two of them. But it overflowed, onto the tops and down the sides, to where they dropped away for a thousand feet, into the valley below. Across the narrow valley were sheer walls of other mountains. And everywhere we looked, still more came into view and faded and were lost in the clouds. In that place the Incas built their palaces and temples and open courts, of great stones, shaped and fitted by hand, to stand for a thousand years.

Between, they cut steps out of the solid rock and all aound, they built narrow terraces - held in place by stone walls - on which to grow their food. The roofs of straw had disappeared but otherwise, most of the buildings were in fine shape - they could be put back into service quicker than you could find a hundred virgins - but we saw no carvings. Maybe the priests had other things to do. The buildings were gray, like the rocks on the mountains and there were pathways of crushed stones, here and there. But everything else was green. Every terrace was covered with lush grass, each dip held a bush or a tree. Even the tops of the walls were green. And everything you touched was damp.

318

Of course, it was raining intermittently in those clouds. It must always have been damp there.

Going from one part of the city to another was not easy, for the paths were often steep. And soon it began to rain quite hard, so we went to the mountain top hotel, for soup and beer. Our friends were there and we all agreed that the site was very impressive, with fine engineering in stone. But Steve pointed out that even up there, the Incas felt they needed two lines of defence against attack by the Spaniards. Steve and Joan had a room at the hotel (which they said was expensive and not as good as Leonard's Lodgings) but we were going back to Cuzco that day, so we left them and took a bus down the steep road to the railroad station.

Small boys slid straight down the hillside, racing the bus to the next corner. Usually, they were ahead of it and the cheering tourists tossed coins from the windows.

The train was still there, so we climbed up into it and found our seats and waited for it to leave at 4:00 PM. But the time came and went and nothing happened. By five o'clock, the passengers were wondering what was wrong. And at six, the word came that it could not leave. There had been a landslide, 500 yards long, 5 miles away and a bridge was damaged.

There was a sudden, dramatic exit from the train. People who had been sitting, sedately waiting for the return trip, were now pushing and shouting toward the parked busses. The race for a room at the hotel was on. We stayed behind in our seats, knowing the small hotel could not possibly feed and sleep all those people. We heard loud arguments about being charged a fortune by the bus drivers to return to the top. But finally a price was agreed upon, the busses left and quiet returned to the few of us who had chosen to stay behind.

The station master locked the toilets, because it was the proper time, but the passengers made it clear that lynching was not out of the question, so he unlocked them again. And nearby, there was a shop that sold everything we needed.

Patrick walked across the tracks to a shack that served food of sorts and sold a few provisions. He returned with our dinner and a candle.

Our small compartment on the train had a table, between the seats and at 8:30 we sat down to a supper of tuna, served on crackers, with bananas and chocolate, by candle light. The candle stood on the lid of the tuna can and the food was placed on napkins. We had to take turns to spread the fish with my knife but otherwise, it was quite elegant. As we ate, a tall stranger came by and remarked, in good English, on how self-sufficient we looked. He was an editor of Playboy magazine - the one who selected the jokes. He worked at home (in Maryland, I think) and each day he sorted through great piles of tem, looking for new ones. The trick was to read the punch line first (nine times out of ten, he already knew it) but what he liked best were limericks. In fact, he wrote many of those himself and then he was paid $ 25 for each one, as well as his regular fee.

When he left, we went out for an after dinner stroll. It was a lovely, moonlit night in the deep valley, with a few small clouds between the mountains and dark shadows lower down. Back on the train, it was quiet. Some of the people were playing with home made cards - pieces of cardboard, torn into squares and marked 'Ace' or '9' or whatever - but most of them were talking quietly. It was all very civilized.

We heard no complaints. People acepted the situation, not from stupidity or impotence but with the grace that you would expect of intelligent beings.

The coach was not heated and the seats were too short to lie down on but we slept quite well, in various positions, and everyone awoke about 5:00 AM. At seven a work train went past, with two bulldozers and many ties - it had come up the valley, the other way - and they said the mud was 4 feet deep, on the tracks, ahead of us. I offered to round up some male passengers to come and help. But the workmen just laughed, as if they did not expect such an idea to be taken seriously.

As the work train left, someone said that landslides had been quite rare, since the railroad was built, in 1926. It was overcast and cool, by then. In our train, the passengers were reading and chatting and playing cards quietly. And a man from the railroad said they hoped to get us through - to a train on the far side of the blocked section - about noon. But soon a train full of Indians went by and at 10:25 the engine came back, to hook us up. There was much laughter among the passengers and they cheered, as we left. Then the word came down the train that five people had been killed. They were a family of campesinos (farmers) in their house when the land came sliding down. One of the bodies had already been found, in the river. Those things happened every six years or so but that one was unusually bad.

When the train stopped, we all got out and walked along the track, to where it ended in the mud, then picked our way over a trail, between huge boulders - some as big as busses - which had come down the mountain from above. Five hundred yards of track were gone. It would probably be months, before it could be fixed. But there were tourists - some of them women in high heels - coming the other way. No one had told them about it, for tourism must go on. The mud was gray and full of smaller boulders. The bridge must have been swept away, because we all crossed the river on a temporary one two tree trunks, with planks between them - and beyond the landslide, the mountain went almost straight up, from close beside the railroad track.

The slide must have been more like an avalanche of boulders, bouncing down the nearly vertical slope, with the thick grey mud following them. Anyone or thing on its path would have been helpless. The river, that had been clear the day before, ran rapidly past us now, full of debris - brown, foaming water. Someone pointed at the river, where he said there was a body. Everyone stopped and stared, I couldn't look. Finally the column of people started moving again, scrambling over the rocks, then along banks of grass until the railroad track appeared. We asked several people going the other way. They had not been told of the landslide until the train suddenly stopped, just before it. They were given the choice of returning to Cuzco or climbing over the rubble to the train we had just left.

When we arrived, there was no train - it had gone off to put its engine on the other end - but soon it backed up to us and everyone rushed to climb into it. We fetched up with a fat travel agent from California (pleased with himself because he was not paying for anything) and a very serious Dutchman, who took pictures of everything, as we went up the valley and over the pass and down the zigzag tracks into Cuzco. That was Monday evening and we were due to fly on Tuesday morning but we had trouble getting our tickets from the travel agent. If we missed our flight. we might never get a refund. so we tried three times and finally a man found them, in a drawer. Then, at Leonard's Lodgings, we met Steve and Joan. They had expected us to go back to the mountain top hotel when the train did not leave Macchu Picchu, so they kept space for us in their room (everyone was doubling up). And eventually they gave it to some other people. But we had not missed much, because the place was a mad house, all that night.

Now the four of us went out to dinner, at one of the best restaurants in Cuzco, which was all right but nothing special. It had very few customers and most of those were Americans. But Steve and Joan told us how they travelled. They went by public transportation (as we had been doing, for the last few days) and stayed in guest houses. And seemed to be spending about as much as we were. But we much preferred having our truck and avoiding the tourist places. Also we met more local people in the camp-grounds, garages and shops. But we could not have reached Macchu Picchu - or even Cuzco - by road, at that time of the year.

At breakfast we said good bye, for they were staying in Cuzco, then went out to the airport. It was a fine day and the plane was full but we left on time and rose into the blue sky, over the crumpled green mountains, and dropped down to land at Arequipa. And by 9:45 we were at the tourist hotel. It was all so easy - if you do not count the paper work. Minim was in the yard, behind the hotel and there was no sign that anyone had tampered with her. It was good to have her again, to be free to travel when we pleased, without asking for tickets or waiting in line or fighting for seats. But there was no need to rush off and we felt we should stay for one night, after using their parking space all that time, so we took a room and called the Sol Reefer's agents in Lima. They had also Telexed Miami, on Friday but had no news yet, so I said I would call them from there. Then we went into town, to relax and saw the Convent of Santa Catalina - all white stone and silence - where one nun had spent her whole life and was on her way to sainthood. But in the Plaza - with its green lawns and palm trees - a small boy tried to put the bite on us, though he never approached a local person, however wealthy they looked.

The bed at the hotel was rather short for me. They often were, in Central and South America, though I was just six feet tall. And when (as in this case) they had boards at both ends, it was hard for me to sleep. But we could breathe all right at 7,500 feet and the morning was clear and sunny. It took us a while to get going and we had forgotten that the desert, bare and barren, starts right outside Arequipa. But it was good to come to the junction, where we had picked up the detective, and know what was down each road ahead. To the left were Arica, La Serena and Puerto Montt - all places we remembered well. And to the right was Lima, where we came into South America. But beyond it were miles of ocean. If we found no ship, there would be other roads, we did not know, across northern Peru, Ecuador and Colombia, to the shore of the Caribbean Sea, And then we must find a way across it.

Soon we crossed the bright green oasis, between the bare hills, where we had slept on Christmas night. Then the highway went down to the coast and along it, beside the great hills of sand. Again the sand was deep, in places, on the road. And for lunch we stopped on a bluff, over the Pacific Ocean. While June got out the food, I slid under the truck. By then, the exhaust pipe had rotted through and hot gasses were coming out where they should not. Already we knew better than to close the windows but now it was clear that we must fix it soon, or the locker where we kept spare gasoline might become hot enough to promote a small explosion.

There were few control points that day and no one wanted to see our papers but a Mickey Mouse was parked beside the road near a town and a policeman in it flagged us down, looking for a sticker on our windshield, then waved us on, when he saw that Minim was not a full-sized truck, after all. She must have looked like one, from the front and we were often flagged by hitch hikers. Usually they expected to pay for their rides in South America and their attitude showed it. They waved with firm authority, as if hailing a bus.

As we passed though Chala, it was getting dark but soon the road left the coast, climbing a little, and went through a desert that looked as though it had once been the bottom of an ocean - smooth, level sand with reefs of jagged rocks, ten to twenty feet high, here and there - so we pulled off the road and went behind one, about 100 yards away. And there we set up our tent, with a view of the sea down below. After supper, it was dark and still. We saw the lights of trucks in the distance but none came near us. At 1:00 AM there was brilliant moonlight, with a faint breeze off the land. Then at six, the sun came up but the big moon was still high. As we ate breakfast, a truck went down to the sea, left off a man and a boy and came back, past us, to the highway. When the wind came off the ocean, there was a quiet roar of surf. It was cool and pleasant, then. But when the sun rose into the sky, white and hot, it was time to leave.

Quite soon we passed Nasca, where we had set up our tent for the first time in South America, then we started across the barren desert, toward Lima. About half way, just off the road, was the town of Pisco. And having become fond of the drink made there, we went to see it. But it was only a sea port, with one main road and somehow disappointing. Still we got fresh bread and bought wine - though it was expensive - from a woman at a roadside stand (she had money, hanging in a basket overhead, to make change) but there was no grape juice, just Pisco, white or amber colored.

Going across the desert, it was hot in the afternoon but toward evening it cooled off. There were no control points, all that day and the few policemen we had met since coming back to Arequipa were relaxed and kind. But the traffic increased as we approached Lima. If we went into the city, it would be late to find a place to sleep. So we decided to camp for the night. And about 30 miles out, we found a suitable site. Off to the side of the road was a valley, with tracks in it, so we followed them for a quarter of a mile and came to a place that might have been a gravel pit, or a garbage dump, or both. It was not very attractive but we did not think any Bad Guys would find us, so we set up the tent. There were too many rocks to set the pegs but with just a light breeze, they were not needed. And except for the faint noise of distant traffic, it was quiet and peaceful. It would do.

While June was cooking dinner, I checked our security. The hills around us were blackened by smoke but nothing was burning, just then. And there were trails up the barren hill, close behind us. I wondered what made them. Goats, perhaps? But Minim and the tent were hard to see, at any distance. We could scarcely improve on them, for our kind of travelling. And the slightly official look of the truck was helpful, for it tended to keep away petty intruders. The wine we bought in Pisco was grapey but okay. And once it was dark, there was little chance of anyone finding us, so we turned in. We had finished the trip that we had set out to make, around South America. Now we must find a way to get Minim home - which was beyond the Equator and half way across the world. But we would think about that in the morning.

11 - NORTH OF THE EQUATOR

At dawn the garbage dump was wreathed in fog. We had both slept well and in the damp silence, June made breakfast. It was cool, at that hour. But as we folded our tent, the sun came out and soon we were on the highway, heading into Lima. Before nine we were at the German pension in Miraflores, where we hhad stayed before. The manageress was not there and a young man phoned her at the annex. But she did not come, so I went outside and met her on the sidewalk. Glancing at our car, she was very cool. As I followed her to the pension she said "You wrote me one letter," then "You did not leave it here." I asked if she had a room for us and she said "No", quickly and quietly. Her whole manner was suspicious. And I felt sure that she had personally stolen June's necklace. We thought of reporting the theft to the police, or maybe the Tourist Office. But we decided that it would be useless. In Cuzco, Steve had told us that when Americans cashed traveller's checks with that woman, they had turned up in the black market. She seemed to be well known already and it was unlikely that we could do anything to change things. So we drove into the center of the city and while June watched Minim, I walked to the First National Bank, where our money should be.

The girl at the Information desk found a draft for $ 500 right away, then asked my wife's name (it must have been a test question, to be sure it was me) and how much I wanted in soles, how much in traveller's checks. Getting cash took longer, with three forms to be filled out in quadruplicate, but that was the Peruvian governmen's system. The bank was quick and efficient. In fact, the money came by Telex the same day that it was sent. But they did not have the other draft - for a thousand dollars - that should have been transferred from La Paz.

It was a fine day and warming up but still hazy overhead. For some reason, there were often clouds - or thick haze - over Lima that seemed to be why the climate was so pleasant. It reminded us of San Francisco. But the latitude of Lima is about 12 degrees South - well in the tropics - and without that haze, it would surely have been too hot for city life. At the Sol Reefer's agents, we were told that the Panama Canal was closed, by a strike of United States personnel. And they had no reply yet, either from David Humphreys in New York or the ship's office in Miami. They called a few shipping lines in Callao but none of them had space for our truck. One small ship, then in Guayaquil, was coming south and might take Minim to Guatemala (we would have to fly) if there were no problems with charges for offloading - there was nothing else to go off there - and if the captain thought he could get her safely to shore by lighter. The agent looked in a book and said there was a three ton crane on the dock. So I asked him to telex the captain and told him we would keep in touch.

We had heard of another pension, owned by Sally Griswold, in a part of Lima called Miramar, so we went out there and it looked fine - a large brick house, facing the sea across a quiet road, some grass and a cliff. In front of the house was a formal garden and beside that was a driveway, leading to a secure parking place. In the house were a dining room and a bar, with doors opening out to a large garden - all flowers and trees and grass - behind it. And along one side of the garden was a new building, with kitchens on the ground floor and half a dozen rooms above them. One of those was available and though it was expensive by our standards, it was pleasant - with an outside walkway along the front and a stairway down to the garden - so we took it and stayed for a nice lunch, served by Indian maids.

There must have been a dozen or so people eating in the dining room. They were all very quiet. The food couldn't have been more unimaginative. Perhaps that made people somber. But Patrick liked the meal. And I liked the nice room we had, with a proper bath and lots of hot water.

Then we went on a crowded bus to a travel agent, in the center of the city. A man there said the Grace Line only went to Los Angeles - which was out of our way and far too costly - and the German Line would be no help. So our only hope was that he might be able to get us on a ship of the Italian Line, sailing on April First for Cristobal. That assumed the strike would be over by the time we got there but if not, then he had no idea what would happen. He seemed to resent our refusal to book passage on that but we said we would think about it and revert to him on Monday.

I was dead against the Italian Line. There had to be a better way.

Next we went into the nearby Sheraton hotel, to phone the Sol Reefer's agents and tell them we would be at Sally's place. The hotel - like the United States Embassy - was so fancy, it stood out sharply, as a symbol of an opulent life style. Going back to Miramar, we thought how nice it was to know enough Spanish to be able to take busses around town, without feeling awkward. And we were at Sally's place in time for tea, served in the garden, just as it would be in England. One man there spoke good English, so I asked if he came from the U.K. and he did. But he was retired and lived in Lima now, though he went back once a year to visit his wife.

We were sad to know that June's necklace had really gone. I felt sure the woman sold it within a few days of stealing it, from her manner. And was mad that she got so little for it, when my letter came. But it was unreasonable to have hoped she would get it back for us. We must simply forget it. And I should stop riding busses in my best 'shore going' pants, which had pockets that were far too easy for anyone to 'dip'

At dusk it was cool and pleasant. Down in the bar, we met an American woman who lived in Spain and various young Englishmen, in Lima on business. After dinner we went out for a stroll around the neighborhood There was a lighthouse nearby but away from the sea, the scene was like Paris when I was young, before World War Two: The quiet streets of gray, introspective houses. Small corner shops, run by women in black. A dog trotting along a sidewalk, anxious to be somewhere else. But we found wine and chocolate. And going back we noticed shacks on the land between the road and the cliff. Someone lived out there.

In the morning we sat in our room, at a desk overlooking the garden, figuring routes home and the cost of each. Now it seemed that the best would be via the Sol Reefer, all the way to Miami, or to drive north across

Ecuador and Colombia (if it were possible) to Cartagena and find a ship to Panama. Either would be about $ 500 cheaper than the Italian Line. So we must check with the Colombian tourist people. But how could we fit more visas, for all the countries of Central America, into our passports, which were already full of stamps? We were told that none of the embassies would be open on a Saturday, so we started typing the notes for this book. Later we set up our tent, in the parking place, to dry. And we found what was wrong with Minim's fuel gauge. There was a great bunch of wires underneath her - in the rear, right hand corner - and when we wiggled them, the needle moved. So we secured the whole lot with a big safety pin and the gauge was fine.

On Sunday morning, the sky was overcast and the air was cool and birds were singing in the garden. We were late getting up but it was good to slow down, once in a while. After lunch we walked down the road, along the cliff and watched the people surfing off the beach below. Then back to work, typing these notes. June phoned Michigan to ask for more money to be sent to Lima, in case the draft from La Paz never did arrive, and her mother said that more than 100 ships were waiting to go through the Panama Canal. It was on the news in America. On Monday, we went to the United States Embassy and they put some extra pages in my passport, which was more full than June's because it had several notations about Minim in it. But the pages were made of special paper and the people could not find any more of that, so June did not get hers.

At the Colombian Embassy, a woman told us it was possible to drive to Cartagena but we must get a transit permit, so we applied for that. We had to leave the Carnet and both our passports and she did not give us any receipt for them but we had no choice, so we hoped to get them back. A man told us that Cartagena was a very nice seaside resort - also that we could camp along the way - so we began to feel more hopeful. In the Embassy of Ecuador, they checked the visas that we got in Texas and said they were in order. We had estimated our date of arrival accurately enough. So there was nothing further that we needed. Then they gave us some literature for tourists but there were no maps of the country available. On Tuesday, we went back to the Colombian Embassy, where we got the transit permit (and our documents back) and tourist cards, good for 15 days. But the money had not arrived, at the bank. If it were sent by cable, it would take 2 or 3 days. And we drew a blank with the shipping agent. Nothing was available except the Italian Line. If the Sol Reefer did not come and get us, we had better drive north to Cartagena.

The odds were quite high that she would not come, so we started preparing for the trip north by road.

We already had visas for Costa Rica, valid for 12 months, so we tried the Panamanian people, who gave us them right away and told us that the problems at the canal had been settled for the moment, though they might recur at any time. But the embassies were only open in the mornings, so we went back to Sally's, got Minim and drove out to the edge of town, to a muffler shop, where they made a new tail pipe from thicker metal and put it on, while we waited. They had no lifts for the cars or trucks but a whole row of big, clean pits with metal guard rails, arranged diagonally for ease of entry. When we pulled over one, a man took off the old pipe, another man made new one (using a bending machine) and the first man put it on. It was very efficient. A tail pipe is a 'tubo de cola' in Spanish, for 'cola' means tail. And Coca Cola, which is poular, means Coca Tail. On Wednesday we got Mexican tourist papers and Nicaraguan visas. But our visas for Honduras would not be ready until the next day. And then it was lunch time again.

We travelled all around town, to the different embasies, by bus. It took time, but we had plenty. It was nice, frittering away the days. And I did not have to spend all my time guarding Minim.

But in the afternoon we had a set of spark plugs cleaned and back at Sally's, we filled our water cans. We were warned to beware of bandits in northern Colombia and told to look for a smaller vessel at Santa Marta, if we did not find a ship in Cartagena, when we got there. And it was good to be planning a whole new trip, into places we did not know. On Thursday we picked up our passports, at the Honduran Embassy. Then we had all the visas we needed, to drive back to the United States - if we found a ship across the Caribbean - and Minim was ready to go. But our money had not arrived, from La Paz or from the States. So we phoned

Michigan and asked to have the drafts traced, from that end. And film for our camera was $ 20 a roll in the city, so we did not buy any.

On the bus back to Miramar, we considered the situation, If we stayed in Lima, we might run out of money, before the Sol Reefer arrived - even if she did. And a weekend was coming up, so the bank would be closed for two days. If we did not get any news on Friday, we had better head north. But first we should let Sally know that we were leaving. We had never met her but we sent word that we wanted to pay our bill and she appeared - large and quite overpowering - and hovered in the background, while her small, timid servant counted our money. Then we had $ 174 left, to get to Quito in Ecuador, which was more than 1,300 miles away.

In the bar, that evening, we met two men from England who had been waiting four months to get a shipment of machinery off the docks in Callao. They had not even been allowed to see it, so they had no proof that it was still there. They said that it was processing equipment - for the benefit of Peru - which they had to set up and get working, when it was in place. They were not surprised or concerned, it seemed. They were comfortable at Sally's and someone else was paying the bill.

I was so glad to be leaving that place. The food was monotonous, the people were monotonous, even having baths in hot water was getting boring.

It was hot and sticky, that night. And there were sand fleas - I think - in our bed. So we did not sleep much. Or perhaps it was the tension we always felt before starting on a new journey into countries we did not know. After breakfast, we went shopping for food and by ten we were at the bank. No money had come or us, so we asked them to send it to Quito, when it did. Then we went to the shipping agent and he had a letter for us. The Sol Reefer would not be coming. We must go back on our own. By noon we were on our way to Route 1 (the only passable road to Ecuador) which followed the coast to the northwest. And at the edge of the city, where the buildings ran out, the desert started again.

It seemed great to be back on the road. No matter that we had so little money left. We knew there would be enough for gas and food, along the way. We were much happier on our own, than tied to the routine of that boarding house.

For about 40 miles, the highway had four lanes and where it reverted to the usual two there was a control point. As always, the policeman who checked us wanted our documents. But this time he noticed that our Carnet had never been stamped by the Touring Club in Lima. So he went into his act. First he told me it was a serious matter and demanded that I pay him a large sum of money - I forget how much - as a fine. Then, as he saw that I was going to stand there and argue all day if necessary, he softened his tone and reduced the amount. Toward the end, he was practically whining and eventually I ageed to give him four dollars. So he tried to pocket a ten and when that failed, he let us proceed. He did not give me any receipt for the money, or make any notation on the Carnet, so we could still be hit up by another one, down the line. But I thought it best to take a chance on that - at four bucks a crack, they were not expensive.

It was cold that afternoon, for there was fog along the coast. And we saw many fishing boats, close inshore. But the land was still desert, with oases now and then. And fields of crops   it looked like sugar cane occasionally. Toward dark, we were looking for a place to camp and saw a sandy hill, beside the road. So we drove around, behind it. But a red truck was already there, with men in it. And we went back to the highway, to continue for a while.

We tried not to let anyone see where we camped at night. If they found us in the morning, it was okay. But if anyone knew where we were sleeping, they just might decide to make a fast buck, at our expense and inconvenience.

Then we saw a line of bushes and small trees, following a dry wash, away from the road. That would do, if we could get to it. But the white sand looked soft, beside the road and we might get stuck. So I walked along, until I found a good place to cross it and June followed in Minim to a fine site, between the trees 100 yards away. But we did not want to take any chances of being seen, so we had dinner early - using a shielded light - and went to bed. The sky cleared, after dark and Orion was overhead. We had gone 22,723 miles, since leaving home and June's stool had just worn out. She must be heavier that me. Or wiggle more.

FROM LIMA TO
BUENAVENTURA

PAMAMA

COLOMBIA

BUENAVENTURA

AMAZON BASIN

ECUADOR

PACIFIC

OCEAN

PERU

LIMA

The only difference between the two stools was that one had just worn out. Of course, it must be mine. From then on, I had to balance a cushion over the frame and hope it would stay in place through the meal.

It was still in the night but at dawn we heard sounds of movement nearby. And through the bushes, I saw two donkeys, then a man and behind him, a modest shack. We had camped close to his place but he did not seem to mind. So I decided not to approach him for permission to be there. It was a bit late. By eight o'clock, when I finished checking the truck, the sky had clouded over and the air was cool. The farmer who lived behind us came past - perhaps to have a look at us, more likely on his way somewhere. We were a little uneasy, that day, with a whole new trip to do and the uncertainties of finding our money in Quito or a ship when we got to Cartagena.

Minim's odometer showed 129,106 miles, that morning. She was no longer young. We hoped that she would hold together and not need anything major, for a few more thousands of miles. I suppose the shortage of cash made us worry about things that might happen.

Then we drove all day, across deserts and through fields of sugar cane. That was the most highly developed part of Peru, with plants making fish meal, along the shore and barrios, here and there - rows and rows of modest houses, just the same and each with a high TV antenna beside it. That afternoon, we bought gas. Then we had $ 6.00 left, in soles. And it was still daylight, when we found a place to camp. But we had not seen one for a long time and there was nobody in sight, either way, so we pulled off the road it was open range country - and stopped behind a clump of trees, with bushes under them, which would protect us from wind and view. Again we dined early, just using a tiny flashlight, so as not o attract attention and give our location away. A truck stopped, on the highway but then went on while we peered at it from the bushes. And by 8:00 PM we were in bed. A pig came by twice, in the night - walking close around our tent - but its footsteps were different from a man's, so we did not panic much. And the morning was bright and sunny, with green trees nearby and gray mountains in the distance. And birds singing. And occasionally a truck on the highway.

If all went well, we should reach Cartagena about the time that some money would be available for us, in Vermont. So if we could find a reliable way of getting it to Colombia, we would be able to pay for Minim to be shipped to Panama. When we packed up to go, it was already hot and we wished we had started at dawn. For the road was so far from the coast, at that point, there was no fog, that day. At noon we spent the last of our Peruvian soles on beer and gas. And soon we came to a junction, where the road went left or right. We had no maps of Ecuador but the AAA one of all South America was quite clear: The road to the left was paved, as far as the border of Ecuador. And after that, it was narrow on the map - a secondary, gravel one. But the one to the right was a major highway - partly gravel, partly paved - which went across Ecuador to Quito and on to Colombia.

It was even shown in red, on the AAA map, as part of the famous Pan American Highway, which turned out to be a fancy name for some roads that happened to be there, sometimes.

So we turned right, toward the border village of La Tina and quickly the road went from pavement to gravel to dirt. But a man at a control point assured us that we were on the proper road, as did some men - building an aqueduct - whom we stopped to ask. So we kept going and things changed rapidly. First there were small fords to cross - after so long in the desert - then we came to a wide river, running with clear water but full of rocks. And near the middle, we hit a big one with Minim's under part. The problem was to find where to go, in such a ford. But on the far bank, I checked and did not see anything bent or broken, so we went on.

There were three control points, one after another. And at each one, the police looked into everything, including the case for my glasses and our Flair pens. But at one, they found June's Tampax and decided that it was some kind of explosive - you lit the wick and threw it? - and it took us a while to convince them that the things were really quite harmless. Then we came into tropical jungle - with pouring rain - and the road was deep, black mud for hundreds of yards at a time. Once we got stuck in mud so deep, it was up to the door for the truck but we put her in reverse and she want back to higher ground and we found a better way. For a while, we were unsure of getting through but a Volvo came from Ecuador and if he could make it, we could. And we churned through the mud - flinging it up, behind us and sliding from side to side - all the way to the village at the frontier. It was just a few small buildings, beside the narrow road, ending at a bridge over a river to Ecuador. Though it was too late for us to cross that evening, various officials demanded to see our papers and asked questions, until one said:

"How long have you been married?"

"Twenty years."

"How many children do you have?"

"None."

Then they all crowded around the truck, saying:

"What do you use?"

So June wrote down a name for 'the pill' on many pieces of paper and the men all became very friendly. When we asked if we could camp for the night, they showed us a small brick building that was under construction. The roof was on - though it had no doors or windows - and we were welcome to stay there. Inside, it had four small rooms and the floors were still dirt, littered with pieces of brick. So we swept out the first one and set up our tent there. The rain had stopped and some of the officials came over to watch us. They wanted to buy it but we explained that we needed it, to live in and the rain started again, so they went away.

Steadily the rain got heavier, until it was a downpour. And we looked up 'La Tina' in a dictionary. It was 'the bathtub' - of course, we should have known. It was dark in the village, that night, for there was no electricity. The only light we saw was a candle, in a building across the road. The rain, pouring down, hid everything else. So we ate a cold supper and went to bed at eight.

The rain, bouncing off the tin roofs of the village houses, deadened all other sounds. We fretted a while about Minim sinking deeper into the ever increasing puddle outside the door. And wondered about what sort of jungle creatures might seek shelter under our roof. But hopefully, our tent was snake proof, so we slept.

At dawn the sky was overcast and there were noises of the jungle behind the small building but the rain had stopped and the road was nearly dry. A man went by with some garbage, which he threw off the bridge into the brown, rushing river. Our tent was dry, in the building. But the truck was very muddy and crawling underneath it, I could not find where we hit the rock, the day before. Then at 8:00 AM the border opened and for an hour, we were busy with paper work. And in one office we were told that we had taken the wrong road. The paved road, back at the junction, led to a paved road across Ecuador. There was no need to go though all that mud or to spend the night in La Tina - unless of course we were on our way to somewhere nearby, in Ecuador. Which we had not intended. But we were now, so we asked about the road ahead. The man said it was worse than the part we had just come over, in Peru. But going back was not attractive, so we decided to try it.

The AAA map was wrong again. But we did get into a lot of interesting situations, by following it.

As we crossed the bridge, the sun came out and by the time we had cleared with all the authorities in Ecuador, it was hot. The village there had deep ditches with steep sides, by the road and it would have been easy to fall into them but they drained off the water very well and there was none left. Two men changed ten US dollars for us and we bought gas - at 30 cents a gallon - then headed north, on the only road out of there. It was far better than the road to La Tina - firm gravel with good bridges. There were many landslides, in the first section - we saw a small one happen - but the road was cleared promptly. There were crews out doing it.

The officials in La Tina must have known that the road in Euador was better. Did they not dare to say so? Or were they unwilling to admit it? I suppose, in isolated areas like that, a common hate is one of the few things that will keep a village together, or maintain an imaginary line between two countries.

As we climbed up, away from the river, the landslides were fewer and soon there were no more. At noon we got gas and Extra was 25 cents a gallon, so it would cost less to get to Cartagena than we thought, for we had been told it was about the same in Colombia. And the drivers on that road were better than the ones in Peru, so we could relax and enjoy the

336

trip. Still climbing, we went up through cypresses, into very fine scenery - rather like Guatemala - where the road wound over the tops of mountains. And the people were nice. At Loja we stopped to get ice but a woman who owned a shop had just bought the last big piece and there was none left. So she let the man sell us the small chunk we needed, off hers.

We liked Loja. The mountain air was cool. The cobbled streets were wide and clean. There was traffic, it wasn't a sleepy place, but still people took time to chat.

Then we went on, through a narrow gorge with many houses between the trees, on either side. And up onto a mountain; into rain and out again, above the clouds and over a col and down - past many precepices - in the gathering dusk. And at last light, we parked on a grassy spot by the road at 8,600 feet. The road was paved and straight, angling down the side of the mountain toward a village ahead. On the left, the land went steeply up and on the right it dropped down into woodland, with houses here and there. We had not found a better place to stop, so we chose a spot between two houses - where some bushes would give us a little shelter - and ate our dinner in the truck. But the wine we bought in Loja was terrible, so we drank Pepsi Cola and Grand Marnier with our meal, instead.

We parked much too close to the road but there was no other place. I was a bit nervous about it and hurried us through our meal so that if there was any trouble, we would be ready to jump into the car and move.

When the stars came out, we could see the Big Dipper, so we must be approaching the Equator. There was little traffic but a man and woman came by to chat. They were small people of the mountains and both shook hands, as they left.

We asked them if they thought it would be alright for us to stop there for the night. They said it was a very nice place, no one would mind. Patrick showed them the bed in the truck. They didn't express surprise. I got the impression that if one had a truck, of course one slept in it.

Then there was a strange rushing noise, coming down the mountain in the darkness. And a small cart went down the middle of the road, with two boys on top of a load of firewood.

We had no idea what could make a noise like that and I was terrified, by the time it reached us. Then to see those little boys, at top speed, rushing headlong down the pavement, shouting with glee, totally unconcerned that each second they were on the verge of injury, made me stop and ask myself what I had to be afraid of.

We slept in the truck and heard footsteps, in the night. The single ones concerned us a little but none of them stopped near us. And about 4:30 they started going uphill, probably to work in the fields and woods, higher up the mountain. When daylight came, we both felt rather second hand. And Minim's oil needed changing - it felt gritty, when I rubbed it between my finger and thumb. A man came by on a mule and asked June politely what she was doing. Cooking breakfast. He went up the hill, looking puzzled. As we finished, a 'lenadoro' came up the hill, with his cart. He made a living gathering 'lena' (firewood) on the mountain and selling it to people in the village below. His cart was just two long poles, with three short ones lashed across them and four tiny wheels. But it was light to carry uphill - we saw such men taking short cuts up the mountain with their carts on their backs - and surprisingly, it held a great pile of firewood for the trip down, with the owner on top steering the front wheels with a rope.

I supose he was in his twenties but it is so hard to tell. The mountain people are small and their life expectancy can't be more than forty years. They look like wise, weathered children. His suit was black, made from a coarsely woven rough cloth. He wore a white homespun shirt under his jacket and on his belt was one of the most beautiful silver buckles I've ever seen. A black leather, wide brimmed hat sat squarely on his head and a silver handled machete was tied to his belt.

He stood, chatting easily, watching us finish washing the breakfast dishes and packing the truck. We pulled out our map of South America, to show him where we had been so far. We pointed out Ecuador. He recognized that. The name and the shape of the country were known to him. But he moved his hand across the whole continent and said "Is that the world?" We pointed into the air around the map, where the United States, Europe, Africa were. He'd heard of none of those places. Our chatter slowed. There was too much to speak of. We watched him lift his cart over his wide shoulders. His lungs must have been huge, developed through generations to work with ease at mountain tops. He smiled and turned up the road. It was getting late and we all had a busy day ahead.

The road north was rather hairy at first. The surface was good but it was narrow and had precepices, most of the way. But later it climbed up on top of the mountains and got much better. And early in the afternoon we came to Cuenca, a nice clean town with much building going on.

When we saw a village, it would be a cluster of half a dozen stone houses. The road kept near the mountain tops, in this section less rugged, more like rounded hills. Often it was no more than two ruts, with grass growing between them. There were sheep grazing, in the pale green fields, and sometimes a wooded section. We wondered how those few trees had managed to withstand the lenadoro's machete.

There we changed $ 50 into sucres and the bank gave us 26.50 to the dollar. Back at the border, the two men had only given us 22.00 but we only changed $ 10 there, so they made $ 1.70 between them. Hardly too much. And that plan, by which we changed a few dollars at the border and the larger amounts farther inside the country, worked very well. Then we had Minim cleaned and her oil filter changed and her steering gear checked. But evidently we had not done any damage when we hit the rock in Peru, so we bought food and beer and went back to the highway. And toward evening we saw a section of old road - curving away from the new one, through some pine trees and back to it - at the top of a hill.

Not far away was a house, so we asked for permission to camp there. It turned out to be an experimental tree farm - a government project - and the guardian's wife was sure that it would be all right, so we went around the curve until we were out of sight of the highway and pitched our tent, at the side of the road, in the shelter of the tall pines. While June made supper, I walked along the old road - it had a fine view of the valley below - and at the far end was a line of boulders, to stop trucks from using it. So I went back to our end and put some across there. Few people would get out of a vehicle to heave them out of the way, so we should not be run over, while in bed in our tent, with luck.

It was cool that evening and calm in the lee of the trees and the tree frogs were chirping loudly. But in the night they were silent, for it was very cold. And by morning it was damp   the tent was wet with dew. When the sun came up, it started to dry but we were not feeling good, after sleeping at 10,500 feet in the cold and damp. And we had not had showers since leaving Lina, five days ago. So June had a wash in the tent. While she was in there - naked and wet - the guardian of the tree farm came by for a chat. He seemed to think it odd that she spoke through the canvas, rather than come out, or at least open the door. But he was polite and so was I - he had a big knife - and he said that Peace Corps people, from Mexico and Canada, had been there in the past 15 years. After he left, two other men came on horses and stopped for a chat, sitting on them. One of the horses pissed and it made a fine splatter on the road. But they both had guns and we were far too polite to say anything about it.

By that time, I had managed to dress and opened the tent flap. Patrick stood off to one side, with one of the horsemen, but the other nudged his mount closer to the tent, where he could have a good look inside, In a very quiet voice, he asked if we had any guns. If I said "No", he might pull his. If I said "Yes", he might draw his and tear everything apart, looking for ours. There wasn't time to consider the consequences of saying maybe. I told him the truth, we had none. But added hastily that we didn't need any, because people were so nice, and besides, we had nothing of value with us. He said something to his friend and they rode off. We wondered what would have happened, if we'd had guns.

The road north was paved and stayed high in the mountains but there were several landslides along it and suddenly it came to an end. Ahead was a gravel road, that we were advised not to try (a man said it was worthless) and to the left was a narrow, gravel one which went quickly down - with many switchbacks - to a tropical valley, a thousand feet above sea level, with banana plantations and fields of sugar cane and small rain clouds that moved across them, between patches of sunlight. We had been told to look for the junction at Calle, which should be about 60 miles ahead, so I asked a young man, sitting at a gas station, how far it was and he said: "Sir, I have no concept of the distance to that place" But when we came to the junction, there was a fine, paved road and we were told that we could have come from the border of Peru that way. So following the AAA map had cost us two days of expense and discomfort - not to mention being pissed on by a horse - but then, if we had a proper map, we might never have known the mountains or people of southern Ecuador.

Going northeast on the paved road, we passed many women selling fruit and stopped to buy a bunch of good bananas from one - a friendly, cheerful person - for ten cents. Then up we went, through rain and clouds, into the mountains again. Past Riobamba, the highway turned north and was even fancier, with smooth pavement and signs and an overlook (our first in South America). But with nowhere to spend the night. Darkness came early, for the sky was overcast and it was raining then. But in the gray, fading light we saw an old road and took it. There was just a short section - maybe a hundred yards - and it was parallel with the highway. But there was an earthen bank between them and near the middle, parked beside it, we could not be seen by passing vehicles. Of course anyone who took the old road would find us but we chose to take that chance, rather than keep going. The altimeter said 10,700 feet and as a rule, it was safer to sleep in high places than low ones, because the mountain people were generally more reliable and honest than the people of the lowlands. Still. we should not be careless. I rigged a ground sheet over the back of the truck, so that June could heat some soup without the flame of our stove being seen. We ate by flashlight - the small one, carefully shaded - and went to bed in Minim, with the doors locked and the ignition key in place, surrounded by the enveloping darkness of the rainy night.

Actually it was rather fun, stting under our makeshuift shelter. We managed to get the table under it, too. So dinner was fairly civilized, in spite of the downpour washing around our feet.

When we awoke, it was 6:00 AM. We had slept for ten hours. The dawn was gray and cloudy, with quite a breeze on the bare mountain, so we had juice and bananas and packed up to go. Minim's engine did not start easily (nor had it the day before) but maybe that was because of the altitude. Before long, the highway dropped down into Quito - a fine city at 9,500 feet with a big central park and we soon found the First National City Bank but it was not open yet, so we had breakfast at an hotel nearby (in a small, high walled parking lot, some cheerful men moved another car sideways, bouncing it on its springs, to make room for ours).

We were enchanted with the hotel. It was a second rate businessman's type but it seemed like the Plaza to us. You know you've been a long time on the road when something that ordinay looks posh.

But when the bank did open, our money was not there. So we walked across the park, to the telephone company's office, and called Lima. The New York bank, though which it had been transferred, had sent it by air mail, instead of Telex and it had just reached Lima. So I asked the girl to send it on, via Telex, to Cartagena. And she said "Okay". By then, the sun was out and it was warm and pleasant in the park, with its green grass and tall, shady trees and clear views of the cars and people and buildings on every side. In a money shop, we changed the last of our dollars into Equadorian sucres ($ 10 worth) and Colombian pesos ($ 30 worth). And some girls advised us to stay at the Hotel Intercontinental Quito - we could charge eveything to our credit cards. At the United States Embassy, June got more pages put in her passport and driving across town, we saw many policemen on traffic duty - they did a better job than lights. Also cops on motorcycles (Moto Guzzis) that matched their uniforms.

The few control points we had seen in Ecuador were not for cars at all - just for commercial vehicles.

At the hotel, they did indeed take our credit cards. But they had no room for us. However, perhaps in a short while there might be one. So we went to the coffee shop for lunch and when we finished, they had a nice room for us on the ground floor, looking into a garden. So I moved Minim to a safer location, while June sent off our laundry.

We both took long, hot showers and then napped though the afternoon. It seemed so good to be doing nothing.

But by evening, we had relaxed too long, so we went up to the rooftop bar for drinks and saw the lights come on. That was a beautiful city, with mountains all around it. And one by one, the lights appeared, all across the valley. For dinner we went across the street to a French place - complete with a man doing business in a corner and an owner who checked our bill and good food at high prices - then back for a night in the wide, soft bed, far from harm's way. In the morning, the sky was blue, with white clouds.

And there were palm trees outside. Breakfast, in the coffee shop, was served by Indian girls in native dress and they were good, fast workers - the place was well run.

Minim was fine in the parking lot, so we took a bus into town, looking for money. June tried to hit up the U.S. Consul but he would only give her five dolars - his tiny 'slush fund' was just enough for people to phone home for money - so she did not take it and we tried the Bank of Amarica. There we met an Oklahoman - one of the executives - who gave us $ 150 as a cash advance, on June's credit card (I had Master Card and she had BankAmericard). He also advised us to avoid camping, after the first day, in Colombia. For theft was a national characteristic there.

That would get us to Cartagena and surely the big sum would reach us by then. We would have to be very thrifty but we were used to that.

Then we took another bus, to the top of a steep hill, in the city, where a huge statue of an angel - maybe 80 feet high - was being erected. But the wings did not seem to be attached to the body very well (just by a few bolts) and in a high wind I would not like to stand undeneath them.

But there was a good view of the city from there, and it was like all such places, where people go to stand and look out, anywhere else in the world.

The narrow road down from there clung to the side of the hill and at one point a sweater fell of a rack, covering the driver's eyes. But he pulled it off without slowing down. On a hairpin bend, he just barely avoided a head-on collision with another bus and shook his hands over his head, in a gesture of triumph, as we rushed down the hillside. Near the bottom, he stopped for passengers and I gave my seat to an old lady with a child. But as I ushered her into it, a man tried to shove her aside and grab it. So I told him, politely but firmly, that I had only risen for her sake and he went off down the bus, looking surprised.

She was an Indian woman. Perhaps that was why the man was so rude. We had heard stories of discrimination but hadn't seen much of it, in our way of travel.

It was nice to be able to do such things on our own, to wander freely around the city, as the mood took us, wihout any need of help, beyond the simple directions that a visitor from another part of Ecuador might want. That was a great thing about South America. You could go from one country to another and always feel at home, because the language and the customs were essentially the same and the people were invariably polite when spoken to. Film for our camera was only $ 6.00 a roll there (cheap, by Peruvian standards) but our small bundle of laundry, at the hotel, was $ 12.50. We would not be back in Vermont in time to pay our Income Tax (poor us) so we wrote to them that evening and asked or an exension. We were Out of State.

Much of our clothing was ruined, too. Patrick's socks would fit a twelve year old. I know it was dirty, we'd been on the road so long. But did they have to boil it?

Dinner in the restaurant upstairs was served with a great deal of show - the whole place smelled of burning margarine, as they flamed things - and it was not that good but we decided to use hotels in Colombia, to avoid the bandits.

By that time, we were getting bored with hotel life. It was time to get off on our own and stop being at the mercy of the mediocre who run the tourist trade.

And at breakfast, the coffee shop was full of old ladies. There were two bus loads of high school teachers from the USA - on a thing called 'people to people' - but one of them labelled 'Official' paid the bill and they all trooped out. Then we paid our bill, at the front desk and found it had cost us about $ 70 a day there. But with so little cash, we had to stay in hotels that took our credit cards.

We could have stayed in a Spanish style hotel for half as much and we wold have preferred it. So the bank's inability to send our money properly was costing us double.

As we left the city, we came to a control point but it was no problem - just a quick check of our papers - and there was fog in the valleys but blue sky and sunlight above. Then we crossed the Equator, just before Cayambe and were back in the northern hemisphere, after three months. At Ibarra we bought ice and food, to use up our sucres. But no lunch, for we had eaten too much in Quito. The road to the northeast was paved and the going was good. It was a joy to meet trucks on a highway so wide that it was not danmgerous, or even difficult, to get by them. By 2:00 PM we were at the frontier and were cleared by the customs people but had to go back into Tulcan to have our passports stamped, before crossing the border. In Colombia, on the other hand, we were cleared by the immigration people but had to go into Ipiales to have our Carnet stamped by the customs officer, who was at home on a Saturday. That was a crummy little border town and it took us a while to find his house - a plain, adobe one - and inside, it was very simple, with little furniture in sight. But when he appeared, he was in a fine, clean uniform (perhaps his Sunday best) and quickly stamped our Carnet, for a small fee.

Beyond the town, the road was still good and by 6:00 PM we were in Pasto. Back in Lima, a man we met at the Colombian Embassy had told us that his favorite place was a resort east of there, called Laguna La Colcha. So we turned off toward it and followed a gravel road, up a valley. Just as it got dark, we picked up a hitch hiker, a student, who knew the place and after going over a col, we dropped down to the lake. Since it was late, we asked where we should stay and as he got out, he showed us the way to the Chalet Guamuez.

By that time, it as raining hard. The directions were to take a right fork then a left fork, then turn left - or was it the reverse? The road was muddy and hard to follow in the dark. There were no signs. But we had little choice at that time, except to keep going. I thought we would never find it.

It was just a mile or so ahead and looked like a hunting lodge, with a big roof, among the trees. But in the parking lot were several cars, so we went inside. It was all stone and big wooden beams, with a fireplace in the dining room and people at most of the tables. In the bar, we asked for gin and tonic and it was made with Schweppes. The owner, who served us, was Swiss and spoke English, among other languages. After chatting for a while, we asked about staying for the night and were taken down a passage to a cozy room, with a view of the lake.

It was dark and raining hard by that time. We couldn't see the lake but it didn't matter. We had stumbled into a fairyland of warm fires, good food, happy people and comfortable beds. The soggy world outside was of no interest.

The dinner was good and as we ate, some young people came by. They were German, Swiss and English, travelling together in two vans and had just arrived in South America at Buenaventura, so they would like to talk to us, when we finished. In the bar, we answered their questions and asked about the road to the north of us. They had only joined it at Cali but said there were many camp sites, north of there, with all facilities and multiple swimming pools, that were crowded on weekends but quiet all the rest of the week. They were sleeping in their vans, in the parking lot, so we went out to admire their gear, which was rather crude by our standards but okay. After all, they were young.

At breakfast someone told us we were in the Amazon Basin since we came over the col from the main road. It did not look an different but it was nice to have been there. And our bill - for the two of us, including tips, for the drinks, dinner and room and breakfast - was just $ 22.00. The road back over the col was easy enough in daylight and at Pasto we got gas (Extra) for 40 cents a gallon. At that rate we should get to Cartagena without running out of money.

But we would still have to find enough to have our truck shipped across the Caribbean, when we got there.

Beyond the town was a control point but the young man we spoke to was polite and efficient. And later there was a check point, for documents. Then the road changed to gravel, and went winding up and down, over green mountains. The land was rumpled, as in parts of northern California and though it was lush, more of it was open fields and trees. Often there were houses, with white walls and brown roofs. And there were many people on the road, especially in the villages along the way. Also there were slow moving trucks. So progress was not rapid and by the afternoon, we were wondering where to look for a safe place to sleep, that night. But at 5:30 we came into Popayan and at a gas station the pump for Extra was blue and showed a lower price than the Comun but you doubled it. After sorting that one out, we asked if there might be somewhere to stay and indeed there was.

The Monastery hotel, next to the police station, was in a fine old building - probably a real monastery - set back from a pleasant street in the quiet town. It was run by the Government Tourist Agency and they had done a good job of not altering it. Our room - which had three single beds in a row - opened out onto a balcony with a fine view across town, toward the airport (where camping was allowed, since they only had one plane a day) and I could keep an eye on Minim, in the courtyard below.

The whitewashed building was two storeys high, with long passages and winding stairs. We would have loved to explore its secret places but the management seemed stern and sober. We thought it best not to ask. Instead we walked along the open balconies that ringed a lovely central courtyard. The pillars, archways and ornately carved doors made us wonder if the building hadn't perhaps been a palace before becoming a monastery. The yard was full of flowers. There were pots of geraniums everywhere.

A serious man in European clothes came to wash Minim - with a bucket of water and a rag - and gave us a receipt showing how many tires, radios and such there were, when he started. But he did a good job and soon she looked much better. Then we had drinks in the empty bar and a good dinner in the vast, empty dining room. Which seemed a pity, for the rates were modest (9.00 a night, for 2 people) and the whole place had a great deal of charm, in a quiet, peaceful way. We had trouble communicating with people in Colombia, at first, because their Spanish was different from the variations we knew - not so much in the accent, as in the choice of words - but we would soon get over that. We always did.

We did not have to work at it. Just by listening to the people, we soon picked up the local dialect.

As we left in the morning, a man was painting a wall of the building, along one side of the courtyard. But having no brush, he was dabbing it on with a cloth, bunched in his hand. And there were big drops of white paint, soaking into the fine old stone walkways, wherever he had finished. From Popayan, a good paved road went across flat country, with fields of sugar cane, all the way to Cali. And beyond the city, we came to irrigated farm land, with just a few trees for shade. About 5:00 PM we found ourselves on the wrong road (the AAA map was all wet, there) but we got a local map, that showed us how to get back onto the road northward.

Then it climbed up into mountains and there were many slow moving trucks with neat tarpaulins but few cars. By 6:30 it was dark and we saw nowhere to spend the night. There were truck stops with lights, presumably to discourage thieves, run by roaring generators but no place off the road for us, so we kept on going. At 7:30 we crossed a bridge, after a control point, and went up a steep hill. And there, set back from the road but easy enough to see, was a new motel, run by the government. It was a single storyed building on the hillside and few people were staying there. The rooms were airconditioned, for it was hot, even at night. But all the water was cold. Perhaps no one wanted a hot shower. The restaurant was large and open - just a glassed-in area, under a wide roof - and we could see lights, some of them moving, in the valley below.

Our room was not clean. The faucets dripped, the windows didn't open. Same country, same government but not the same sort of hotel as the one we had stumbled upon, the night before. But then the building itself, while looking modern and impressive, was truly shoddy. And, too, we were now nearing the coast. For the last few days our route had followed a gradually descending line down the Andes to the ocean. The air was muggy, the vegetation lush and jungle like. We seemed to have crossed the imaginary line between the mountain and lowland people.

Breakfast – in the cool of the morning – was served on a terrace outside. There were white cows in the green fields of the valley. And the river we had crossed the night before. And a railroad. And trucks already, coming up the hill. Behind the motel were four swimming pools and camping was allowed, beside them - we had not thought of that - but no one was there. So we asked what was available to the north and were told there was another government motel, at Caucasia - between Medellin and Cartagena. Or we could camp beside a different one that was privately owned, 15 kilometers past it. By 8:30 we were under way and two hours later we came to Medellin - a big, dirty industrial city in a valley. There we found a bank, in a row of low buildings, where they changed $ 30 into pesos for us. All the tellers were male and they had a soldier outside guarding the bank, and Minim and June, while I was in there. Such service.

All through Central and South America, soldiers seemed to be protecting the government from its opposition - and the rich from the poor - not the state from other states. So clearly the trick was to look rich enough to get their protection - but not so rich as to be worth the attention of the bandits. The road north was paved but soon it left the valley and climbed up into mountains, winding and twisting. It had many trucks on it - going slowly uphill or very fast downhill - and was quite dangerous. We saw at least four accidents that day. The sky was overcast and gray, with occasional rain. And early in the afternoon, we stopped for gas at a town built on top of a hill, about 9,000 feet above sea level. The door of the toilet was of bare wood, weathered gray, and centered near the top of it was a carving of a butterfly, maybe six inches high, in the same wood - the colour and grain matched perfectly, shade for shade and groove for groove. But when I touched the door, it flew away. Going down the mountains, we made good time, since we had to keep up with the trucks, in their headlong dashes (or take a chance of being side swiped as they passed us). And in the low, flat country further north, we met a long convoy of Ford trucks - bare chassis, brand new - coming from the coast.

Probably they used a lot of trucks, there. And us with no insurance. We had forgotten that,

Then we followed a brown river, through swampy land. Near a grim village of tin roofed shacks, an iguana about five feet long crossed the road, ahead of us. And at 5:00 PM we came to the government motel in Caucasia. Ir was not nearly so nice as the one before but an airconditioned room was $ 10.00 which sounded better than camping in a tropical swamp 700 feet above sea level, so we took it and turned the thing way up. The noise drowned everything, even our thoughts, and though it rained in the night, we did not find out until morning. When we left, we had to sign our bill (as well as pay it) but the manager explained that in Colombia, all motels had to provide insurance for their guests, by law. So evidently he was covering his tail, like any government employee.

For six hours we drove across flat country   most of it cleared for farming - with small, poor villages. But as we approached the coast, the sky cleared and by two o'clock that afternoon, we were in the outskirts of Cartagena. On our way, we stopped at the airport to ask about flying

Minim to Panama, for it was less than 300 miles and we might save enough by not having to wait for a ship - to pay for the extra cost of transporting her that way. But no one, at the terminal or in the general aviation area, had any idea of what it might cost, or even if it were possible. Then we went past a poor, outlying section of the old sea port - now a bustling city - and on though its crowded streets to a modern resort, on a peninsula to the southwest, with tall buldings and green trees and a white, curving beach and beyond it the Caribbean Sea, shining blue in the sunlight. On a quieter street, down the middle of the peninsula, we found a travel agent who phoned Avianca, the Colombian airline, for us but said we must go to their office in the center of the city, to find out about flying a car to Panama. So back we went though heavy traffic to the central park and across a street, we found the airline's office,

While June looked after Minim, I went inside but as I waited in line, there was a commotion in the park and everybody in the office stopped to watch it, through the big storefront windows. Beyond the busy street was a wide expanse of grass, dotted with trees. And people came running across it - fanning out, as though trying to get away from something - then behind them came policemen, with truncheons and clear plastic shields, and behind those came soldiers with guns, driving everyone out of the park, into the crowded streets and alleys of the city. Some of the people looked young enough to be students but most of them looked like ordinary citizens who just happened to be in the park when the trouble started. Anyway, the police and the soldiers showed no interest in who was who. They just drove them all out, beating the ones they could reach.

I asked the next person in line what the score was and he said it was a small political riot, nothing to worry about. And everyone went back to business as usual. When my turn came, the senior official convinced me that no one put cars in airplanes, so I gave up the idea and went back to the travel agent, to ask him to find us a ship. Then we enquired about an hotel, not too expensive and he suggested Las Velas (the sails) nearby, so we went there. It was a tall, new building on the beach, with a restaurant, a coffee shop and a safe place to keep Minim. Most important, we could put everything on our credit cards, so we moved in. It would make a good base for us, while we figured how to get our truck to Central America.

Las Velas didn't attract American tourists. Most occupants seemed to be from the inland ciies - Bogota, Medellin or other centers of wealth. All were Spanish speaking. And it was a family place. They had come for a week at the beach and spent the days in the pool or in the ocean that sparkled in the high sun, just a few yards from our view.

The dinner was good, in the hotel but we were bitten by fleas in bed. The shower was tepid and water was dripping from the ceiling, outside our room but it was large and had a fine view of the Caribbean Sea and the beach far below. The coffee shop was okay and over breakfast, we made plans for the day's work. That was Thursday, the 8th of April, so we should try to get Minim on a ship to Panama before the weekend.

We were back in sand flea country. But they didn't really bother us anymore. We were a bit tougher skinned by then.

Minim was fine, so we took a taxi into the city and went from one shipping agent to another, looking for space on a ship to Panama - or anywhere else, within reason. But none, that we tried, had anything available in the near future.

We were duplicating the work that we had asked the travel agent to do. But we did not expect him to succeed. That kind of work required more persistent effort and experience of shipping agents than we thought he could muster.

At the bank, we found the $ 500 that had been sent on by Telex from Lima (with no charge, which was civil of them) so we bought traveller's checks with it. But the thousand dollars we had sent to La Paz had not caught up with us yet. And the banks in Colombia were not allowed, by law, to give cash advances on credit cards (though some hotels did, they said). Then we tried another shipping agent and were lucky. They had space on the Republica de Ecuador, leaving on Saturday and arriving in Cristobal on Monday morniong. We rushed to the hotel and back to their office, with all our documents. It was a large office - down an alley and up a flight of stairs - with several agents and the one who was dealing with us sifted though our documents, keeping Minim's Carnet and my passport. Then he had me sign about two dozen blank forms and papers. Some of them were just blank sheets of paper - with no writing on them, at all - but he measured the place for me to sign each one (usually near the bottom). Later he would put in the details, above the signature. But that was a risk which we had to take, if we wanted to get our truck home.

It was a government owned shipping line, so the papers would likely be even more bizarre than usual.

He would need 24 hours, to prepare all the documents, so we went back to the travel agent, on the peninsula, who had not done anything yet and thanked him and told him that we had things under control. He looked relieved. At the hotel, they had a new room for us, nicer than the first one and without fleas - the girl said people brought them up from the beach, in their clothes. It was a few dollars more but still reasonable, so we moved our things to it. Cartagena felt like a cross between San Juan, Puerto Rico and Miami Beach, Florida. And it was a far better place to be stuck in that either Guayaquil or Buenaventura. There were very few beggars and even the taxi drivers were honest. But perhaps we would not be stuck there for long. We were due to take Minim to the docks the next day, if all went well.

In the afternoon, we went to another travel agent, whose office was there in the hotel, to buy air tickets for Panama, since the Republica de Ecuador did not take passengers. The girl had us leaving at 9:00 AM to catch a 10:30 flight which landed 15 minutes later at Barranquilla. Then we must wait until 4:35 PM for the hour's flight to Panama, by which time no connections would be available to Cristobal. But it was the best she could do and she would take our credit cards (except for the flight to Barranquilla) so we asked her to go ahead and in due course she made up our tickets. At least that was all set. Feeling we had achieved a lot that day, we retired to our airconditioned room with the fine view and typed out the notes for this book. The restaurant downstairs was glamorous, all the tables were angled to look out, through long windows, onto the swimming pool, in a setting of palm trees (and general tropical splendor) and the food was good and we were smug.

At dawn we went down to prepare Minim for shipment, as we had in Panama, before - taking off the mirrors and hubcaps, the tachometer and altimeter, stowing everything in the lockers and screwing them down, then putting plastic wood on the screws and staining it, to make the whole thing look permanent. And at breakfast in the coffee shop, a small deer came to eat a bush, in front of the window but was shooed away by a man delivering parrots - from Rent a Bird, I suppose.

When the bank opened, our thousand dollars had still not arrived, though it was 15 days since we had asked the bank in the United States to trace it, so we cashed $ 400 worth of the traveller's checks (that we bought the day before) and walked to the shipping agent's office. By 9:30 we were there, reading trade magazines, to the rattle of Telex machines and chirping of radios (with messages from ships) and at 10:30 he came. The stevedores were on strike, against the police and wanted them swapped for ones from Barranquilla. The ship was due to arrive on Saturday and we might be abe to deliver the car then. But if not, it would probably be Monday (or later) for there was no work on the docks on Sunday. Also, we would need the Original Bill of Lading to get our car back, in Cristobal.

The situation was no longer clear, except that it was fouled up, as usual with ships and docks.

Meanwhile, we should go back to our hotel and wait to see what happened, so we did. And some people we met told us that the police had been beating students in schools, the day before but that things were worse in Barranquilla. Then we went to our room and waited or the telephone to ring. We had done all we could, for the time being and thought it best to stay there and be available if anything changed. At 12:30 it rang but it was a wrong number. And we both stared at it with genuine resentment, for a while. But by two o'clock we had had enough of that and went to see the agent. The strike was over and the ship would dock on Saturday but she would not sail until Monday and we must wait for the Bill of Lading, so we could not fly until Tuesday.

But we had to deliver the car at 8:00 AM on Saturday. Then he started adding up our bill - going from one room to another, consulting people and adding figures - for loading our truck on the ship and carrying her to Panama and unloading her there, plus insurance and taxes and extra charges for this and percentages for that. And the grand total, that he gave us with some pride, was close to a thousand dollars. In theory we had that much, floating around in the bank's internal organs but we had given up any real hope of getting it before we left South America and for practical purposes, all we had was the $ 400 we had brought with us. So we showed him that and told him it was all we could get, there.

His reaction was surprising. Instead of saying there was nothing he could do about it, he started probing - asking what else we had on us. Maybe traveller's checks? So we admitted we had $ 100 left in those but explained that we had other things to pay, before we could get to a bank in Panama. Then he asked a few more questions but evidently he was satisfied that we were telling the truth, because he started to 'adjust' our bill - reducing a percentage here, taking off an item there, going back over his calculations - until it came to $ 466.17 and at that point, he made it clear that we were getting his best, rock bottom price for the job. That would leave us nothing to spare - by the time we got to Panama, we would be lucky to have ten dollars left - but we believed it was his best price, so we paid him. Then he gave us a receipt, saying we could pick up the papers on Saturday and the Bill of Lading on Monday afternoon.

That left us $ 33.83, plus the few dollars we had in our pockets and the odd bits of change lost in the bottom of my purse. If we could just get to Panama. a bank there might give us some cash on a credit card.

Back at the hotel we went to the travel agent's office, to have our flights changed from Sunday to Tuesday. But there was no way of doing that, so the girl called up the airline to cancel our flights, then tore up our tickets and credit card slip, then made new reservations and we had to sign another slip (for the same amount as before) and said that we could pick up our tickets on Monday afternoon. For she was too busy to write them up - with so much going on - that day.

We arranged to be called at 6:30 on Saturday morning. And at breakfast it was raining hard but a toucan was fighting with the parrots, outside. By eight, we were at the shipping agent's office with Minim and by 8:30 we were at the docks. Then there were two whole hours of inspections, papers, lists, formalities and bribes. The agent did a good job of handling it but we were not allowed to put her in the warehouse (though we saw a car in there) and had to park her in the open. The dogs around were to

354

smell for drugs, they said. So the only thing to stop thieves, apart from one guard, was a chain link fence.

I was worried about leaving her there, for two days (and nights) and I resented being forced to take what I felt was an unnecessary risk of having our gear stolen from her, but we had no choice - as usual - so I gave the guard some money and said that I would greatly appreciate his keeping an eye on her. Now we had no car, so we took a taxi back to the agent's office in the city and on the way, I remembered we had forgotten to take off the fire extinguisher, that was in a bracket on the side of the driver's seat in Minim. But I had painted it brown, to match the truck and maybe the thieves would not see it.

We had also left a whisk broom, between the seats and a couple of small cushions. Everything else was glued or nailed down.

The agent said we must be there at 8:00 AM on Monday, to have Minim's Carnet stamped. Then we took a bus to the hotel. But Holy Week was starting and our nice room had been reserved long ago, so we were moved to another one, on the 17th floor - under the rooftop bar - with no airconditioning. But we took cold showers and hung our clothes up near an open window, in the hope that they would dry. Then there was nothing more that we could do until Monday but sweat and fret. On Sunday morning, there was a Trade Wind and it was cool and sunny in our room, with small white clouds in the blue sky over the Caribbean and many people on the beach down below, for the holiday. So we finished typing out the notes for this book. Then at noon, we took a bus to the Old City.

There were few people in the narrow streets, as we wandered around, admiring the old white buildings. Most of them had living quarters above, with elaborate balconies jutting out over the sidewalks and usually an awning to shade the windows up there. But downstairs, at street level, they were shops, now shuttered but with things like NCR looking incongrous in red letters on the horizontal slats of bare metal. Down by the sea was a fort, built to protect the old city from pirates in sailing ships. And wandering into another section, with wide streets and apartments and green trees - we saw the end of a bicycle race. People stood in twos and threes - along a sidewalk and on a central divider - looking down an empty street, as if expecting something to come up it. So naturally we joined them. And soon two cyclists appeared, heads down over low handlebars, side by side and so closely matched that the leader was no more than two feet ahead of the other as they passed us. Then came five motorcycles, escorting them. And well back was one lone cyclist, cruising along in third place. Then much farther back were seven more, their brightly colored shirts all soaked with sweat, battling to be fourth. Going back to the hotel, I decided that even if some of our gear were stolen from Minim, it should not stop us from completing our journey, back to Vermont. And we could replace it easily enough, in the United States. So I really should not worry about it. We were both relaxed, by then - after the pleasant day - and ready to make the trip north.

Monday started badly. We woke up at 6:00 AM, bitten by midges. Our room was hot and sticky, with no wind. And we saw a leaflet that said we could have an aiconditioned room for half what we were paying, if we had been able to go to an hotel which did not take credit cards. That bank in New York City had really fouled things up for us.

Riding a bus into town, we were at the shippinmg agent's office by eight. He took my passport and the Carnet and told us to return at eleven. We no longer asked why. When the bank opened, our money was not there. And the travel agent had us booked on a 6.00 AM flight to Barranquilla with a 3 hour layover but we took it, anyway. So far, so good. But at eleven, the shipping agent told us that the Carnet could not be stamped (or Minim leave the enclosure on the dock) because the serial number on the chassis was wrong. I must go to the Customs House with him at 1:00 PM that day. At the hotel, there was a message for us to call Avianca. It was urgent. And when we did, they said there were no flights on Tuesday. We must go on Wednesday afternoon.

Evidently the travel agent had booked us on a nonexistent flight. And if Patrick couldn't sort out the chassis number with the customs people, there wold be further delays - and demands for money. I wondered about the limits of our credit cards. Best not to voice concern, then. We had enough to worry about.

Now if we solved the mystery of Minim's chassis number and got her unstuck from the docks, she would be in Cristobal early on Tuesday but we would not be able to get there until Thursday morning, which would give any thieves at that end two nights to select the items they preferred. So we went into town and split up - June to do battle with Avianca while I joined the shipping agent and went to the Custom House on the docks.

At least with Minim locked away in the docks I was free to do battle with the airline while Patrick tackled the customs.

We were ten minutes early and Minim was nearby, so I went over to check her and nothing seemed to be missing so far. But there was nowhere to wait, except a big metal shed and that was hot, inside. Finally we compromised by standing in the doorway, still in the shade but with some breeze, going though it. Then the shipping agent told me to give him some money, it was not a large amount, so I did and he put it in a pocket. The customs officer finally arrived - half an hour late - and showed us that one digit in a long number on the Carnet did not agree with that on the truck's chassis. How it got that way was a mystery but even more surprising was that no one had seen it before, in all the countless controls and inspections we had been through, in sixteen foreign countries.

An inspector had noticed it, as we entered Uruguay. There was a little fuss but we had both forgotten it by then.

Then I remembered that they never looked at the chassis number, which was down on the frame of the truck, but checked the engine number, that was easy to see (if you knew where to find it). So I showed him that and said all those things - as he peered at the new number - and after making noises like an elerly school master in a snit, he went off - with the agent - to a small office inside the metal shed. For a long time I waited outside - trying to look like a man confident that all was well - and eventually they came out. The matter had been dealt with, the necessary papers had been prepared and I could have the Carnet back. The customs officer said "Numbers are for checking" and left. Minim would be loaded that afternoon, on the deck of a ship, which was due to sail that night, non stop for Cristobal. So I gave the guard more money - to keep up the good work - and went back, with the agent, to the city.

June was in his office. Our money had still not arrived at the bank. And

Avianca had no flights to Panama on Tuesday. But I was most anxious not to leave Minim lying around on the docks in Cristobal, so we went out to the airport to see the general aviation people about an air taxi. The smallest airplane available for charter was an Aero Commander - fine for a small group but far too expensive for just two people - but we discovered, for the first time, that Avianca was not the only airline flying to Panama.

Maybe we should have known that if the Panamanians let the Colombians fly that route, they would also.

Back in the city, we went to the shipping agent's office and after waiting for three quarters of an hour, we were given Minim's Original Bill of Lading. That was the last document in the series. We shook hands with him and left.

We both believed Minim would be in Cristobal in the morning. We had nothing more to do in Colombia and all that we wanted was to get to Panama, as soon as possible.

Then, at the hotel, we saw the travel agent and I must have been less than pleasant but under questioning, he admitted that we could have flown to Panama on Tuesday, by another airline. Of course he had excuses for not telling us. Such people always do. But I believed that he was either out to maximize his commissionm or under pressure to 'sell' the government airline. Still, he convinced us that it was too late for us to fly on Tuesday. And he said the first flight he could arrange was on Wednesday afternoon, too late to go on to Cristobal. That meant we would not be there until Thursday. And with Easter coming, we might not get Minim until the following Monday. Under further questioning, he admitted there was a flight out of Barraquilla at 10:00 AM on Wednesday. But he said that we could not get there, in time to catch it. So I said we would take a bus - it was only 85 miles - and stay at the airport all night, if we must. Then he said there was a flight, at 6:00 AM on Wednesday, to Barranquilla. It was a small airplane and very dangerous but if I insisted, we could go on it. We insisted quite firmly and the agent - a smooth, round man with a mustache - retired to a back room, leaving his girl to handle the details. For a while, we sat reading out-of-date magazines, while other customers came and went. But eventually she gave us the tickets. And as we left, she asked why we wre so angry. But I saw no point in trying to explain it.

June demanded a martini - which was most unusual for her - so we went to the rooftop bar, And in the night, we had severe indigestion, due to worry about Minim and the possibility of our gear being stolen and the problems of getting her off the docks in Cristobal and finding money to go on from there. Tuesday was a dead loss. All morning we sat around, with nothing to do but worry, In the afternoon, we took a bus to the bank but our money had still not arrived, so we asked them to send it back, if it ever did. And I was unhappy with the travel agent, who prevented us from flying that day. On Wednesday, we awoke at 4:15 AM so we packed our things and by 5:30 we were outside the hotel, waiting for a taxi, in the first cool light of dawn. At the airport, the fare for the first short flight was only $ 3.00 each. And the airplane we were to go on was unusual - built in Iceland and narrow, it had no center aisle and many outside doors - but with two pilots, three engines and the ability to land anywhere, it was probably the safest kind imaginable, for that flight.

Our spirits bounded high. The little plane was fun and best of all we were on our way at last. I don't think either of us could have remained sane another 24 hours in Cartagena.

With a full load of 12 passengers, it took off on time at 6:30 - the engines were turboprops, which hummed quietly - then climbed to 4,000 feet for a smooth flight across the low, level country to Barranquilla - a port city on a river, with barrios of poverty around it - and landed softly at 7:05. After breakfast, at the airport, I went toward the men's room but two men an two women were talking in the doorway of the ladies' room and one of the men came over to tell me that they were both out of service for cleaning. So I pretended not to understand him and went in. No one was there. But evidently they had a schedule and it must be adhered to. At the International Departure Lounge, there was an exit tax   for tourists - of $ 10.00 a person. But we had used up our pesos, so we paid in dollars and were given $ 7.00 change in pesos. They had plenty of dollars but it was against their policy to give them out. So we sold the pesos or $ 6.00 worth of Panamanian coins, at a gift shop in the same room.

And so another unpleasant, aggravating incident. I think if I'd had a thousand dollars in my pocket at that stage, I'd have shoved them down the throats of all those petty people. And then spend the rest of my life in a Colombian jail. There are some arguments in life you just can't win.

Then we were cleared by the immigration people and went out to the airplane, a BAC 111 jet, operated by Lasca. And at ten we took off, bound for Panama and the road home.

Gracias a Dios.

12 - THE ROAD HOME

The airplane climbed up to its cruising altitude and when it levelled off, we were far out over the Caribbean. Then June saw the San Blas Islands, down below. And soon we were descending - the engines quieter - toward green land, with white beaches and jostled through a small cloud, to land at Panama. At the airport, one of our suitcases was missing. All the others were taken away, until there were none left and still we could not find it. Then we caught a glimpse of it - standing on end - behind a pillar. And by noon, we were on our way into the city, sharing a taxi with two fat salesmen. After dropping them at hotels, the driver took us to a bus stop, on a busy street of shops and offices, Then he overcharged us - tourists are for clipping - and left.

For a while, we stood on a wide sidewalk, until a bus for Colon arrived. It seemed to be quite full but the people in it - mostly black - were friendly and helpful. The driver put our luggage on the floor, near the door. And someone on a back seat made room for us, as the bus pulled out into the traffic. Beyond the city - on the narrow, winding road across the isthmus - it stopped often, to let people off. And there were few aboard, when we came to Colon. so the driver put them off at the last stop. Then he took us and our luggage, in the bus, to the shipping terminal at Cristobal.

He offered that service at a small extra charge, so we took it - we were in a hurry to get to Minim.

It was two o'clock, when we arrived, so June stood under a metal shade at the bus stop, outside the gates of the terminal - guarding our luggage - while I went to the shipping office, with Minim's papers. Everything had been paid in advance, including a charge for unloading her. But I must get her admitted to Panama, before taking her out of the terminal. And all the offices would be closed at 4:00 PM for the Easter holidays.

Patrick came by, at one point, and told me that the docks would close at four o'clock for a 5 day Easter holiday. There was nothing to do but stand in the hot sun by our bags and wait and wait.

At the custom house, the Panamanian officials went through their pro-ceedures with all deliberate speed, while I counted the ticks of the clock on the wall. Then I ran back to the terminal, where I was dircted to the freight department.

Patrick passed by again but didn't stop. Actually there was little hope, at that stage. I could have been sitting in the airconditioned hotel coffee shop, instead of standing in the sun like a ninny. But he had to try.

There I recognized a tall, thin black man (from the time I was there, before) who seemed to specialize in cars. And when he had checked all the papers, he led me out to Minim. She was in fine shape - as far as I could see - so he gave me the key and I drove out of the gates, to pick up June and our luggage, with nearly twenty minutes to spare.

Could the sun be geting to me or was that really Minim?

It was so nice to be free again, even the old Washington Hotel sounded good, so we went there for iced coffee and asked about staying the night. But they could not take credit cards, though the clerk said the big hotels in Balboa did, and off we went, down the winding road across the isthmus. The carpet for our tent was still in its brown bag, down behind the seats. And the cushions which made our bed were all in place. Even the fire extinguisher was still in its bracket. But one thing had gone: A medal of St Chistopher - the patron saint of travellers - from my late mother's car, had been torn off the dashboard, probably with a crowbar.

It was a pity, for we could never replace it. But then we had been far luckier than we had expected. So we determined not to let its loss bother us. And soon we were in Balboa. We had heard there was a Holiday Inn, so we asked a local man for directions and he insisted on leading us to it in his sports car, then waved and drove off, when we saw it. And before dark, we were settled in, with Minim parked outside. Our room had a view of the water and airconditioning and even a television set - we had not looked at one, for months - and after taking showers, to wash off the sweat of the day, we went down to a patio - under the stars - where the drinks were free, because the place was quite new. It was a great relief to be in Panama - and on the road home - at last. Now everything seemed so easy and pleasant. At breakfast we read Newsweek, to see what had been happening in the world outside. Then we checked Minim and found the thieves on the docks had taken more that we thought.

The small whisk broom, down beside the driver's seat, was gone. So was the cushion between the seats, that June had made and covered with brown cloth, to sit on when we had a passenger. And someone had tried to open the back of the truck but had not succeeded, because we had changed the lock. Evidently the thieves would take anything that was not an obvious part of the truck - like the seats or fitted cushions - but would not break in to do it. So we assumed that evidence of breaking in, or actual parts of the vehicle missing, would lead to investigations they preferred not to have. Losing the cushion between the seats might be a pain in the ass, before the journey was over. But the brush would be easy to replace and with nothing else missing - except the St Christopher medal - we thought ourselves lucky.

Though Baloa was next to Panama City, the difference was dramatic. Instead of old, run down buildings, there were modern ones, freshly painted, on clean streets. Instead of poverty, it had an air of affluence. For it was in the Canal Zone, that was controlled (and financed) by the United States. Not far away were several banks and the third one we came to handled June's credit card, so they tried to call Vermont by Telex but could not get through. Probably it was too early there. And all the banks in Balboa would close at 11:00 AM that day, until Monday morning, for the Easter holidays. While the girl tried again, the man who was handling our requst said the Panama Canal had been closed by a strike of the American pilots, when we were in Lima, until the President threatened to send the U.S. Army down to run it. He also said that foreign charges on credit cards could take months to be processed, so that we would probably be home before the last ones were debited to our accounts.

At 9:30 the girl said she could not get through. She tried three times but there was no answer. But the man decided to let us have $ 150 anyway.

And while she was doing the paper work, he told us how to get to another bank, just a few blocks away, where they handled my kind of credit card. By 10:05 we were there and a girl immediately got through to Vermont on the Telex - we were in the same time zone and the bank in Burlington had just opened - and by 10:10 she had their authorization to give us two hundred dollars. With what we had, that would get us back to the United States. Outside, it was a warm, sunny, breezy day - there was no rain in Panama, that time - and soon we had food, liquor, beer, ice, water, gas - just about everything we needed for the next 5 days. It was surprising how quickly one could get things done in the environment of the United States. And again there was a feeling of relief, at being this side of the Darien Gap, with a road that we knew leading all the way home.

It was noon when we crosed the bridge over the canal - the last time we saw it was from the deck of the Rossini - then we drove on the good road, southwest to Santiago and west to David in much holiday traffic, all though the afternoon. At the frontier, the time changed (back an hour) and we had to clear with five different departments in Panama. But in Costa Rica, they were quick and efficient. We paid $ 1.70 for tax and insurance on the car for a week, which was fair enough but we had forgotten about insurance. As we drove off, to the northwest, we thought about buying some but it did not seem to be worth while, for a few days in Central America. Maybe when we got to Mexico, we would do something about it.

How our standards had changed. A few months ago, we had been horrified at the thought of having to drive for a single day without insurance.

Just before dark, we saw a motel and since we were still in the lowland jungle, we stopped there. It was quite modest - just the owner's house, with a few small units nearby - and no food was available, so we had rum and tonic and tuna and bread in our room, glad to have crossed the frontier. which would be closed at 10:00 PM for the holidays, they said.

At last, luck was running with us. To get Minim off the docks, find money and cross the border - all in the nick of time. We felt very pleased with life. The contrast between our night's lodging and that of the night before, in Balboa, was something we could find amusing.

It was hot and sticky, so we left our door open - to let out some of the heat - and various people and dogs came into our room, during the night but no snakes (that we knew of) and at dawn a cock crowed nearby, so we had breakfast on Minim's tailgate, under a gray sky, in the damp stillness of the early morning. By 6:00 AM it was full daylight and as we left, the owner (an American) said "Have a nice trip". So we said "We're going home" and he said "Have a nice trip, anyway" The road was quite level, through the lowland jungle and soon we came to a pig, with a plant in his mouth, who tried to race our truck. For a few moments, he made it, galloping ahead (though we slowed down) then he pulled over to the sde of the road and slid to a stop - with all four feet angled forward - and huffed off, into the undergrowth beside us.

Then at San Isidro del General, the road started up into the mountains - where our brakes faded, coming down - and went winding up, into the clouds and though them, to the pass at the top and down, beneath them, to Tres Rios. Beyond the Singing River, we were on roads we had driven three times already and hardly felt we needed a map but they were very quiet - almost empty - for it was Good Friday and we barely slowed down, going though the city of San Jose and on, down the wide, green valley to the westward.

The traffic in San Jose was usually wild. But that day the streets were empty. How long would our good luck last?

Everything was so easy, after South America. To go into a city like that and out on the othe side, without being stopped and questioned and having all our posessions examined, at least twice, was a strange, new experience for us. And the roads were so easy to drive on, with their smooth pavement and guard rails and more signs than we needed, showing where all the towns were and how far each was away. Past the turnoff to Puntarenas, the road went northwest, over the gentle hills and just beyond Liberia - on the right - was the trailer park, where we stayed before. It was only 3:30 but we stopped there,for it had showers and a bar, beside the swimming pool and grassy sites, on which to camp. Then we took Minim's instruments, hubcaps and mirrors, from the lockers and put them in their places and she was back to normal. It was a relief to be in a camp site with a fence around it - just a split rail one but enough to make it clear that we had a right to be there - and nice to have a water tap nearby. We were happy, then   relaxing, after Cartagena - and at seven o'clock, when we went to bed, it was quiet, with a juke box in the bar just audible and very little traffic.

We had barely slept, the night before, and after one gin and tonic, neither of us could keep our eyes open.

When I got up in the night, Orion was bright in the sky. And just before dawn, we both awoke, having slept very well. By 5:35 it was full daylight and cool and pleasant in the tent (much more so, than the hotels) with birds singing and cocks crowing and the sun slowly coming up into the clear sky. While June made breakfast, I checked Minim's engine and by seven, we were on our way, down the road to Nicaragua. It only took an hour, at the frontier, to clear with all the authorities in both countries - no longer than it would to go through a couple of control points, in Argentina - and then we were on the level road past the Lake of Nicaragua, with two volcanoes in it and mountains far across it. As usual, we took the back road - past Nick's place - to avoid the city of Managua. And beyond it, there was a volcano, quite near the highway, with smoke coming from it. Or maybe it was steam. Anyway, we were glad to leave it behind and soon we were at the frontier of Honduas. Again we were cleared by all the authorities, on both sides, in an hour and by six o'clock, we were at Gringo Jim's place in Choluteca.

It was still hot - near sea level - and none of the sites were taken, so we set up our tent in the shade of a tree and as we finished our supper, Gringo Jim came by. We had heard that the frontiers would be closed, the next day but he said we could go though them, at triple rates. And he told us that Mexico was being kind to tourists, after losing millions of dollars, but Coata Rica was hassling Anericans with phony traffic tickets and taking their license plates until the fines were paid, due to Russian influence. But Panama was okay now. And he said that 20 people, who were on their way to Costa Rica, had all turned back, when they met one couple coming out and heard about the conditions there.

I often wonder if he ever tells others of our trip. That we went all the way and came back and loved it. And that it encourages them to go on, too. Or do people want to hear tales of woe, to give themseles an out?

The contryside was very dry and he said they had had no rain for five months but the wet season was expected to start at any time, two weeks earlier than usual. And it rained hard, in the night. At dawn, our tent and its carpet were wet. And the sky was overcast and a dark, menacing cloud came over us, so we packed up and left for El Salvador. There were many children at the border, offering to show us where to go and though we knew quite well what departments to visit, in which order, it was easier to pay one his fee and let him keep the others at bay, while we did it. Then we took the coast road, across El Salvador, through the level farm country and past the well kept houses along the shore and through the 5 tunnels (so easy, after South America) to the border of Guatemala, where the formalities were quickly dealt with and the extra charges were modest. And soon we were on our way, toward the town of Esquintla. At the bridges, on that road, there are topes (bumps) to make you slow down and if you did not take them seriously, you could easily break something. But after the first one you are expecting them and slow right down, to walking speed, and then your head does not even hit the roof of the truck. The road from Esquintla to Guatemala City was busy with Easter Sunday traffic, climbing up into the mountains - in an almost continuous line - at the speed of the slower vehicles. But the local rules did not prohibit one from passing another car on the right and Minim, being suitable for rough terrain, went quickly up it, mostly on the gravel shoulder.

I'm sure it was against the law but the law didn't happen to be around. Patrick drove like a maniac, up the shoulder, for fifteen or twenty miles. Only when the road narrowed as it rose up the mountainside - and the shoulder ceased to exist - did he start driving normally. By that time, I was at least 20% grayer than I had been, at the start.

Then we found the bypass, around the Capital - after all those years - to the road for Antigua and by seven o'clock we were at the Patio. All the guests except two had left, for the Season was over, then. And when we had hung our tent up to dry, we sat down to dinner with Tom and Erika.

It was dark by the time we entered Antigua. We had trouble finding our way to El Patio. Some of the streets were blocked off and the buildings we remembered at certain intersections weren't there. The street lights weren't working. After several minutes of confusion we spotted the clock in the arch that spans Fifth Avenue, then saw the cathedral called La Merced beyond it and knew that would find our friends at the next corner

The earthquake - that we had read about, in Buenos Aires - had been centered between Antigua and the Capital. Many lives were lost and many houses were destroyed, especially the adobe ones, of the poorer people. But most of the people whom we knew had survived. The Patio had a few cracks in its walls but they were thick and strong and Tom had some men cutting channels in the outside and putting in steel girders at strategic points, to reinforce them in case it happened again. In fact, there were two earthquakes and when the second one happened, Erika was in her kitchen. All her pots and pans fell on the tiled floor, then an American woman - one of the guests - came rushing in to help and went skidding across the room, in a huge pool of ketchup.

We sat on the verandah that rings the garden, listening to the old parrot scolding and chortling on his swing near the kitchen door. The evening was cool and pleasant. Stars shone in the clear sky above. It was so like the many evenings we had spent there - swapping stories, lulled by the tranquility of the scene - that we were unprepared for the destruction we found, in the harsh daylight, the next morning.

But there would not be another one, for many years, so we felt quite safe and slept soundly, in our silent room. And when daylight came, we walked to John's house. The long drifts of dirt in the streets were the remains of adobe houses, carried there by the wind. And the lovely old public 'pila' with its high, carved facade was lying in pieces on the ground. But John's house looked all right and when he came to the door, he was fine. Bob and Cynthia and Julie were okay - he told us - and so were the Bells. Bob was head of CARE in San Lucas Sacatepequez. We should go and see him.

John had to go to work then, in the Capital. But we arranged to have dinner with him, that evening.

Then we went to the house where Victoria lived and found her safe and well - fat and happy - so we headed back to the central park and our friend the beggar was in his usual place, looking as good as he ever did. But we had trouble finding our way around Antigua, after the earthquakes, with so many houses down and the piles of rubble in the streets. Several churches were now unsafe and services were being held in open fronted huts, outside them. And the post office was in a hut, in the central park, for its building was unsafe also. And we wondered when the city would be as we had known it, again. Perhaps never. What we had known would be part of a long line of memories, in an ever changing world.

When we got back to the Patio, it was a fine, sunny day. While June saw to our laundry, I worked on the truck, rotating the tires, changing the plugs and checking the engine. Then we went off to see Bob. There were few cars in Antigua and no one-way streets, any more. But the road up to the main highway had been cleared and soon we arrived in San Lucas. The whole town was flat - like central London, after the bombings, in World War Two - and standing in a street, if you could find one, you saw clear across it. Nothing higher than a few feet remained, except a small, white building, so we went there and it was Bob's headquarters. Inside were big stacks of corrugated metal and behind it, on a wall, was a big drawing of a framework to support a roof, with struts at each corner, to prevent it from collapsing in an earthquake.

Bob was fine - he and Cynthia were at their finca, in the jungle, when the first earthquake happened and immediately set out for the Capital, to help with the rescue work - and now Cyn was running the finca, but she was in the Capital, that day and would be at Julie's house, the next morning. As head of CARE in that town, Bob seemed to be doing very well. With his quiet, easy going manner and superb command of Spanish, he could get people to do what was needed and already they had over 300 roofs up - just the roofs - in the time that it took another agency to build one house. With the rainy season coming, it was roofs that mattered and his technique was simple. He put out the word that he would give anyone the tools and materials to build one - for himself and his family - if he would agree to construct it, as shown in the drawing, to be safe in an earthquake. Then the owner could finish the house - adding walls and so on - in any way that he pleased and when it was done, it was his.

There was no paper work, at all. The man just came in and Bob's assistants, who knew everyone in the area, said he lived nearby. Then Bob explained the method of construction, shown in the drawing, and told him why the roof must be built that way. If the man agreed, they shook hands and the deal was made. Then he would take the tools and materials that he needed and in due course, his family would have a house again. The Guatemalan Army was supervising the work, on behalf of the government and every few days, a couple of men came by. So Bob drove around with them, looking at the new roofs, then they would all have a drink together and he assured them that everything was fine and they would go back to their superiors and report that things were under control.

It was market day and a few women had gathered in the open square, vending produce from makeshift tables, keeping jostling children and dogs from upsetting the fragile displays. There was not much to choose from. We bought fruit, tomatoes and beans. Everything was bruised and spotted. Bob told us that most of the gardens had been destroyed. There was little food to be had. But the women seemed anxious to sell it. They needed money too.

Julie had a new house in the pine woods outside the town of Chimaltenango, so we went there and found her painting. She was asleep in her van with another girl, down in the lowlands, when the first earthquake came and they were both flung across it, from side to side. Her old house fell down that night but no one was in it and most of her pictures had survived, so she had been lucky and now she was going ahead with the work. But she invited us for breakfast, the next day, to see Cynthia and Bob, on our way to the Mexican border.

We had been prepared to squeeze Julie into the truck and take her back to the States with us. We were so relieved to find her alive and unharmed, for we knew the old house she lived in could not survive a good quake. But she would not consider leaving Guatemala. In spite of everything, she was painting and she was happy there.

Then we took the back road to Antigua - past Swan Lake - that June used when she went to work at Dr. Berhorst's hospital in Chimaltenango, the year before. And after putting ice, food and water in Minim, we were ready to leave again. At dinner that evening, John told us he was in his house when the first earthquake came. There had been no warnings but he heard a window rattle, so he went quickly to an archway and stood there, while the stone floor heaved in waves - just like the sea - and all the big stones in the building moved. It was the most helpless of feelings. But the house did not fall down and when it was over, he was still alive. As head of the medical section of AID in Guatemala, he had to decide where to put the field hospital that soon arrived at the airport from the United States. So he led the convoy of trucks to Swan Lake and it worked out quite well, for there was plenty of water and it was off the main road but near the towns which had been hardest hit by the earthquakes.

There were far more deaths than he had expected, because so many people were choked by the dust from the crumbling adobe houses. Probably 80 percent of the people died that way. A man was found dead in his house, that was undamaged, trying to find his way out of it, with a flashlight. And he had nothing wrong with him, except that his lungs were full of dust. About 25,000 people were killed. And another 65,000 were injured by falling buildings, so there was a great deal to do, for a while. But help came, from all over the world - Mexico sent an airplane full of civil engineers to get the roads open – and now the first, critical period was over. But the work of reconstruction would take a long time. Meanwhile, life went on, much as before. The minor damage to his house was now repaired. And his cottage, high above Lake Atitlan, was fine, It was so new that the putty in the windows was still soft, when the earthquakes happened and not a pane of glass was broken. So he was lucky. But those who lived well did not usually suffer in disasters like that. It was the poor who lost so much and all that he could do was continue his job of teaching them how to look after themselves.

In the morning, as we drove out of Antigua, we went past Musa's house and saw a wide, jagged crack down the front wall. But that could be fixed - she must be away - and the roof line was straight, so the structure was all right. Then at Julie's house we found Cynthia. When she arrived in the Capital, after the earthquakes, John had sent her out to remote villages - reachable only by motorcycle or on foot - to arrange for the wounded to be picked up by helicopters. And she had to decide, each time, who could be saved. If a man or woman or child were so badly hurt that their chances of survival were too slim, she had to say "No" and put aboard someone else, with more likelihood of living, for there were too few places available to waste on the dying. And since the Mayan people took care not to show their pain, it was hard to know which ones had internal injuries. So that was a trying time.

But now she was running their 'finca' and things were easier. She was alone in the jungle, full of poisinous snakes, but it scarcely seemed to bother her. One day, she found a feu-de-lance (the most deadly of all) inside a closet but she chased it out of the house with a broom, since she never killed things, if she could help it. She had a gun at the house, to scare away intruders. But it was stolen. And someone had hung chicken feathers, dipped in blood, outside her door. But she was going back, that day. And she seemed to be as calm - almost placid - as ever. Such people do not scare easily. She would be all right.

After breakfast, we left but soon a yellow truck passed us, the driver honking his horn and waving. It was Ron Parker, another friend, who was now head of CARE in Chimaltenango, and his wife Cathy was working for a different agency, so we went there to see her. The town was almost as badly damaged as San Lucas and they told us that Dr. Berhorst's hospital had fallen down, when the second earthquake struck. It had survived the first one, so it was full of injured people, when someone shouted a warning and all the staff ran out of the building, just as it collapsed. They had no time to save anyone, except themselves. But at least they were still available, to care for the hundreds of people who were injured by the other buildings which fell down. Now Ron was getting roofs put up - by the same technique that Bob had developed - before the rainy season came. And all of them were glad to have jobs, so we left them and headed norteast, on the mountain road to Mexico.

For a while, there were metal roofs, geaming in the sun, near the highway but later, as we drew away from the center of the earthquakes, they were fewer and beyond Totonicopan we saw no more. Then we went down through the gorge, to the frontier, where no other people were crossing and we were quickly passed through. And continued over the green mountains to the trailer park, near San Cristobal de las Casas, that we had seen on our way to Guatemala, in the previous fall.

We had rushed through Guatemala. There was so much destruction and nothing we could do. Every daylight hour was painful. For a country that, a few months before, had been gay with sunshine was now drab with dust. The people's faces were lined with sadness. And everywhere along the road were clusters of metal roofed shacks. Our friends had faced the work that had to be done. They were busy and by now hardened to the scene around them. But we were outsiders. It was best that we moved on.

The park was new and set back from the road, in the pine trees, with bathrooms in a small building where beer and other things were sold. But all the sites were empty, so we took one in the lee of the tall trees and though it was raining hard by then, we set up our tent. It was good to be back in Mexico, so close to the United States and so civilized. By dawn, the sky was clear and when the sun came up, our tent started to dry, while I worked on Minim, adding the last of the Argentine oil and cleaning the distributor. But when we drove off, she was still running poorly, with little power. At Tuxtla Gutierrez we changed $ 80 into pesos but the insurance company we used had moved, so we went on again. And at the top of a hill, we came to a mechanic's shop - a gray shed - where a man set the points by eye, in less than a minute and charged us fifty cents and the engine was fine again.

Then we dropped down, from the mountains, to the control point at Ventosa, where the policemen had a kitchen, in their new house but no pots or pans to cook with. Near Tehuantepec a sign directed the Mexico City traffic to go by a new road and our old one, that climbed up toward Oaxaca, had much less than usual. But by seven it was dark and we were still winding over mountains, with lightning ahead, above the city. And at eight we arrived at the trailer park, in a thunderstorm, with strong wind and heavy rain. Most of the spaces were empty, so we took one (without checking in) and sat there, tired and hungry but too cheap to go to a restaurant or a motel. At nine, the rain eased off, so we got Cinzano, crackers and cheese from the back, to eat in the truck. And at ten, as the storm moved away   still rumbling and lashing   we set up our tent, in light, steady rain and went to bed.

Most of the night, it rained and a white dog slept on our door mat (under the front fly of the tent) and growled at June, when she looked out. But at dawn, the sky was clear and soon it was a bright, sunny day with noises of the city in the distance and the ground and our tent quickly started to dry. A young Canadian couple came by, looking worried. They had been thoroughly searched by the police, on the road up to Oaxaca from the coast. But that was known as a route used by amateur smugglers and while they seemed to be sensible people, they looked 'hippie' enough to have tried it. But the park was made horrible by a car with a loud radio, so I went into town for insurance while June dried our gear and then we left for Puebla, by a new road, to the north, which was narrow and winding but quiet and pleasant.

Oaxaca was an 'in' place for North Americans to hang out. It still is a beautiful city but next time, we will bypass that tourist's campground. We'd have been much bettter off in a quiet hotel or even the local gravel quarry.

At lunch time we sat on Minim's tailgate in a hot, still desert, after passing through a lush, level valley between two mountains. Then we took the toll road past Puebla and stopped at a roadside shop for rum, tonic and food. And at 6:00 we set up our tent in a corner of the usual trailer park (called Las Americas) at Cholula, west of the city. It was cool, overcast and windy but we were all right, in the lee of a high wall and there we had our own water tap and drain and electric outlet, luxuries we had almost forgotten and hardly felt we needed. But it was cold in the night, so we used our electric heater for the first time since we were in Mexico, on our way south, half a year ago. The morning was cold and clear, with birds singing, and a factory whistle sounded nearby. Then it was quiet in the park and soon it was warm and sunny and very pleasant. But we could not get used to the luxury of having showers each day and clean clothes and water and electricity and drains.

Minim's engine was using some oil, which was unusual but I thought it was due to a small leak. And after leaving there, we stopped to have her cleaned and greased. We found marks on the paint in two places, made by slings used to put her on the ship at Cartagena or take her off at Cristobal. But otherwise, she was fine and off we went - taking our usual route over the high, open country   to Pachuca and followed Route 85 (the old mountain road) to the Posada del Rey in Zimapan. There were no other campers, so we set up our tent in the shelter of some tall trees and while June made dinner, I looked around. The swimming pool was half full of green slime and when I peered into the poolside building - through a hole, where a window had been - a bat flew out. The only facilities available were toilets in the hotel and those were dirty. But a sign said it was reccommended by the AAA. Curious.

Soon after dark, a thunderstorm was overhead, with a strong wind and heavy rain. But we had worked on a lightning research vessel, in our days at sea, so we sat on the rubber mattresses, to avoid the ground currents that would develop, if a tree were hit near us and counted caterpillars (seconds) between each of the flashes and its thunder, to measure the distance. Some were within half a mile, all around us but in less than an hour, the storm moved away, so we adjusted the tent's top fly - which had been blown askew - and lowered the front fly, so that the water would run off it better and went to bed in steady rain, with no wind and the lightning moving away from us.

By dawn, the sky had cleared a little and the white pony made a pest of himself, as I checked out the truck. The brakes needed adjusting but I decided not to do it there and at 8:00 AM we went on, through the mountains - using the gears to control our speed, as we dropped down into Tamazunchale. Beyond it, the hills were less steep and at Ciudad Mante we stopped to buy food, then carried on and at 5:00 PM we arrived at Ciudad Victoria, in another thunderstorm. So we went to the trailer park beside the Motel el Jardin, at the far end of the bypass road, because it had high, dense trees which would give us more shelter than the low palms at the other one. And there we set up our tent, in heavy rain again.

We no longer thought anything of setting the tent up in a rain storm. And going to a motel, trying to sleep on a bumpy bed, just to keep dry, was too much trouble. Tomorrow the sun would shine - the tent would dry. Tonight we would eat our can of tuna, our bread and cheese, as we had the night before. We were totally adjusted to the nomadic life.

But on Sunday morning it was dry, where we were - though the sky was gray and there was a thunderstorm to the east of us - so we packed up quickly, then spent the last of our pesos on gas and headed northeast - on good, straight roads - into light rain and out beyond it into sunshine. At El Tejon, we took the quiet road for Reynosa and at noon we crossed the bridge, over the Rio Grande, into the United States. It was so simple. On the Mexican side, we handed 3 small papers - one each and one for the car - that we had been given when we entered the country, to a man in a booth. Then, on the American side, we stopped under a high roof, where the customs and immigration people cleared us in 15 minutes. They were very thorough but wasted no time on paper work and were not interested in our purchases. Their main concern seemed to be stopping drugs from entering the country and when they were satisfied about that, they let us through. Then we drove on, into Texas and suddenly I had the feeling that I had stepped through a looking glass like Alice - back into the real world, from one that maybe never existed. For it was hard to believe that beyond those border towns, the road went on, through Mexico, to all of South America. And by driving it for long enough, we could again see all those people. But reality itself takes getting used to. We stopped for hamburgers - our first, in half a year and they were awful, made of plastic meat, on plastic buns, served in an atmosphere of enforced sterility on plastic tables and tasting resolutely of genuine, one hundred percent cardboard. The road northward just a small one, on the map was magnificent but dull and Minim ran better on the good American gas and June was singing, as we hummed along.

There was nothing else to do. In only two thousand miles, we would be sleeping in our own bed. There were gas stations and hamburger stands every 10 miles. The road was always paved and never disappeared over a precepice. I didn't even have to watch the map, for either of us could find Vermont, from Texas, blindfolded. Besides, I like to sing.

We lost an hour - the time changed - but still we were in Corpus Christi by 5:30 and picked up our mail (the truck's new registration and license stickers) at the yacht club, which was very glamorous after Latin America, with so many yachts - not just a few for the rich - rocking gently, in row after row, on tiny waves in the wide, sweeping curve of the bay. There were palm trees, along the water front. And across the road was a Ramada Inn, so we moved in there and telephoned June's mother, in Michigan. Our money was on its way back from Cartagena. And after dinner we sat in our room, watching color TV, glad to be back in the United States.

The wealth, the comfort on display everywhere glittered at us. Even the slummy areas of towns looked modern and posh. We had been away long enough to forget how luxurious and easy life in America was.

At eight o'clock on Monday morning, we went to the local International Harvester garage, to have Minim's brakes relined and her engine tuned up. And by 5:00 PM it was done. But the 4 front spring bushings also needed changing, so we went back at 8:00 AM on Tuesday and it was noon when we left Corpus Christi to head northward again, across Texas. Toward evening, we came to a small trailer park near the village of Lexington - just a few sites on a grassy knoll, by the owner's house - and there we set up our tent, in the shade of a big, spreading tree. There was an overhead light, on the tree, with a switch lower down, to control it. And hot showers nearby. The few people around were quiet and pleasant and the birds were singing, in the trees and it was good to be camping again, after two days in a motel. And our dinner - of chicken and raspberries - tasted far better than restaurant food, even though the materials that June used were packaged. As we went on, in the morning, all the roads seemed flat and large and empty. The sheer abundance of luxury impressed us, after Central and South America - so many fine bridges and guard rails and so on, even on the smaller roads. Early that afternoon, we were on a super-highway, that was still safer but more dull. And there we were nearly clobbered. June was driving when a wheel fell off a big truck that was heading toward us at maybe 55 miles an hour. And since we were doing the same, it came across the median - bouncing and spinning in the air - at an approach speed of about a hundred and ten miles an hour, which left her little time to consider the matter. But she calmly gauged its line and put Minim into a gentle curve - without touching the brakes - that missed it by several feet, as it went across our lane.

At least we hadn't yet lost our instinct to survive. We were still watching, still on the defensive. We wondered if we would keep alert, all the way to Vermont, or if the easy life around us would lull us into a stupor, and we would expect the other guy to be responsible for us.

Our campground, that night, was just a patch of gravel in a small town, behind a store. And at dinner, we had the heater going in our tent, for we were in northern weather, by then. In the news on the radio, we heard that 15 inches of snow fell on Colorado, the day before. And the next morning there was a cold wind, out of a bleak, gray sky. But we felt much better, after two nights of camping, than we had after spending two nights in the fancy motel, back in Corpus Christi. There was much humor and singing in our truck, that day, We both kept yawning - we were bored by the easy driving - but everything looked so good: The prosperous farms with their well kept fences and freshly painted houses. The small towns, each with everything people needed. The many cars and all that farm equipment, in the fields around the barns. Toward evening, we left the highway and took a country road to a campground in the woods. No one else was there - it was early in the year - but we found a level place among the empty trailers and set up our tent, then went off to call June's mother from a phone booth in a quiet village, where a cuckoo was singing and children were playing.

Back in our tent, it was cold and pleasant and soon after dawn we were up and about. Before eight we were on our way and that evening, we were in Benton Harbor. Our money had still not arrived from Cartagena but it should, next week, they said. So we picked up the things we had left there in November and went eastward, past the shore of Lake Erie, to Vermont. Again there was a feeling of relief, as we came into our own State, where we knew people and anything that might go wrong could easily be fixed. Soon we were on the road that we knew so well, from Burlington to our village, then the mountain road beyond it and suddenly we were home, with 31,000 miles and 16 foreign lands behind us and enough memories for a lifetime. So we parked Minim and went inside.

Inside, to another world, where everything was just as we had left it. But we are not the same. For in quiet times, those memories return. The

378

morning mist, swirling around the black hatted woman, tending her herd of long necked llamas. The sound of ancient bagpipes leading lines of red skirted revellers down pale green mountain paths to the fiesta in the meadow ahead. The leathery smell of the old Indian who rode with us up the hill. The crack of the glacier, near the tip of the continent, as it dropped a chunk of ice into the blue lake, The rainbows touching the earth at both ends, for hours at a time. And the people who have no concept of the size of their world. They are all still there, just as they were a hundred years ago and before that too. For we saw another time, we have lived other lives. And we thank you, South America.